th on

an architectural guide

edwin heathcote
photographs by keith collie

theatre london

an architectural guide

• • • **ellipsis**

•••

BRITISH LIBRARY CATALOGUING IN PUBLICATION
A CIP record for this book is available from the British Library

For Kriszti

PUBLISHED BY •••ellipsis
2 Rufus Street London N1 6PE
E MAIL ...@ellipsis.co.uk
WWW http://www.ellipsis.com
SERIES EDITOR Tom Neville
EDITOR Rosa Ainley

ISBN 1 84166 047 7

PRINTING AND BINDING Hong Kong

For a copy of the Ellipsis catalogue or information on special quantity orders of Ellipsis books please contact us on 020 7739 3157 or sales@ellipsis.co.uk

contents

Introduction

The history of theatre building in London is a spectacular cycle of boom and bust, a more-or-less continuous tradition stretching back to the Elizabethan period. Shakespeare's life (1564–1616) coincided with the first great theatre-building boom which saw the original development of the South Bank as an arts and recreation centre, theatres springing up alongside bear-baiting pits, cock-fighting rings, brothels and so on. Drama, alcohol and sex for sale have always huddled together in the crowded streetscape of London. Later in the seventeenth century, the Puritans put a stop to the fun and the next phase did not start until after the Restoration of 1660 with the building of the two premier venues, the Theatre Royal, Drury Lane and The Royal Opera House. The Georgian era, remarkably, witnessed another mini-boom, despite a ban on straight drama which lasted until 1843.

The real boom years came towards the end of the Victorian era and lasted until the outbreak of the First World War. Shaftesbury Avenue was cut through the Soho slums and became the centre of London theatre, while the streets around Covent Garden and Soho became clogged with frothy theatre façades. The next wave of theatre building arrived with a new urgency caused by the competition from talking pictures and led to a dazzling outbreak of jazzy art-deco buildings in the years around 1930. A war came along to spoil that boom too.

Apart from a brief flourish in the 1970s, which saw the first intervention of the state in London's theatre building and embraced the Barbican (see page 6.2) and National Theatre (see page 7.8), the next big boom is the one we're in now. The lottery-ticket-buying classes have generously subsidised a huge programme of rebuilding and new theatre construction. This is a boom that gives the impression of being hurried and ill thought-out and that has led to a number of disappointing and unremarkable, if articulately modern, structures and a few truly worthwhile schemes.

The development of theatre architecture in London

The roots of London theatre lie in its streets, marketplaces and cathedral precincts which formed the backdrop for the medieval mystery plays. The city itself was both auditorium and stage. The comedy characters in these religious plays gradually came to dominate proceedings and the sacred gave way to the profane as the bawdy sideshows which arose from the need to keep audiences amused became entertainment in their own right. Shows moved to the courtyards of inns as landlords realised there was money to be made (the link between alcohol and theatre is long-standing and powerful, just try to imagine a theatre without a bar).

The earliest permanent theatres were based on one of two models. The first was the bear-baiting ring, a circular structure that was, in effect, the inheritor of the Roman arena for blood sports. The second was the courtyard inn, a rectangular plan with galleried sides and standing room at the centre. Banned from the City of London by its puritanical burghers who feared rioting mobs and biting satire and used Protestant morality as an excuse, theatres sprang up on the outskirts. The first, The Theatre (1576) built by Richard Burbage, was in Shoreditch. The focus subsequently moved to the red-light district, Bankside. The Curtain, Rose, Swan, Globe, Fortune and Hope theatres followed in quick succession and provided venues for a genuinely popular theatre which cut across class divides. The essential elements of these theatres were thatch-roofed galleries, a central pit for standing spectators and a covered stage which protruded into an audience that surrounded the players on three sides. Despite this unparalleled burst of creativity, London theatre's golden period was surprisingly short. The wind of the Renaissance blew through the court and swept the creative focus from the crowded pits of Bankside to the gilded luxury of palace and court theatres.

Inigo Jones, England's foremost stage designer of the period, completed the Banqueting House in Whitehall in 1622 as a venue for elaborate masques and plays, keeping nobles and courtiers amused. Twenty years after its completion it abruptly ceased to be a venue of amusement for nobility when the king awaited his beheading there. The Suppression of the Theatres Act of 1642, born out of the puritanism of the Civil War, was to remain a serious hindrance to the development of London's theatres for two centuries after the war had ended. Theatres were branded decadent and sinful but were really suppressed for political reasons, for fear of the same mob that had terrified the city fathers of Shakespeare's day. There was, for instance, a riot at the Theatre Royal, Drury Lane in 1737 when footmen were refused free admission, and again during the Gordon Riots of 1780 after which a company of guards was posted, a custom which lasted until 1896, a demonstration of the continued fear of the link between theatre and mob.

The Restoration led to the establishment of two new London theatres which both survive. The Theatre Royal, Drury Lane (1662) and the Royal Opera House (1732) were given royal licences and a monopoly on serious drama. Based on Italian and French Renaissance models, these were self-consciously sophisticated and continental theatres, a world away from bear pits and inns attended by the unwashed masses. Theatre became the place to be seen. A select band of cynical snobs went as much to be seen as to watch the play, a noble tradition that continues to this day and can be best observed at Covent Garden. Those keenest to be seen would often bring their own stools and sit on the sides of the stage. This custom was eventually formalised into boxes at low level to either side of the stage where a foppish king and his courtiers made themselves the centre of attention. To attract attention back to the stage a barrage of technical innovations and special effects were introduced, including the flytower. The stage was separated from the auditorium with the introduction of the proscenium arch and became a magical space and a separate world.

Theatres continued to be built, despite the ban on dramatic performances. Musical numbers and sales of hot chocolate and coffee were introduced as ruses to get around the ban. It was exactly the kind of sedition and cynical wit that the authorities had been trying to avoid that fuelled theatre building in the Restoration and Georgian periods. In 1843 the royal licensing system was finally abandoned and controls on theatres were loosened. This coincided with an explosion in London's population and with the arrival of music hall which allowed the working classes to enjoy theatres for the first time since the Shakespearean era.

Just as early theatres had developed from the courtyards of inns, music halls grew out of the side of pubs. Landlords were once again well placed for huge profits and made money from alcohol rather than ticket sales. Music hall burgeoned; packed, smoky halls became gold mines. Opera singers and actors would often rush to these crowded rooms after performances at the premier theatres and sing arias or act scenes to drunken crowds for huge fees that far outweighed their West End earnings. The architecture of music hall was modest. Essentially a hall, usually with a gallery, there was little or no stage machinery. More akin to the routine at a modern comedy club, acts came on in quick succession with few props. The oeuvre is well represented by a few remarkable survivals, the most incredible of which is the hauntingly atmospheric Wilton's (see page 6.12).

The success of music hall and its less risqué cousin, variety, inspired impresarios to build colossal new venues for the entertainment of the masses. Looking to the Romans for inspiration, huge theatres like the Hippodrome (1900), the Colosseum (1904) and the Palladium (1910) were erected to provide entertainment for all sections of London's fast-growing population. The Victorian era also saw the last major remodelling of London's streets: the clearance of Soho slums and the construction of Shaftesbury Avenue (1886) and later of the Aldwych (officially opened 1905) provided a focus for entrepreneurs keen to build new theatres.

This brings us to one of the great oddities of the London theatre: the West End is a purely commercial venture. London is alone in Europe in having relied on the private sector for its stock of theatre buildings. While kings and governments elsewhere were building great opera houses and national theatres in capacious boulevards and squares as expressions of national pride, London architects were squeezing dozens of theatres into narrow sites on crowded streets. This situation, and the huge demand for new theatres, led to the emergence of a clique of architects who became known for their ability to design practical, economical theatres and deliver them on time, shoe-horning maximum seats into minimal plots.

Restoration and Georgian theatres were often built by the country's finest architects: Wren, Vanbrugh, Adam, Benjamin Wyatt and Robert Smirke all contributed designs to London's theatres. The Victorian and Edwardian theatre-building world, however, was dominated by specialists who were little known outside their circle. W G R Sprague, Frank Matcham, C J Phipps and Bertie Crewe, despite building Theatreland, remain relatively obscure names and at the time were looked down on by the architectural establishment as vulgar and commercial. Their buildings, in the West End at least, have survived better than many of those of their contemporaries.

The Victorian and Edwardian theatre-building boom coincided with great advances in construction technology. Steel cantilevers allowed the construction of deep balconies with no columns. This meant that long, thin sites, rather than the traditional horseshoe shape, became viable. Stage machinery was enhanced by pneumatics, hydraulics, revolving stages and elaborate effects. Electric lighting dramatically reduced the risk of fire which had consumed dozens of London's theatre buildings in the nineteenth century alone.

The growth of the population and the development of the suburbs led to vastly expanded audiences for West End theatres and to the development of local theatres, most of which have since been demolished. The Hackney Empire, Theatre Royal Stratford and Richmond Theatre (see pages 6.8, 6.16, 8.16), all by the ubiquitous Frank Matcham, are fine survivals. London theatres grew up around railway stations, in the Strand, near Charing Cross and around Victoria station. These theatres afforded a taste of plush velvet, marble and golden putti to a population suffering long working hours and grim conditions. The theatres remain a fascinating testament to the engrained English class system with separate doors to the cheap seats in the upper balconies so that top-hatted toffs wouldn't have to rub shoulders with the proles. The higher you rise in these theatres, the cheaper the finishes become, from fine marble and stucco downstairs to wipe-clean glazed brick and tile in the gods.

The First World War brought a sharp end to the Edwardian boom. A new burst of building activity arrived in the late 1920s, bringing the flash and glamour of Parisian art deco to London for a brief but brilliant few years.

Theatre architecture remained virtually untouched by modernism and only in the post-war period were any real innovations in design realised. Socialism and modernism combined in the ideal of the state-funded theatre, a new concept to England. By the time the National Theatre and the Barbican were built in the 1970s, the thrust stage had become virtually compulsory, the proscenium unfashionable. State-funded theatres seem alien to the London tradition, a fact underlined by their location outside the West End. That both the National and the Barbican are perceived to unlovely lumps of rain-stained concrete looming up from cold, damp walkways beneath low London skies has not endeared them to a (still, though decreasingly) architecturally conservative British public. Yet at their best both are very fine theatres and among the best large modern stages in the world.

The current state

We are moving towards the end of the current building boom. Lottery money has ensured the creation of a number of prestigious projects in sleek new buildings while – as ever – theatre companies struggle to survive. Some are good, some less so. Gleaming modern foyers tend to lead to boring black boxes. The holy grail of versatility combined with a fascination with found space has led to a paralysis in the architecture of the auditorium. Architects seem unwilling to engage with the heart of the theatre and are often content to tinker with the bits around it. Sometimes this is a good thing; occasionally simplicity is the key – the Cottesloe, the Tricycle (see page 5.14) and the Donmar (see page 2.40) illustrate that. Sometimes found space needs little attention; the Almeida (see page 5.10) and the retained auditorium at the Royal Court (see page 8.2) needed only tweaking. At other times, theatres encourage their architects to create the blandest of black boxes for fear that they might get something completely unusable rather than merely something lacking in charisma. The black box is the easy option. Its widespread acceptance as the standard is also the reason that there has been no truly innovative or daring theatre design in London for more than a quarter of a century.

The architecture of the front of house is now compulsorily modernist. Even the Royal Opera House is only a wearing a little classical fancy dress on the outside. Inside, like the other modern theatres, is a world of cold, slick corporate modernism which can equally be found at the Soho Theatre (see page 1.52) and at Sadler's Wells (see page 5.2). It is middle-of-the-road modernism for those who aren't quite convinced – MORchitecture. Only the wonderfully redesigned Royal Court fully escapes it.

Perhaps this new puritanism makes the velvet and gilding of the West End look warmer and more inviting. It remains as tacky and commercial as ever and exists on as precarious a knife edge as always, everything constantly threatening to go out of business. Yet it remains vital and genuinely popular (partly due to a glut of long-running and money-spinning musicals) and has survived remarkably intact. The last major theatre to be demolished was the St James's in 1957, a far better record than New York where so many old theatres have been destroyed.

The survival of London's theatres and the constant revitalisation of the buildings over the last 500 years creates an endlessly fascinating theatrical landscape. Yet despite the amount that is written about what happens on stage there is a dearth of material about the physical fabric of the city's theatres. The aim of this book is to point out a few details and to give audiences something to do in the idle minutes before a performance, to amuse them during the interval or to use as a quick guide when walking around the city. Whether a theatre is a faded West End tart with worn velvet seats, sticky carpets and dust-caked, gilded putti; a scuzzy workshop with duct-tape embossed floors and wobbly plastic chairs; or an evocative music hall with crumbling walls and rusting pillars, there is always something worth looking at away from the stage.

Further reading

Remarkably, there have been no substantial books devoted to the architecture of the London theatre. There are, however, a few books that will give a good background to the broader subject of the development of English theatre design or which include useful information about London theatre buildings. As well as these there are a number of books solely devoted to individual theatres which I have not mentioned here, most of which have surprisingly little to say about architecture.

Mander, Raymond and Joe Mitchenson, *The Theatres of London*, London 1961, revised 1975. A good book with succinct but detailed entries on the architecture of London theatres as well as dramatic productions. Incredible amount of information. Mander and Mitchenson, whose archive of theatre-related material is phenomenal, were also responsible for *The Lost Theatres of London* and *British Music Hall, A Story in Pictures*, both useful but hard to find.

Leacroft, Richard, *The Development of the English Playhouse*, London 1975. Good overall history with excellent, clear cutaway drawings tracing the historical changes in both front-of-house and backstage areas.

Hartnoll, Phyllis, *A Concise History of the Theatre*, London 1968 and subsequent editions. A fine basic study in Thames and Hudson's World of Art series.

Mackintosh, Iain, *Architecture, Actor and Audience*, London 1993. Opinionated, witty and erudite, this is among the best accounts of building for theatre, essentially a plea for architects not to get too clever.

Earl, John and others, *Curtains!, A New Life for Old Theatres*, Eastbourne 1982. A very succinct but comprehensive survey of Britain's historic theatres at a time when their future looked uncertain. Unusually, it includes information about stage machinery.

Carlson, Marvin, *Places of Performance: The Semiotics of Theatre Architecture*, New York 1989. Far better than the subtitle suggests, this is a truly readable study of meaning in theatre architecture and of the place of the theatre within the context of the city. Good international context.

Day, Barry, *This Wooden O: Shakespeare's Globe Restored*, London 1996. The whole story.

Gurr, Andrew, *The Shakespearean Stage 1574–1642*, London 1992, Good overall survey of the period incorporating recent research, archaeological evidence and contemporary documents. Readable and interesting on playhouses and staging.

Eccles, Christine, *The Rose Theatre*, London 1990. Interesting account of archaeology and the story of the Rose fiasco.

Walker, Brian M, *Frank Matcham: Theatre Architect*, Belfast 1980. The only biography of a major theatre architect. Gives an idea of the breadth and sheer quantity of Matcham's work.

Mulryne, Ronnie and Margaret Shewring, *Making Space for Theatre: British Architecture and Theatre since 1958*, Northamptonshire 1995. A catalogue accompanying a British Council exhibition, mostly about provincial buildings but with a few interesting essays and studies.

Sachs, Edwin O and Ernest Woodrow, *Modern Opera Houses and Theatres*, London 1896–98. This monumental work recorded the great nineteenth-century theatres in fastidious detail through a series of meticulous drawings. An unparalleled work which was reissued in 1968. Incredible, unliftable and unlikely ever to be equalled in range, scope and beauty.

Theatre-related places of interest

The George Inn 77 Borough High Street, London SE1. London's last-surviving fragment of a galleried inn, giving an idea of the inn-model on which many early theatres were based. The old part dates from the 1670s and, despite extensive rebuilding, the atmosphere of old London survives. Shakespeare plays are occasionally performed here.

The Banqueting House Whitehall, London SW1. The setting for court masques designed by the building's architect, Inigo Jones. Jones brought Italian ideas about stage design to London, including perspectival architectural sets. This, London's first significant classical building, signalled the arrival of the Renaissance in England. Masques, balls and performances were held here after the building's completion in 1622 but ceased when it was realised that smoke from the lights was damaging Rubens' porky nudes and cherubs on the ceiling. Open to the public.

The Theatre Museum 1 Tavistock Street, London WC2. A branch of the Victoria and Albert Museum, the Theatre Museum is housed in a converted flower market in Covent Garden. Very good collection of stage designs and costumes in particular, as well as temporary exhibitions. Appointments are necessary to visit the fine archive in the basement.

The Theatres Trust 22 Charing Cross Road, London WC2. Set up by Act of Parliament in 1976 to protect theatres, the Theatres Trust houses a large archive of theatrical resources and photographs.

French's Theatre Bookshop 52 Fitzroy Street, London W1. Excellent bookshop with a very wide selection of play texts and books on the theatre.

National Theatre Bookshop Right on the riverside frontage, a very well-located and good bookshop.

Offstage Theatre and Film Bookshop 37 Chalk Farm Road, London NW1. Good theatre bookshop with ephemera, programmes and second-hand books in the basement.

Dress Circle 57 Monmouth Street, London WC2. Theatrical ephemera and posters.

David Drummond Theatre Ephemera and Books Cecil Court, London WC2. Attractive, crowded little shop in Cecil Court, the very civilised alley at the centre of London's antiquarian book trade.

Museum of London London Wall, London EC2. Good museum with bits and pieces about the city's entertainment.

Pollock's Toy Museum Scala Street, London W1. Unusual and highly evocative collection of toy and puppet theatres.

Note All phone numbers given are for the theatre box office.

west end

Her Majesty's Theatre

The origins of Her Majesty's Theatre stretch back further than any other London theatre with the exception of the Theatre Royal, Drury Lane (see page 2.58). In fact its roots lie in mismanagement at Drury Lane which prompted the playwright and architect Sir John Vanbrugh to build a rival theatre, The Queens, in 1704. The theatre's first manager was another prominent playwright, William Congreve. An unsuccessful beginning led Vanbrugh and Congreve to leave and the theatre (contemporary accounts describe it as practicality sacrificed to grand architecture, and a failure in terms of sightlines and acoustics) was turned over to Italian opera, the first permanent opera house in England. In 1789, the original burnt down. A new opera house, regarded at the time as one of the finest in the world (only La Scala in Milan was larger), was built in 1790–91, designed by Michael Novosielski, a successful architect born in Rome of Polish parents who was also a prominent stage scenery painter. Between 1816 and 1818 the theatre was reconstructed by John Nash (who laid out the plans for Regent Street and Regent's Park and who was also architect of The Theatre Royal on the other side of the road) and George Repton. This remodelling work included an elegant shopping arcade, now the only survival of the theatre's earlier history, which explains its seemingly odd name 'Royal Opera Arcade'.

In the middle of the nineteenth century, Her Majesty's became the centre of the social scene – the place to be seen. The theatre once again fell victim to fire in 1867 and was rebuilt, this time by Charles Lee. In 1896 it was acquired by actor/manager Herbert Beerbohm Tree who commissioned C J Phipps to rebuild it completely. This is the theatre we see today. The elaborate stone façade is executed in French Renaissance-style with a grand central dome and loggia. A good ironwork canopy shelters the inevitable queues at street level. The lobby is an odd affair, an

C J Phipps 1897

Her Majesty's Theatre

C J Phipps 1897

unsuccessful blend of polychromatic Tudor and rococo plasterwork which seems underscaled for this huge theatre.

The auditorium, however, is wonderful. Phipps based the design on Ange-Jacques Gabriel's opera house at Versailles (Gabriel was also the architect of Petit Trianon and the Place de la Concorde) and achieved a good mix of Italian opera-house drama and French frilliness. The proscenium is crowned by rich reliefs and painted panels and framed by scalloped cupolas and boxes between marble columns. A saucer dome completes the picture, displaying a series of panels painted in an eighteenth-century fashion. Grand and imposing, it looks like an opera house should, with all the bits in the right places and some of the faults in its sightlines can be forgiven.

The loggia to the dress circle bar behind the heavy columns and bold torches and overlooking the Theatre Royal is one of the grandest theatre terraces in London.

ADDRESS Haymarket, London W1 (020 7494 5400)
UNDERGROUND Piccadilly Circus

C J Phipps 1897

C J Phipps 1897

Theatre Royal, Haymarket

London's grandest venue for straight drama lies behind the monumental Corinthian façade that dominates the view down Haymarket. The Theatre Royal was one of the three London theatres to be granted a royal licence for drama (together with the Royal Opera House and Drury Lane) in the days when drama was seen as seditious and potentially dangerous.

The Haymarket received its licence through curious means. The first theatre, dating from 1720, was housed in the building next door, since demolished. Its founder defied the government by putting on drama without a licence (or patent) and this defiance continued when Henry Fielding became the manager in 1735. For the next couple of years his scathing political and anti-royal satires attracted the interest and wrath of the authorities. These were ultimately responsible for the Licensing Act of 1737 which saw the installation of the Lord Chamberlain as a censor, an institution which handicapped expression in British drama until 1968.

Fielding himself was forced to quit drama and went on to become a great novelist. The next manager, Samuel Foote, attempted to get around the theatre's lack of a licence by serving tea and hot chocolate with the entertainment as 'background'. Foote was finally successful in gaining a patent in 1766.

The current theatre dates from 1821. Its architect, John Nash, had been responsible for transforming the West End of London into an urbane and elegant set piece: the planning of Regent's Park and Regent Street right down to the Duke of York's monument are all part of his grand scheme. The columnated portico of the Theatre Royal, Haymarket was conceived as the termination of a view from St James' Square along Charles II Street, which is why the new building was moved sideways, slightly south of its original site. In a typically theatrical gesture, Nash knitted his building into the urban fabric while ensuring it became a pivotal landmark, its

John Nash 1820–21 and C J Phipps 1879–80

Theatre Royal, Haymarket

John Nash 1820–21 and C J Phipps 1879–80

royal cipher visible all around St James'. The generous shelter afforded by the portico was originally designed so that horse-drawn carriages could draw right up to the entrance of the theatre and visitors could alight under cover.

The theatre's frontage has survived remarkably well but the auditorium has undergone a series of radical transformations. Despite the grand appearance of the façade, Nash's original auditorium was a failure. During the middle years of the nineteenth century the auditorium was drastically altered and then, in 1879–80, the theatre was subjected to yet more alterations, this time under the auspices of C J Phipps. Phipps' work essentially created the theatre we see today and his skill is evident in one of the capital's best and most atmospheric playhouses. The works included London's first complete picture-frame proscenium and the boxes which can still be seen. The gorgeous auditorium seems to glow in the light that bounces around the dripping gold details, the lush marble columns and the deep red velvet of the upholstery, and focuses the attention on the shimmering gold royal cipher surmounting the stage. The dark, moody paintings on the dome and on the walls were executed by Joseph Harker, a well-known stage designer.

Behind the dress circle is a sensuously curving gallery, glazed off from the auditorium, which allowed latecomers to be admitted without disturbing the audience, and the dress circle bar retains its original counter. The small but perfectly formed box office is another elegant survivor: look at the wonderful joinery details and grilles around the central window.

It is also worth walking around to the back of the theatre. The stage door to Suffolk Street is the most elegant back-of-house area of any theatre in London, seamlessly blended into this smart little cul-de-sac.

John Nash 1820–21 and C J Phipps 1879–80

Theatre Royal, Haymarket

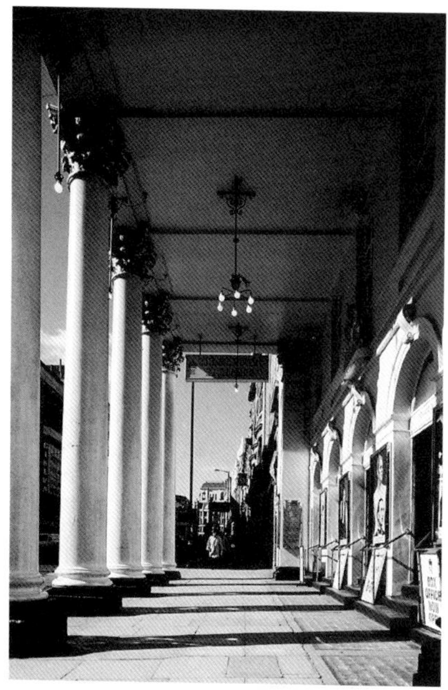

John Nash 1820–21 and C J Phipps 1879–80

Theatre Royal, Haymarket

There is a plaque here commemorating the theatre as the venue where a number of Oscar Wilde's plays were first produced although he was more associated with the nearby St James Theatre which was demolished in 1957.

The Theatre Royal, Haymarket remains very popular with both actors and audiences; the sightlines in the auditorium are impressive and the acoustics excellent while the interior succeeds in the difficult objective of creating an atmosphere at once cosy and grand. It remains a model of theatre design.

ADDRESS Haymarket, London SW1 (020 7930 8800)
UNDERGROUND Piccadilly Circus

John Nash 1820–21 and C J Phipps 1879–80

John Nash 1820–21 and C J Phipps 1879–80

Comedy Theatre

Perhaps the most intimate and best-preserved Victorian theatre in London, The Comedy is a very pleasant surprise. Tucked away in an unpromising little street near Leicester Square, the building's self-deprecating little French-influenced stone façade only modestly declares its presence. Even the tiny canopy (an addition dating from 1980) is bashfully insecure, with none of the usual brash, self-promotional vigour of London canopies. The entrance is surmounted by a rather disinterested and limp torch-bearing lady. The foyer (dating from a 1911 reconstruction) is refined but forgettable.

The auditorium, however, is much better. Crowned by a delicately decorated central panel of garlands, busts and complex, pierced grilles, the ceiling sets the tone for this theatrical gem. Dating from before the widespread use of cantilevers, the sightlines are interrupted by spindly cast-iron columns but the seats are so close to the stage and the whole auditorium remains so intimate that they do not disrupt too greatly the unity of the space. Decoration is kept subtle throughout, in great contrast to the usual Victorian and Edwardian bombast, and this too helps to evoke the idea of a private or court theatre and to diminish the barriers between the tiny stage and the audience. The theatre was in fact extensively rebuilt in 1954 but, with the exception of the Criterion (see page 1.14), it has retained its Victorian atmosphere better than any other in the West End and remains a dignified and important survivor.

ADDRESS Panton Street, London SW1 (020 7369 1731)
UNDERGROUND Leicester Square

Thomas Verity 1881

Thomas Verity 1881

Criterion Theatre

The tiny, intimate auditorium of the Criterion Theatre is discovered, beautifully preserved, at the end of a complex sequence of tiled passages and stairs. Completely subterranean (it is London's only completely underground theatre), the discovery is akin to a kind of archaeological find, a wonderful burial chamber which has survived only because it was lost beneath the layers of the city.

Originally conceived as a concert hall, and part of the complex that includes the glittery gold Criterion restaurant next door, it only became a theatre half-way through construction. The wonderfully preserved Victorian tiled panels (by William de Morgan) that line the walls of the stairs from the foyer still bear the names of composers, rather than playwrights, as testament to the original intention. On the other hand the curious blend of glazed tiles, painted and gilded ceilings, timber panelling and pink wallpaper makes for an uneasy, if not ugly combination. The box office and foyer opening from Piccadilly Circus is the best illustration of this lurid, eclectic mix. The newly restored paintings on the ceilings are particularly dire. The auditorium, however, is elegantly simple, calm and intimate, a far more successful space. With a capacity of a little under 600, all the seats are close to the stage and the slender iron columns supporting the balconies hardly impinge on the spatial intimacy.

When first opened, in 1874, the theatre had to have a pumped air supply to allow the audience to breathe in the confined underground auditorium. A decade after its opening the building was expanded and properly ventilated but it has always suffered from damp and floods, one of which was responsible for extensive damage in 1985. During the bombing in the Second World War, the theatre's underground location made it the ideal venue for BBC radio broadcasts.

The presence of the building above the theatre negates the possibility

Thomas Verity 1873–74

Thomas Verity 1873–74

of a flytower. This has meant that the Criterion has always staged smaller-scale shows. It is one of London's neatest and best-preserved Victorian theatres.

Opposite the Criterion you can see the London Pavilion which was a famous music hall from 1861. The current building dates from 1885, when Shaftesbury Avenue was built, and was designed by R J Worley and J E Saunders. It became a cinema in 1934 and now houses a rock waxworks exhibition.

ADDRESS Piccadilly Circus, London W1
(020 7369 1737)
UNDERGROUND Piccadilly Circus

OUT TO FOYER

Prince of Wales Theatre

The cylindrical tower at the corner of the Prince of Wales is one of the most effective and distinctive signposts of any of the London theatres. Originally, the building's striking corner was highlighted with a series of attenuated neons which betrayed the architect's status as one of the most successful cinema architects of the era. The elaborate pattern of neon strips has since disappeared but the illuminated signs are still wrapped around the body of the corner tower, a prominent and permanently crowded corner between Leicester Square and Piccadilly.

By 1937, when the Prince of Wales was built, art deco had undergone a transformation from the blocky, Aztec-influenced forms of its early years to curvaceous, streamlined forms that echoed the shapes of speed; the smooth surfaces of locomotives, cars and planes. At the same time art deco was slowly giving way to an architectural conservatism. This had always lurked in the background of British architecture throughout the gaudy excesses of deco, considered vulgar and populist by both conservative and modernist architectural establishments.

Robert Cromie's building displays tendencies from both streamlined art deco and the vein of classicised modernism that had been gaining momentum from the 1920s onwards. The curve of the corner allows the building to announce its presence to the broadest possible part of the city as well as dramatically terminating the block, while the slender tower ingeniously accentuates the height of the building, even if it is in fact lower than the neighbouring buildings even at the tower's apex. The pilasters and columns that run the height of the Oxenden Street façade, sprouting out atop the tower, are all smoothly rounded off, giving an impression of stripped classicism and seeming to regulate the otherwise rather disorganised elevation.

The lobby retains elements of the original streamlined art-deco details,

Robert Cromie 1937

Prince of Wales Theatre

Robert Cromie 1937

including the terrazzo floor, and parts of the circulation areas still betray the theatre's glittering early years. But unfortunately the large stalls bar, which had been a sparkling mirror-clad vision of LA glamour, has been turned into a dull cellar, though it is enlivened by some of the original disk-shaped column capitals, glass-block bar and a fine collection of antique theatre posters.

The auditorium has an intimate feel, partly due to the circle being brought very close to the stage. Cromie's skill in planning can be seen in what appears a spacious auditorium – in fact double the size and capacity of C J Phipps' 1884 theatre, originally on the same site and demolished to make way for the modern building. The original, vaguely art-deco reliefs and decoration within the auditorium have survived (particularly around the front of the circle) and the seats retain their distinctive sides. The abstracted drapery of the side walls and a few nice jazzy touches hidden away in corners make the interior worth exploring during the interval.

More of Cromie's stripped moderne architecture can be seen at the London Apollo Hammersmith (1932), the Regal (now Odeon) cinema in the Broadway, Wimbledon, and the Regal (now Cannon) cinemas in Streatham High Road and Beckenham High Road.

ADDRESS Coventry Street, London W1 (020 7839 5987)
UNDERGROUND Leicester Square/Piccadilly

Robert Cromie 1937

Robert Cromie 1937

Piccadilly Theatre

Dwarfed by the backside of the Regent Palace Hotel and set within the tight urban fabric of the edge of Soho, the light bulbs that flash around the canopy of the Piccadilly Theatre could be mistaken for signposts of one of the nude revues for which this area is better known. It comes as a surprise then to find that this lacklustre grey stone façade with its half-hearted curve stands in front of one of the West End's largest theatres which, when it was built in 1928, had a capacity of 1400.

The original impressive gold and green art-deco interior by Marc-Henri and Laverdet was unfortunately messed up in 1955 when a new, duller scheme was introduced which has stripped away most of the charm the theatre may have had. Some nice art-deco metal and glass light sconces remain scattered throughout the building which I assume are tenacious remnants of the original interior.

The theatre is entered via an understated elliptical lobby which is generously spacious compared to many West End theatres and leaves plenty of room for the box office. Within the auditorium, the proscenium is curved and begins to wrap around the stalls; the seating answers this curve with its own broadly sweeping, fan-shaped arrangement and this in turn echoes the form of the building's façade.

The view from outside, looking down towards Westminster via Piccadilly Circus, is one of London's best.

ADDRESS Denman Street, London W1 (020 7494 5070)
UNDERGROUND Piccadilly Circus

Edward A Stone and Bertie Crewe 1928

Piccadilly Theatre

west end

Edward A Stone and Bertie Crewe 1928

Lyric Theatre

The Lyric's sprawling, lacklustre brick façade is overshadowed by its larger and more obviously theatrical neighbours but it is, in fact, the oldest surviving theatre on Shaftesbury Avenue. The clumsy canopy and tacky shops which spoil its façade do the building few favours which is why it is a surprise to enter into a glittering, curvaceously art-deco foyer. The ceiling over the semi-circular space is a silvered half-dome with a wavy cornice, illuminated from behind by hidden lighting. A neat little box-office window fits seamlessly into one side and glass doors with lovely art-deco grilles lead through from the foyer into the stalls bar.

The bar itself is pure modernism which contrasts with the glitzy sliver glamour of the foyer. The plain walls are clad in restrained wood veneer and the edges of the openings are rounded in sleek gesture of deco streamlining. The excellent pendant light made up of three disks of glass and the minimal clock face set above the bar make this one of the few theatrical spaces in London where you can see the serious, elegantly reductivist side of 1930s modernism. These spaces were the work of Viennese-born architect Michael Rosenauer who remodelled the theatre in 1933. His brand of consistently elegant modernism can also be seen inside the Cambridge Theatre and at the excellent Time-Life building (1951–53) in Bruton Street.

The auditorium, however, remains firmly the work of the theatre's original creator, C J Phipps. Well-proportioned and finely detailed, it is a very fine Victorian auditorium with three balconies and and deep proscenium arch enveloping two pairs of boxes contained between finely modelled Corinthian columns. The proscenium itself is of brown and white alabaster. The tympanum above the arch features good relief work depicting a pair of winged hybrid creatures, a lyre and a lot of scrolls against a background of rich gilding. A circular ceiling of pale green and

C J Phipps 1888

Lyric Theatre

C J Phipps 1888

gold envelops the auditorium with a surprisingly understated Victorian elegance. It is this restraint and the essential simplicity of Phipps' work that differentiates it from the ebullient, garish vulgarity and brash, sculptural modelling of the great Edwardian theatre builders who followed him, Matcham in particular. It seems quite appropriate that his well-finished, good quality design should have been complemented by Rosenauer's stripped modernism which similarly reeks of high-class finishes, materials and attention to detail.

From street to auditorium represents an unusually rich journey encompassing the grimy Flemish brick and kitschy shopfronts of the façade through the futuristic shimmering silver of the foyer, on through the sleek modernism of the bar and finally into the rich golden embrace of the auditorium. One of the most varied and complete West End theatres.

ADDRESS Shaftesbury Avenue, London W1 (020 7494 5045)
UNDERGROUND Piccadilly Circus

C J Phipps 1888

Lyric Theatre

C J Phipps 1888

The Apollo

Elegant and well-preserved, The Apollo is one of the most urbane of the theatres along Shaftesbury Avenue. The façade is crowned by a pair of cupolas, each framed by a couple of impressive, stiff-nippled art-nouveau angels in flowing dresses, a very rare appearance of this flamboyant *fin-de-siècle* style in London's architecture. Some ironwork on the façade also comprised art-nouveau flourishes though most of this has disappeared.

The auditorium continues the uncluttered but frothy feel of the façade. The elegant space with a capacity of nearly 800 is notable for the complete absence of columns and the unobstructed views from most seats – highly unusual for 1901. The sophisticated auditorium and rather eccentric pit were apparently based on Richard Wagner's ideas from the Bayreuth Opera House. The orchestra pit was constructed as an oval with glazed walls surrounding it while a three-tiered rostrum (standing on glass legs) formed a series of different levels for the musicians to sit on. In this way it was hoped that all the instruments would be allowed to project without any of the muffling or confusion of notes that was usual in theatres.

The sculptures and gilded decoration of the auditorium are finely modelled and subtle, never overpowering the essential simplicity of the space. The figures supporting the boxes and the putti above, in particular, are beautifully modelled. In the dress circle an odd mascot is visible, a flying lizard framed by a pair of rampant lions, the badge of a tribe of German gypsies who had been associated with the estate (now in Poland) of the theatre's patron and builder, Henry Lowenfeld.

The Dutch-type building to the right of the theatre on Shaftesbury Avenue, originally the Apollo Restaurant, was also designed by Sharp.

ADDRESS Shaftesbury Avenue, London W1 (020 7494 5070)
UNDERGROUND Piccadilly Circus

Lewen Sharp 1901

Lewen Sharp 1901

Gielgud Theatre

The Gielgud originally stood as half of a grand architectural ensemble – the neighbouring Queen's (now rebuilt with a crushingly dull modern façade; see page 1.32) formed the other half and it is easy to see how impressive they must have looked together. Originally known as Hick's Theatre and subsequently as the Globe, the Gielgud represents some of the best work of its architect, the ubiquitous W G R Sprague.

The corner treatment is robustly Edwardian, crowned with a bold hemispherical cupola which encourages the eye to swing round from Shaftesbury Avenue into Soho. The detailing of the stonework is typically Edwardian free-classical, robust, inventive and pompous, while the iron brackets to the canopies display hints of art nouveau in their delicately wrought details. The corner entrance leads to the foyer via a perfectly formed semi-circular vestibule. Look at the original radiators en route.

The generous foyer itself is dominated by the elliptical hole in its ceiling revealing the lovely bar above. The fine gilded details and cherubs betray the Francophile taste of Edwardian London and the whole theatre continues in a strongly Louis XVI vein. The auditorium is well-preserved and elegant with the same cherubs (bizarrely part fish, part putti) which can be seen in the foyer reappearing on the balcony fronts and with urns, garlands and very fine reliefs (some featuring Pan and fauns) everywhere you look. It is almost trying too hard to be French and refined, so the whole thing becomes a little detached and cold. Good, nevertheless.

ADDRESS Shaftesbury Avenue, London W1 (020 7494 5065)
UNDERGROUND Piccadilly Circus

W G R Sprague 1906

Gielgud Theatre

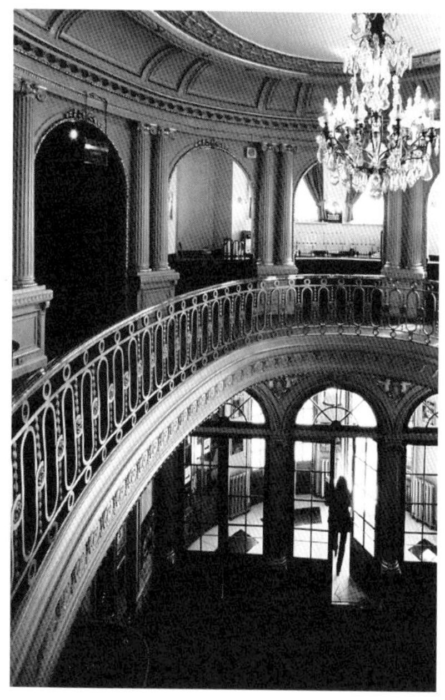

W G R Sprague 1906

The Queen's

Bit of a surprise, this one. This utterly undistinguished modern block standing on the corner of Shaftesbury Avenue and Wardour Street desperately needs the bright neons announcing current productions, without which there would be few clues that this was any kind of place of entertainment. Of these clues through, the most successful are the tactile brass door-handles in the shape of dramatic masks that adorn the glass doors. The foyer is as grim as the façade suggests but beyond, the auditorium is a very fine example of the work of W G R Sprague (1907), an exuberant and elaborate piece of Edwardiana.

The façade was rebuilt in 1959 as a result of bomb damage sustained in 1940 which also took out much of the interior. The auditorium, however, was restored and to get an idea of what the original elevations might have looked like it is only necessary to take a look at the Gielgud down the road (see page 1.30); the two theatres were designed as an architectural pair. The auditorium is capped by a very elaborate shallow dome painted in red, blue, cream and gold and sub-divided into four quarters each framed by a pair of *fin-de-siècle* classical nudes. Below these hangs a ring-shaped light fitting in the form of a huge garland of flowers. Vaguely art-nouveau figures adorn the walls beneath the ceiling and there is a highly eclectic blend of putti, Adam-style garlands and not-quite erotic nudes.

The Queen's boasts an interior that delights in its theatricality and which, like the Lyric Hammersmith (see page 8.8), pits the grimness of post-war design against the reckless exuberance and stick-on decoration of the Edwardians. The Edwardians win.

ADDRESS Shaftesbury Avenue, London W1 (020 7494 5040)
UNDERGROUND Piccadilly Circus

Westwood, Sons and Partner with Hugh Casson 1959

The Queen's

Westwood, Sons and Partner with Hugh Casson 1959

Palace Theatre

This huge theatre stands as a monument to Richard D'Oyly Carte and his dream of a building devoted to English Opera. D'Oyly Carte had built the Savoy in 1882 (see page 2.8) to produce the light operas of Gilbert and Sullivan. Later in the same decade massive slum clearances in Soho provided him with an opportunity to buy a huge site in the West End for his plan to erect a Royal English Opera House. He turned to the architect with whom he was later to work on his Savoy Hotel, Thomas Collcutt. The building itself was a fantastic success. The problem was that there were really no decent English operas. A year after it was completed it became the Palace Theatre of Varieties.

The Palace is one of the very few free-standing theatres in London, and it is among the most impressive, both inside and out. The grand façade facing Cambridge Circus forces the other buildings around it into submission and dominates the scene, acting as a kind of guardian of the gateway into Soho. A shining example of Victorian townscape, the façade is an uncertain Francophile amalgam of Romanesque and railway terminal. Framed by two pairs of domed turrets, the subtly curved main elevation is wonderfully busy and full of movement but doesn't really go anywhere. At street level the whole thing is tied together with a glazed canopy that features a series of well-wrought iron brackets and that gives shelter to lost tourists, beggars and motorbike couriers on two sides of the building. Entrances to the various balconies within the auditorium are spread all around the walls but everyone now enters via the main foyer.

The foyer itself presents a strange contrast with the brick and terracotta of the exterior. Clad completely in heavily grained marble, the space is superbly theatrical with a dramatic stair, inspired perhaps by a Florentine palazzo. An illusion of theatrical depth is created by a series of arches, columns and balustrades. One window in particular is a masterpiece of

T E Collcutt and G H Holloway 1888–91

T E Collcutt and G H Holloway 1888–91

the absurd; a marble arch springs from the middle of the round opening creating what I think is one of the best, if most bizarre, windows in the capital.

The theatre is planned so that the ancillary spaces cluster around the edges of the building and insulate the auditorium from the noise of the city outside. The auditorium itself is huge (seating 1450) and takes full advantage of contemporary innovations in steel construction and cantilevering with three enormous balconies stacked up on top of each other with no columns or other restrictions. In fact, the Palace was the first London theatre to be built using this new steel construction technology and it revolutionised ideas about theatre architecture.

The vertical ascent through the building can be read as a physical manifestation of the engrained Victorian class system with boldly modelled reliefs picked out in gold and fantastic strapwork decorations giving way gradually to austere brown glazed bricks of the type you see in Victorian public lavatories in the balcony (cheapest tickets). Easy to keep clean, too – an important consideration in dealing with the unwashed masses. The balcony is also raked at an alarming angle which, although it provides relatively good sightlines, is not recommended for vertigo sufferers.

Most of the embossed wall decorations are encrusted with years of accrued paint and have lost their sharpness and detail. According to the theatre's archivist, the reason so many of the interior surfaces are coated in a deep aubergine colour is that the theatre obtained a job lot of paint from one of the railway companies privatised after the Second World War, and that colour was the railway's livery. Even the lush marbles framing the proscenium arch have been cruelly painted over in an effort to minimise reflected light.

The gently curving stalls bar which follows the line of the back of the

T E Collcutt and G H Holloway 1888–91

auditorium is one of the finest theatre bars in the West End. The embossed decorations on the ceiling, walls and bar itself seem to glow in the golden light cast by the elaborate wall-mounted candelabras and expansive mirrors reflect and refract the light back into the space. It is at once fussy and generous, pompous and yet welcoming, a jewel of overblown high Victoriana and a sparkling antidote to the gloom of an auditorium suffocating under heavy overcoats of dull, heavy paint. The exterior was renovated and cleaned in 1987, the auditorium is still waiting.

ADDRESS Cambridge Circus/Shaftesbury Avenue, London W1
(020 7434 0909)
UNDERGROUND Leicester Square/Tottenham Court Road/
Piccadilly Circus

T E Collcutt and G H Holloway 1888–91

Prince Edward Theatre

This monumental theatre with its massive brick façade somehow manages to blend in to the narrow, lively streets of Soho without creating a fuss. Its blocky, rather austere exterior gives only a few hints of the rich depth of its interior in the wonderful art-deco doors and grilles. The faux-deco canopy is a little too heavy and the four massive torches a little too large but it all falls into place once inside. In the circular foyer, glamour is provided by the restored glass frills decorating its edges, Egyptian-influenced light fittings (appearing as column capitals around the walls) and a fine central light fitting.

The interior decoration was carried out by Marc-Henri and Laverdet who were also responsible for bringing a touch of Parisian art-deco fizz to the Whitehall Theatre, designed by the same architect, Edward A Stone and which opened a few months later (see page 3.2). There is something satisfying about the combination of Stone's massive and stony-silent façades and Marc-Henri and Laverdet's dazzling deco.

The auditorium is a fantastic riot of jazzy detail, some dating from an extensive restoration of the building by architects RHWL in 1993 and some surviving from the original scheme. The architects attempted to reproduce what had been there when the theatre was built in 1930. It is a large auditorium, seating more than 1600, and has a curious series of boxes descending from the dress circle down towards the stage. These are left over from a period when the theatre was used as a casino and dinner/dance venue. It was converted from solely theatrical use in 1935 and the stage was extended out towards the stalls in a large curving apron to form a dance floor. The stepped boxes are the remains of grand stairs which swept down to the dance floor; the stalls were occupied by dining tables. The cavernous kitchens were situated beneath the stage.

The ceiling is centred on a huge deco light fitting and its sunburst

Edward A Stone and Marc-Henri and Laverdet 1930

Edward A Stone and Marc-Henri and Laverdet 1930

pattern is echoed all around the walls. There are so many fine original details that it is impossible to list them all but it is particularly worth looking at the dramatic lights on the side walls of the auditorium, each a stacked series of glass vessels surrounded by typically 1930s, Aztec-influenced pyramidal patterns and exuberant sunbursts. The metal grilles to the lighting panels in the ceiling formed by the underside of the balconies (and indeed throughout the building) are delightfully varied. Look also at the stylised fountain motifs at the back of the stalls, the ceiling grilles in front of the proscenium arch and the pierced metal friezes at the back of the stalls as well as features dating from the restoration including reproductions of original wallpapers. The bars too are extravagantly period with wonderfully tacky sculptural mirrored shelves for drinks, deco-chinoiserie bar fronts and delicately moulded ceilings. Even the stairs feature little illuminated display cases with stylised floral-patterned glass and chequerboard mosaic borders. An art-deco jewel.

ADDRESS Old Compton Street, London W1 (020 7447 5400)
UNDERGROUND Leicester Square/Tottenham Court Road/ Piccadilly Circus

Edward A Stone and Marc-Henri and Laverdet 1930

Phoenix Theatre

Bits of this odd little theatre humbly poke out from behind an overbearing and dull brick block on the Charing Cross Road. It looks as though the delicate theatre has been stamped on and squeezed out to the edges of the site. It is a surprise then to find a well-preserved and delicate interior in which the atmosphere of 1930 survives intact. The theatre was designed by a remarkable team that included Sir Giles Gilbert Scott, who two years after the completion of this theatre designed Battersea power station. He later went on to design the Bankside power station (now home to the Tate Modern gallery) in the same heroically monumental vein. Also involved in the design were Bertie Crewe, a survivor from the Edwardian theatre-building boom, and Cecil Masey, an architect who sprang from Crewe's office to success in his own right. To ice the cake Theodore Komisarjevsky was brought in, and the Phoenix's wonderfully theatrical (and rather tacky and two-dimensional) interiors are thanks to the Russian-born maestro of gilt, chandeliers and stick-on Hollywood glamour, better known for his definitive work on cinema interiors as palaces of escapism.

Perhaps the ugliest box office in London gives no hint of an interior that is among the most intricate and flamboyant of this remarkably fecund period of London theatre architecture. Shallow, sexy, funny and luxurious in turn, the foyers and bars revel in scarlet and gold, in mirrored ceilings and walls and scalloped niches; this proved the perfect venue for effete 1930s comedies. It is a stage-set vision of luxury, all rather flat and designed to exert maximum effect, the perfect frothy theatrical backdrop and an eloquent answer to the new threat from the cinema.

The auditorium is good, if unspectacular. Both the tiers have good sight-lines and the whole space has a kind of elegant beaux-arts feel compounded by the banal copies of late Renaissance paintings (executed

Sir G G Scott, B Crewe, C Masey, T Komisarjevsky 1930

Sir G G Scott, B Crewe, C Masey, T Komisarjevsky 1930

by Vladimir Polunin, a frequent collaborator of Komisarjevsky's) which do nothing to enliven the space. Some of the other public areas of the theatre feature a kind of spindly, two-D classicism (also visible on some parts of the façade), reminiscent of the kind of architecture popular in Scandinavia at the time, particularly in the work of Swedish master Gunnar Asplund. The light fittings throughout are wonderfully sculptural creations which blend art deco with all kinds of eclectic stylings. Each one is worth a look, but particularly the elaborate chandelier in the auditorium.

The big surprise is to find a superb façade tucked away in Phoenix Street. Twisted columns support a wonderful faïence arcade while a slender ironwork canopy is decorated with little cast phoenixes. The iron fanlights are exquisitely delicate while the original little box offices are wasted, being open only just before the show. Beyond is a wildly polychromatic bar with a vaulted, coffered ceiling and loads of atmosphere. Also worth looking at is the original entrance foyer which is on Charing Cross Road and looks diagonally towards Foyles bookshop. It is not now used for its original purpose as it is absolutely tiny but its cylindrical form, elegant gold-encrusted columns and marble floor make it one of the most intimate, best-defined and most compact spaces in the building. You can see it by peeking in through the theatre's rounded corner.

ADDRESS Charing Cross Road, London WC2 (020 7369 1733)
UNDERGROUND Tottenham Court Road/Leicester Square

Sir G G Scott, B Crewe, C Masey, T Komisarjevsky 1930

London Palladium

The stage-set classicism of the Palladium's overblown Roman temple façade is a perfect introduction to London's largest theatre. The façade incorporates elements from the 'Corinthian Bazaar' that had originally occupied the site. *Ben Hur*-style Roman statues crown the building while the richly veined marble of the foyer draws the public in through the gleaming brass and bevelled glass of the elaborate doors. Once inside, the camp grandeur is almost over-powering; highly polished brass railings and lions' heads fight for attention with elaborate gilded plaster mouldings and marble columns. This is the perfect escape from the awful cheap squalor of Oxford Street and the crowded attempt at grandeur of Oxford Circus. Built by theatre architect supreme, Frank Matcham in 1910, the Palladium somehow remains the home of British variety (or vaudeville) even though variety itself seems to have been long dead.

The site had previously hosted a building housing a circus. This gave way to an ice-skating rink and was acquired as a venue for variety and music hall during the height of their success when the enormous Hippodrome (now a Leicester Square nightclub) and Coliseum (English National Opera, see page 2.14) also functioned as music halls. In common with those two buildings, also designed by Matcham, the Palladium is enormous. Two cantilevered tiers and a spacious auditorium ensure that more than 2200 people have clear views of the large stage.

The decoration is exactly the kind of over-elaborate escapism that you would expect inside such a building, the gaudy, golden excess which defines music-hall interiors. In fact the sumptuous marble finishes and gilded details were found to be overpowering when the venue switched from variety to theatre. Some marble was over-painted to tone it down in the hope that the surfaces would become less distracting. When the theatre was opened telephones were installed in the boxes so that those

Frank Matcham 1910

London Palladium

Frank Matcham 1910

seated within them could talk to those in other boxes. The royal box can be distinguished by the cipher on its front.

The Cinderella Bar, which serves the dress circle, is worth looking at; a rococo fantasy worthy of its fairy-tale title, the white furniture dribbles with gilding, the curvy bar luxuriates in gleaming brass fittings and the whole is reflected over and over in mirrors. It exudes a brash, vulgar idea of elegance, enjoyably theatrical and unselfconscious. The Palm Court (now Palm Court Bar in much-altered form) was originally capable of accommodating up to 1000 people for tea. It is also worth looking at the framed pictures of stars who have appeared at the Palladium over the years; these line the walls of the corridor leading to the box-office. The pictures give a good idea of the status of the theatre in showbiz history.

ADDRESS Argyll Street, London WC1 (020 7494 5020)
UNDERGROUND Oxford Circus

Frank Matcham 1910

Soho Theatre and Writers Centre

Though very near London's theatreland, Soho's Dean Street is known for self-consciously trendy bars and restaurants and the appearance of a new theatre here is genuinely unexpected. Just a couple of doors away from the house where Karl Marx lived in the 1850s, this building was formerly the West End Great Synagogue. The original building was retained rather than replaced but the auditorium has not simply been put in the space the synagogue used to occupy. Instead, the ground floor is taken up largely by a restaurant and café (which shares its sleek horseshoe-shaped bar with the theatre and provides crucial rental income) and the box office while the theatre was hitched up to first-floor level. The transparency and openness of the ground floor and the cool modern lines of the box office produce the feel that prevails throughout the building.

The theatre itself is small, intimate and highly flexible, adaptable to performances in the round, with a thrust stage or in a traditional arrangement. A pair of structural columns on either side of the stage are a reminder that this is a reused building and seem to hint at a proscenium which isn't actually there. Blue suede bench seats produce an air of Elvisy comfort and there is a closeness both to the stage and your neighbours though the theatre space is a little sterile. The internal spaces are all given a metallic feel by cool detailing that picks up the metal grid of the façade which denotes this as a theatre. The grid is intended as a vehicle for installations and as a kind of theatrical lighting rig to enliven the streetscape. Compact and self-consciously fashionable, it is a good, if perhaps cold, reuse of a bland building as one of the West End's very few venues for new writing.

ADDRESS 21 Dean Street, London W1 (020 7287 5060)
UNDERGROUND Tottenham Court Road

Paxton Locher Architects 1999–2000

Soho Theatre and Writers Centre

west end

Paxton Locher Architects 1999–2000

Dominion Theatre

The Dominion is a slightly schizophrenic building, straddling the border between super-cinemas which were becoming popular at the time it was designed and the West End theatres which the cinemas had replaced as the mass entertainment of choice. It was designed to accommodate both movies and stage-shows and remains a versatile venue. The stone façade to Tottenham Court Road certainly suggests a cinema with its elegant blend of classicism and art deco and it is a shame that the architecture is usually covered by hoardings. At least the curved attic storey and its fine ironwork always remains visible. The enormous foyer carries the deco movie-palace feel right into the building. Revelling in the size of the scheme, the architects installed a pair of grand staircases, stone-balustraded balconies, mirrored walls and odd-looking, almost Chinese-style chandeliers. Considering the amount of space, it seems odd that the box office is squeezed into a hole beneath the stairs.

The auditorium itself is enormous, seating more than 2000 (it was nearly 3000 in the 1930s) but it is disappointing after the art-deco promise of the façade. More lantern-type chandeliers add a touch of interest and the scale at least impresses.

The site was formerly occupied by a huge brewery where in 1814 an enormous vat of ale burst, drowning eight people in a flood of alcohol.

ADDRESS Tottenham Court Road, London W1 (020 7656 1888)
UNDERGROUND Tottenham Court Road

William and Thomas Ridley Milburn 1929

William and Thomas Ridley Milburn 1929

covent garden and the strand

Adelphi Theatre

You can see the most dramatic bit of the Adelphi just by peering into the foyer. The fantastic, crystalline light fitting lurking at the centre of the jagged, faceted ceiling like a spider in its web is one of the most unusual gems of London art deco. Its inspiration seems to have come from what was known as cubist architecture, a movement that flourished only in Czechoslovakia in the 1920s, just before the Adelphi was built. Characteristically faceted and jewel-like, the lobby light fitting is a very rare example of cubist-influenced design.

The current Adelphi is the fourth theatre on the site, the first, the Sans Pareil ('unparalleled') dating back to 1806. The third version of the theatre (1901) was designed by Ernest Runtz, incorporating parts of the 1887 theatre. If you look at the theatre from the Strand, the elaborate, colonnaded building neighbouring the Adelphi to the right is a survival from this design, the theatre originally stretched right along the street frontage. The current elevation (1937), clad in hospital-white faïence, is unadorned except for an odd-shaped window and the angular lettering which surmounts it acting as a cornice. This flat façade is in great contrast to Schaufelberg's original highly sculptural elevation.

Hard to envisage now, but the 1930 design featured a prow-like bay above the window (picked out in black to contrast with the white of the façade) and a series of stepped-back, ziggurat planes creating a dramatic cornice. The window, which can still be seen, was originally crowned by a more jagged head, with a zig-zag opening. This façade would have been a real eye-opener in a street of almost pure historicism and must have constituted one of the most strikingly modernistic façades in central London. I find it strange then that the building's architect has received so little attention and Schaufelberg's name now languishes in complete obscurity.

Ernest Schaufelberg 1930

Adelphi Theatre

Ernest Schaufelberg 1930

Adelphi Theatre

The art-deco exuberance of the lobby can be seen as an answer to the silvery flash of the Savoy Theatre opposite and the wonderful interiors of the Strand Palace Hotel, also completed in 1930 (all now ripped out but stored in the Victoria & Albert Museum). The interiors were recently restored in a bland deco pastiche and are a very pale shadow of the original. When built, the lobby featured Lalique glass fountain lights, sun-ray trough lighting (whatever that is) and a staircase clad in black marble. The auditorium features a few 1930s touches, notably the wonderful angular ceiling light which echoes the fittings in the lobby, and the unusual contemporary hexagonal windows in the doors. Otherwise it is rather undistinguished.

Bull Inn Court, a tight alley linking The Strand to Maiden Lane, retains a very good collection of colourful ceramic tiles on its walls incorporating signs pointing the way to the Adelphi gallery entrance, presumably survivals from the 1901 theatre. If you take this passage you emerge near the separate Royal entrance (with a crest above the door) beside the stage door in Maiden Lane.

ADDRESS The Strand, London WC2 (020 7344 0055)
UNDERGROUND Charing Cross

Ernest Schaufelberg 1930

Adelphi Theatre

Ernest Schaufelberg 1930

Vaudeville Theatre

A victim of consecutive rebuilds, each of which incorporated bits of the previous building, the Vaudeville nevertheless manages to retain a semblance of elegance. The unobtrusive façade to The Strand is perhaps the least theatrical elevation in this highly theatrical area, only the modest canopy beginning to announce that this is not an office or apartment block. The foyer is light and uplifting in a fussy, Edwardian kind of way with plenty of rococo gilding and mouldings. The timber booth of the ticket office however is ugly and obtrusive and ruins the integrity of this main public space. Above the foyer and behind the row of arched windows on the first floor can be found a bar which originally served as a summer smoking room in an age when smokers were shunned and segregated from polite society.

The façade dates from a later reworking of the building by the architect of the original 1870 building, C J Phipps. The auditorium, however, dates from 1925–26 when the original horseshoe-shaped interior was gutted and replaced with a rectangular version designed by Robert Atkinson. Unspectacular and workmanlike, the theatre functions well and provides an intimate experience but remains architecturally forgettable.

ADDRESS 404 The Strand, London WC2 (020 7836 9987)
UNDERGROUND Charing Cross/Covent Garden

C J Phipps 1892 and Robert Atkinson 1925–26

C J Phipps 1892 and Robert Atkinson 1925–26

The Savoy Theatre

The interior of The Savoy Theatre brought a touch of jazz-age glitter to the world of theatre at a time when the stage was in serious danger of being eclipsed by the advent of the talkies and an explosion in cinema audiences. It would be good to say that The Savoy interior is one of London's finest surviving examples of art deco, but it would not be true. What you see now is a very convincing reconstruction (by Whitfield Partners) of an interior that was completely destroyed by fire in 1991.

The Savoy has a long and important history in the London theatre scene. It originally opened in 1881, built by the impresario Richard D'Oyly Carte (who also built the Savoy Hotel), and it became the home of Gilbert and Sullivan's operas, which D'Oyly Carte produced. The original theatre (designed by C J Phipps) had been the first public building in the world to be illuminated with electric lighting and was also pioneering in its use of a simple, uncluttered interior, in great contrast to the fussy plasticity that dominated nineteenth-century theatre design. When the Strand entrance to the Savoy Hotel was jazzed-up with a gleaming canopy of glass and chrome, the theatre was also brought up to date. In 1929, Frank Tugwell and Basil Ionides (who was responsible for the wonderful deco interiors at Claridge's Hotel) redesigned the theatre in an explosion of metallic art deco that easily matched the excitement of the movies.

Although little detail survived the 1991 fire, the building had been well documented and the recreation of the original features was achieved with a painstaking attention to detail which allows us to get the feel of the original even though it is hardly more authentic than the reconstruction of the Globe (see page 7.2). The theatre is entered from Savoy Court and its front blends in with the silvery-sleek hotel entrance. From the elaborately modelled rams on the door handles to the metal and glass doors

Frank Tugwell and Basil Ionides 1929

The Savoy Theatre

Frank Tugwell and Basil Ionides 1929

themselves which are framed by gilded curtains, the tone of theatricality is set. The elegant but small box office gives a good indication of the mood of the theatre beyond with marble floor, decorated niches and an ornately layered ceiling.

Motifs tend to repeat themselves throughout the interior and as you take the stairs opposite the counters look out for the niches in the wall. These feature classic art-deco patterns within mini-prosceniums, stepped arches framing eagles, Aztec motifs and sunbeams. The first such niche features a kind of baboon atop a swirl of art-deco skyscrapers, seeming to hint at King Kong on the Empire State Building, except that the film was not made until four years after these designs were first executed. The panels were recreated using casts of the originals which had been kept in case of just such an emergency.

The auditorium too benefits from the recreation of a plethora of original art-deco panels. The line between the proscenium and the auditorium is blurred by the insertion of a band of silver framing the stage through the side walls and ceiling. The coffers on the walls each create frames for an individual stylised vignette, most based on some scene from a Gilbert and Sullivan opera and executed in a vaguely Japanese style. These too are reproductions of the original 1929 designs, as are the air-conditioning grilles above the circle which also feature this hybrid of deco-japonisme. The coffering in the walls and ceiling is curiously distorted and it becomes apparent from the centre of the theatre that they create a false perspective leading the eye inexorably toward the centre of the stage.

The royal box is also worth a look. The original box was extended outwards slightly (thus obscuring the view from a few of the circle seats) to accommodate the bulky form of Winston Churchill, who always sat there when at the theatre. Behind the royal box a small ante-room centres

Frank Tugwell and Basil Ionides 1929

around a remarkable ceiling with a series of gradually reducing star-shaped motifs cut into it, a light fitting illuminating the whole from the centre. The spiky, crystalline form of the starred ceiling suggests the influence of expressionism, an architectural style almost unknown in London.

Although the star-shaped ceiling cut-away occurs only behind the royal box, the foyers and bars throughout the theatre feature elaborate wavy designs (illuminated by unseen lights) evoking cloudy skies. Scalloped surfaces, etched-glass light fittings, geometric designs in the wallpapers and on the floors, silvered details and brass fittings make the whole interior sparkle like a brash diamond. Yet despite its jazzy exuberance the auditorium is elegant and simple, the decoration never overbearing. The atmosphere is heightened by the wonderful journey from foyer to seat, a rich sequence of jewel-like spaces that builds up to the climax of the performance itself.

ADDRESS Savoy Court, London WC2 (020 7836 8888)
UNDERGROUND Charing Cross/Embankment/Temple

Frank Tugwell and Basil Ionides 1929

The London Coliseum

2.14 Like that of the nearby Hippodrome, the name of this theatre was intended to evoke the grandeur of Ancient Rome, and the pompous title neatly reflects the scale and ambition of the project. When it opened in 1904 the Coliseum was the largest theatre in London with an enormous capacity of more than 2350, and the great illuminated globe which surmounts it became one of London's most recognisable theatrical landmarks. It was built by Oswald Stoll who chose Frank Matcham (who had designed the Hippodrome four years earlier) as his architect; together they created one of the defining monuments of Edwardian architecture.

The blocky tower lurking at the Trafalgar Square side of the composition is grossly out of proportion to the rest of the building and capped by an absurd wedding cake of columns, statues and cupola that culminates in the famous globe. Four statues representing art, architecture, music and science sit at the corners of the stocky, rusticated tower and on the next level up four lions echo those in Trafalgar Square. The rest of the building is a magical example of crowded and exuberant Edwardian baroque mixing heavy Piranesian arches, over-scaled aedicules around the windows and projecting canopies with aplomb and scant regard for proportion. The foyers exhibit more taste but an equal urge for antique splendour and fine Byzantine-influenced golden mosaics can be seen in the spandrels and the shallow dome above the information desk, though unfortunately the mosaic floors are now covered by carpet.

The theatre itself boasted a barrage of incredible technical innovations which made it the most modern as well as the grandest arena of the Belle Epoque. Among these innovations were a marvellously elaborate revolving stage (the first of its kind in Britain), consisting of three separate concentric rings that could revolve independently of each other, apparently at speeds of up to 20 mph. The building also boasted lifts to take

Frank Matcham 1904

Frank Matcham 1904

guests up to the Terrace Tea Room (a glazed winter garden that stood above the St Martin's Lane elevation was demolished in 1951) and to the upper levels. Every level had its own tea room, each decorated in flamboyant art-nouveau style. In the terrace-level tea room a band performed four times a day. Most incredible, to me at least, was the device employed to avoid royalty coming into contact with the plebs. A royal anteroom constructed on wheels could be rolled along the public corridor between the royal lift and the royal box, as the circulation could not be solved any other way. Royals in a box on wheels. Surreal.

In contrast to the rather bloated features of the elevation, Matcham's auditorium is absolutely magnificent, probably the most impressive in London. A wonderfully light shallow dome seems to float over the grand space like a canopy and unifies the audience with the 15-metre-wide proscenium arch. Three tiers of seating rise above the stalls and the interior features much of the Roman kitsch that populates the terracotta front of the building including dusty sculpted lions pulling chariots, friezes, medallions featuring Roman emperors and richly veined marble columns and gilded capitals.

Despite the magnificence of the venue, the huge cost Stoll incurred in its building took its toll almost immediately and the viability of the theatre was always to be plagued with uncertainty. A little over a year after it opened, Stoll was forced to close the theatre due to debt. Big variety productions of the sort the theatre was intended to house proved extravagantly expensive to stage and even with four shows a day the venue couldn't be saved once the novelty value of the building itself had worn off. The Coliseum had been positioned close to Charing Cross station in an effort to attract crowds of suburbanites and the entertainment had been aimed at families in deliberate contrast to the coarseness of much

Frank Matcham 1904

music hall. The policy was not a success. The Coliseum has subsequently reopened as a serious theatre, music hall, opera house, musical venue, one of the first TV theatres and a cinema. This last necessitated much damage to the spectacular interior, particularly to the dress circle where the projection equipment was housed. In 1968 the Coliseum was converted back to theatre use when the Islington home of the Sadler's Wells Opera proved too small for expanding audiences. In 1974 The Sadler's Wells Opera became the English National Opera and the theatre remains the venue for popular opera sung in English at more affordable prices than the Royal Opera in Covent Garden.

The globe that acts as the building's billboard to the West End currently gives the appearance of spinning through a series of electric bulbs timed in a particular way. The original sign physically revolved on its axis but as soon as it began working Westminster City Council took Stoll to court for contravening the strict London Building Acts which forbade kinetic sky-signs. Stoll and Matcham argued that the globe was an integral part of the structure rather than a separate sign – after a lengthy court case the current compromise was reached.

ADDRESS St Martin's Lane, London WC2 (020 7632 8300)
UNDERGROUND Leicester Square

Frank Matcham 1904

The London Coliseum

Frank Matcham 1904

The Duke of York's

This theatre was the first to be built in St Martin's Lane, then a backwater, although the area has since become a link in the theatrical chain that ties Shaftesbury Avenue to Covent Garden. The modest and restrained façade to St Martin's Lane proves a good introduction to a pleasantly elegant little theatre, a rare example of the Victorian in a West End dominated by brasher Edwardian theatres. It was built in 1892 by architect Walter Emden, who despite lacking formal academic training, nevertheless developed a thriving office which excelled in designs for restaurants and hotels as well as theatres, including the nearby Garrick.

A very spacious and elegant dress-circle bar opens on to a small terrace in a loggia on the St Martin's Lane frontage and benefits from enormous and elaborate gilded mirrors, one with a marble console. The auditorium is compact and quite tall, capped with a neat little shallow dome and, unusually, the theatre sells cheap standing tickets for the upper circle. Due to its small size, many of the seats towards the rear of the theatre have terrible views of the stage, further interrupted by lighting rigs. Nevertheless the intimate feel of a small Victorian theatre is well preserved.

During the war the Duke of York's was damaged by bombing and was closed between 1940 and 1943. In 1950 it was redecorated to the designs of Cecil Beaton. Look out for the ceramic plaque in the side room of the dress-circle bar that commemorates the mass meeting of actors held there in 1929 at which it was decided to form Equity, their union.

ADDRESS St Martin's Lane, London WC2 (020 7836 5122)
TRANSPORT Leicester Square/Charing Cross

The Duke of York's

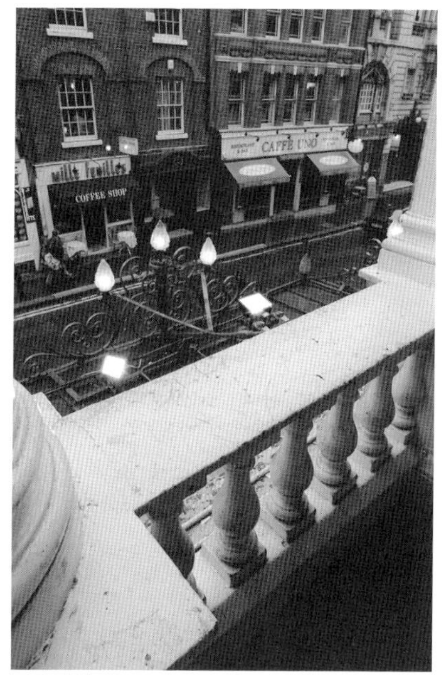

Walter Emden 1892

Garrick Theatre

The heavy, columnated stone façade of the Garrick at the end of Charing Cross Road fronts one of the lightest and finest theatrical interiors in London. The compact semicircular foyer with its original box-office windows sets the tone for the whole building with an unusual lightness of touch and the delicacy of its Italianate decoration. Every relief is interesting and finely detailed, even the curious sphinxes on the ceiling. The upper-circle bar with its coffered ceiling, chandelier and good reliefs all help to set the frothy late-Victorian tone. The terrace (situated behind the colonnade) provides a welcome breath of fresh air in the interval and an excellent vantage point for watching West End life. Also have a look at the fine pierced copper radiator covers in the bar.

The auditorium (which, surprisingly, is placed parallel to the street frontage) is both airy and intimate. Its refined dome, one of the best in London, features groups of allegorical figures. There is no real proscenium, merely an arched opening between the boxes which themselves frame the stage. Above the upper boxes, caryatids (this type of half-human/half-structural pilaster is sometimes known as a herm) support the ceiling on their heads while the arches contain classical busts. Putti and tragic/comic masks on the balcony fronts continue the theme of Roman/Italianate decoration while a crystal chandelier completes a decadent sense of luxury, cleverly contained within the bounds of good taste.

ADDRESS 2 Charing Cross Road, London WC2 (020 7494 5085)
UNDERGROUND Leicester Square/Charing Cross

Walter Emden and C J Phipps 1889

Garrick Theatre

Walter Emden and C J Phipps 1889

Wyndham's Theatre

The front of Wyndham's Theatre on Charing Cross Road is one of the liveliest in London. Always crowded, always buzzing, the building's lively and well-proportioned stone façade adds a touch of class to a jumbled, incoherent streetscape. The composition of curving balconies, elaborate timber windows and delicate palazzo details brings the stone façade to life. The sculpted herms on the attic storey and the putti beneath the canopy to Charing Cross Road are easily missed but well worth raising your eyes for. The perfectly formed little circular lobby whisks you into a world of frothy *fin-de-siècle* elegance.

In fact Wyndham's is the ultimate *fin-de-siècle* monument: the last London theatre to be built in the nineteenth century, it defines the age. Walls of Wedgwood blue and cream, gilded details and a finely painted circular panel (mellowed and yellowed by age) set into the ceiling introduce the visitor to the most delicate, compact and well formed of West End theatres. The painting of angels and cherubs which surmounts the lobby is inspired by the rococo frilliness of François Boucher and presages the larger series of four painted panels that decorate the shallow dome of the auditorium, and owe a similar debt to the French artist.

The auditorium itself carries on the atmosphere set up in the foyer, one of frilly (but always tasteful) playfulness. Three tiers of boxes surround a picture-frame proscenium, crowned by a pair of winged angels holding garlands and a pair of portraits depicting the playwrights Goldsmith (on the left) and Sheridan. The palm-winged figure at the centre of the composition probably represents Mary Moore, the leading lady of the theatre's founder Charles Wyndham. She later became his second wife and her society connections helped Wyndham to raise the money needed to build the theatre. He moved here from the Criterion in Piccadilly and the new theatre was built on land owned by the Marquess of Salisbury, who was

W G R Sprague 1899

Wyndham's Theatre

W G R Sprague 1899

prime minister at the time the theatre was built. The piece of land stretched back a long way and Wyndham subsequently constructed the Albery (then the New Theatre) on the remaining part of the site. The two theatres share a stage door, despite being separated by an alley, and are linked by a bridge clad in corrugated metal which is significantly less elegant than their respective interiors.

The Marquess of Salisbury is memorialised in the pub behind the theatre in St Martin's Lane that bears his name and features one of the best Victorian pub interiors in London, with sparkling etched glass, shiny brass and rich, dark wood. The pub offers a tantalising glimpse into the thriving theatrical social life of the capital.

ADDRESS Charing Cross Road, London WC2 (020 7369 1736)
UNDERGROUND Leicester Square

W G R Sprague 1899

W G R Sprague 1899

The Albery

> Mr W G R Sprague, the Architect, has excelled himself, in this, his thirtieth theatre, and from an architectural point of view Sir Charles's New Theatre is the acme of perfection.

That is how the opening-night souvenir programme began to describe the theatre, then known as the New Theatre but which has been known as The Albery since 1973. But then they would say that, wouldn't they? The same programme is just as gushing about the interior features:

> Perhaps the most noteworthy feature of the Theatre is the exquisite treatment of decoration, which is of the period of Louis XVI and has been adhered to, even to the minutest details, throughout ... Over the Proscenium will be seen a perfectly modelled gilt trophy emblematic of Peace and Music, while on the other side are models of Cupids, illustrating Winter and Summer, copied from bronzes in the collection of Mr Claude Ponsonby.
>
> The panels in the Auditorium are decorated with beautiful portrait medallions of the French Kings and Queens.

There doesn't seem to be a lot more to say: the contemporary PR machine was in full flow and didn't leave much to the imagination. But we could add just a little history to this description of the acme of perfection.

The theatre was built by the actor/manager Charles Wyndham (who earlier built the Criterion) on land left over after he built Wyndham's Theatre (see page 2.24) which stands on the other side of The Albery. Wyndham employed the same architect as he had for his eponymous theatre, the prolific W G R Sprague. Like its sister theatre, The Albery is a sophisticated work that effortlessly slots in to the theatrical milieu of St Martin's Lane. Sprague cut his teeth working for Matcham whose

The Albery

W G R Sprague 1903

spectacularly overblown work can be seen over the road at the Coliseum. Sprague's work was always more restrained than his master's and The Albery is a good example – as the opening-night blurb commented, 'The front elevation is of the free classic order, and is at once dignified and effective.'

The auditorium, which has three upper tiers and excellent sight-lines, leads on naturally from the façade and from the posh-looking foyer with its gilded ceilings, solid, conservative doors and bevelled glass, a civilised and elegant interior capped by a large shallow dome and plenty of unobtrusive decoration. The torches that illuminate the auditorium are unusually well-preserved, as is the large central chandelier while the cartouche above the proscenium arch has already been mentioned and one mention is enough. The royal box comes complete with a very tasteful retiring room. The dress circle bar (now royal circle bar) is also among the most elegant in the West End. The acme.

ADDRESS St Martin's Lane, London WC2 (020 7369 1730)
UNDERGROUND Leicester Square/Charing Cross

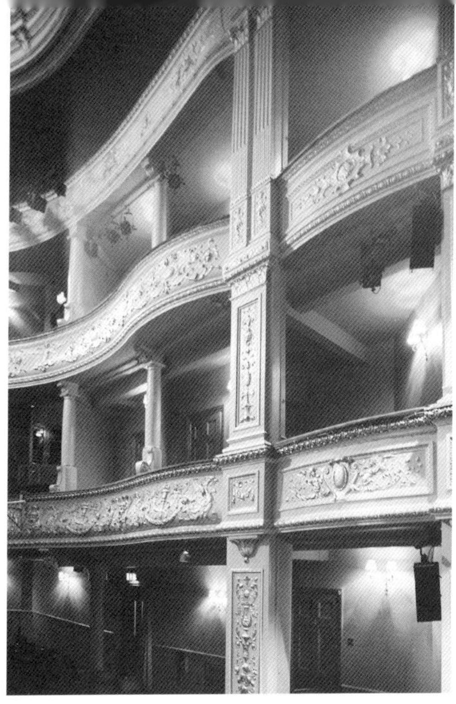

W G R Sprague 1903

New Ambassadors

The unassuming and restrained façade of the New Ambassadors hardly exudes theatrical excitement. The stolid, dense classicism of the elevation signals the end of the era of Edwardian exuberance. Less than a decade earlier its architect, W G R Sprague, was designing the frothy, exquisitely detailed theatres, the Aldwych and the Strand (see pages 2.76 and 2.74). Sculptural, almost over-enthusiastic modelling of the façades and the auditorium encapsulated the Francophile appeal and elegance of *fin-de-siècle* style. The Ambassadors, built the year before the outbreak of the First World War, represents the beginnings of the severe reaction to all that inconsequential frilliness.

Things soften up a bit as you get inside, though. At the time of writing the compact circular lobby is adorned with a spindly, junk-chic chandelier and deliberately trashy light fittings – all part of an attempt to reduce the ostensible glamour of the theatre by the Royal Court (see page 8.2) when it was temporarily in residence here. The stripped, bare plaster walls are part of the same process of democratisation. The auditorium is fancier than the outside would suggest but still a far cry from the splendour of Sprague's earlier theatres. The decorative scheme revolves around a series of ambassadorial crests (a play on the theatre's name) around the top of the walls and above the proscenium. One tall box to either side of the stage sets the scene for the productions and decoration is generally confined to a minimum of frills and flourishes. The original chandelier survives intact, as does most of the decoration. The theatre provides a compact and satisfying venue; most seats are close enough to the stage to create real intimacy between audience and actors.

ADDRESS West Street, London WC2 (020 7369 1761)
UNDERGROUND Leicester Square

W G R Sprague 1913

W G R Sprague 1913

St Martin's Theatre

The last theatre of the Edwardian era, the St Martin's is elegant and unique, but destined to remain an enigma to most Londoners. The reason for this is that the same play, Agatha Christie's *The Mousetrap*, has been running here, and previously next door at the New Ambassadors, continuously since 1952. A shame because the auditorium of the St Martin's is well worth seeing. Ironically, it's probably perfectly suited to the turgid country-house murder plot of Christie's interminable play.

Sprague designed the St Martin's and the neighbouring New Ambassadors as an ensemble in this cramped corner of theatreland. Designed in 1913, the outbreak of the First World War delayed construction and it was only completed in 1916. The façade is in a severe classical style with four chunky columns rising through it. A cartouche used to surmount the centre but was destroyed by bombing during the Blitz and the elevations still seem incomplete. The foyer is pretty but sober, its most interesting feature a board displaying the inexplicable number of performances *The Mousetrap* has achieved.

The sobriety is taken through to the auditorium. The frippery of the Edwardian auditorium has been abandoned altogether in favour of a severe, heavy classicism. The weighty columns that appear on the façade are echoed in the solid Doric columns framing the side walls. The ceiling is lightened by a delicate glass dome, giving the impression of a winter garden during daylight hours. At night, however, the solidity of the rich, dark hardwood highlights the flimsiness of the sets. The theatre displays the transition from Francophile frilliness to English solidity and understatement.

ADDRESS West Street, London WC2 (020 7836 1443)
UNDERGROUND Leicester Square

W G R Sprague 1916

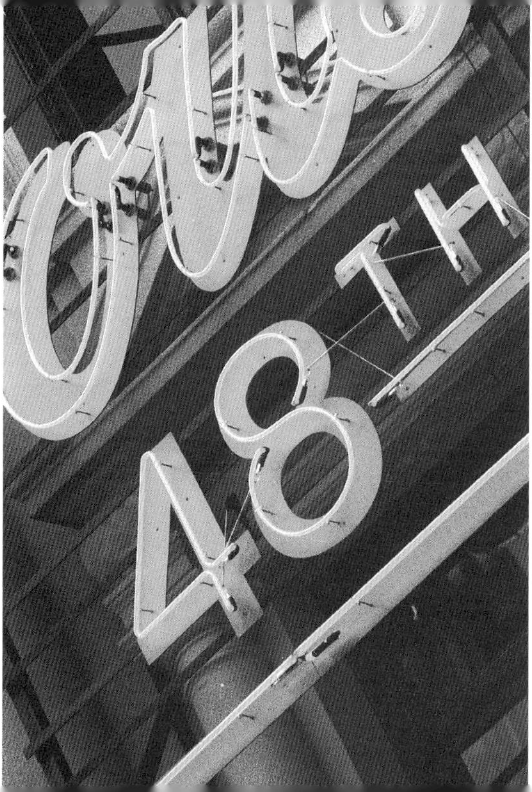

Cambridge Theatre

The severe, blocky wedge of stone sitting between two of the seven roads that converge on the junction of Seven Dials does little to suggest that the Cambridge Theatre contains one of London's best art-deco interiors. The round entrance lobby, however, immediately gives the game away – classic 1930. On entering you are confronted by a relief frieze of figures frozen in awkward, balletic stances. This symmetrical grouping recalls the straining athleticism that characterised the worship of the perfection of human form characteristic of both fascist and communist regimes of the 1930s. Moving on into the foyer similar friezes can be seen on either end wall, these more reminiscent of Hollywood musical extravaganzas. The two ends of the oval foyer are tied together with a silver ceiling and at the centre sits the box office which draws attention to itself via a fine brass front featuring a series of incised geometric motifs. The same geometrically patterned brass also adorns a number of doors throughout the theatre, including those to the stalls, which can be reached from the foyer along a slick, curved corridor with a vaulted ceiling, illuminated by lights concealed behind coving. The slight ribbing to the ceiling creates an unusual, theatrical effect which betrays the influence of German expressionist architecture.

The auditorium is a wonderful space, very different to other West End theatres. Unusually it is curved in both plan and section and the space seems to embrace the visitor in an organic form, in stark contrast to the austere angularity and the inexpressive stone of the façades. The designer of the interiors was the Russian emigre, Serge Chermayeff, later the partner of Erich Mendelsohn. Both architects were responsible for bringing a blend of expressionism and avant-garde modernism to England. This theatre is probably Chermayeff's best surviving London interior. The ceiling arcs across the heads of the audience in a theatrical

Wimperis, Simpson and Guthrie/Serge Chermayeff 1930

Cambridge Theatre

Wimperis, Simpson and Guthrie/Serge Chermayeff 1930

sweep and a series of receding vaulted ribs bridges the gap between the proscenium and the auditorium. The boxes feature a pair of highly stylised and geometric art-deco tableaux picked out in gold: one depicts an urban scene by moonlight, representing night, while the other shows a sun radiating very 1930s rays of light over an idealised landscape and represents day. The fronts of the balconies feature a continuation of the kind of geometric patterns that can be found throughout the building – not a very English kind of decoration, they seem more typical of Vienna or New York, which makes the theatre such a refreshing change from the usual West End fare. A pair of slightly awkward (not to say naff) light fittings frame the proscenium opening and take the form of cascades of crystal emulating water spouting from urn-shaped uplighters.

One detail to look out for when walking around in the interval is the wall-mounted ash trays. The gleaming brass fittings with their archetypal deco script request 'Ashes please'. Much of the credit for restoring these details can be given to designer Carl Toms who oversaw an extensive overhaul of the theatre in the 1980s. This included the restoration of colours similar to those originally used (the whole theatre was painted red in the 1950s) and highlighting details such as the brass doors and box office which had been covered up and painted as art deco went out of fashion after the Second World War.

ADDRESS Earlham Street, London WC2 (020 7494 5080)
UNDERGROUND Covent Garden/Leicester Square

Wimperis, Simpson and Guthrie/Serge Chermayeff 1930

Cambridge Theatre

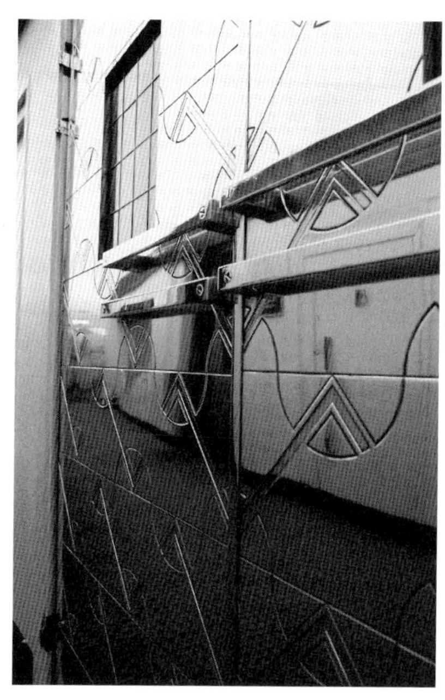

Wimperis, Simpson and Guthrie/Serge Chermayeff 1930

Donmar Warehouse

London's most dynamic studio theatre is internationally recognised for what happens on its stage, less so for its building which just sits in the background and lets the drama happen, keeping the focus firmly on the stage. As its name suggests, the Donmar is set in a building which formerly functioned as a warehouse (in fact as banana store), but also saw life as a stable and brewery. It was used first as a rehearsal room from 1961 onwards and housed the Royal Shakespeare Company in the period before they moved into the Barbican.

Unpretentious and very basic, though clean and modern, the front-of-house facilities are a workmanlike break from the Victorian gilding and cherubs that dominate Covent Garden, and are exactly what was required. The elemental, unfussy feel continues into the auditorium which is simply a rough brick box, its stark, bare walls (the existing structure of the warehouse) painted black. A wooden floor marks out the stage and simple fixed benches seat around 250 in very close proximity and on three sides of the actors. A suspended metal balcony is picked out in kind of 1980s semi-high-tech, industrial red scaffolding, a red echoed throughout the building. A self-effacing architecture that modestly allows the attention to fall on one of London's most consistently enthralling and intimate stages.

ADDRESS Earlham Street, London WC2 (020 7369 1732)
UNDERGROUND Covent Garden

RHWL 1992 (part of new development and shopping arcade)

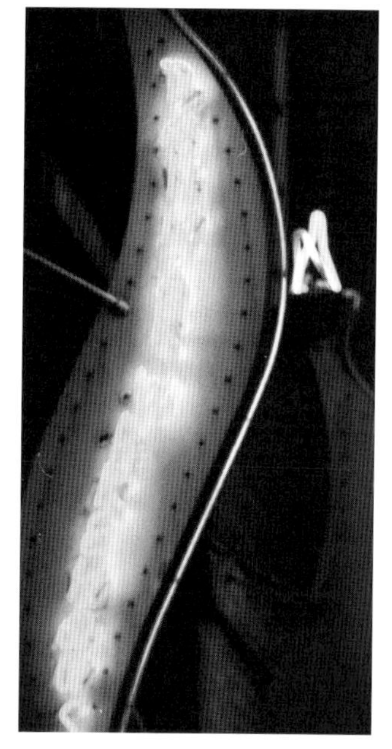

RHWL 1992 (part of new development and shopping arcade)

The Shaftesbury Theatre

This theatre appears to be lost in the wrong bit of Shaftesbury Avenue. Even its appearance seems to suggest some kind of grand Edwardian municipal building, a town hall perhaps, rather than a theatre. Squat, heavily rusticated and with an odd assortment of baroque and mannerist-influenced windows and openings, the rather inadequate tower that rises from the powerfully articulated corner seems to encapsulate the architect's almost successful attempt at grandiosity. But the municipal blend of pomposity and grand inelegance is quickly forgotten on entering the theatre. The generous foyer, its details picked out in gilt, brass and mahogany (with gold mosaic tiles on the pilasters) leads into a long bar that curves away from the foyer in a grand sweep.

The well-lit, rather strained elegance of the bar only begins to prepare the visitor for the auditorium. From the outside the building looks rather underscaled, its details more ambitious than its size but, with the stalls set well below ground level, the auditorium is much larger than you'd expect, and grander too. The theme is what the contemporary journal *The Era* called 'Modern Renaissance'. Two grand arches frame the proscenium on either side above the boxes. Into these arches are squeezed four Michelangelesque sculptures (representing comedy, tragedy, poetry and music) with putti at their feet, sat atop oversized and over-detailed plinths. The domed ceiling, which could be retracted in hot weather, originally featured a series of symbolic paintings that have since been painted out. The spandrels above the arched proscenium exhibit a pair of finely modelled and elaborate reliefs. Panels of highly figured marbles are still to be seen throughout the auditorium and the original scheme also featured a considerable amount of gold mosaic (of which only a few straggling tiles can still be seen in the foyer). The creamy hues in which the interior is now painted give the whole scheme a slightly anaemic appear-

Bertie Crewe 1911

The Shaftesbury Theatre

Bertie Crewe 1911

ance, rather like the decorative icing from a wedding cake that has been put away as a souvenir and gone dusty in a cupboard.

Nevertheless, there's an awful lot of detail to look at and the auditorium is impressive both in its scale and as a functioning theatre. The sightlines seem generally good for a building of this scale, although its size means that from the back of the stalls the top part of the stage is cut off from view. It is interesting to compare this theatre with The Piccadilly (1928) and the Phoenix (1930), both also designed by Bertie Crewe. Less than two decades separate the Shaftesbury and these other theatres yet the difference in approach is staggering, from the overbearing, over-detailed neo-baroque to the stilted simplicity of art deco – the change from the frivolity of the period before the First World War and the sobriety of the years that followed it could hardly be greater.

ADDRESS Shaftesbury Avenue, London WC2 (020 7379 5399)
UNDERGROUND Piccadilly Circus/Leicester Square

Bertie Crewe 1911

The Shaftesbury Theatre

Bertie Crewe 1911

New London Theatre

The architecture of the New London is fashionable again. A glass curtain wall wraps itself around the theatre on Drury Lane and billows out into a shallow curve on the Parker Street façade. This gentle curve reflects the sharper curve of the auditorium, visible from outside as a heavy concrete wall. There is, however, none of the harshness of brutalism at the New London. Whereas the Barbican, designed around the same time, provides a grim streetscape of car access, service entrances and massive concrete walls, Michael Percival here created a building which responds well to its tight urban site. The foyer and box-office areas form a podium upon which the glazed building sits. Designed as a shop window for the theatre, the ground floor is transparent and inviting. The rounded corners of the metal window frames and the facing of the box-office window to the street (now closed) are a nice period touch and a rare survival of 1970s detail.

The entrance though, is abysmal. As soon as you enter you find yourself beneath the underside of a concrete stair. Oppressive and off-putting, this is a real low-point. A grand stair should billow down and suck visitors up with tantalising glimpses of the world beyond, as does the nearby Theatre Royal, Drury Lane. Here you find yourself in what looks like left-over space and the ascent is actually made via an inauspicious escalator off to the right which would look more at home in a provincial 1970s shopping mall.

Ascending through the building, things begin to get better. Despite the greyness of the concrete finishes and the touch of extra greyness provided by the smoky-tinted glazing, the composition of walkways, galleries and the sweeping curve of the auditorium walls is complex and interesting. At night the life inside the building affects the street which is otherwise almost deserted and quiet. The views outwards bring the city into the

Michael Percival 1971–72

Michael Percival 1971–72

foyer so that you do not spend the intervals isolated in a blind box.

The auditorium was highly innovative and this remains one of the most ambitious modern theatres in London. Built in an era when versatility was king, this is an awesomely flexible venue. The stage, the orchestra pit and the front rows of the stalls are capable of revolving through 180 degrees so that a conventional proscenium-arch configuration can become an amphitheatre with the stage thrust into the middle of the auditorium. The walls are composed of a series of panels mounted on pivots and tracks which can revolve and move to tailor themselves to the appropriate configuration. The louvred ceiling is arranged so that scenery can be lowered, and from the centre of the space when needed. Despite the size of the auditorium, all seats are close to the stage in all configurations and the intimacy achieved is impressive.

The site has a long history of theatres and music halls stretching back to the early nineteenth century. It was occupied by a Frank Matcham theatre from 1910–11 until its demolition to make way for the current building. The current occupant of the site is not particularly beautiful – even fashion can't turn around enough for this to become a much-loved and popular theatre – but it is innovative and it is undoubtedly one of the best modern theatres in the London. Looks pretty cool at night, too.

ADDRESS Parker Street/Drury Lane WC2 (020 7405 0072)
UNDERGROUND Holborn/Covent Garden

New London Theatre

Michael Percival 1971–72

The Peacock

The first new theatre to be erected in the West End for nearly 30 years, The Peacock appears undistinguished from Kingsway, buried in a large office block, its entrance self-effacingly tucked away in Portugal Street. Incredibly, to make way for this indifferent building, the London Opera House, an enormous theatre designed by Bertie Crewe in 1910, was demolished.

A new theatre was, however, grudgingly incorporated around the back of the new block. A spacious, clean, modernist foyer leads down to the subterranean auditorium. Unspectacular but workmanlike, this boasts an adjustable proscenium and good sightlines from both stalls and balcony. Virtually all the original decorations and fittings, but for the handrails and a few forlorn marble panels, have been removed. A shame because they sound riotous: a contemporary description describes features including three-dimensional mosaic figures of tragedy, comedy, harlequinade, dancing and music above the entrance and a 'rear illuminated concrete and glass screen which depicts a royal procession'. This latter was a reference to the theatre's original name, The Royalty. Other features apparently included a marble-panelled bar with a zig-zag counter reflected in a faceted mirror 'to sparkle like a giant cut diamond' as well as a mixture of superb period finishes encompassing gold and white vinyl, flock wallpaper and rosewood and maple panelling. Probably as close as 1960 came to Frank Matcham.

ADDRESS Portugal Street, London WC2 (020 7314 8800)
UNDERGROUND Holborn

Lewis Solomon and Kaye and Partners 1960

Lewis Solomon and Kaye and Partners 1960

Lyceum Theatre

The first Lyceum opened in 1772 as an exhibition and concert hall. Three years later it was converted into a theatre. In 1802 it became the first venue for Madame Tussaud's waxworks. After a brief stint hosting the Drury Lane company, the theatre was rebuilt in 1816 as the Royal Lyceum and English Opera House by architect Samuel Beazley. In 1830 the theatre burnt to the ground and was rebuilt by the same architect in 1834; the grand classical portico dates from then. The theatre was demolished in 1904, leaving only the portico and walls standing.

The new theatre was built as a huge music hall (in competition with its contemporary, the Coliseum, see page 2.14) by Bertie Crewe. The theatre was over-ambitious as a music hall and began to be given over to melodrama. Just before the outbreak of the Second World War the theatre was purchased by the London County Council as part of a major scheme to cut through Covent Garden to create a grander approach to Waterloo Bridge. The war forced the LCC to abandon its ambitious plans and the building was sold off for use as a dance hall.

In 1996 the theatre was renovated in an extensive scheme that involved demolishing and completely rebuilding the stage and backstage areas to meet modern technical demands. The impressive auditorium was extensively renovated but the overall result is curiously sterile. The front-of-house spaces are fantastically dull in their feeble attempt at mock period design – a kind of corporate notion of what Edwardian theatres should look like. Dreadful. Nevertheless the theatre is functioning again, its façade remains one of London's most elegant and recognisable frontages, and the auditorium remains a good place to see a show.

ADDRESS Wellington Street, London WC2 (020 7314 2888)
UNDERGROUND Covent Garden

Bertie Crewe 1904

Lyceum Theatre

Bertie Crewe 1904

Fortune Theatre

Oppressed by the bulk of the Theatre Royal, Drury Lane on the other side of the road, the Fortune is an odd little theatre that could easily be missed if it weren't for the neon glowing rather underwhelmingly in the shadow of its massive neighbour. It was the first theatre to be erected in London – and the first in Europe – after the First World War and it is a very early manifestation of art deco, a style that did not catch on in London until a few years later.

The theatre is wrapped around the Scottish National Church, remarkably built over, around and under the church; quite a feat of planning. The architect, Ernest Schaufelberg (who designed the art-deco Adelphi six years later; see page 2.2) based the design for the elevations on a spurious drawing of the original Shakespearean Fortune Theatre. Either it was very freely adapted or an extremely odd drawing. Austere and rather blank, the façade only gives a clue that something interesting might be going on inside with an unusual sculpted frieze that runs right around the building, a wavy line sculpted in relief. At the centre of the façade (above the arched window) stands an ineffectual little semi-nude dancer, apparently either Terpsichore, the Greek muse of dancing, or Fortuna. Although her awkward balance seems an unlikely tribute to dancing, it is in fact a beautifully modelled little figure in bronze (now painted white) and it is a pity it is so underscaled.

The garlanded doors begin to hint at a little of the glamour of the stage and lead into an absolutely tiny foyer with perhaps the smallest box office in London. The ticket window is placed in a prow-shaped protrusion clad in brass which is richly modelled in abstract art-deco motifs; a charming period survival. The walls are clad in creamy marble, striped in places with black bands. The square light fitting that sits beneath the ceiling as the stairs ascend into the circle is worth looking at for its elegant

Ernest Schaufelberg 1924

Ernest Schaufelberg 1924

simplicity, and the way in which the light is incorporated into the architecture rather than just stuck on.

After the compact and thoughtful elegance of the foyer, the auditorium itself is a bit of a disappointment. Small, intimate and with excellent sightlines throughout, all the seats are close to the stage. The decoration continues the themes begun in the foyer but the luxury of marble and brass is surrendered to more pedestrian plaster. The general feel is of a kind of chinoiserie art deco, the geometric motifs echoing Far Eastern forms, a change from the Aztec and Egyptian motifs that would later dominate the style. Above the proscenium can be seen a glaringly blank panel. This was originally covered in a saucy art-deco mural of bathing nymph-types against a geometric, stagey background. Apparently the church, which has to co-exist in such close proximity to the theatre, found them offensive and the mural was painted over. Still there beneath the coat of paint, it would be good to see the mural restored one day. The final point to make is that the Fortune was the first British theatre to be constructed entirely out of reinforced concrete (then known as ferro-concrete), making it a pioneering building in structure as well as style.

ADDRESS Russell Street, London WC2 (020 7836 2238)
UNDERGROUND Covent Garden

Fortune Theatre

Ernest Schaufelberg 1924

Theatre Royal, Drury Lane

There has been a playhouse on this site since 1636, giving it the longest continuous history of any theatre in the country. The original temporary structure fell victim to the puritanism that followed in the wake of the English Civil War. The first permanent theatre was completed in 1663 by King Charles II only a few years after the end of Cromwell's short-lived regime. That theatre was destroyed by fire in 1672 and it was replaced by a new (but apparently not very special) building designed by Sir Christopher Wren, a year before he began working on his designs for St Paul's Cathedral. In 1775 the Adam brothers were employed to make substantial alterations both inside and out, including a fine new façade. The theatre was rebuilt once more, reopening in 1794, this time by architect Henry Holland.

Designed to be completely fireproof and the safest theatre in the world, it was provided with a battery of water tanks, a cast-iron fire curtain and other precautions; it promptly burnt down in 1809. Sheridan, the dramatist and politician who was responsible for building the new theatre, watched it burn down from a nearby tavern. When his friends tried to pull him away from the sight he is reputed to have said, 'Nay, leave me, leave me, 'tis a pity if a man cannot take a glass of wine by his own fireside.' The burnt-out ruins of Sheridan's theatre were replaced with the building we see today, completed in 1812 by the architect Benjamin Wyatt (who designed the Duke of York Monument and Apsley House), the design inspired by the Grand Theatre at Bordeaux (1777–80) by Victor Louis.

Entering through the portico (an addition from 1820) the visitor comes across one of London's grandest and most theatrical entrance sequences. The marble-clad lobby with its statues of Shakespeare and Coward sets the scene for a magnificent staircase and the 'rotunda', a colonnaded atrium that rises up to an impressive coffered dome above. The Grand

Benjamin Wyatt 1812

Benjamin Wyatt 1812

Saloon boasting a vaulted ceiling, enormous chandeliers and very fine relief plasterwork is among the poshest of London's theatre bars (and makes up for the other bars which are oppressively awful).

The auditorium itself is impressive but more restrained than the front-of-house grandeur would indicate. It is rather disappointing to learn that it was completely rebuilt in 1922 by architects including Emblin Walker and Robert Cromie. On the other hand it functions remarkably well as a theatrical space, retaining a surprising intimacy for an auditorium seating more than 2000 people (a thousand less, incidentally, than it did in 1812) spread over three tiers and the stalls.

One of the best stories about the theatre is the explanation for a royal box and a separate Prince of Wales' Box. The Prince Regent once arrived late to a performance causing a commotion on his arrival. His father (King George III), so incensed by his son's insensitive behaviour, apparently boxed his ears. After this it was thought better to separate the warring factions and their boxes were placed with separate staircases, which are still labelled 'King's Side' and 'Prince's Side'.

The massive bulk of the Theatre Royal is a critical part of the dense urban landscape of Covent Garden. Its huge blank walls dominate the area and only when the side doors are open and you are able to see the backstage workings of the building does its scale (and in particular the size of the stage) become truly apparent. The rear of the theatre is occupied by hangar-like workshops, scene-painting rooms and props stores and it is worth walking beneath the Russell Street arcade (added in 1831) to try to catch a glimpse through the vast doors. Some of the lighting on this side of the building is still fuelled by gas. The ugly and incongruous fountain (1896) stuck on to the Catherine Street façade commemorates Augustus Harris whose time as manager during the second half of the

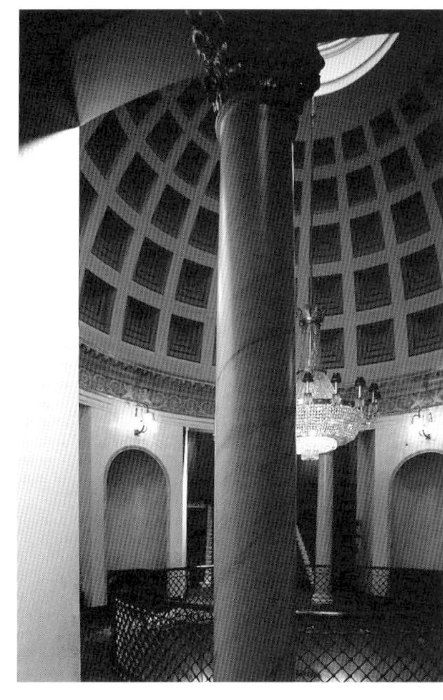

Benjamin Wyatt 1812

nineteenth century saw the theatre become the home of extravaganzas and pantomimes. It seems odd that London's most historic and important playhouse is now regarded as the home of the musical but it fits in with the tradition of the last century and a half of grand and popular productions.

ADDRESS Catherine Street, London WC2 (020 7494 5000)
UNDERGROUND Covent Garden

Benjamin Wyatt 1812

The Royal Opera House, Covent Garden

Architect Jeremy Dixon is fond of saying that the Royal Opera House is like a whole city in itself, much more than just a theatre. The rebuilding of the opera house was a monumental achievement and one which stretched back to the architects' appointment in 1984 – it finally took an incredible 16 years. The scale of the design is daunting; only the Theatre Royal in Drury Lane has a longer theatrical history than the Opera House. The first theatre on the site, designed by Edward Shepherd, was built in 1732 and was then the most luxurious London had ever seen. The second, built in 1808–09, was probably the most impressive of the theatres to have occupied the site. It was designed by Robert Smirke (who later designed the British Museum) and was the first major Greek revival building in London, modelled after the Temple of Minerva in Athens, and it was responsible for setting a new fashion in the capital's architecture. The fine reliefs (by Flaxman) which can be seen behind the portico come from this building and were reused when the theatre was rebuilt. Smirke's splendid building was used as a venue for drama and opera but was never financially successful and, in 1856, it fell victim to a fire.

A new theatre was built by Frederick Gye, manager of the Royal Italian Opera Company, who was a bit of a cheapskate. Although the auditorium was finely conceived and built, the front-of-house facilities were mean and the façades were of stucco rather than stone. Conscious of the endless capacity of a big theatre to lose money, Gye was keen to bring in other businesses to help share the costs. Thus, he built the big conservatory of the Floral Hall next to the portico, a space that he rented out to the flower sellers of Covent Garden market. It is easy to criticise Gye for his meanness with the country's premier opera house, but it is also easy to forget that it was all done with private money – other countries throughout Europe were building lavish state-funded opera houses at the time.

E M Barry 1857–58 and Dixon Jones BDP 1984–99

E M Barry 1857–58 and Dixon Jones BDP 1984–99

Bearing this in mind his achievements are not at all bad.

Gye was in many ways a pioneering figure. He conceived a kind of fast-track construction and assembled a building team who had recently worked together on the Houses of Parliament. His architect was E M Barry, son of Charles Barry who had designed the Houses of Parliament. Much of the structure of the opera house consists of huge iron girders and beams; the auditorium sits within the building almost entirely as a separate entity with its own iron structure. Even the central dome was just a sham, hung from iron girders attached to a complex timber roof structure. Barry made a good job of making do with what he had but the economies he was asked to provide show in the building's cheap frontages and (characteristically English) stingy front-of-house spaces, although he managed to persuade a reluctant client to build the opera's grand portico. The glittering luxury of the auditorium, the lush curves, nymphs and angels of the balconies and the sculptural work above the proscenium are the work of Italian sculptor Raffaelle Monti, who was brought in by Gye as an artistic consultant.

With the exception of a rebuilding of the stage and flytower between 1899 and 1902, the opera house remained substantially unaltered until the 1980s. The saga of the rebuilding of the house became a national cause célèbre and the catalyst for a much-needed debate about public subsidy (i.e. the working-class supporting the opera-going class through the National Lottery), about snobbery and about urban design. Architects Jeremy Dixon and Edward Jones spent a significant chunk of their careers on this gigantic scheme and are prepared to admit that the monumental delays and the constant furore around the scheme finally allowed them to realise a better design.

In answer to criticisms of elitism the architects finally opened the

E M Barry 1857–58 and Dixon Jones BDP 1984–99

theatre up to become a public building, one which can be enjoyed even without an outrageously expensive ticket. A new arcade successfully completes Covent Garden Piazza (London's first proper square, laid out by Inigo Jones in 1631) and creates a route from the busy square through the theatre and a new box office. In creating a retail arcade the architects are following the precedent of Gye and his efforts to subsidise the opera through commerce. Gye's Floral Hall, for years a useless appendix, has been reborn as a public space, the heart of the new scheme. Rising up through the escalator in the Floral Hall, the visitor gains access to spacious new bars, the amphitheatre and a terrace overlooking the piazza with superb views across the city. To create more room for the stage, half of the Floral Hall has been cut off and a mirror wall inserted to give the impression of a larger space while allowing views down from the bar and a long public gallery. The fan-shaped frontage, barrel-vault and complex iron structure have been reconstructed. Among the most important changes is the abolition of the class apartheid of separate entrances – the whole audience now enters through these generous common areas.

The auditorium was always internationally respected as a fine venue with good acoustics and although seating has been tweaked to provide better sightlines, it has remained substantially the same. The biggest changes occurred above and behind the stage. In an area which used to be alive with markets and workshops and which has become a kitschy, if successful, arm of the tourist industry, the enormous and fascinating world of backstage production has brought back an air of industry and arty creativity. From wig-making workshops in the garrets to hangar-like stage-painting facilities, the whole of the opera house is surrounded by a labyrinthine network of production, an opera factory. Much more could have been made of the fascinating, hidden world by opening it out to the

E M Barry 1857–58 and Dixon Jones BDP 1984–99

public realm. The building has become a kind of arts ghetto behind massive walls, rather than a public display of urban activity.

The opera house has been critically well-received. Conceived in an era when post-modernist architects were questioning the supremacy of modernism and reassessing the role of the traditional city plan, the designs and ideas have survived well. There are, inevitably, question marks including the dressing-up of the new flytower in Victorian icing and the reconstruction of the Floral Hall. This was a white elephant to start with (which now, with its 'grand' escalator, looks like a sterile, pastiche 1980s shopping mall) but it is precisely the architects' attitude to the building as a (typically London) collection of parts that allows it to blend so well in this complex area of the city. By acknowledging the Victorian nature of a building in stucco and gilt as well as iron and glass, the way in which the architects of the nineteenth century were not afraid to mix modern and historical languages, the architects of the rebuilding have succeeded in creating a new building which maintains the spirit of the old. Thus, although classical columns, forms and proportions have been used in the piazza, the new steel and glass insertions inside the building are crisply modern, as striking a juxtaposition as the Floral Hall must have seemed next to the portico in 1858. The elevations are considered and urbane and the new scheme is self-effacing yet on an imposing enough scale to stand up to Barry's 1858 original. The rebuilding of the opera house has opened up one of London's great theatres to a public all too often excluded from opera.

ADDRESS Bow Street, London WC2 (020 7304 4000)
UNDERGROUND Covent Garden

E M Barry 1857–58 and Dixon Jones BDP 1984–99

The Royal Opera House, Covent Garden

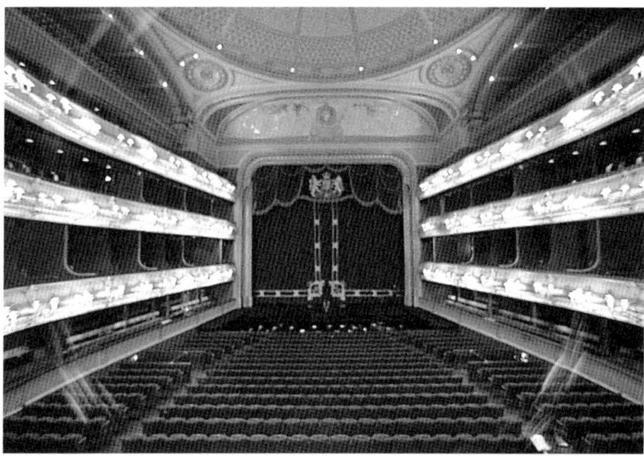

E M Barry 1857–58 and Dixon Jones BDP 1984–99

Duchess Theatre

This is an exact contemporary of all those Tudorbethan semis that frame the suburban A-roads around the edges of London. Architecturally too, it is their peer. While the glittering art deco of the Savoy and the Adelphi (see pages 2.8 and 2.2) were being planned in The Strand nearby, Ewen Barr was building his version of stockbroker Tudor in Catherine Street. A series of three stone bays lethargically climbs up the dull façade and the attempt at enlivening the elevation with some spurious heraldic mouldings fails dismally.

Despite the painfully dull façade, better suited toan undertaker's than a theatre, the architect showed great skill in handling the complex design and handling of the structure. Hampered by planning restrictions and the need to provide light to neighbouring buildings, Barr was forced to create a circle which is smaller than the stalls and hung the structure from steel beams in the roof.

The original interiors were designed by Marc-Henri and Laverdet, who designed the exuberant art-deco interior of the Whitehall Theatre the following year (see page 3.2). In 1934, Mary Wyndham Lewis, the wife of J B Priestley, who had become associated with the theatre's management, oversaw a reworking of the interior scheme. Highlight of the redecoration was a pair of bas reliefs cast in bronze by the sculptor Maurice Lambert, framing the proscenium to either side. Depicting figures bearing tragic and comic masks above pairs of clapping hands, these panels are undoubtedly among the very worst pieces of sculptural art in the capital and demonstrate perfectly why Britain was largely left behind in the revolution of modernism which swept the continent between the wars.

ADDRESS Catherine Street, London WC2 (020 7494 5075)
UNDERGROUND Covent Garden

Ewen Barr 1929

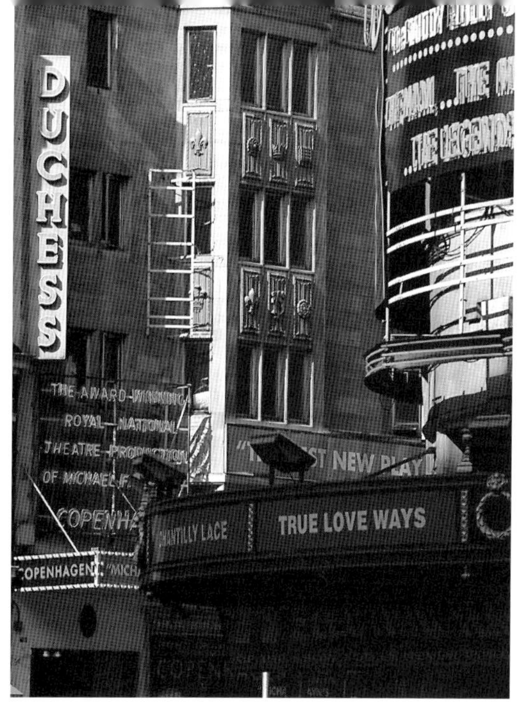

Ewen Barr 1929

Strand Theatre

Being bombed in one world war is bad luck. Being bombed in both begins to look like carelessness. The Strand Theatre was bombed during a Zeppelin raid in 1915 and then during the Blitz in 1940. It looks remarkably good, considering.

The Strand, originally known as the Waldorf, is the twin of the Aldwych Theatre (see page 2.76). The exteriors are almost identical, both rich with reliefs, sculptures and detail. The solid Edwardian façade reveals a sumptuous lobby adorned with elaborate fittings (including a pair of very fine sculptural light fittings that frame the dress-circle stairs) and which in turn leads to a handsome auditorium.

The focus is undoubtedly the relief of Apollo in his chariot surmounting the proscenium. This decorated tympanum is framed by a pair of elegantly curving vaults and sculpted, gilded putti gathered round a bowl overflowing with fruit. These sculpted groups sit atop a cornice over the boxes, themselves framed by fluted marble pilasters crowned with golden capitals sitting on elegant brackets which tail away into fine gilded decoration. The painted and gilded circular ceiling is also worth craning your neck for.

The theatre remains in very good condition, its rich decoration surviving almost intact; well worth seeing. Unlike its twin, the Strand has three tiers and was the last such theatre to be built in London as soon after its completion the LCC prohibited three-tier auditoria.

ADDRESS Aldwych, London WC2 (020 7930 8800)
UNDERGROUND Temple/Covent Garden

W G R Sprague 1905

Aldwych Theatre

The construction of the Aldwych and its twin theatre, the Strand (see page 2.74), were a part of an enormous slum-clearance and rebuilding programme in the early years of the twentieth century. Aldwych and Kingsway were conceived as spacious and elegant new streets in a Parisian style and the scale of the urban fabric here is one of the few places in London where that grand continental influence can be strongly felt. The theatre's monumental neighbours, the Waldorf Hotel and the nearby BBC Bush House conspire to dwarf the theatre and it needs all its neons and flashing lights to make its presence felt.

The façade is elegant and urbane, neatly folding around Drury Lane with a drum-shaped corner. The entrance is on that corner and is handled with panache via a semicircular porch and a few steps to the fine and well-preserved lobby. The original, elaborately-detailed little box-office survives facing the old fireplace and if you look up you will see a circular hole in the ceiling which allows views up to the bustle of the dress circle bar. Like the lobby below, the bar is incredibly well-preserved, retaining a host of period detail genuinely rare in the West End theatres which have been subject to so many insensitive refurbishments.

The auditorium, though, is a bit of a disappointment. The Royal Shakespeare Company during their tenure here (before they moved to the Barbican) were responsible for much vandalism including stripping out the stage boxes. The basic shape of the auditorium remains unaltered but that's not much to boast about as the sightlines from many positions are pitiful. The rear of the stalls is claustrophobic with the floor of the circle looming low above the seats and cutting off the top half of the stage. Unusually, some of the best sightlines and most spacious seats are in the upper circle.

Many little details have survived and are worth looking at in passing,

W G R Sprague 1905

W G R Sprague 1905

including lovely original brass fingerplates on the doors (with an arts-and-crafts feel) and a stingy little royal box which nevertheless boasts a wonderfully compact retiring room and its own little WC featuring all the original tiles and fittings. Apparently the original Edwardian canopy with its stained glass survives almost intact beneath the clumsy box that now greets visitors. Its delicacy is hinted at by the very fine wrought-iron brackets that can be still be seen holding it up.

ADDRESS Aldwych, London WC2 (020 7416 6003)
TRANSPORT Temple/Covent Garden

W G R Sprague 1905

Aldwych Theatre

W G R Sprague 1905

whitehall and victoria

Whitehall Theatre

The unadorned, white façade of the Whitehall Theatre with its tall, attenuated arches evokes the surreal cityscapes of De Chirico's paintings. It stands in stark contrast to the fussy buildings that crowd in on it to either side. A contemporary architectural critic, Charles Reilly, wrote that the theatre was 'so clean and simple in its line that it makes the new Government offices, banks, and public houses of that great thoroughfare look as if they need a shave.'

The building is an early and well-preserved manifestation of art deco in the conservative heart of civil-service London yet its exterior displays little of the jazzy moderne penchant for decoration. It was designed in 1930 by Edward A Stone, an architect more associated with cinemas in which he used a blend of exotic features from the Moorish to the classical to create 'atmospheric' places of entertainment. The blank whiteness of the Whitehall Theatre represents a major shift towards substantial form and a more serious, solid approach, perhaps in deliberately marked contrast to the frivolity of cinema design. This assumption would be ironic with the knowledge that the theatre has subsequently become famous for farce and comedy. The façade also undoubtedly displays a faint echo of the white marble walls and shadowy arcades popular at the time in Mussolini's Italy. The walls step back towards the parapets in a typically 1930s detail, seeming to suggest the mass of some Mayan pyramid while the blank, solid walls and dark, slim arches also imply some kind of massive bunker below.

The interior, however, provides some of the jazzy frivolity that the elevation so emphatically denies. Once past the oppressively awful executive-hotel-style lobby groaning under the weight of polished brass, the original interior decoration, by Marc-Henri and Laverdet, is among the finest examples of art deco among London's theatres. Although much was

Edward A Stone 1930

Whitehall Theatre

Edward A Stone 1930

destroyed, including a cubist mural in the bar and streamlined art-deco boxes, a lot of good stuff has survived. It was the first English theatre interior to be painted entirely in black (in order not to distract attention from the stage) and the dark background serves to highlight the metallic decoration which is picked out throughout the auditorium. The focus is on a panel above the stage centring on a Venus emerging from a seashell amid waves and swirling tendrils and this kind of organic flourish is echoed in details throughout the interior. Metallic stripes all around the auditorium produce a curiously late-1970s post-modern feel but the wonderful geometric, vaguely cubist murals found around the walls sparkle in the blackness. The best of these murals, executed in a range of gold, sliver and copper colours, can be seen around the boxes. The ceiling too is resplendent in its art-deco glory, a shimmering metallic octagon lurking in the roof like a flashy diamond ring.

ADDRESS Whitehall, London SW1 (020 7369 1735)
UNDERGROUND Charing Cross

Edward A Stone 1930

Edward A Stone 1930

The Players

Slotted beneath the brick arches below Charing Cross station, The Players theatre is an unlikely venue, but it displays a name with a long history. The current theatre has only been in existence since 1990 when its forebear, also under a railway arch, was squeezed out by the crushing weight of Terry Farrell's overbearing Embankment Place. The old Players opened in 1867, four years after the completion of Charing Cross station above it. Originally known as 'The Arches', it seems to have been a blend of coffee-house, pub and restaurant and became one of the earliest music halls. It survived remarkably well until Farrell's elephantine post-modern monument to the Thatcher era obliterated it. The Players company was relocated down the road to another set of arches off Villiers Street and an attempt was made to recreate the feel of the original.

In the spirit of music hall the long, narrow auditorium is served by a bar at its rear and the audience can take drinks to their seats, some of which have tables. The bar itself, a nice piece of Victoriana complete with etched-glass fittings, was rescued from a building site where it had been dumped. The theatre is simple; a billowing, stripey textile ceiling makes the subterranean space surprisingly cheery; otherwise there is a proscenium and small galleries to either side. It could be looked on in the same way as the Globe – a building with no inherent historical interest but one that attempts to reproduce the atmosphere of an age which can never really be recreated.

ADDRESS Villiers Street, London WC2 (020 7839 1134)
UNDERGROUND Embankment/Charing Cross

Terry Farrell and Sandy Brown Associoates 1990

Terry Farrell and Sandy Brown Associoates 1990

The Playhouse

Grafted on to the side of Charing Cross Station and Hungerford Bridge, this theatre was originally built by a sharp operator who apparently thought he would be able to make a quick profit by selling the site and building for a hugely inflated amount to the railway company when they needed to expand the adjacent station. The station was not expanded and, remarkably, considering the short-termism of its conception, the theatre survives. The first theatre was built in 1882 by architects Fowler and Hill. The restrained, curving, stone façade dates from this first building (it was originally capped by a series of sculpted figures) but the auditorium was rebuilt in 1905. During this reconstruction, part of Charing Cross station collapsed on to the theatre, killing six workmen and severely interrupting building work. The new work was completed by Detmar Blow and his French partner, Fernand Billerey, in 1907 with decoration by Mortimer Menpes – a restored version of that is the theatre we see today. The foyer with its black and white marble floor is a picture of late-Edwardian elegance, its sparse but fine decorative details picked out in gold. The auditorium is also better than average; the balconies sweep and billow in grand curves and the walls, vaults and ceiling are enlivened by huge rococo paintings. The proscenium contains within its depth two tiers of boxes, the upper tier supported by very fine female terms (anthropomorphic columns).

The simplicity of the balustraded balcony fronts is a change from the usual garlands and cherubs. Their graceful curves, together with much subtle and well-executed plasterwork, make this a very successful auditorium.

ADDRESS Northumberland Avenue, London WC2 (020 7839 4401)
UNDERGROUND Embankment

F H Fowler 1882 and Detmar Blow and Fernand Billerey 1905

Victoria Palace

This sculptural Edwardian theatre rises incongruously from the urban mess surrounding Victoria station. The figures crowning it echo the fine sculptures on the façade of the station on the other side of the road. Its slightly clumsy but enthusiastically eclectic façade, topped by a baroque cupola, betrays the ubiquitous hand of Frank Matcham. Built in 1911, it replaced a music hall from 1886, which had itself replaced one of 1863. The growth of London's suburbs in the early twentieth century provided a mass market for the halls and the Victoria Palace was well placed to accommodate the crowds that poured out of the station.

The contemporary spiel was that the 'main object has been to combine a maximum of comfort and convenience with a prevailing note of simplicity'. For audience comfort the auditorium was provided with an opening shallow dome which moved to allow fresh air in and clouds of tobacco smoke out. The cupola was originally crowned by a figure of Pavlova which the ballerina herself apparently disliked and would never look at (and after seeing a contemporary photo I am not surprised). The figure was taken down during the war in an effort to save it from German bombing, and never re-emerged. The façade still boasts a fine mosaic depicting two figures of drama and music in a vaguely Pre-Raphaelite style on a gold background, placed in the tympanum above the main canopy. Unfortunately the arch is usually covered by billboards.

From the finely detailed, spacious foyer with its wedding-cake mix of white marble and polished brass, to the well-preserved and harmonious auditorium, the building has retained its integrity and gives a good impression of the exuberant atmosphere of an Edwardian music hall.

ADDRESS Victoria Street, London SW1 (020 7834 1317)
UNDERGROUND Victoria

Frank Matcham 1911

Victoria Palace

Frank Matcham 1911

Apollo Victoria

Sleek, streamlined and elegant, the twin façades of the Apollo dragged London architecture into the 1930s and were pivotal in introducing and popularising the idea of modernism to both clients and the general public. They don't, however, even begin to indicate the contents of the bizarre interior. The elevations are a fascinating blend of art deco and modernist styles with a long street frontage, its length emphasised by horizontal banding that is taken up again on the other side of the entrance to blend back into the existing building line. The entrance is emphasised by the dynamic insertion of a vertically fluted section above a deep cantilevered canopy. Two wonderful art-deco panels frame the entrance to either side. Designed by W E Trent, they depict audiences watching films (one a romance, one a thriller). These used to be sheltered by a pair of smaller canopies which have now disappeared. Otherwise a surprising amount of the very fine original details have survived, inside and out. Before you go in, look for the sculpted exit and stage-door signage on the granite walls and a little Charlie Chaplin figure to the right of the entrance.

The foyer is a highly individual cocktail of art-deco, modernist and populist motifs in an elegant scheme of black and silver. The space was originally focused on a central light; the void it left is now occupied by a 1970s insertion that looks like an upside-down fakir's bed of nails. The eclectic mix of 1930s styles is compounded by the insertion of chinoiserie motifs which can be seen throughout the building on grilles on the façade as well as in the glazing bars of the doors and the metalwork throughout the interior. The mezzanine of the main stair is lifted by a slightly clumsy relief frieze in gold and silver of a dancing girl in diaphanous dress which seems influenced by the cool stylisation of Scandinavian art.

Moving through the network of passages and corridors to the main auditorium, the decoration is rich and unusual. It seems that architects

Ernest Wamsley Lewis 1930

Apollo Victoria

Ernest Wamsley Lewis 1930

faced the same kind of problems as they do today; Wamsley Lewis was asked by the client what the 'theme' of the building would be and, on the spur of the moment, he improvised with 'mermaid's palace'. Thus the ceilings are adorned with stylised fish swimming in circles, with ripples and waves and niches stuffed with abstracted scallops and stiff-looking mermaids, all delicately illuminated.

The auditorium itself is spectacular and remains one of the most impressive and influential built in Britain during the twentieth century. Ernest Wamsley Lewis spent the late 1920s on a sojourn studying theatre architecture in Germany. Architects in Berlin in particular were conducting serious experiments in innovative theatre and cinema building which were unparalleled elsewhere. Whereas cinemas in the USA and in Britain were being built either in historical fancy dress or in odd variations of the atmospheric theme (in Italian palazzi or oriental courtyard design), German architects were building serious-minded modernist cinemas with an eye to expressing the function of the building outside and in. Wamsley Lewis blended the expressionist ideas of Hans Poelzig with the sleek modernism of Erich Mendelsohn and Rudolf Frankel.

Thus the exterior and foyer of the Apollo are thoughtfully functional but the auditorium is an expressionist fantasy. Expressionist architecture largely passed London by, which is why the stunning auditorium of the Apollo is such a rare delight. The walls are sculpted with stacks of scalloped sconces. Each layer was originally uplit from within while the ceiling centres on a crystalline rose that echoes the icy visions of the early expressionists who used mountains of crystal as their vision for a pure new world. Stalactite light fittings used to hang above the front of the circle; other crystalline lights can still be seen towards the back. All the sculpturally cubist lights (including the central rose) have black screens

Apollo Victoria

Ernest Wamsley Lewis 1930

above them that could be withdrawn to allow natural light in from above. The dramatic lighting which shone from behind every feature and cornice is currently out of commission and the baroque layering and intricate organ-pipe decoration of the proscenium arch is obscured by the bleak intrusion of the extended stage and sets for *Starlight Express*. It deserves a full restoration. Unmissable.

ADDRESS Wilton Road, Victoria, London SW1 (020 7494 5070)
UNDERGROUND Victoria

Ernest Wamsley Lewis 1930

Ernest Wamsley Lewis 1930

Westminster Theatre

Like The Queen's theatre and the Lyric Hammersmith (see pages 1.32 and 8.8), the Westminster, currently under threat of demolition, has a tough, modern shell which gives way to a soft centre. The grey slate-clad façade is forbidding and it is a surprise to come across the delicate interior with its glittering gold dome and deep reds. Unlike The Queen's and the Lyric, the auditorium is nothing special and on second glance it is in fact the dark but well-articulated brutalist elevations and roofscape which are the more interesting parts of the scheme.

The building's odd history culminated in it being the only dry theatre in London. The site was originally occupied by an eighteenth-century chapel that fell into dereliction. The shell of the chapel was used as the basis of a cinema from 1923 and in 1931 the old crypt was converted into dressing rooms and a bar. In the years around the Second World War the theatre gained an impressive reputation for staging avant-garde productions. In 1946, however, the theatre was acquired by Moral Re-armament, an organisation dedicated to restoring society's morals who took over control of the theatre from 1960. This explains the ban on alcohol. It was extensively rebuilt by John and Sylvia Reid in 1965 – the offices wrapped around the existing auditorium and the elevations date from this period. The unusual, powerful-looking trusses which emerge like some insectoid exoskeleton from the walls to support the roof structure, and the building's lurking, heavy presence make it worth regarding as one of the better examples of 1960s London architecture, an era that saw much of Victoria changed beyond recognition. Still no bar.

ADDRESS Palace Street, London SW1 (020 7828 9361)
UNDERGROUND Victoria

Arnold Dunbar Smith 1931 and John Reid and Sylvia Reid 1965

Westminster Theatre

Arnold Dunbar Smith 1931 and John Reid and Sylvia Reid 1965

The Institute of Contemporary Arts (ICA)

When The Mall was created in about 1660, it quickly became London's most fashionable promenade. By the time John Nash built his exquisite terraces it had fallen rather out of favour and it remains an oddly dead, if beautiful, thoroughfare. There is something fascinating about the positioning of the ICA, which has some claims to be the country's most avant-garde arts institution, on the Queen's front path and it undoubtedly invigorates at least that little bit of The Mall. The ICA moved into these premises in 1968 and, although its primary purpose is to support the visual arts, the complex includes a small theatre.

The theatre itself is a simple black box with staged seating but the surroundings are far more interesting. A very slick bar on a gallery was redesigned by 24/7 during 1999 while another little café can be found downstairs. As well as galleries there is a good bookshop and a small cinema and the place has a constant arty buzz.

ADDRESS Carlton House Terrace, The Mall, London SW1
(020 7930 3647)
UNDERGROUND Charing Cross

John Nash c. 1660 and 24/7 1999

The Institute of Contemporary Arts (ICA)

John Nash c. 1660 and 24/7 1999

bloomsbury and fitzrovia

Cochrane Theatre

Built on to the side of Central St Martin's College of Art, the Cochrane was originally the venue for student productions and experimental stage designs. In 1992, the front of house underwent a radical facelift and the banal 1960s block was ripped apart to make way for a more welcoming façade. The original building can still be seen poking its head up above the first floor. The remodelling opened out the first floor into a long bar which wraps itself around the theatre and creates good views of Holborn through entirely glazed walls. The wavy copper-clad bar makes a good focus and the deep, rich colours combined with the glazing make this a pleasing space to be in while helping to maintain a funky ambience.

The auditorium is intimate and it comes as a surprise that it seats more than 300 in a single, raked block. Simple proscenium layout and an orchestra pit which is usually covered over mean this is not a particularly versatile theatre yet it retains a good, cosy feel and a closeness to the stage throughout.

ADDRESS Southampton Row, London WC1 (020 7242 7040)
UNDERGROUND Holborn

LCC Architects Department 1965/Abiodun Odedina 1991

Cochrane Theatre

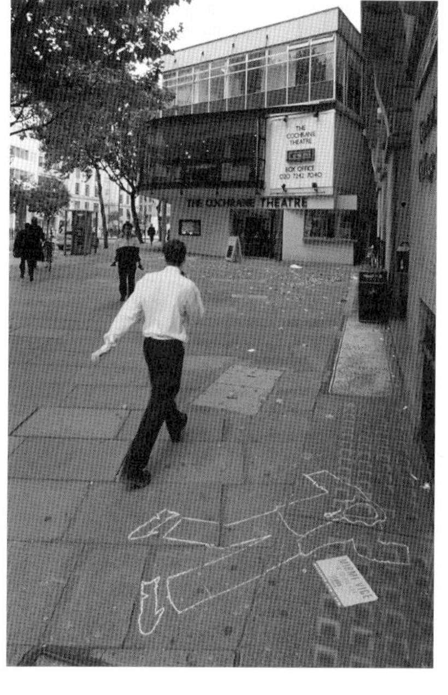

LCC Architects Department 1965/Abiodun Odedina 1991

The Vanbrugh, Royal Academy of Dramatic Art

RADA, Britain's leading drama school, was founded by Sir Herbert Beerbohm Tree in 1904 in the dome of His (now Her) Majesty's Theatre, where Tree himself also had an apartment. Later in the same year the new school moved to Gower Street where it has remained ever since. The strained but relatively elegant neo-Geo Gower Street façade (1927) has been retained. The entrance is flanked by a pair of good, chunky sculptures representing comedy and tragedy (their masks the reverse of their expressions) by Alan Durst in the style of Eric Gill. Behind this, the building has been dramatically altered.

A new 200-seat theatre, The Vanbrugh (open to the public) has been built on the second floor, replacing the original theatre. The horseshoe-shaped auditorium has bench seating in the stalls and two balconies but is flexible enough to be used with conventional proscenium or thrust-stage layouts. It is expressed simply with elegantly considered handrails to the balconies, sweeping curves and a minimum of fuss. A flytower rises above the stage and is expressed on the Malet Street elevation as a grid infilled with terracotta panels that help its solid mass to melt into the grimy Bloomsbury brickwork. The grid sits on top of a bowed, opalescent glass wall (indicating the curving rear wall of the auditorium) and canopy, behind which is the café.

The long streak of a site necessitated skilful planning to accommodate all the facilities (including a 60-seat studio theatre and a large workshop) and ensure natural light in the depths of the building via light wells. Unassuming and urbane, this is an elegant solution.

ADDRESS 62–64 Gower Street, London WC1 (020 7580 7982)
UNDERGROUND Goodge Street/Euston Square

G Norman 1927, Avery Assocs/Theatre Projects Consultants 2000

The Vanbrugh, Royal Academy of Dramatic Art

G Norman 1927, Avery Assocs/Theatre Projects Consultants 2000

The Place

Essentially a dance venue, The Place is occasionally used for drama and would not really merit an entry here but for an interesting remodelling scheme by Allies and Morrison. Like the Drill Hall (see page 4.8), it was built for a regiment of artist/soldiers, in this case the Bloomsbury Rifles, as a place for sensitive, artistic types to practice warmongery. It was sold to the London Contemporary Dance Trust in the 1960s. Over the years further buildings have been acquired and the site has become deeper and now runs right through the urban block to Flaxman Terrace.

Allies and Morrison's design rationalises the building across the site and provides a lot of extra accommodation for the dance school that now inhabits the site. The theatre space is placed near the Duke's Road entrance and consists of a simple box with few outstanding features. What gives The Place its vitality is the dance school which ensures that all the spaces are stuffed with people all day and remains buzzing at all times. Allies and Morrison's interventions consist of considerable remodelling of the front-of-house spaces and a good new basement café. The most interesting part of the reconstruction will take place at the rear of the site and includes a very transparent and crisp new entrance to the dance facilities from the Flaxman Terrace end and three floors of studio and workshop spaces.

ADDRESS Duke's Road, London WC1 (020 7387 0031)
UNDERGROUND Euston/King's Cross

Colonel R W Edis 1888–89, Allies and Morrison 1999–2000

Colonel R W Edis 1888–89, Allies and Morrison 1999–2000

The Drill Hall

The grimy brick façade of this odd little Victorian building does nothing to suggest that it may contain a theatre. Built in 1882, it was designed as a drill hall for the Bloomsbury Rifles, an unusual outfit of patriotic artists volunteering to do their bit. In 1975 a section of the building became a theatre and in 1984 the theatre was moved to the main hall and the other spaces were converted into rehearsal rooms and studios. It remains an incredibly active little complex.

The façade to the street is a typically Victorian affair with bits of Queen Anne and gothic blended into a rather dismal concoction. The terracotta moustachioed heads which adorn the window hood mouldings offer the only light relief. The building is entered through a dark porch and a surprisingly generous bar. The theatre itself is unusual in being much wider than it is deep so that all 200 seats are close to the stage. The result is intimate and potentially intense. The metal trusses of the roof remind you that this used to be a utilitarian drill hall. The original shooting gallery (with an incredibly low ceiling) has been retained to one side of the stage and the actors have to pass along it, ducking their heads, on their way from changing rooms to stage. The rehearsal and studio spaces upstairs are surprisingly good – light, airy and spacious.

The building was due to be replaced by a sleek modern design by Rick Mather which caused some excitement at the time. Now, in the light of changes to lottery funding, it looks likely that this Victorian oddity will remain in place for a while to come.

ADDRESS Chenies Street, London WC1 (020 7637 8270)
UNDERGROUND Goodge Street

Samuel Knight 1882–83

Samuel Knight 1882–83

Open-Air Theatre, Regent's Park

Cold, wet and muddy, London is a disastrous place for open-air theatre. This makes the survival of the Regent's Park theatre, open since 1933, a remarkable tale of the English refusal to accept defeat. Until recently a trip to this theatre involved a long, wonderful walk through one of London's glorious parks followed by a stark confrontation with a ramshackle heap of huts, portakabins and algae-coated plastic sheeting culminating in mild hypothermia. Aspiring to the form of an Ancient Greek theatre, the seating is arranged around a central stage with the front part being carved out of the ground and the rear being built up in reinforced concrete. With the colonnade of trees which wraps around the rear of the theatre and the scraggy shrubbery behind the stage, there is also a hint of the clearing in the woods and the pantheistic pagan temple.

Haworth Tompkins were faced with a problematic task when asked to bring the temple up to post-pagan standards. Their ingeniously unobtrusive proposals rely more on landscape than architecture and somehow manage to maintain the ad-hoc air that has become characteristic of the theatre's survival against the odds. With greatly improved, yet raw and unpretentious 'front-of-house' (*sic*) facilities and a picnic-lawn ballooning out to one side, the original impression of approaching the theatre via a derelict battery farm has been replaced with a dignified yet straightforward entry. Foliage, trellises and fairy lights (an installation by David Ward) blend into a slightly kitsch, am-dram concoction both charming and wholly appropriate. A long bar curves around beneath the canopy of the cantilevered seating and creepers are guided up around the new metal structure in casings wrapped around the columns. A very great improvement.

ADDRESS Inner Circle, Regent's Park, London NW1 (020 7486 2431)
UNDERGROUND Regent's Park/Great Portland Street/Baker Street

Haworth Tompkins Architects/Camlin Lonsdale (landscape) 2000

Open-Air Theatre, Regent's Park

Haworth Tompkins Architects/Camlin Lonsdale (landscape) 2000

north

Sadler's Wells

This theatre owes its existence to the well which can still be seen through a glass plate behind the stalls. The well was discovered in 1683 and was claimed to be that of Clerkenwell Priory, whose water had been ascribed magical healing powers in the Middle Ages. It became a destination for sick and superstitious Londoners and the well's astute developer, Thomas Sadler, created a kind of Restoration leisure centre on the site to squeeze a few more pennies from these travellers. Situated away from the constraints and censorship of the burghers of the City of London, the original 'Musick House' and its successors thrived as venues with a reputation for bawdiness. By the middle of the nineteenth century it had been transformed into a respectable and important playhouse with a huge capacity of 2500 in a building designed by C J Phipps. In 1893 it reverted to popular entertainment and became a music hall, this time redesigned by Bertie Crewe and, with the decline of that genre, the theatre itself ran into trouble and closed after a brief interlude as a cinema.

The roots of the modern theatre were laid by Lilian Baylis who was responsible for commissioning a new theatre as a north London equivalent of her Old Vic (see page 7.14). The new building, a stolid bricky pile, was designed by F G M Chancellor and completed in 1931 and eventually became the home of the English National Opera (before it moved to the Coliseum; see page 2.14) and the Royal Ballet. The idea of the building was to bring opera and lyric theatre to the artisan classes at affordable prices – this was a kind of socialist theatre in Clerkenwell, historic home of British socialism (even Lenin lived nearby for a while) and political free-thinking. When the 1931 theatre was demolished, the brief for the new theatre called for the same egalitarianism and pragmatic affordability that had characterised the thinking behind the old theatre and the ideals of Lilian Baylis in bringing theatre to the people.

Arts Team @ RHWL and Nicholas Hare Architects 1998

Arts Team @ RHWL and Nicholas Hare Architects 1998

The shape of the old auditorium has been retained, the walls and the cantilevered structure of the balconies of the old theatre were left in place. The auditorium sits at the centre of the building and the bits of left-over site around it have been built up to follow the boundaries of the site. This dislocation at the heart of the building gives it the odd shape and the architects have obviously struggled to give the building an interesting outline. The effect looks a little French in its naïvely angular geometry with a few wilful, angled planes to create an identity. The theatre is contained within massive brick walls while the foyer area is made transparent with a huge glass wall to emphasise the openness of the building to the public. In fact it makes it look a little like a developer's atrium office block but the multi-levelled foyer and bars do communicate some of the vibrancy of the interior to a rather dead street, just as the New London did in the 1970s. The glass wall is dominated by a polyvision screen which is used both as a sign to the street and to the patrons. The height of the atrium allows huge works of art to be displayed on a four-storey wall in a space that works quite well.

The auditorium fulfills the brief with a sparse, utilitarian appearance and no unnecessary frills. It is comfortable but by no means luxurious and is designed so that the members of the audience are aware not only of the stage but of each other. The stage is framed by pivoting mesh panels that allow the space behind to be used as an extension either of the stage or of the auditorium as boxes and galleries. These mesh panels, which also occur on the ceiling, are an effective way to cover services and they lend a workman-like aesthetic to the space yet still present a finished interior. The large square stage is blessed with what is claimed to be the first totally computerised flying system in the world. Huge stage doors, one on to Rosebery Avenue, would allow a double-decker bus right through

north

Arts Team @ RHWL and Nicholas Hare Architects 1998

the theatre. The disabled seating is in the best, rather than the worst part of the stalls and allows for carers or friends to sit next to wheelchair spaces. Indeed the whole theatre is beautifully fitted out to cater for disabled people with low counters and bars and ramps throughout, an absolutely exemplary approach.

The building also encompasses the Lilian Baylis Theatre, a good small studio space seating 200 and a café and bar for both artists and public, education centre and community facilities.

On the whole, better inside than out.

ADDRESS Rosebery Avenue, London EC1 (020 7863 8000)
UNDERGROUND Farringdon/Angel

Arts Team @ RHWL and Nicholas Hare Architects 1998

Arts Team @ RHWL and Nicholas Hare Architects 1998

The Tower

One of the most eccentric settings for any London theatre is this eccentric building incorporating a dark brick tower just off Canonbury Square. The house was built for the priors of St Bartholomew in the early sixteenth century but passed into private hands after the dissolution of the monasteries not long after its completion. A number of rooms in the house survive from this time in incredibly good condition with panelling and plasterwork intact.

The theatre, though, is located in a less-than-interesting building put up in the early years of the twentieth century as a social club and recreation hall for the residents of nearby Canonbury and Clerkenwell estates; its future is now uncertain. Despite the shambolic, rather rural atmosphere of the hall, there is a kind of dark, haunting nature to the space and to the whole complex. The entrance is through a quaint courtyard and there is also a pubby little bar.

The really interesting, historic rooms belong not to the theatre but to the Canonbury Academy. The mark of the builder, William Bolton, can be seen above a surviving monastic door at 6 Canonbury Place: an arrow (bolt) passing through a barrel (tun) is a play on his name.

Nearby, in Compton Terrace, is the Addams-Family-gothic of the Union Chapel Project, a monumental High Victorian red-brick church and its grim appendix of a god-fearing Sunday School and hall which have been turned over to theatre use. Designed in 1876 by architect James Cubitt, its cavernous interior works oddly well as an atmospheric, lofty performance space.

ADDRESS Canonbury Place, London N1 (020 7226 3633)
UNDERGROUND Highbury & Islington

William Bolton early sixteenth century

The Tower

north

William Bolton early sixteenth century

Almeida Theatre

From operating theatre to working theatre: the Almeida, one of London's finest and most sympathetic stages for drama occupies a space built as a science lecture theatre originally used for dissections and other gory spectacles. The elegantly controlled cubic façade of the building off Islington's Upper Street previously concealed a library; the amphitheatre lecture theatre occupied the rear half. The building, which dates from 1837, was converted into a theatre in phases between 1981 and 1986, the first performance taking place in 1984.

The auditorium is roughly horseshoe-shaped but facing in the wrong direction. The back of the stage (rather than the seating) is defined by a curving brick wall interrupted by structural piers. A gallery, supported on cast-iron columns, wraps around a stage roughly the same size as the seating area. The stalls seating stretches right to the front of the stage which is sometimes built up or raked to improve sightlines, sometimes left flush with the stalls' floor. A pair of boxes to the sides of the stage compound the feeling that the audience is surrounding the stage. The architects attempted to change the space as little as possible and to retain the quality of the interior; it works extremely well. There is an impressive stripped-down feel (which seems to have inspired the rebuilding of the Royal Court), creating intimacy but also the inclusivity of watching a work in progress or being present at a workshop. Excellent.

The theatre bar is executed in the same stripped bare-brick and metal aesthetic as the auditorium and works equally well. The building is due to undergo minor alterations in the near future.

ADDRESS Almeida Street, London N1 (020 7359 4404)
UNDERGROUND Highbury & Islington/Angel

Burrell Foley Fischer 1981–86

Burrell Foley Fischer 1981–86

Hampstead Theatre

Dramatically, the Hampstead Theatre is among the most important and influential London theatres outside the West End. Architecturally, it is not. This situation is due to change with the building of an entirely new theatre by Bennetts Associates. Replacing the 1962–63 theatre (by Ian Fraser and Associates with A D Gough), the new building promises a dramatic and sculptural theatre. A long, low, transparent façade will front a new plaza with the volume of the auditorium expressed visibly beyond in the form of a curving wall protruding above the roof line. The theatre is at the heart of the plan, surrounded by a café and education rooms as well as generous backstage facilities. Slightly simplistic but elegantly clean and unfussy, this promises to be an important new theatre in a city where lottery money has been poured into a few elephantine schemes and new theatres remain a rarity. Certain to become a key stop on London's arts pilgrimages.

ADDRESS Eton Avenue, London NW3 (020 7722 9301)
UNDERGROUND Swiss Cottage

Bennetts Associates 1994–2000

Hampstead Theatre

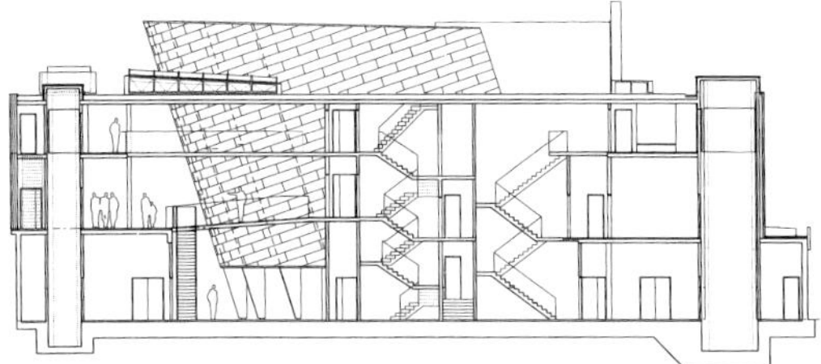

north

Bennetts Associates 1994–2000

Tricycle Theatre

A stack of scaffolding in the shell of a 1920s dance hall may not sound like the pinnacle of modern theatre architecture. Yet the Tricycle has remained consistently one of the very best places to see fringe theatre. Built in 1980, the red-painted scaffolding of the auditorium seemed to have some relationship with the fledgling British high-tech architecture which was to dominate the coming decade. Industrial fittings, garishly painted scaffold-poles and bolted pipes hold faint echoes of the Pompidou Centre. In fact this was low-tech at its best. The architecture's self-deprecating quality represents an alternative functionalism, based on the need for economy, adaptability and immediacy rather than on an aesthetic.

The structure and dimensions of the auditorium were modelled on the Georgian Theatre in Richmond, Yorkshire, the most intimate of Britain's historical playhouses. Like the Georgian Theatre, the Tricycle consists of a roughly cubic space contained by galleries on either side of the stage. The unfussy roughness of the scaffolding, rope and canvas construction complements the famously stark, stripped nature of Tricycle productions. The theatre was partly destroyed by fire in 1987 and, when confronted with rebuilding, the clients asked for a reinstatement of the original structure, attesting to the success of the design.

In 1998 the Tricycle added a cinema and rehearsal and workshop spaces to the complex. The building can now be entered from Buckley Road; the visitor is greeted by a refined canopy and a wall of glass. The foyer and bar are crisp and spacious and accentuate the rough construction of the theatre. One of the simplest and finest modern theatres.

ADDRESS 269 Kilburn High Road/Buckley Road, London NW6
(020 7328 1000)
UNDERGROUND Kilburn

Tim Foster/Theatre Projects Consultants 1980, 1987 and 1998

Tim Foster/Theatre Projects Consultants 1980, 1987 and 1998

Rudolf Steiner House

The Steiner House, London's only expressionist building, is one of the city's best-kept architectural secrets. Rudolf Steiner developed anthroposophy, which he defined as 'becoming aware of one's humanity'. He went on to design a pair of profoundly influential buildings in his native Switzerland dedicated to Goethe who had initially inspired his philosophy. Steiner's architecture was organic and flowing; he believed that people's souls were constrained in buildings full of right angles and straight lines. He assiduously avoided rectangular windows and door frames, justifying his approach by saying that these forms did not occur in nature. The architect of the Steiner House, Montague Wheeler, drew on these ideas to create a structure in the finest Steiner tradition.

The elevations are restrained but the way the arched window openings meet the ground and the shapes of certain doors and windows betray the building's organicism. The fine bulbous doors give way to a wonderfully curvaceous stairwell which acts as the building's core. Its sculpted handrails seem to flow upwards and the trickling sound of water from a lily-shaped fountain and pool permeates the stairs. The stairs, bookshop and foyer were remodelled in 1990 but the organic backbone of the design is Wheeler's.

The theatre is off to the left, a cavernous but effective space with a deep stage to accommodate the eurythmy for which is was essentially intended – though it is often used for straight drama. Odd but enigmatically fascinating.

ADDRESS 35 Park Road, London NW1 (020 7723 4400)
UNDERGROUND Baker Street/Regents Park

Montague Wheeler 1926–1937

Rudolf Steiner House

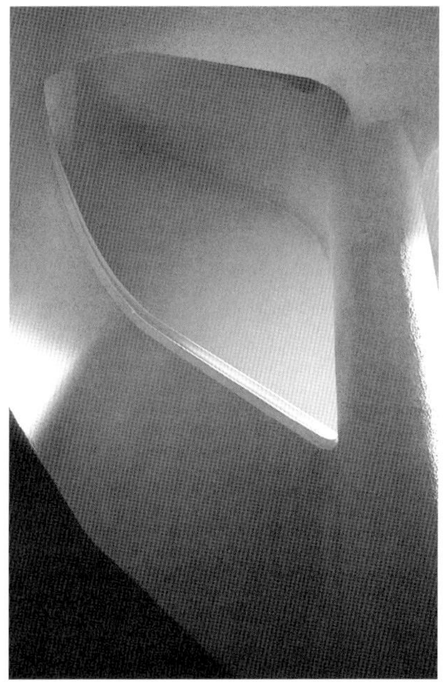

north

Montague Wheeler 1926–1937

east

The Barbican

Of all the grand or subtle architectural devices that could have been used to direct the visitor to London's premier Shakespeare theatre – the long vista, the picturesque route, the string of events along a lively street – a streak of yellow paint on the pavement is perhaps the feeblest and least sophisticated. But this dismal yellow line which is supposed to direct the visitor to the cultural delights of The Barbican is the perfect cipher for the problems of the complex.

The Barbican stands on an area which was flattened by bombing in 1940. Built between 1956 and 1981 by Chamberlin, Powell and Bon, this huge complex is unique in London in terms of both scale and ambition, comprising housing, schools, public spaces and cultural centres. The cultural facilities are housed within the Barbican Centre, a confusing melange of spaces at the north-east end of the development which encompass a concert hall, art gallery, library and restaurants and cafés as well as the theatre. The approaches are a gruesome mess; forbidding grey concrete, covered walkways with oppressively low ceilings. Long, meandering walkways conspire to make visitors feel that they can't possibly be going in the right direction. The aesthetic is one of service entrances, gangways and loading bays, all the rage in late 1960s brutalism and enjoying a bit of a revival in fashionable architectural circles as the essence of urban cool (the perfect antidote to suburban twee).

My reservations notwithstanding, The Barbican has become one of the hippest places to live in London and its architecture is gathering a die-hard following. I am not yet convinced. This was the era of streets in the sky and sun-drenched plazas which must have looked very impressive on dynamic circulation diagrams and architects' perspectives but bear little relation to the London reality of windy, inhospitable public spaces and hard-to-find entrances. It is a relief finally to find the spacious water court

Chamberlin, Powell and Bon 1965–82

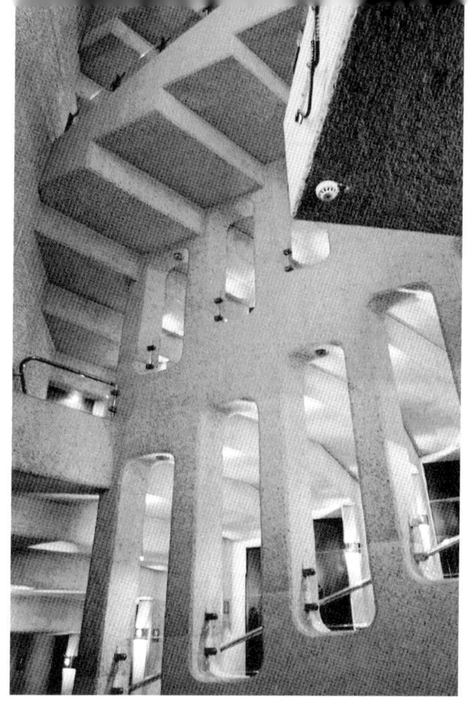

Chamberlin, Powell and Bon 1965–82

and the theatre's foyer but the interior, it transpires, is no more logical or well arranged than the exterior. There is no clarity in the spaces within the building. Although the areas are generous there are too many levels, desks, bars and huge intrusive columns to interrupt the visual flow and the constant oppression of low ceilings minimises the spatial pleasure of galleries and bars.

The difficult approach sequence is a disaster without even the virtue of absolute architectural failure; it is direly dull rather than tragically bad. After this the theatre itself is a pleasant surprise. Peter Hall, then artistic director of the Royal Shakespeare Company, collaborated with the architects in the design of the theatre. The thrust stage brings the action right into the audience while the three narrow circles rise up one on top of the other at alarmingly steep angles. The effect of this (though not for those with vertigo) is to bring the whole audience very close to the actors, the furthest seat being only around 20 metres from the stage and the lack of a permanent orchestra pit brings the front seats right to the front. Each row has its own doors, eliminating the need for aisles and increasing the unity of the audience as a single mass. Just before the performance begins the doors close automatically in a highly theatrical gesture of expectation. Comfortable, intimate (despite seating around 1200) and with excellent acoustics and sightlines, The Barbican finally rewards the odyssey of the off-putting approach with one of the most successful modern theatre interiors.

Situated under the main theatre,The Pit provides a small and flexible studio space.

ADDRESS Barbican Centre, London EC2 (020 7638 8891)
UNDERGROUND Barbican

east

Chamberlin, Powell and Bon 1965–82

Hoxton Hall

The incredible survival of this rare example of an almost intact music hall is due, with biting irony, to the efforts of the temperance movement. Most music halls owed their roaring profitability to alcohol sales but, unlike the majority of these theatres, Hoxton Hall was not attached to a pub (compare Wilton's, page 6.12). Nevertheless, it was described in 1878 as a 'place of the lowest repute' by the Quakers who took over the empty building as a base for their crusade against the evils of alcohol.

Built in 1863 as Mortimer's Hall, it was enlarged and two balconies were added in 1867 (when it became Macdonald's Hall) but it survived as a functioning theatre only until 1872. First it became a temperance hall and later a Quaker hall. It survived the twentieth century as a kind of community centre at the centre of a building that has been changed around it. Essentially, only the interior remains, but it gives an excellent idea of the scale and feel of a Victorian London music hall. The two tiers of balconies have good cast-iron fronts and are supported on slender columns with acanthus-leaf capitals picked out in gold. The steeply stepped stage is a newer addition and there is only a kind of suggestion of a proscenium below the ceiling. Small and incredibly intimate, this is a very surprising and powerfully atmospheric survival.

ADDRESS 130 Hoxton Street, London N1 (020 7739 5431)
UNDERGROUND Old Street

Architect unknown

Architect unknown

Hackney Empire

The complete lack of restraint demonstrated by Frank Matcham (architect of the Coliseum, see page 2.14) in building the Hackney Empire makes it perhaps the most exuberant and enjoyable Edwardian theatre in the capital. The brick and terracotta façade is a typically free composition of oddly juxtaposed elements. A statue of Euterpe (the Greek muse of lyric poetry and music) crowns the building and is framed on either side by a pair of strange cupolas with a Byzantine flavour. Both the statue and domes were replaced with replicas in 1997 after their stupid removal by the then owners of the Empire. Also replaced at that time was the wrought-iron canopy enlivened by brightly coloured stained glass. More stained glass can be seen in the curving windows on either side of the entrance. These feature wonderful, organic art-nouveau designs and are surprising survivals. The entrance is an ebullient stew of every kind of material in a typically odd blend: brightly coloured mosaic on the steps (which continues inside, now concealed by carpet), curvaceously sexy brass door furniture (wonderful handles, and check out the letterbox) and elaborate doors of an absurd design.

The foyer continues in the vein to which the façade accustoms us. The wall to the left is adorned with portraits of great composers (Haydn, Handel and Mozart), the counterpart oval panels on the right are filled with more art-nouveau coloured glass. The space is stuffed to bursting with decoration and colour from extravagant gilded plaster mouldings to marbled columns and a richly sculptural coffered ceiling. It may be hard to believe, but the foyer was originally even richer with painted panels on the ceiling and walls and mirrors throughout. Operatic double stairs lead to a landing focused on a pink marble bench, apparently a gift from Queen Victoria who was given it by the Shah of Persia. There is more excellent stained glass and original tiling en route to the auditorium.

Frank Matcham 1900–01

Frank Matcham 1900–01

Hackney Empire

After this display of garish good humour, it comes as no surprise that the auditorium is a magical space. Matcham was a supreme populist and the Empire remains an uplifting delight at the heart of one of London's most perennially deprived boroughs. Matcham mixed elements of art nouveau, rococo, baroque and Islamic decoration with consummate ease and a complete lack of discrimination or taste. The result is spectacular. The proscenium arch is a doll's-house concoction of rococo paintings, a swirling cartouche, delicately pierced tympanum framed in black marble and finished off by wonderfully sculpted angels at the uppermost corners. To either side a pair of curry-house domes sit beneath trellis-work moulded pendentives. Below these lie cherubs and a pair of blank screens. Intriguingly, these were the Edwardian equivalents of monitors; lights would be back-projected showing the performance so that patrons could take their seats at the parts which interested them.

The auditorium carries on in the same style with three tiers of seating, all beautifully fronted, and a complex ceiling. Throughout the theatre it is worth looking around you as every surface is crammed with remarkable detail. This makes it all the more incredible that the construction of the building was completed in only five months. Unmissable.

ADDRESS 291 Mare Street, London E8 (020 8985 2424)
UNDERGROUND Bethnal Green then bus 106, 253, 277

Frank Matcham 1900–01

Frank Matcham 1900–01

Wilton's Music Hall

The most hauntingly atmospheric of London's theatres, Wilton's Music Hall is a staggering survival in an area robbed of so much of the physical fabric of its rich stew of history. The music hall was built by John Wilton behind his pub, the Prince of Denmark. The pub's name derived from the strong Scandinavian connection of a docks area handling Baltic timber. Grace's Alley, once a dark lane squeezed into the space grudgingly left between buildings, has been turned into a sterile access road for a number of unimaginative new housing developments. But the rich floral reliefs and the crumbling plaster around a pair of large doors hint at an altogether different world behind the brick façade which sits in the middle of the lane. Like most music halls, Wilton's is buried in the surrounding urban fabric. It is entered through the remains of the pub where only a few original details, such as an elaborately decorated beam and brackets, remain. As the visitor drifts inside it becomes obvious why this little space has become one of the most frequently used theatres for filming and, as a result, one which may be oddly familiar after appearances in *Chaplin*, *Interview with the Vampire* and innumerable videos and ads.

The hall itself is a simple space covered by a vaulted ceiling with a single balcony running around three sides and an arched proscenium that replaced an apse-like stage in the 1870s. Another apse, which presumably matched the opening for the stage, can still be seen at the rear of the hall. The stage is tiny and there are no wings as this kind of venue was designed for musical acts needing only minimal backdrops. The greatly elevated stage allowed performers to be seen over the assorted top hats and bowlers of the audience. The centrepiece of the room was originally a 'sunburner' chandelier composed of 300 gas jets and 27,000 cut crystals, the light from which was reflected and refracted in mirrors lining the walls. The truly odd cast-iron columns supporting the balcony are among

Jacob Maggs 1858–59

Jacob Maggs 1858–59

the best survivals with shafts like caricatured barley-sugar twists, topped with elaborate capitals. The curvaceous balcony fronts are budget models made of a kind of papier-mâché (explaining the big holes). Pierced structural ribs in the ceiling provided outlets for the smoke which used to saturate the space so much that the hall had to be repainted four times a year.

The spaces around the hall are also worth a quick look: particularly unusual are a series of huge flagstones used on floors and galleries – medieval stones found on site. The foundation stone of 1858 has been incorporated into the wall near the toilets. Unable to meet rigorous new fire regulations, the building ceased functioning as a music hall as long ago as 1885 and became a mission. A refuge for strikers in the 1898 dock strike, it became the base for the anti-fascists during the infamous Battle of Cable Street (1936) when Mosleyite fascists were prevented from marching through the East End. It later became a rag warehouse and John Betjeman was instrumental in a campaign to avoid its demolition in the 1960s. Now back in use as a theatre, the owners, the Broomhill Opera, keep an open house.

This is one of the great survivals of the London theatre. Its crumbly decrepitude is richly evocative and the juxtaposition of the scarred plasterwork exposing the bricks beneath and the richly sculpted plasterwork is one of the most atmospheric theatrical sights in the city. Ron Arad is designing a number of insertions and a few minor improvements are scheduled – I hope it will be nothing too drastic as it is the inevitability of its decay that gives it such charm. Not to be missed.

ADDRESS Grace's Alley (behind Cable Street), London E1 (020 7702 2789)
UNDERGROUND Tower Hill

Jacob Maggs 1858–59

Jacob Maggs 1858–59

Theatre Royal, Stratford East

Definitely not to be confused with Stratford-on-Avon, the Theatre Royal provides the centrepiece to the seemingly oxymoronic Stratford Cultural Quarter. The latest phase in the regeneration of this vision of urban squalor is a performing-arts centre designed by Levitt Bernstein that will create a more sympathetic context for the old theatre, which the same architects restored from 1992 onwards. The Theatre Royal was designed by J G Buckle in 1884 as a good suburban theatre and was then subject to some alterations by Frank Matcham. What survives of the exterior is of little importance but the auditorium is terrific. Two tiers of balconies supported on cast iron date the building to the pre-cantilever age. Despite the columns, sightlines are good and the lush red and gold of the interior envelops the audience comfortably like a snug dressing gown, a luxury made more noticeable by the theatre's alienating surroundings. A glittering gold-framed proscenium and arched boxes surround the stage which is crowned by a finely detailed cartouche and frieze, the latter continuing beyond the boxes.

To the west of the Theatre Royal is the new performing-arts centre which houses a 300-seat performance space as well as a series of smaller studios, rehearsal and educational facilities. The architects' intention with this new building is to reinstate a version of the original street plan – its destruction in the 1960s redevelopment of the area left the old theatre stranded in an urban wasteland. This new scheme, which is transparent, modern and modest, should reintegrate the area into some kind of urban framework and create a functioning series of public spaces again.

ADDRESS Theatre Square, London E15 (020 7534 0310)
UNDERGROUND Stratford

J G Buckle 1884/Levitt Bernstein Associates 1992–2000

J G Buckle 1884/Levitt Bernstein Associates 1992–2000

Greenwich Theatre

The Greenwich Theatre has its roots in music hall and, like most music halls, was built around a pub. Originally known as the Rose and Crown Music Hall, the theatre became Crowders Music Hall and Temple of Varieties and, in 1879, gained the even grander title of the Parthenon Theatre of Varieties. In 1885 the theatre was rebuilt by J G Buckle, who had designed the Stratford Theatre Royal the previous year. The building's fortunes declined along with audiences for music hall and variety and, after suffering bomb damage during the war, it was closed down in 1949.

In the 1960s the building was leased by the council and earmarked for theatre once again. Brian Meeking, the architect commissioned to carry out works to reopen the theatre, originally wanted to reuse the surviving original auditorium space but the GLC deemed the gallery too steep and the building a fire hazard and so the new auditorium is at a higher level than the original. Unspectacular, it is a typical product of its time; thrust stage, a pair of vomitories and a single block of seats rising within a stark black box. Yet it is a successful performance space with an intensely intimate feel and no distractions. The new brick façade with stairwell slit windows to Crooms Hill is dire; an earlier, more sculptural side wall can be seen around the corner in Nevada Street.

The facilities originally included an art gallery but now the box office flows through to a café space at a lower level. This floor was rejigged by Brookes Stacey Randall in 1999 and the result is an inviting and generous set of spaces. The open concrete shuttered stairs are a well-preserved piece of 1969 but even better are the donors' bricks at the top which include local shops and tradesmen as well as famous theatrical types.

ADDRESS Crooms Hill, London SE10 (020 8858 7755)
DLR Cutty Sark

Brian Meeking 1969

Greenwich Theatre

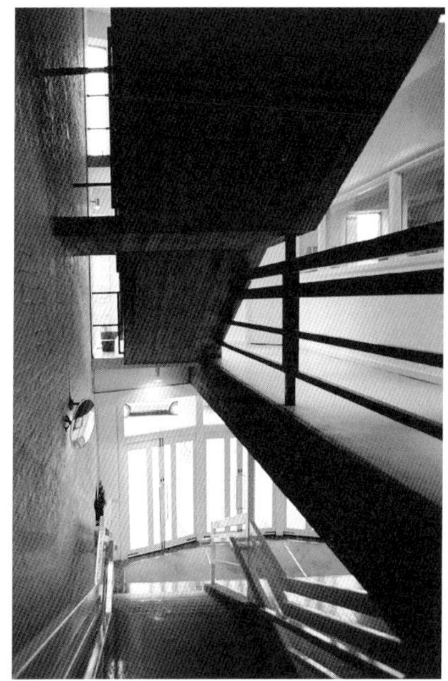

Brian Meeking 1969

bankside and the south bank

Shakespeare's Globe

The Bankside area of Southwark used to be a seedy stew of brothels, inns, bear-baiting pits and all the other pleasures that were forbidden by the puritanical City authorities on the other side of the river. Bankside is once again becoming a kind of (slightly more refined) pleasure garden opposite the City with the Tate Modern and all the stuff that will undoubtedly follow. The building of the Globe was one of the earliest steps in the redevelopment of this formerly industrial area of wharves and warehouses. The idea of the reconstruction of the Globe came from the American film director and actor, Sam Wanamaker, who provided the impetus and a good deal of the money for the project, setting up the Globe Playhouse Trust in 1970. Southwark Council came up with the current riverside site a couple of hundred metres away from where the original theatre stood.

The first Globe was built in 1598–99 by Cuthbert and Richard Burbage, partly using materials salvaged from The Theatre in Shoreditch, London's first permanent playhouse. Its name derived from the figure of Hercules (rather than Atlas, apparently) who appeared on the theatre sign bearing the globe on his shoulders. Shakespeare was both shareholder and actor at the theatre and it seems that the famous line from *Henry V* about 'this wooden O' probably referred to the Globe with its circular form. Like all the Bankside theatres, the Globe was built of timber with a thatched roof which made it susceptible to fire – it duly burnt down in 1613 when flames from two cannon fired during a performance of *Henry VIII* sparked a blaze in the roof. According to a contemporary account only one man was injured in the fire: 'his breeches on fire that would perhaps have broyled him if he had not with the benefit of a provident wit put it out with bottle ale'. After the fire the theatre was rebuilt with the help of a royal grant and reopened in 1614. In 1642 it was closed down by the Puritans and two years later it was demolished.

Theo Crosby and Pentagram 1997

Shakespeare's Globe

Theo Crosby and Pentagram 1997

Reconstruction was hampered by lack of knowledge of how it originally looked. Evidence was limited to a few contemporary panoramic engravings and maps, written descriptions and much speculation. In 1989, during the building of the new theatre, the foundations of The Rose Theatre were excavated nearby and a lot of information about the shape of the Elizabethan theatre, particularly the stage, gleaned from the archaeological dig was incorporated into the building of The Globe. The remains of The Rose (1586–87) can still be visited. Situated in a dark pit beneath a grim office block, there is almost nothing to see and you are charged for seeing it. The remains, uncovered during the construction of the offices in 1988, had to be covered up in sand, concrete and water to stop them decaying due to exposure to air. What you see today is a pile of concrete with a few forlorn markers sticking up. Dark and staggeringly unimpressive, the remains are almost impossible to present with any interest yet they present an effective antidote to the theme-park atmosphere of the reconstructed Globe.

The Globe itself was finally completed in 1997; it is sheltered by the first thatched roof to be built in London since the Great Fire of 1666. The theatre is circular in form, open to the sky, with covered galleries running all around. The stage, which protrudes into the circular courtyard, is covered by a canopy supported on a pair of columns. The underside of the canopy is painted with a fantastical picture of the heavens while the shafts of the columns supporting it are painted in imitation of marble. The timber framing which constitutes the structure of the building (executed by McCurdy & Co) is a remarkable achievement and was in itself an important research exercise in Elizabethan construction techniques.

As a museum and an exercise in historical research, Shakespeare's

Shakespeare's Globe

Theo Crosby and Pentagram 1997

Globe is wonderful. But there is a muted theme-park vibe to the whole complex. The touristy shop and dull, clean foyer and toilets bring home the hopelessness of attempting to recreate the theatre of Shakespeare. The Elizabethans needed an open roof to let in light. With artificial lighting, this need no longer exists and in England's dreadful climate a roof is a genuine advance in theatre technology. The open roof also means that acoustics are poor and actors have to shout to be heard. Modern audiences, used to a proscenium arch, tend to move to the front of the stage and line up as if they were sitting in the stalls. They do not wrap around three sides of the stage as they would have done 400 years ago. In this way, the actors are forced to act to the front, just as they do in any West End theatre.

We cannot recreate the real conditions of the Elizabethan theatre, and – with the unwashed groundlings, bear-baiting, rowdy, drunken audiences and widespread illiteracy of the time – why would we want to? Authentic the building may be, but the desire to see Shakespeare's theatre as his contemporaries would have seen it cannot be fulfilled.

It seems to me that during the last four centuries we have moved on to warm theatres with seats, roofs, reasonable sightlines and acoustics. These developments have generally made theatre-going much more pleasant, but if The Globe holds no other interest for you, it is worth visiting to see how lucky you are to live in the twenty-first century.

ADDRESS New Globe Walk, London SE1 (020 7401 9919)
UNDERGROUND Mansion House/Cannon Street/London Bridge

Shakespeare's Globe

Theo Crosby and Pentagram 1997

The Royal National Theatre

One of the few public buildings to address the magnificent flow of the Thames through the city, The Royal National Theatre is at once one of London's most maligned and most successful modern structures. Its architect, Denys Lasdun, conceived the theatre as a kind of fortified miniature hill town on the bank of the river. Its layers of expansive terraces and broad walkways were meant to open the building out to the public realm and create a series of stages on which the audience themselves would perform, drinks in hand, against the backdrop of the city. Unfortunately, Lasdun mixed his metaphors a little too liberally. While the massive concrete towers and battlement-like terraces do succeed in creating the effect of some concrete castle, and Lasdun did well to break up the theatre's monolithic form into a complex and intriguing series of strata, the image of a fortified enclosure militates against the ideas of openness and accessibility. Instead we are left with what looks like a defensive bastion to protect the sensitive theatre-going classes against the rabble outside. This effect is particularly unfortunate as the building is among the finest modern theatres in the world and a structure of a complexity, intricacy and intelligence that did not generally touch London's architecture of the period.

The idea of a national theatre had been mooted in London for most of the twentieth century (in fact even as far back as 1848) but it was not until the Labour government of 1945 to 1951 that the idea of subsidised theatre began to look a realistic proposition. The choice of the South Bank site, which had housed the Festival of Britain in 1951, was controversial. Critics, Bernard Shaw among others, argued that positioning a national theatre outside the West End would compromise its success. The site was chosen partly in an effort to revitalise what was then a working-class area of warehouses and docks, though one in terminal decline. Lasdun's first

Denys Lasdun 1967–76

The Royal National Theatre

Denys Lasdun 1967–76

design of 1965 encompassed a new national opera house facing the national theatre but the scheme was pared down to the theatre alone for the 1967 version. It was finally completed in 1976, after a tortuous process which had been going on since 1949.

On entering the complex, the mass of lobbies and walkways and the network of columns, bars and terraces is confusing. Essentially it consists of two large theatres – the Olivier, with an expansive apron stage, the Lyttleton, a smaller proscenium theatre – and the much smaller Cottesloe, a studio theatre completed in 1977 round the back of the building in a gap beneath the Olivier.

The Olivier reflects Lasdun's love of Ancient-Greek architecture. It is a huge amphitheatre, an ambitious single space in which stage and seats really are unified. The auditorium is fan-shaped and contains steeply raked seating, rising slightly at the sides, and a looming circle. It is comfortably spacious yet there is enough proximity to both neighbouring seats and the stage to maintain a level of closeness with audience and actors. It has a straightforward yet grand appeal. Intimate it is not; like the theatre of the Greeks, it is a place for tragedy and grand vision.

The Lyttleton is less impressive, if effective – a simple two-tiered, rectangular auditorium with a broad stage.

The tiny Cottesloe, designed by Lasdun in conjunction with Theatre Projects Consultants, is perhaps the most successful of the three theatres – and it was almost left out of the scheme. Highly flexible, intimate and the least pretentious of the three, it takes the form of the courtyard theatre with two stacked, narrow galleries and a stage that can be anywhere between.

The sides and rear of the building reveal an almost constructivist approach with huge cantilevered volumes and flying concrete braces

The Royal National Theatre

Denys Lasdun 1967–76

giving a highly sculptural dynamic. The massing of the complex, rising to a crescendo in the huge form of the Olivier's flytower (which anchors the building), is impressively articulated. The spaces between the auditoria – lobbies, galleries and terraces – are an odd blend of brutalism, dated 1970s details, oppressively low waffle ceilings and an often fascinating play of interlocking volumes and spaces. The stairs are contained within concrete shafts which are pierced with little slits like arrow holes in castle walls giving glimpses of the lobbies, crowds and, occasionally, the river. These lead up to a series of open-air terraces which reveal fantastic views over the Thames to Somerset House and the City. As these terraces are staggered they provide canopies for the spaces below so the audience can pop out for a cigarette or breath of air even when it's raining.

The National Theatre is not beautiful; concrete often looks grim under grey, low-hanging London skies and it can appear forbiddingly rocky and jagged. It is, however, a fine building once you begin to look at it closely. A key work of British modernism.

ADDRESS South Bank, London SE1 (020 452 3000)
UNDERGROUND Waterloo

Denys Lasdun 1967–76

The Royal National Theatre

Denys Lasdun 1967–76

Old Vic

One of London's most important theatres, the Old Vic has an odd history. It was opened in 1818 after a tortuous building process and partly constructed from the remains of the Savoy Palace Theatre on the other side of Waterloo Bridge, demolished to create a larger road across it. Designed by Rudolph Cabanel, an architect from Aachen, it opened as the Royal Coburg Theatre. A couple of years later it was given a curtain made up of 63 large sections of mirror-glass which itself became a major attraction but had to be taken down soon after, as it was found to put too much stress on the roof structure. In 1858 16 people died in a stampede caused by a false fire alarm and for most of the nineteenth century the theatre struggled from crisis to crisis.

In the years before and after the First World War Lilian Baylis made the theatre famous by staging Shakespeare at affordable prices and presenting the whole of his oeuvre for the first time. In 1941 the theatre was damaged by a bomb and did not reopen until extensively renovated by architect Douglas Rowntree in 1950. By this time it had become accepted as the national theatre, a position it held until the official version took up its home at the newly built complex nearby (see page 7.8).

Nineteenth-century engravings of The Cut show a bustling street of market traders, barrow boys, well-stocked shops and promenading families. Now that kind of liveliness seems hard to imagine as traffic and architecture have killed off the more pleasant aspects of urban life. The theatre's subdued façade with its split pediment and royal cipher seems a little out of place in this grim, traffic-deluged location. However, the monumental blind brick arcades that adorn the long sides of the building do seem to echo the grimy grandeur of the Victorian railway arches that dominate this part of south London.

Like much of the rest of the theatre, the pediment (a recreation of an

Rudolph Cabanel 1818

THE
CAR
MAN

earlier incarnation), dates from a comprehensive restoration in 1982–83 by architects RHWL. Unfortunately the building fell victim to the cliché of being 'restored to its former glory', a spurious 1980s attempt at Victorian elegance which almost certainly never existed. The front of house and foyer have been redecorated in a competent impression of a provincial hotel foyer and have lost any semblance of character. The auditorium is better, though also slightly sterile for a theatre that had been famed for its bohemian shabbiness.

The neatly decorated boxes and balcony fronts (the balcony was considerably enlarged as part of the restoration) and the flags and royal cipher above the proscenium arch add to the impression of a kind of doll's-house theatre – pretty but unconvincing. Yet despite these criticisms it remains, with a well-proportioned, intimate auditorium, a very good place to see a play.

ADDRESS The Cut, London SE1 (020 7928 7616)
UNDERGROUND Waterloo

Old Vic

Rudolph Cabanel 1818

Young Vic

An odd sight from the street, the Young Vic consists of a long, low, messy collection of structures with an absurd-looking old house sticking up at its centre and with a permanent building-site aesthetic. The appearance is low-cost high-tech, a result of function rather than fashion: its exposed steel structure is placed on the outside to avoid the necessity for fire-proofing rather than as a style statement. Nevertheless, the concrete block and steel cross-bracing seems ahead of its time and successfully introduces an unpretentious workshop feel to the little theatre.

Bizarrely, the theatre is entered through the remnants of a butcher's shop. The old gold letters of the shop sign (Wilson Brothers) can still be seen above the entrance and the wonderful green and white tiles of the interior have been left more or less intact. The tiled space houses a basic foyer and box office, and a good-looking modern café can be found on the left. The theatre itself is off to the right. The unpretentious auditorium has a square plan with chamfered corners and a gallery on three sides; it can be used with a thrust stage or in the round. Originally built for a lifespan of only six years, it has survived 30 years as one of London's most intimate theatres, and it remains resolutely among the best modern small theatres in the capital.

ADDRESS The Cut, London SE1 (020 7928 6363)
UNDERGROUND Waterloo

Howell, Killick, Partridge and Amis 1970

Howell, Killick, Partridge and Amis 1970

west and south

Royal Court

Deep in the heart of London's poshest shopping and residential district stands the bastion of radical new theatre, the Royal Court. The theatre draws its power from curious juxtapositions; one of the world's most consistently progressive theatres, it is situated in the genteel world of the wealthy and in an utterly conventional Victorian playhouse. When, in 1995, architects Haworth Tompkins redesigned the theatre they needed to be very careful to maintain the paradoxes embodied in the building.

The auditorium, renowned for its intimacy, is loved both by actors and audiences. It largely dates from a 1952 rebuilding after war damage to Walter Emden's original design, and so is tied in deeply with the building's prominent theatrical past as well as being central to the Royal Court's success. The proportions and the proscenium have been retained but the interior has been stripped naked. Frilly garlands and cosmetic plastering have been discarded to reveal the powerful bare bones of the building. The bolted iron plates and the rust-coloured finishes seem to echo the aesthetic of the tube tunnels that run on one side of the theatre, whose rumbling sound still quietly intrudes on performances.

The tight site conditions created by these tunnels – together with the pitiful remains of the Westbourne River (which now, ingloriously demoted to a sewer, runs diagonally across Sloane Square station in a huge iron pipe) – left limited possibilities for expansion. New facilities have been located above the auditorium and in an elegant, slim annexe to the side, sheathed in a screen of Cor-ten steel mesh. Expansion of the public parts of the building has taken place below ground. An atmospheric undercroft housing the lofty restaurant and bar has been created beneath the pavement and road and can also be reached via a stair in Sloane Square itself, descending into a space that used to be a public lavatory, bringing a kind of Ortonesque humour to the scheme. A glass pavement in front of the

Haworth Tompkins and Theatre Projects Consultants 1995–2000

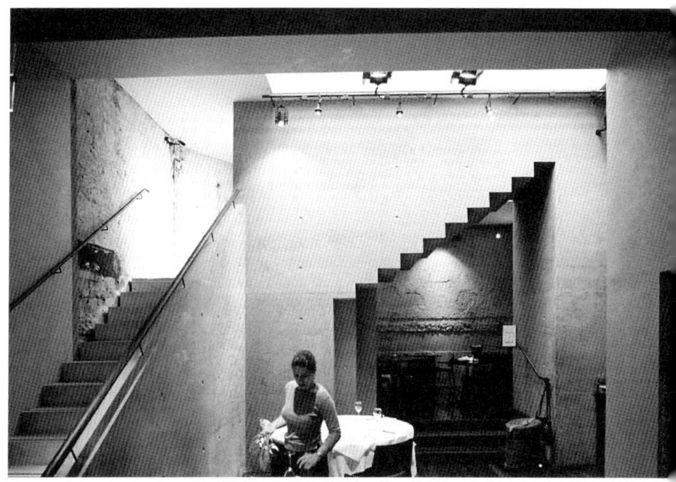

Haworth Tompkins and Theatre Projects Consultants 1995–2000

theatre allows the light from this new restaurant/bar space to illuminate the street above. The beautiful dark timber used throughout the building is reclaimed from a number of sources including railway sleepers and laboratory worktops. Bringing its own history to the building, it blends in with the dominant aesthetic of a working place with its history engrained in its fabric. There is no jarring between old and new materials.

Expanded windows in the theatre's foyer, with its sumptuously curving wall daubed in layers of bright red paint by artist Antoni Malinowski, have opened it up to the public realm. This burning red can be glimpsed throughout the building and projects powerfully into the street like the glowing coals of a brazier. This is compounded by subtle lighting and signage on the Sloane Square façade which give the building a warmth and makes it a natural focus for the public space.

The theatre remains focused around the two performance spaces: the main auditorium, which has been tweaked to give better sightlines, with its new, luxurious soft leather seating, and the Theatre Upstairs which remains a versatile and intimate space seating 60–100, with the bonus of superb views down the King's Road. Finishes throughout are robust and highly textured. Avoiding preciousness and peeling back the skin to reveal the structure (including rough concrete repairs of wartime bomb damage), the theatre proudly reveals its scars and imperfections. The architects have managed to maintain the air of louche but slightly kitchen-sink artiness on which the Royal Court thrives. The theatre that gave birth to the Angry Young Man retains its position as a dependably radical part of the London scene, scarred and stripped but implacably powerful.

ADDRESS Sloane Square, London SW1 (020 7565 5000)
UNDERGROUND Sloane Square

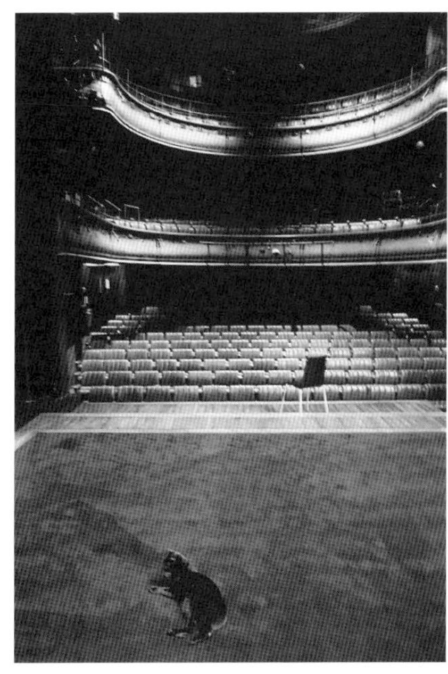

Haworth Tompkins and Theatre Projects Consultants 1995–2000

Gate Theatre

A good example of the London pub theatre, the Gate has been transformed from a simple room above the Prince Albert pub to a well-designed little theatre that is among the most successful small auditoria in the capital. The reconstruction dates from 1993 when, with a lot of juggling around, removing walls and using extra space that previously belonged to the pub, Tim Foster Architects managed to expand the seating capacity from around 50 to 130. From the industrial finishes of the foyer and the galvanised-metal surfaces that dominate the redesigned theatre, it is clear that this is a bohemian place where the focus is on the stage. Tough and durable, the aesthetic here is of a functioning small theatre built to withstand knocks, an antidote to the West End's plush velvet and gilded putti. Retaining a good, arty, workshop atmosphere, the architects have managed to maintain the intimacy of the auditorium and the intensity of seeing drama close-up in a confined space.

The pub-theatre genre is an indispensable part of the more edgy end of the London scene. Other very good pub theatres can be seen at the King's Head (115 Upper Street, N1), the Man in the Moon (392 King's Road, SW3) and the Bush (Shepherd's Bush Green, W12), among a host of others.

ADDRESS 11 Pembridge Road (door to the side of the Prince Albert pub), London W11 (020 7229 0705)
UNDERGROUND Notting Hill Gate

Tim Foster Architects 1993

west and south

Tim Foster Architects 1993

Lyric Hammersmith

I think it's fair to say that everything that went wrong with modernism can be seen at the Lyric Hammersmith. From the hideously articulated (in fact inarticulate) façade to the pitifully inadequate box office, the building does its best to squash any expectations. The bar you pass on the way up is at least a little more spacious but the surprise comes with the auditorium. The rich Edwardian interior forces you into a double-take: this is one of London theatre's most surreal experiences.

The original theatre by Frank Matcham (1895) was reckoned to be one of London's finest. In 1972 it was sold for redevelopment and demolished but the Greater London Council saved the best bits. When the new development was built to include a theatre, these pieces were dusted off and used to recreate Matcham's auditorium. Where details only survived in part, moulds were taken and used to reproduce the original. Some changes were made to accommodate a widened proscenium but the whole project was executed with subtlety and intelligence by the Hammersmith Borough Architects and Theatre Projects Consultants so that you feel you are in an Edwardian auditorium. An architectural time machine.

ADDRESS King Street, Hammersmith, London W6 (020 8741 2311)
UNDERGROUND Hammersmith

Hammersmith Architects Dept/Theatre Projects Consultants 1979

Hammersmith Architects Dept/Theatre Projects Consultants 1979

Riverside Studios

Despite the slick, neo-modernist, toothpaste-white façade, Riverside Studios is based in the shell of an old foundry. The industrial roots show through in a series of stark, functional studios that retain a kind of rawness many other arriviste workshop theatres can only dream of recreating. Originally built in 1913, after only a few decades in operation as a foundry the building was converted to an early BBC television studio. It was converted again into the arts centre in 1979 and is still used for TV broadcasts.

Big expanses of glass and a wide, uncluttered space create an excellent airy foyer with a tiny café slotted into a corner. A new studio immediately on the right of the foyer, the smallest of the three main performance spaces, was added by architect Clyde Boalch in 2000; the foyer itself dates from a 1994 revamp by Burrell Foley Fischer. Moving on through the building via a spacious and well-designed café/bar, there are two larger studios, one currently used for TV and the other a good-sized, unfussy space with a very generous stage. The building also houses a fine cinema.

Nearby, on Hammersmith Broadway is the Hammersmith Apollo, formerly the Hammersmith Odeon and the Gaumont Palace before that. An occasional venue for musicals and rock concerts, it is one of London's seminal music venues. The building was originally one of the city's best art-deco cinemas with a broad, sweeping deco-classical façade, curving foyer and good interiors. It was designed in 1932 by Robert Cromie who worked on the designs for the rebuilding of the auditorium of the Theatre Royal, Drury Lane as well as designing dozens of theatres and cinemas in the 1920s and 1930s.

ADDRESS Crisp Road, London W6 (020 8237 1111)
UNDERGROUND Hammersmith

RHWL 1979 and Burrell Foley Fischer 1994

RHWL 1979 and Burrell Foley Fischer 1994

Battersea Arts Centre (BAC)

Outside, Edwardian red-brick municipal, inside an Edwardian version of a Renaissance palazzo. The building housing Battersea Arts Centre was originally a town hall, and it shows. Yet its operatic staircase of white and coloured marbles is grand and well-lit, and from the relief cherubs which enliven the coving above the stair to the bees in the mosaic floor, there are plenty of rich details to feed the eye. The bees, by the way, are a traditional symbol of thrift and conscientiousness, the perfect metaphor for Edwardian municipal values of community, not to mention a moralising enjoinder to work hard and put up with it.

The main theatre space is in the old council chamber; its two doors were originally the exits for the Ayes and Noes, the markings can still be seen above the architraves. Flexible and black-painted, the auditorium is a disappointment after the luxury of the grand stair. There are also two smaller studio spaces, rehearsal rooms, a decent café and a gallery.

The elevation to Lavender Hill is archetypal Edwardiana, a kind of free French Renaissance concoction, well worth looking at. The well-carved stone relief figures on the front of the building apparently represent labour and progress, art and literature instructing a young figure representing Battersea. The architect, Edward Mountford, built much around Battersea and Wandsworth but is best known for the monumental Sessions House at the Old Bailey.

A short walk away, opposite Clapham Junction, is the Grand, a superb Matcham theatre with a fine façade and odd chinoiserie interior. Last in use as a music venue, its future always seems to be in doubt, though it is one of London's best theatre buildings.

ADDRESS 176 Lavender Hill, London SW11 (020 7223 2223)
TRAIN Clapham Junction

Edward Mountford 1893

Battersea Arts Centre (BAC)

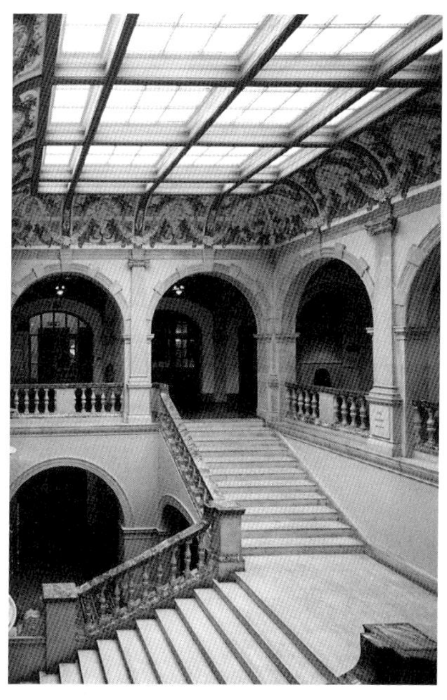

Edward Mountford 1893

Questors Theatre

The design of the main auditorium at the Questors produced one of the most radical theatre buildings of its age; capable of use in the round, with a thrust stage or a traditional proscenium (even stretching to an orchestra pit), the theatre built to house this respected amateur company represented a ground-breaking achievement. The Questors was built in an age when versatility was the holy grail of theatre design. The downside of versatility, though, is compromise and the experiment was not entirely successful. Sightlines from the sides of the auditorium, for instance, are abysmal. Yet the intimacy and closeness to the actors achieved here gives a good idea of just how radical was this departure from the conventional proscenium theatre then still ubiquitous in England.

The site also houses a number of studio theatres, rehearsal spaces and an impressive array of workshops and technical facilities. The contrast between the Questors and glitzy West End theatres that populate much of this book could hardly be greater – there is almost a kind of anti-aesthetic at work here. Questors looks like a kind of theatre factory.

The buildings were rationalised and brought together in a recent lottery-funded scheme that has produced a grimly nondescript lobby and given the whole complex the look of the back end of a poorly designed municipal office. Nevertheless, this remains a lively and innovative theatre and an important link in the development of theatre architecture in Britain.

ADDRESS Mattock Lane, Ealing, London W5 (020 8567 5184)
UNDERGROUND Ealing Broadway

W S Hattrell and Partners/Norman Branson 1964

Questors Theatre

W S Hattrell and Partners/Norman Branson 1964

Richmond Theatre

Set into a corner of the idyllic and perfectly English eighteenth-century Green, Richmond Theatre enjoys one of the finest settings of any theatre in Greater London. The bold modelling of the terracotta and brick façade and the eclectic mannerist and baroque detailing sit a little awkwardly with the restrained simplicity of the surrounding buildings but also mark the theatre out as a place of entertainment. Richmond Theatre is Frank Matcham's best-preserved work in the London area and one of the most intimate and enjoyable theatres of the era.

The front elevation is a typically odd blend of features including a pair of green copper-domed towers, a multitude of mannerist pediments and sculptures and all kinds of permutations of windows: an enjoyable, frothy mess. Ascending the steps to the foyer however, the quality of the detailing and the character of the building become evident at close scale and the theatre becomes far more engaging. Snug and intimate, the foyer is both luxurious and welcoming, appointed in expensive materials and lit by a glamorous chandelier. The circular painted ceiling panel from which the chandelier hangs depicts a heavenly scene with putti and angelic figures bearing the drawings (plans and elevations) of the theatre itself. The brass details (particularly the lovely finger-plates on the doors) display a blend of baroque and *fin-de-siècle* influences with art-nouveau curves faintly showing through.

Moving through into the auditorium, the same attention to detail is carried right on into every aspect of the building. The interior is caked in rich decoration like a kind of sugary icing, from the shallow-domed ceiling with relief-work depicting scenes from Shakespeare's plays to the figures of tragedy and comedy that crown the columns to either side of the marble proscenium. This is one of the richest of all Edwardian auditoria. It's well worth taking your seat five minutes early and checking out

Frank Matcham 1899

Frank Matcham 1899

the sheer amount and quality of the relief work, often overdone, for instance in the occasional bizarre attempts at Elizabethan details. Every figure – from the putti on the curvaceous balcony fronts to the figures at the corners of and in the coving on top of the marble-framed proscenium – is well executed and entertaining, adding to the delightful hotchpotch of Edwardiana. The boxes, in particular, with rich arcading above them and angels at their centres, are delightful. Detailing aside it is also a very good place to see a play with good proportions, acoustics and an intimate auditorium. The bar also has a terrace overlooking the Green, one of the best views from a London theatre bar. A very civilised break from the West End.

ADDRESS Little Green, Richmond (020 8940 0088)
UNDERGROUND/TRAIN Richmond

Frank Matcham 1899

Richmond Theatre

Frank Matcham 1899

Orange Tree Theatre

The Orange Tree Theatre takes its name from the pub across the road in which it was founded in 1970. Twenty years later it moved to a converted Victorian school on its current site. The idea was to create theatre on a nearly domestic scale and the tiny acting area (and it is an acting area rather than a stage) at the centre of this theatre in the round forces an incredible intimacy and closeness to the actors. It is almost the lack of architecture that has made this theatre such a resounding success. The slim galleries are supported on the most elemental of wooden columns, no fuss, no over-detailing. Like other schemes in which Iain Mackintosh and Theatre Projects Consultants have been involved, including notably the Tricycle and the Cottesloe, the Orange Tree is modelled on the courtyard theatre and the intense yet homely intimacy of British Georgian theatres.

The theatre's inconspicuous presence in the townscape, tucked away behind a truly grim modern office block, is due to be greatly improved in a proposal put forward by architects Pawson Williams. A prominent corner block and highly transparent foyer and bar are planned to give the building weight and a recognisable urban presence, and reveal the active life of the theatre to a rather dreary piece of streetscape currently dominated by heavy traffic. The planned building will also add a circular rehearsal space, partly visible from the street, and should rationalise the existing facilities in a thoughtful and elegant framework.

ADDRESS Clarence Street, Richmond (020 8940 3633)
UNDERGROUND/TRAIN Richmond

Theatre Projects Consultants 1990–91

Orange Tree Theatre

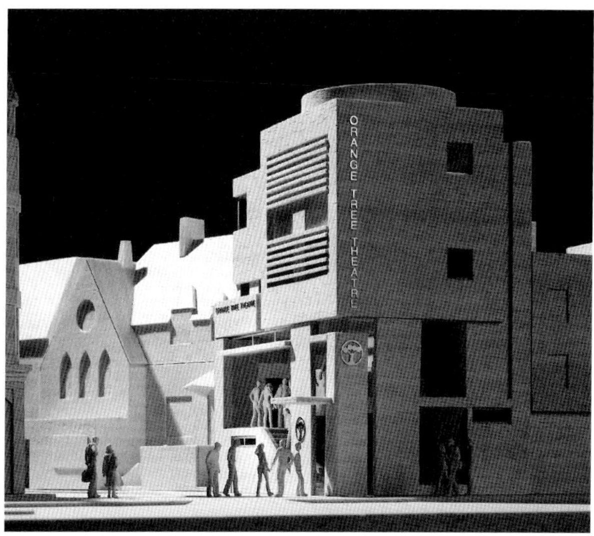

Theatre Projects Consultants 1990–91

Normansfield Hospital Theatre

John Haydon Langdon-Down, pioneer of mental-health care, and instrumental in the recognition of Down's Syndrome, founded the Normansfield Hospital in 1868. He was ahead of his time in his recognition of the need for stimulation for the patients in his private asylum and provided them with a chapel that also functioned as a fully working, perfectly formed little theatre.

An undistinguished Victorian exterior gives way to an enchanting surprise. Enveloped by a hammer-beam roof with a 'sunburner' gas light hanging from its centre, the focus of the space is the exquisite little proscenium and stage. Framed by painted panels within gothic arcading, with the original elaborate iron railings to the side stairs intact, the proscenium is a peculiarly eclectic and Victorian blend of classical and gothic detailing. It is the stage scenery and machinery however that makes this little theatre such an incredible survival. It has retained its original groove system of wings which can slide in and out, and more than a hundred original stage paintings have survived.

The hospital became part of the National Health Service in 1951 and the future of the theatre has been uncertain ever since. The site has been bought by a developer for housing and the theatre's future seems more secure within this development than it has been in the past. It remains difficult to visit the theatre but it is worth seeing. Like a full-scale toy theatre it has a wonderfully eccentric doll's-house feel.

ADDRESS Kingston Road, Teddington
TRAIN Hampton Wick

Rowland Plumbe 1879

Normansfield Hospital Theatre

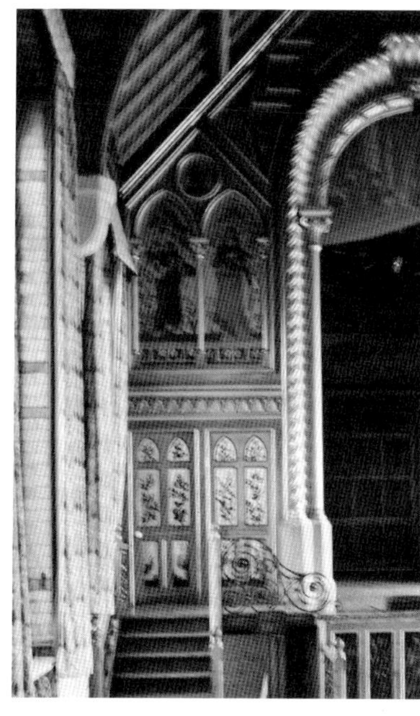

west and south

Rowland Plumbe 1879

Wimbledon Theatre

The dome of Wimbledon Theatre is a rare landmark in the south London landscape, and apparently was used by German bomber pilots in the Second World War as a beacon along their route. As a result the original figure which sat atop the globe crowning the dome was removed and subsequently lost. A replica (representing gaiety) was installed in the 1990s. The original model can now be seen above the box-office window.

From the outside the building looks clumsy, unsuccessfully blending Lutyens-style brickwork and clunking baroque and mannerist details, impressing only through its scale. The interior is another matter. Colourful stained glass recalls the influence of the waning arts-and-crafts movement, with tulips, garlands and bunches of fruit. The original box office also features well-preserved stained glass and the details throughout the lobby spaces and the stalls bar beyond have survived well, even down to the terrazzo floor. The lush detail carries through into the impressive auditorium, one of the best outside the West End. The feel is based loosely on an Italian opera house; the unusual iron balcony fronts lend a Mediterranean appearance. The ceiling is unorthodox, dominated by a half-dome and a series of gaudy painted panels, apparently approximating what was there originally. The rear of the dress circle features a curved gallery for latecomers, with stained-glass windows that could be raised to allow those standing at the back a view of the stage. A pair of boldly sculpted reclining females adorn the spandrels above the proscenium and fine plaster reliefs of putti, garlands, etc. clutter every vertical surface. A final fling for Edwardian suburban exuberance.

ADDRESS 103 The Broadway, Wimbledon, London SW19
(020 8540 0362)
UNDERGROUND Wimbledon

Cecil Masey and Roy Young 1910

OFFICE

theatres currently in other use

London Hippodrome Frank Matcham 1900
Hippodrome Corner, Cranbourne Street, London WC2
Originally a vast circus and variety venue conceived on an Ancient-Roman scale (featuring gargantuan aquatic spectacles, the water drawn from the Cranbourne river beneath the stage) and seating 1340, the Hippodrome, a complex still comprising mansion flats and shops, remains an imposing and enjoyable West End landmark. The original openwork dome crowned by a Roman chariot survives and the red sandstone elevations remain in relatively good condition although the original interior has been almost entirely destroyed.

In 1958 the building was converted into a dance venue, The Talk of the Town, and it is now one of Europe's largest nightclubs. Well worth looking at for its scale and verve.

The Carlton Theatre Frank Verity and Sam Beverley 1927
62–65 Haymarket, London SW1
Designed with both cinema and stage use in mind, the building retains its elegant stone façade featuring an odd blend of mannerist and Hollywood-villa details although a dirty great illuminated sign-board now obscures its heart. It was conceived as a sister building to the neighbouring Plaza cinema, one of the country's first super cinemas, also designed by Frank Verity.

The London Pavilion J E Saunders and R J Worley 1885
Piccadilly Circus, London W1
Built as a music hall on a site with a history of drinking and entertainment dating back into the eighteenth century, only the stone façades of the London Pavilion survive. It became a cinema in 1934 and the interiors

were rebuilt. The classical Victorian elevations were covered up for years by illuminated signs and were only revealed again when the building was listed in the late 1970s.

It now houses tacky shops and the kitschy Rock Circus.

The Windmill architect unknown 1910/1931
Great Windmill Street, London W1
Buried in one of Soho's seamiest backstreets, the odd French-château turrets of the Windmill poke up from the dark, dank alley to be seen from Shaftesbury Avenue. In an odd reversal of the norm, this was an early cinema dating from 1910 which was converted in 1931 to become a theatre. It is a fine, if forlorn, little building with London sky-grey faïence façades and interesting modelling.

It is now in use as a strip joint.

The Prince Charles Carl Fisher Associates 1962
Leicester Place, London WC2
London's best-known low-budget cinema was, surprisingly, originally a theatre although dramatic performances only lasted three years and the interior was rebuilt. Not very notable, although the French church next door has a good mural by Jean Cocteau.

The Saville Theatre T P Bennett and Son with Bertie Crewe 1931
135 Shaftesbury Avenue, London WC2
This solid and monumental piece of 1930s stripped classicism relies on a single subtle device to indicate that the austere brick and stone pile housed a theatre. A superb stone bas relief, sculpted by Gilbert Bayes, runs the whole length of the elevation tracing the development of

'Drama through the Ages'. Two rosettes on either side of the central arched window portray 'Art through the Ages'. The original auditorium was destroyed when the building was turned into a cinema in 1970. The elevations, however, remain an important and impressive piece of townscape.

The Coronet W G R Sprague 1898
103–111 High Street, Notting Hill, London W11
One of London's best-known cinemas was built as a theatre by London's supreme theatre architect. Smaller and less elaborate than Sprague's West End theatres, The Coronet is nevertheless a surprising survival, its classical façades and dome introducing a touch of architectural theatricality to this part of Notting Hill.

The Arts Theatre P Morley Horder 1927
6–7 Great Newport Street, London WC2
A private club incorporating a theatre (its club status ensured its operation beyond the censorship of the Lord Chamberlain), at the time of writing the building is empty although it will reopen soon. Plain and simple, its elevation is based on the restrained Georgian model fashionable during this period (see also the contemporary RADA building, page 4.4). For a spell in the 1950s and 1960s it was perhaps the capital's most important avant-garde theatre venue.

The Mermaid Elidir Davies 1959
Puddle Dock, London EC4
Currently used for corporate entertainment and almost certain to be demolished, the original Mermaid was an early and effective use of found

space and proved massively influential. Housed simply beneath a deep vault, it was just a long space with raked seating and a stage at one end. It was mucked up during improvements in 1978 (during which it was buried in an unappealing office complex) which stripped it of its simplicity and intensity by expanding the auditorium. Any new development on the site will feature a small theatre to replace it.

Royal Camden Theatre (now Camden Palace) W G R Sprague 1900–01
Camden High Street, London NW1
With a typically theatrically eclectic Edwardian façade and crowned by an odd dome, this Sprague theatre is currently in use as a nightclub and retains many original features both inside and out. A big building, it originally seated 3000 and the auditorium with its galleries and boxes, although chopped and changed, has survived surprisingly well.

Collins Music Hall architect and date unknown
10 Islington Green, London N1
Only the Victorian façade remains here but even that is an unusual survival of the music halls that used to litter the city. A blue plaque is all that's left to reveal its history; the building behind is currently a Waterstone's bookshop.

Tottenham Palace Theatre Oswald Cane Wylson 1908
Tottenham High Road, London N17
This impressive neo-baroque façade is a key monument in the north London cityscape. The building functioned as a variety theatre for less than two decades, becoming a cinema in 1926 and succumbing to its current use as a bingo hall in 1969. The interior survives in generally good

condition, the golden ladies framing the proscenium are notable and the lush plastered and gilded interior is in good shape, considering. An important survival.

Golders Green Hippodrome Bertie Crewe 1913
North End Road, London NW11
A very grand late-Edwardian theatre with a monumental columnated façade framed by twin pavilions and with an ill-fitting corner entrance. The auditorium is based on a Roman theme (with hints of the Coliseum completed a decade earlier) and is fairly well preserved although, frankly, not that special. Its grandeur works better outside than in.

The Hippodrome is currently being used by the BBC as a recording and broadcasting studio.

Shepherd's Bush Empire Frank Matcham 1903
Shepherd's Bush Green, London W12
A bold corner tower crowned by an delicate cupola anchors this large Matcham theatre to the site. Unusually for Matcham, the building is asymmetrical and features rendered elevations with only the details picked out in his beloved terracotta. It was for a long time a BBC TV theatre and is currently a well-established concert venue. Little of interest can be seen inside.

The Bush, a good, well-established pub theatre, is a neighbour also worth seeing.

The Grand Frank Matcham 1900
St John's Hill, Clapham Junction, London SW11
A wonderful, generous suburban Matcham theatre with an impressive

brick and terracotta façade, the grimy Grand is one of Clapham's key landmarks yet it has been under constant threat for as long as I can remember. The auditorium is extant and, with its unusual chinoiserie decoration, is a surprising survival.

The Grand is currently shut after stints housing bingo and as a concert venue. An excellent example of its type, deserves better.

biographies

The zenith of London theatre building occurred during the late-Victorian and Edwardian periods; there was a brief renaissance around 1930. The technical requirements and structural expertise, the constraints of fire legislation, sightlines and the need to cram as many people in to as small a space as possible were so demanding that a few architects became recognised as experts who specialised in theatres and did little else. A kind of clique formed who dominated the scene and built up reputations for completing work quickly, on time and on budget, and for being able to co-ordinate the myriad trades involved in complex construction projects.

A few of these architects moved seamlessly and naturally into cinema design at the beginning of the twentieth century, sometimes combining the two disciplines. But as they tended to work solely in the fields of popular entertainment and were looked down on by the architectural establishment for their populism, they are virtually omitted from the main architectural histories. Details of their lives and works are sadly sketchy. Below are a few basic facts intended to help readers to get a picture of the architects whose names crop up most frequently in this book.

Bertie Crewe (?–1937)
Crewe had worked for three years in Paris during his youth and he brought back a Francophile decorative flair. He worked with two of the best-known theatre architects of the era – Walter Emden and W G R Sprague – and in 1895 he set up his own practice. Concentrating on theatres and later cinemas, Crewe was responsible (occasionally in collaboration with others) for a number of the best late-Edwardian and early-twentieth-century London theatres including the Shaftesbury, the

Phoenix, the Piccadilly and the interior of the Lyceum. He also designed the London Opera House on Kingsway (demolished to make way for offices and the Peacock; see page 2.50), the Palace of Varieties in Manchester (1913), the Pavilion, Glasgow (1909), the Alhambra and Mogador Palace theatres in Paris (both 1904) and another Alhambra in Brussels (1907).

He was among the first architects to design cinematograph theatres, initially in converted premises and later in new buildings. He built London's first 'super cinema', the New Tivoli in the Strand, in 1923 (demolished in 1957). Cecil Masey and Robert Cromie, two of Britain's most successful cinema architects, were given their starts in Bertie Crewe's office.

Walter Emden (1847–1913)
Emden was a mechanical as well as a civil engineer, a member of the Strand District Board of Works, and went on to become a City of London councillor and then mayor in 1903. All this activity left little time for him to develop as a refined architect; nevertheless he made his name with a number of hotels, restaurants and theatres. He worked with both Bertie Crewe and C J Phipps and the latter's talents in particular helped him to realise his better buildings, including the elegant Garrick and the more sober Duke of York's.

Marc-Henri and Laverdet
Marc-Henri Levy and Gaston Laverdet dressed the theatre interiors of the early 1930s in clothes of exquisite Parisian chic. They introduced the glamour of art deco to London's theatres and remnants of their work can be seen at the Whitehall and at the Prince Edward.

They were also responsible for the lavish interiors of the Paramount theatre in Paris.

Cecil Masey (1881–1960)
Starting in the office of Bertie Crewe, Masey became a prolific theatre and cinema specialist. Among the best of his designs are the Wimbledon and Phoenix theatres. On the latter he collaborated with Russian emigre Theodor Komisarjevsky, with whom he also realised some fantastical cinema buildings including the incomparably wacky combination of expressionist deco and Hollywood-gilt gothic of the Tooting Granada.

The Granada (ABC), Walthamstow (Alhambra-style) and the Granada (Gala Bingo), Woolwich (renaissance and gothic) are both also well worth a look.

Frank Matcham (1854–1920)
The most successful and most prolific theatre architect ever, Matcham was a great populist and his theatres are among the greatest Edwardian buildings. Often clumsy, he occasionally transcended his natural lack of taste with a sublime feel for theatricality and modelling. His façades are eclectic and sometimes botched but always noticeable, loudly announcing the theatre behind, and his interiors are usually riotously enjoyable and unrestrained. He peppered the country with more than a hundred theatres, every bit as enjoyable as the masses of pubs he also designed. Naturally, the architectural establishment hated him.

The Coliseum, the Hackney Empire and Richmond Theatre are among his best works.

C J Phipps (1835–97)
Charles John Phipps started out designing buildings in Victorian gothic but went on to become the most eminent theatre architect of the period, setting the rules for the classic Francophile West-End theatre. His work is best represented by the magnificent pile of Her Majesty's which originally formed part of an ensemble with his neighbouring Carlton Hotel, destroyed in the war.

Ernest Schaufelberg (dates unknown)
Almost completely undocumented, Schaufelberg was nevertheless responsible for the wonderful art-deco delights of both the Fortune and the Adelphi; the latter is among London's greatest treasures of the era despite the destruction of the original sculptural façade. Schaufelberg is known to have worked on occasion with Erich Mendelsohn in the mid 1930s. Sounds like a good subject for a dissertation.

W G R Sprague (1865–1933)
Born in Australia, Sprague worked first with Frank Matcham and then with Walter Emden before setting up on his own, designing more than 30 theatres and becoming the architect who, more than any other, created the definitive theatre architecture of London. Sprague had the lightest touch of any of his contemporaries and his buildings are the most sophisticated, both inside and out. His theatres blend seamlessly into the Edwardian townscape and are consistent from elevation through to proscenium arch with well-composed spatial sequences and well-proportioned auditoria.

His finest theatre is the exquisite Wyndham's: other highlights include the St Martin's, Aldwych, Strand and Globe (now the Gielgud). He also designed a number of suburban London theatres which have disappeared though the Coronet, Notting Hill, survives as a cinema. In 1902 he designed the elaborate Edward VII Theatre in Paris.

Edward Albert Stone (dates unknown)
Not being an architect proved no handicap to Stone, who was responsible for three theatres in the mini-boom around 1930. All three – the Whitehall, Piccadilly and London Casino (now Prince Edward Theatre) – have survived. They are, however, more notable for their interiors for which Stone employed top art-deco designers Mollo and Egan and Marc-Henri and Laverdet.

He was better known as a cinema designer (a field in which his career stretched back to before the First World War) and many of his best cinemas survive. These include the Astorias in Finsbury Park and Brixton (the latter now a music venue), which were among the first 'atmospheric' cinema interiors designed in a theatrically exotic Italianate style to emulate fantasy townscapes.

Thomas Verity (1837–91) and **Frank Thomas Verity** (1864–1937)
Between them, the Veritys (father and son) were responsible for some of London's best Victorian buildings. Verity senior was instrumental in the detailing of the Royal Albert Hall (1867–70) and went on to design the Criterion restaurant in Piccadilly Circus (with its awe-inspiringly glittery, almost Byzantine, luxury interior) and the adjoining theatre. The Comedy, which also survives, is another Victorian delight.

In 1889 Thomas was joined in practice by his son who later designed a great number of fine London houses and fashionable apartment blocks, and even worked on the interiors of the state apartments at Buckingham

Palace for King Edward VII. He designed the huge Plaza Cinema in Lower Regent Street in 1926 – this, though messed up inside, still forms an impressive piece of townscape – and the Empire Theatre in Leicester Square. Films were first shown at the Empire in 1896 and the building has since become a cinema.

Index

PICTURES

All pictures are by Keith Collie except:
pages 2.11, 2.13 Matthew Weinraub, reproduced by kind permission of The Savoy
page 4.11 Haworth Tompkins Architects
pages 5.3, 5.5, 5.7 Morley von Sternberg, reproduced by kind permission of Sadler's Wells
page 5.13 Bennetts Asociates
page 6.17 Levitt Bernstein Associates Limited
page 8.12 Eamonn O'Mahony, reproduced by kind permission of Pawson Williams Architects

БЪЛГАР
АНГЛИЙСКИ
РАЗГОВОРНИК

Настоящият "Българско-английски разговорник" е адресиран към всички, на които предстои да посетят Великобритания и страните, в които се говори английски език, независимо дали отиват на гости, на екскурзия, на почивка или на работа.

Разговорникът ви предлага:

• практично и удобно структуриране на темите и разделите

• прецизен подбор на думите и фразите, направен според честотата на употребата и полезността им

• формулиране на въпросите и отговорите така, че да съумеете сами и с лекота да построите фразата, от която се нуждаете в конкретната ситуация

• възможност не само да си служите с езика, но и неусетно да го усвоявате

• и много полезна информация за вашето пътуване и престой, която ще ви помогне да не се чувствате чужденец извън България

Трето преработено издание
Съставители: Даниела Трънколова
Панайот Първанов
Редактор: Миленка Костова
Художник: Красимир Коцев
Печат: "АБАГАР" АД - В.Търново
Формат: 64/108x84
Печатни коли: 26

ISBN 954-8805-19-7

СЪДЪРЖАНИЕ

ОБЩА ЧАСТ

ОБЩУВАНЕ

УСЛУГИ И РАЗВЛЕЧЕНИЯ

СТОКИ И ПОКУПКИ

ПЪТУВАНЕ

ЧОВЕК И ЗДРАВЕ

РАБОТА

Важни изрази и акценти

Речник

Актуална информация

ОБЩА ЧАСТ

▸ АНГЛИЙСКА АЗБУКА ◂

A a	ей	**J j**	джей	**S s**	ес
B b	би:	**K k**	кей	**T t**	ти:
C c	си:	**L l**	ел	**U u**	ю:
D d	ди:	**M m**	ем	**V v**	ви:
E e	и:	**N n**	ен	**W w**	да̀бъл ю:
F f	еф	**O o**	о̀у	**X x**	екс
G g	джи:	**P p**	пи:	**Y y**	уа̀й
H h	ейч	**Q q**	кю:	**Z z**	зед
I i	ай	**R r**	а:		

▸ ПРАВИЛА НА ПРОИЗНОШЕНИЕТО ◂

Ще се убедите сами, че английските букви в думата много рядко се изговарят така, както звучат в азбуката. Тяхното произношение е необходимо да се знае, за да сте в състояние да продиктувате напр. името, адреса си или която и да е друга дума буква по буква. Това е ежедневна практика в английския език и се нарича **spelling** (спѐлинг).

Произнасянето по букви може да ви се наложи по телефона, на митницата или в хотела, т.е. винаги, когато вашият събеседник иска да знае точния правопис на съответната дума.

➢ Ако някой ви помоли:

Would you spell it, please?

[Уд ю: спел ит, пли:з?]

Бихте ли я (го) *(думата, името)* изговорили буква по буква?,

вие следва да разчлените съответната дума по букви и да я произнесете:

G-e-o-r-g-i

джи:, и:, ѐу, а:, джи:, ай

I-v-a-n-o-v

ай, ви:, ей, ен, ѐу, ви:

В английски език се е наложила необходимостта от използване на допълнителна азбука от фонетични знаци, които показват конкретното произношение на буквите в думата. Това е така, тъй като в английския език няма достатъчно букви, които да представят всички звуци, съществуващи в езика.

Фонетичните знаци, използвани в настоящия разговорник, за улеснение на читателя, са взети от българската азбука, но с уговорката, че някои от звуците в английски език нямат точно съответствие в българския.

◈ Със знака [æ] е обозначен звук между българското **а** и **е**. Устата се отваря за **а**, а се произнася **е**.

bad	[бæд]	лош,-а, -о, -и
hand	[хæнд]	ръка
pat	[пæт]	потупвам

◈ Знакът [а] се използва за означаване на звук между българското **а** и **ъ**. Устата се отваря за **ъ**, а се произнася **а**.

funny	[фа̀ни]	смешен,-а,-о,-и
sun	[сан]	слънце
cut	[кат]	режа

◈ Чрез знаците [*т*] и [*д*] са означени два звука, за изговарянето на които върхът на езика се поставя между зъбите, но без да ги докосва. При това положение се опитваме да произнесем **т**. Звукът, който се чува е *т*.

thin	[*т*ин] слаб, тънък
teeth	[ти:*т*] зъби
thank you	[*т*æнк ю:] благодаря ти (ви)

Когато при същото положение на говорните органи, се опитаме да произнесем **g**, звукът, който ще се чуе, е *g*.

those	[*g*оуз]	онези
this	[*g*ис]	този, това
weather	[уè*g*ъ]	време *(метеорологично)*

Тези два фонетични знака илюстрират произношението на буквосъчетанието **th**.

◈ Английското r [р] се произнася, като езикът се подвие към небцето, но без да го докосва. За да добиете нагледна представа за произнасянето му поставете палеца между зъбите и се опитайте да изговорите българското **р**, като не докосвате палеца с език.

red	[ред]	червен,-а,-о,-и
road	[ро̀уд]	път
run	[ран]	тичам

◈ С буквосъчетанието [нг] е обозначен носов звук, при който с горната задна част на езика затваряме гърлото и произнасяме носово **н**. В края се чува едно загатнато **г**.

young	[йанг]	млад,-а,-о,-и
ring	[ринг]	пръстен, кръг
sing	[синг]	пея

◈ Знакът [:] се използва за удължаване на съответната гласна. Често дължината на гласния звук в английски език има смислово-различителна функция:

heat [хи:т] горещина
но:
hit [хит] удар; успех

sheep [ши:п] овца; овце
но:
ship [шип] кораб

Съществително име

Категорията *род на съществителното име* в английски език почти е изчезнала.

worker [уъ:къ:] работник, работничка
doctor [дòктъ] лекар, лекарка
friend [френд] приятел, приятелка

И все пак:

boy friend [бòй френд] приятел
girl friend [гъ:л френд] приятелка

Родът на съществителното име се основава на естествения род на лицето или предмета:

man [мæн] мъж
woman [уỳман] жена
son [сан] син
daughter [дò:тъ] дъщеря

Образуване на множествено число

За да образуваме множествено число е необходимо да поставим в края на думата буквата **s**, която в зависимост от предходния звук се произнася **с** или **з**:

hat ⇨	hats
[хæт]	[хæтс]
шапка	шапки

bed	⇨	bed**s**
[бед]		[бедз]
легло		легла

➢ Когато крайната съгласна е **t**, **k**, **p**, **f**, т.е. беззвучна, се произнася **с**:

ha**t**	⇨	hat**s**
[хæт]		[хæтс]
шапка		шапки
shi**p**	⇨	ship**s**
[шип]		[шипс]
кораб		кораби
hi**t**	⇨	hit**s**
[хит]		[хитс]
удар		удари

➢ Когато думата завършва на звучна съгласна или гласна, се произнася **з**:

be**d**	⇨	bed**s**
[бед]		[бедз]
легло		легла
su**n**	⇨	sun**s**
[сан]		[санз]
слънце		слънца
bo**y**	⇨	boy**s**
[бой]		[бойз]
момче		момчета

Особености: 

➢ Когато думата завършва на съскащ звук *(ч, ш, з, с, ж, кс, дж)*, окончанието е вече **-es**, което се изговаря *из*:

bri**dge**	⇨	bridg**es**
[бридж]		[брѝджиз]
мост		мостове
ro**se**	⇨	ros**es**
[ро̀уз]		[ро̀узиз]
роза		рози
wa**tch**	⇨	watch**es**
[уо̀ч]		[уо̀чиз]
часовник		часовници

➤ Когато съществителното завършва на **-o**, окончанието отново е **-es**, и **s** се произнася *з*:

tomat**o**	⇨	tomato**es**
[тъма̀:тоу]		[тъма̀:тоуз]
домат		домати

➤ Когато съществителното завършва на **гласна + y**, окончанието е **-s**:

b**oy**	⇨	boy**s**
[бой]		[бойз]
момче		момчета

В случаите обаче, когато пред **y** има съгласна буква, **y** се преобразува в **i**, а окончанието е **-es**:

lad**y**	⇨	lad**ies**
[лѐйди]		[лѐйдиз]
дама		дами
bab**y**	⇨	bab**ies**
[бѐйби]		[бѐйбиз]
бебе		бебета

➤ Малък брой съществителни, които завършват на **-f** или **-fe**, преобразуват окончанието си в **-ves**, което се произнася *вз*:

kni**fe**	kni**ves**
[найф]	[найвз]
нож	ножове
wi**fe**	wives
[уа̀йф]	[уа̀йвз]
съпруга	съпруги

➤ Една група съществителни образува множествено число неправилно. Ето само някои от тях:

man	⇨	**men**
[мæн]		[мен]
мъж		мъже
woman	⇨	**women**
[уу̀ман]		[уѝмин]
жена		жени

child	⇨	**children**
[чайлд]		[чѝлдрън]
дете		деца
tooth	⇨	**teeth**
[ту:*т*]		[ти:*т*]
зъб		зъби
foot	⇨	**feet**
[фут]		[фи:т]
ходило		ходила

В английски език съществуват два начина за изразяване на притежание:

❶ Чрез *окончанието* **-'s** (апостроф и **s**), което се произнася по същите правила, както и окончанието **-s** за множествено число на съществителните имена. Този начин за изразяване на притежание се употребява главно за живи същества:

Mr. Jone's car
[мѝстъ: джо̀унз ка:]
колата на господин Джон

Mary's house
[мѐриз ха̀ус]
къщата на Мери

the children's clothes
[*д*ъ чѝлдрънз кло̀у*д*з]
дрехите на децата

Ако притежателите са повече от един, окончанието се поставя след последното съществително:

Jill and Jack's mother
[джил ænд джæкс мà*д*ъ]
майката на Джил и Джак

Когато съществителното е в множествено число, изразите добиват вида:

the boys' car
[*g*ъ бойз ка:]
колата на момчетата

the brothers' house
[*g*ъ бр<u>а̀</u>*g*ъз хàус]
къщата на братята

Възможно е притежаваният предмет да се изпусне:

This is a car. It is **Roger's**.
[*g*ис из ъ ка:. Ит из рòджъз]
Това е кола. Тя е на Роджър.

Предпочита се също и в изрази, които се отнасят до времето, разстоянието и т.н.

one month's salary
[у<u>а̀</u>н м<u>а̀</u>н*тс* сæ̀лъри]
едномесечна заплата

❷ Чрез предлога **of**.

Този начин за изразяване на притежание е типичен за съществителни, които не означават живи същества.

the leaves **of the tree**
[*g*ъ ли:вз ъв *g*ъ три:]
листата на дърветата

the legs **of the table**
[*g*ъ легз ъв *g*ъ тèйбъл]
краката на масата

the name **of the dog**
[*g*ъ нейм ъв *g*ъ дог]
името на кучето

или

the dog's name
[*g*ъ догз нейм]

Неопределителен член

Неопределителният член в английски език е **a** или **an**. Той се поставя само пред броими съществителни (тези, които могат да се броят и имат ед. и мн. число) в единствено число и не носи ударение. Превежда се с *един, една, едно, някой, някоя, някое*, или не се превежда.

➤ **a** се поставя пред броими съществителни, които започват със съгласен или полугласен звук.

Полугласните звуци в английски език са **j** и **w.**

a pen [ъ пен] писалка
a dog [ъ дог] куче
a univercity [ъ юнивъ:сити] университет
a yard [ъ йа:д] двор
a window [ъ уйндоу] прозорец

➤ **an** се поставя пред:

- съществителни, които започват с **гласен звук**
  an egg [ън ег] яйце
  an orange [ън òриндж] портокал
- съществителни, които започват с **h,** което не се произнася (нямо **h**):
  an hour [ън àуъ] час

Определителен член

Определителният член в английски език е **the**.

Той стои винаги пред думата както в единствено, така и в множествено число и отговаря на пълното и непълно членуване в българския език, когато съществителното име е подлог, допълнение или обстоятелствено пояснение:

The teacher is young.
[дъ тѝ:чъ из йанг]
Учителят е млад.

I'm talking to **the** teacher.
[айм тò:кинг ту дъ тѝ:чъ]
Разговарям с учителя.

I went to **the** pharmacy.
[ай уèнт ту дъ фà:мъси]
Отидох до аптеката.

The children are playing.
[дъ чѝлдрън а: плèинг]
Децата играят.

➤ Произнася се [дъ], когато съществителното или прилагателното пред него, започват със съгласна или полугласна:

the dog	[дъ дог]	кучето
the window	[дъ уѝндоу]	прозорецът,-а
the young man	[дъ йанг ман]	младият,-я мъж

➤ Определителният член се произнася [ди] пред съществителни, които започват с гласна или нямо **h**:

the egg	[ди ег]	яйцето
the orange	[ди òриндж]	портокалът,-а
the honest man	[ди òнист мæн]	честният,-я човек

Прилагателно име

Прилагателните имена в английския език не се изменят по род и число, т.е. не се съгласуват със съществителното пред което стоят:

a good man	[ъ гуд мæн] (един) добър мъж; човек
a good woman	[ъ гуд уỳман] (една) добра жена
the good child	[дъ гуд чайлд] доброто дете
good parents	[гуд пѐърънтс] добри родители

Съществуват два начина за степенуване на прилагателните:

❶ Чрез окончанията **-er** и **-est**

Сравнителната степен на всички едносрични и някои двусрични прилагателни се образува чрез окончанието **-er,** а превъзходната - чрез окончанието **-est**.

Превъзходната степен обикновено се членува.

long ⇨	long**er** ⇨	the long**est**
[лонг]	[лòнгъ]	[дъ лòнгист]
дълъг	по-дълъг	най-дълъг
cold ⇨	cold**er** ⇨	the cold**est**
[кòулд]	[кòулдъ]	[дъ кòулдист]
студен	по-студен	най-студен
clever ⇨	clever**er** ⇨	the clever**est**
[клѐвъ]	[клѐвъръ]	[дъ клѐвърист]
умен	по-умен	най-умен

Когато прилагателното завършва на **-e**, то отпада:

brav**e** ⇨	brav**er** ⇨	the brav**est**
[брейв]	[брѐйвъ]	[дъ брѐйвист]
смел	по-смел	най-смел

Когато прилагателното е едносрично и завършва на една гласна и съгласна, последната се удвоява:

hot	⇨ ho**tt**er	⇨ the ho**tt**est
[хот]	[хòтъ]	[gъ хòтист]
горещ	по-горещ	най-горещ

Когато пред **y** има съгласна буква, то се променя в **i**:

bus**y**	⇨ busier	⇨ the busiest
[бѝзи]	[бѝзиъ]	[gъ бѝзиист]
заем	по-заем	най-заем

❷ Друг начин за степенуване на прилагателните е чрез наречията **more** (повече) и **less** (по-малко) за сравнителна степен, и **most** (най-много), **least** (най-малко) за превъзходна. Повечето двусрични и всички многосрични прилагателни се степенуват с **more** [мо:] и **most** [мòуст]:

careful [кѐъфул]	внимателен
more careful	по-внимателен
the **most** careful	най-внимателен
clever [клѐвъ]	умен
more clever	по-умен
the **most** clever	най-умен
energetic [ѐнъджетик]	енергичен
more energetic	по-енергичен
the **most** energetic	най-енергичен

С помощта на **less** и **least** се образуват сравнителната и превъзходната степен на всички прилагателни:

hot	[хот] горещ
less hot	[лес хот] по-малко горещ
the least hot	[gъ ли:ст хот] най-малко горещ

clever	[клèвъ] умен
less clever	[лес клèвъ] по-малко умен
the least clever	[gъ ли:ст клèвъ] най-малко умен
careful	[кèъфул] внимателен
less careful	[лес кèъфул] по-малко внимателен
the least careful	[gъ ли:ст кèъфул] най-малко внимателен

➤ Някои прилагателни образуват сравнителна и превъзходна степен неправилно:

good ⇨	**better** ⇨	**the best**
[гуд]	[бèтъ]	[gъ бест]
добър	по-добър	най-добър
bad ⇨	**worse** ⇨	**the worst**
[бæд]	[уъ:с]	[gъ уъ:ст]
лош	по-лош	най-лош
little ⇨	**less** ⇨	**the least**
[лѝтъл]	[лес]	[gъ ли:ст]
малък	по-малък	най-малък

➤ Ако два предмета или лица са равни по качество за тяхното сравняване се използва **as** пред и след прилагателното в положителна степен:

as ... as... [æз ...æз...]

as good as ...

толкова добър, колкото ...

➤ В отрицателна форма се използва **not so...as** ... [нот сòу ... æз...]

not so good as ...

не толкова добър, колкото

Наречие

за място

where	[уѐъ]	къде?
here	[хѝъ]	тук
there	[*д*ѐъ]	там
high	[хай]	високо
low	[лòу]	ниско
far	[фа:]	далеч

up [ап] горе
above [ъба̀в] горе
down [да̀ун] долу
inside [инса̀йд] вътре
outside [аутса̀йд] отвън
to the South [ту *д*ъ са̀у*т*] южно
to the North [ту *д*ъ но:*т*] северно

to the East	[ту *д*и и:ст]	източно
to the West	[ту *д*ъ уѐст]	западно
anywhere	[ѐниуеъ]	където и да е
near	[нѝъ]	близо
over there	[òувъ *д*ѐъ]	хей там
over here	[òувъ хѝъ]	хей тук
somewhere	[са̀муѐъ]	някъде
to the right	[ту *д*ъ райт]	надясно
to the left	[ту *д*ъ лефт]	наляво
elsewhere	[елсуѐъ]	другаде
around	[ъра̀унд]	(на)около
in front of	[ин франт ъв]	(от)пред
forward	[фò:уъд]	напред
ahead	[ъхѐд]	напред
back	[бæк]	обратно
at the back	[æт *д*ъ бæк]	отзад
everywhere	[евриуѐъ]	навсякъде
nowhere	[ноуѐъ]	никъде
near by	[нѝъ бай]	близо до
close to	[клòус ту]	близо до
straight (on)	[стрейт][он]	направо

за време

when	[уѐн]	кога?
then	[ден]	тогава, после
ever	[ѐвъ]	някога
never	[нѐвъ]	никога
now	[нàу]	сега
today	[тъдѐй]	днес
tonight	[тънàйт]	довечера
tomorrow	[тъмòроу]	утре
daily	[дѐйли]	дневно, ежедневно
yesterday	[йѐстъдей]	вчера
early	[ъ:ли]	рано
late	[лейт]	късно
lately	[лѐйтли]	напоследък
always	[ò:луиз]	винаги
often	[òфън]	често
usually	[ю:жуъли]	обикновено
rarely	[рѐъли]	рядко
just	[джаст]	току́-що

за начин

how?	[хàу]	как?
well	[уѐл]	добре
badly	[бѐдли]	лошо
slowly	[слòули]	бавно
quickly	[куѝкли]	бързо
carefully	[кѐъфули]	внимателно
just	[джаст]	точно
noisily	[нòизили]	шумно
hardly	[хà:дли]	едва
hard	[ха:д]	усилно, яко

за степен

how much?	[хàу мач]	колко?
much	[мач]	много
little	[лѝтъл]	малко
quite	[куàйт]	доста
almost	[òлмòуст]	почти
very	[вѐри]	много
too	[ту:]	твърде
so	[сòу]	така, толкова

Наречията се степенуват по същите правила, както и прилагателните.

Неправилно степенуване имат:

well	**better**	**best**
[уèл]	[бèтъ]	[бест]
добре	по-добре	най-добре
badly	**worse**	**worst**
[бæ̀дли]	[уъ̀:с]	[уъ̀:ст]
зле	по-зле	най-зле
much	**more**	**most**
[мач]	[мо:]	[мòуст]
много	повече	най-много
(за количество)		
many	**more**	**most**
[мæ̀ни]	[мо:]	[мòуст]
много	повече	най-много
(на брой)		
little	**less**	**least**
[лѝтъл]	[лес]	[ли:ст]
малко	по-малко	най-малко

Местоимения

Лични местоимения-подлог

I	[ай]	аз
you	[ю:]	ти
he	[хи:]	той
she	[ши:]	тя
it	[ит]	то
we	[уй:]	ние
you	[ю:]	вие
they	[*д*ей]	те

➤ Местоимението **I** (аз) се пише винаги с главна буква.

➤ Местоимението **you** означава, както *ти*, така и *вие* за множествено число, а освен това се използва и за изразяване на учтива форма.

➤ С местоимението **it** се означават неодушевени предмети и животни. То се използва също и като безличен подлог.

It's late.
[итс лейт]
Късно е.

It's raining.
[итс рѐйнинг]
Вали дъжд.

Лични местоимения-допълнение

me	[ми:]	(на) мен, ме, ми
you	[ю:]	(на) тебе, те, ти; (на) вас, ви
him	[хим]	(на) него,го, му
her	[хъ:]	(на) нея, я, и
it	[ит]	(на) него, го, му
us	[ас]	(на) нас, ни
them	[gъм]	(на) тях, ги, им

Възвратни и емфатични местоимения

➤ Възвратните местоимения се превеждат на български със *себе си, се, си.*

➤ Емфатичните, които по форма съвпадат с възвратните, и с които подчертаваме извършителя на действието, се превеждат със *сам, самият*:

myself	[майсѐлф]	се, себе си
yourself	[йо:сѐлф]	аз (ти, той,
himself	[химсѐлф]	тя, то, ние
herself	[хъ:сѐлф]	и т.н.)
itself	[итсѐлф]	самият
ourselves	[ауъсѐлвз]	
yourselves	[йо:сѐлвз]	
themselves	[gъмсѐлвз]	

Притежателни местоимения

➢ ***Притежателни прилагателни местоимения***

my	[май]	мой,-я,-е,-и
your	[йо:]	твой,-я,-е;ваш,-а,-е,-и
his	[хиз]	негов,-а,-о,-и
her	[хъ:]	нейн,-а,-о,-и
its	[итс]	негов,-а,-о,-и
our	[àуъ]	наш,-а-,е,-и
their	[gèъ]	техен,-а,-о-,-и

След този вид местоимения винаги следва съществително име.

➢ ***Притежателни местоимения***

mine	[майн]	мой,-я,-е,-и
yours	[йо:з]	твой;ваш,-а,-е,-и
his	[хиз]	негов,-а,-о,-и
hers	[хъ:з]	нейн,-а,-о,-и
its	[итс]	негов,-а,-о,-и
ours	[àуъз]	наш,-а-,е,-и
theirs	[gèъз]	техен,-а,-о-,-и

Тези местоимения се употребяват винаги самостоятелно, без съществително след тях.

Показателни местоимения

this	[gис]	този, тази, това
that	[gæт]	онзи, онази, онова
these	[gи:з]	тези
those	[gòуз]	онези
the one	[gъ уàн]	*замества споменато преди това съществително*
this one	[gис уàн]	този, тази, това
that one	[gæт уàн]	онзи, онази, онова
the ones	[gъ уàнз]	*замества съществителни в мн.ч.*
these ones	[gи:з уàнз]	тези
those ones	[gòуз уàнз]	онези
the same	[gъ сейм]	същия, -та, -то, -те

Въпросителни местоимения

who	[ху:]	кой,-я,-е,-и
whose	[ху:з]	чий,-я,-е,-и
which	[уйч]	кой,-я,-е,-и от всичките *(за предмети и по-рядко за лица)*
what	[уòт]	какъв,-а,-о,-и
why	[уàй]	защо
where	[уèъ]	къде
when	[уèн]	кога
how	[хàу]	как

Относителни местоимения

who	[ху:]	който, която, което, които *(за лица)*
whose	[ху:з]	чийто, чиято, чието, чиито *(за лица и по-рядко за предмети)*
which	[уйч]	който, която, което, които *(за предмети)*
what	[уòт]	това, което
that	[ðæт]	който, която, което, които
as	[æз]	какъвто, каквато, каквото, каквито

Неопределителни местоимения

some	[сам]	някой,-я,-е,-и; малко, няколко *(в пол. и вър. изречения)*
any	[èни]	някой,-я,-е,-и; малко, няколко *(във вър. изречения)*
any	[èни]	никой,-я,-е,-и; николко *(в отр. изречения с **not**)*

no	[нòу]	никакъв,-а,-о,-и; *(употребява се винаги със същеcтв. име и глагол в положителна форма)*
many	[мèни]	много *(на брой)*
much	[мач]	много *(по количество)*
few	[фю:]	малко *(на брой)*
little	[лѝтъл]	малко *(по количество)*
each	[и:ч]	всеки,-а,-о (поотделно)
every	[èври]	всеки, всяка, всяко
each one	[и:ч уàн]	всеки,-а,-о (един,-а,-о)
everyone	[èвриуан]	всеки, всяка, всяко, всички
everybody	[èврибоди]	всеки,-а,-о; всички
everything	[èвритинг]	всичко, всяко нещо
either	[àйдъ]	всеки,-а,-о един,-а,-о *(от две лица или предмети)*
neither	[нàйдъ]	нито един,-а,-о *(от две лица или предмети)*
both	[бòут]	и двамата, и двете
all	[о:л]	всички

Местоименията в английски език не се членуват.

Глагол

Спомагателни глаголи

Глаголът be (съм)

➤ **Сегашно просто време**

Този глагол има пълни и кратки форми:

пълна	*кратка*	
I am [ай ем]	**I'm** [айм]	аз съм
you are [ю: а:]	**you're** [йо:]	ти си
he is [хи: из]	**he's** [хи:з]	той е
she is [ши: из]	**she's** [ши:з]	тя е
it is [ит из]	**it's** [итс]	то е
we are [уй: а:]	**we're** [уйъ]	ние сме
you are [ю: а:]	**you're** [йо:]	вие (Вие) сте
they are [дей а:]	**they're** [дѐйъ:]	те са

Въпросителната форма се образува **чрез инверсия:**

Am I ...?	Аз ли съм ...?
Are you ...?	Ти ли си ...? / Вие ли сте ...?
и т.н.	

Отрицателната форма се образува с частицата **not**:

пълна форма	*кратка форма*	
I am not ... [ай æм нот]	**I'm not ...** [айм нот]	Аз не съм ...
you are not [ю: а: нот]	**you're not** [йо: нот]	Ти не си ...
he is not [хи: из нот]	**he's not** [хи:з нот]	Той не е ...

и т.н.

Кратката форма, с изключение на 1 л., ед.число, има и втори вариант:
you (we, they) **aren't** [à:нт]
he(she, it) **isn't** [йзънт]

➢ **Минало просто време**

I **was** [уòз] ... Аз бях ...
You **were** [уъ:] ... Ти беше ...
He **was** ... Той беше ...
She **was** ... Тя беше ...
It **was** ... То беше ...
We **were** ... Ние бяхме ...
You **were** ... Вие бяхте...
They **were** ... Те бяха ...

Отрицателна форма

I **was not** ...
I **wasn't** [уòзънт]...Аз не бях ...
You **were not** ...
You **weren't** [уъ:нт]... Ти не беше ...
He **was not** ...
He **wasn't** ... Той не беше ...
и т.н.

Въпросителна форма

Was I ...? Аз бях ли ...?
Were you ...? Ти беше ли ...?

Глаголът **have**(имам)

➢ **Сегашно просто време**

пълна форма	*кратка форма*	
I have ... [ай хæв]	**I've ...** [айв]	Аз имам...
You **have**... [ю: хæв]	**You've...** [ю:в]	Ти имаш...
He **has** ... [хи: хæз]		Той има...
She **has**...		Тя има...
It **has** ...		То има...

We **have**...	**We've...**	Ние имаме...
[уй: хæв]	[уй:в]	
You **have**...	**You've...**	Вие имаме...
[ю: хæв]	[ю:в]	
They **have**..	**They've...**	Те имат...
[ɡей хæв]	[ɡейв]	

В английски език глаголът **have** обикновено се придружава от **got**, което не се превежда на български.
I've got a house.
[айв гот ъ хàус]
Аз имам къща.

Отрицателна форма

I have **not**	I've **not ...**	Аз нямам...
You have **not**	You've **not**..	Ти нямаш..
He has **not** ...		Той няма...
и т.н.		

Въпросителна форма

Have I ...?	Аз имам ли... ?
Have you...?	Ти имаш ли...?
Has he ...?	Той има ли...?

Глаголни времена

Present Simple Tense
Сегашно просто време

Употребява се за изразяване на обичайни и повтарящи се действия, постоянни състояния или общоприети истини.

WORK РАБОТЯ

I	**work**	[уъ:к]	Аз работя
You	**work**		Ти работиш
He	**works**	[уъ:кс]	Той работи
She	**works**		Тя работи
It	**works**		То работи

We **work**	Ние работим
You **work**	Вие работите
They **work**	Те работят

Отрицателна форма

I **don't work** [ай дòунт уъ:к]	Аз не работя
You **don't work**	Ти не работиш
He **doesn't work** [хи дàзънт уъ:к]	Той не работи
She **doesn't work**	Тя не работи
It **doesn't work**	То не работи
We **don't work**	Ние не работим
You **don't work**	Вие не работите
They **don't work**	Те не работят

Въпросителна форма

Do I work? [ду ай уъ:к]	Аз работя ли?
Do you work?	Ти рàботиш ли?
Does he work? [даз хи уъ:к]	Той работи ли?
Does she work?	Тя работи ли?
Does it work?	То работи ли?
Do we work?	Ние работим ли?
Do you work?	Вие работите ли?
Do they work?	Те работят ли?

(!) Обикновено при отговор към положителната или отрицателна частица се добавят личното местоимение и спомагателният глагол, използван във въпроса.

положителен отговор	*отрицателен отговор*
Yes, **I do.**	No, I **don't.**
Yes, **you do.**	No, you **don't.**
Yes, **he does.**	No, he **doesn't**

Present Continuous Tense
Сегашно продължително време

◉ Изразява действия, които се извършват в момента на говоренето. Образува се от формите за сегашно просто време на спомагателния глагол **be** и сегашното причастие на глагола.

I'm working [айм уъ:кинг]	Аз работя
You're working	Ти работиш
He's working	Той работи
She's working	Тя работи
It's working	То работи
We're working	Ние работим
You're working	Вие работите
They're working	Те работят

Отрицателната форма се образува с частицата **not**:

пълна форма	*кратка форма*
I'm not working	Аз не работя
you're not working	Ти не работиш
he's not working	Той не работи

Въпросителната форма се образува чрез инверсия:

Am I working?	Аз работя ли?
Are you working?	Ти работиш ли?
	Вие работите ли?
	и т.н.

Past Simple Tense
Минало просто време

◉ Употребява се за изразяване на минало действие. В зависимост от контекста може да се преведе с минало свършено, минало несвършено време или преизказно наклонение.

Образува се като към инфинитива на глагола се постави окончанието **-ed**. В английския език съществува една немалка група глаголи, които имат неправилна форма за минало време.

I **worked** [уъ:кт]	Аз работих
You **worked**	Ти работи
He	Той
She **worked**	Тя работи
It	То
We **worked**	Ние работихме
You **worked**	Вие работихте
They **worked**	Те работиха

Въпросителната форма се образува с помощта на миналото време на глагола **do**. Спрегаемият глагол е в инфинитив.

Did I work?	Аз работих ли?
Did you work?	Ти работи ли?
Did he work?	Той работи ли?

Отрицателната форма се образува от миналото време на глагола **do** и частицата **not**: **I didn't** [дидънт] work. Аз не работих.

Future Simple Tense
Бъдеще просто време

I **shall work**. [ай шæл уъ:к]	Аз ще работя
You **will** work. [ю: уйл уъ:к]	Ти ще работиш
He **will** work.	Той ще работи
She **will** work.	Тя ще работи
It **will** work	То ще работи
We **shall** work.	Ние ще работим
You **will** work.	Виеще работите
They **will** work	Те ще работят

Съкратените форми се образуват по следния начин:

I'll	[айл]	work
You'll	[ю:л]	work

He'll	[хи:л]	work
She'll	[ши:л]	work
It'll	[ѝтъл]	work
We'll	[уѝ:л]	work
They'll	[дейл]	work

Предлози

за движение / място

in	[ин]	в, на
into	[ѝнту]	вътре в
inside	[инсàйд]	вътре в
out of	[àут ъв]	вън от
outside	[аутсàйд]	вън от
on	[он]	на, върху, по
off	[оф]	от
from	[фром]	от
to	[ту:]	до, към
at	[æт]	в, у, на, при
by	[бай]	до
beside	[бисàйд]	до
near by	[нѝъ: бай]	близо до
about	[ъбàут]	около, из
round	[рàунд]	около
for	[фо:]	за
across	[ъкрòс]	през
through	[тру:]	през
behind	[бихàйнд]	зад
over	[òувъ]	над
above	[ъбàв]	над
under	[àндъ]	под
below	[билòу]	под
underneath	[андъ:нѝ:т]	под
in front of	[ин фрàнт ъв]	пред
against	[ъгèйнст]	срещу, на
opposite	[òпъзит]	срещу
between	[битуѝ:н]	между
among	[ъмàнг]	измежду

за време

in	[ин]	в, през, на
on	[он]	на, през
at	[æт]	в
from	[фром]	от
to	[ту:]	до (с from)
since	[синс]	от
by	[бай]	до
about	[ъбàут]	към, около
till	[тил]	до
until	[антѝл]	до
for	[фо:]	за
before	[бифò:]	преди
after	[à:фтъ]	след
during	[дюърингг]	през,по време на

Съюзи

and	[æнд]	а, и
or	[о:]	или
but	[бат]	но
if	[иф]	или
as	[æз]	както
because	[бикò:з]	защото
that	[дæт]	че
whether	[уèдъ]	дали
where	[уèъ]	където
(al)though	[(ол)дòу]	въпреки че
when	[уèн]	когато
as long as	[æз лонг æз]	докато
as soon as	[æз су:н æз]	щом като
till	[тил]	докато
until	[антѝл]	докато (не)
as though	[æз дòу]	въпреки че
after	[à:фтъ]	след като
as...as	[æз..æз.]	толкова... колкото
not so...as	[нот сòу æз]	не толкова ... колкото ...
than	[дæн]	от *(при сравнение)*

Числителни	Numbers	Нàмбъз
бройни	**cardinal**	**кà:диньл**
Колко?	**How many?**	**Хàу мèни?**

0	нула	zero	зѝъроу
1	един, една, едно	one	уàн
2	две	two	ту:
3	три	three	*три:*
4	четири	four	фо:
5	пет	five	файв
6	шест	six	сикс
7	седем	seven	сèвън
8	осем	eight	ейт
9	девет	nine	найн
10	десет	ten	тен
11	единадесет	eleven	илèвън

12	дванадесет	twelve	туѐлв
13	тринадесет	thirteen	*тъ*:тѝ:н
14	четиринадесет	fourteen	фо:тѝ:н
15	петнадесет	fifteen	фифтѝ:н
16	шестнадесет	sixteen	сикстѝ:н
17	седемнадесет	seventeen	севънтѝ:н
18	осемнадесет	eighteen	ейтѝ:н
19	деветнадесет	nineteen	найнтѝ:н
20	двадесет	twenty	туѐнти
21	двадесет и един, една, едно	twenty-one	туѐнтиуа̀н
22	двадесет и две	twenty-two	туѐнтиту̀:
29	двадесет и девет	twenty-nine	туѐнтина̀йн
30	тридесет	thirty	*тъ*:ти
40	четиридесет	forty	фо̀:ти
50	петдесет	fifty	фѝфти
60	шестдесет	sixty	сѝксти
70	седемдесет	seventy	сѐвънти
80	осемдесет	eighty	ѐйти
90	деветдесет	ninety	на̀йнти
100	сто	one hundred	уа̀н ха̀ндрид

145 сто четириде- сет и пет	one hundred and forty-five	уàн хàндрид æнд фò:ти файв
200 двеста	two hundred	ту: хàндрид
300 триста	three hundred	*т*ри: хàндрид
400 четиристотин	four hundred	фо: хàндрид
500 петстотин	five hundred	файв хàндрид
600 шестстотин	six hundred	сикс хàндрид
700 седемстотин	seven hundred	сèвън хàндрид
800 осемстотин	eight hundred	ейт хàндрид
900 деветстотин	nine hundred	найн хàндрид
1 000 хиляда	one thousand	уàн *т*àузънд
1 095 хиляда и деветдесет и пет	one thousand and ninety-five	уàн *т*àузънд æнд нàйнти фàйв
1 245 хиляда двеста четиридесет и пет	one thousand two hundred and forty-five	уàн *т*àузънд ту: хàнд-рид æнд фò:ти файв
2 000 две хиляди	two thousand	ту: *т*àузънд
един милион	one million	уàн мùлиън
1 349 890 един милион триста четиридесет и девет хиляди осемс-тотин и деветдесет	one million three hundred and forty-nine thousand eight hundred and ninety	уàн мùлиън *т*ри: хàнд-рид æнд фò:ти найн *т*àузънд ейт хàндрид æнд нàйнти
два милиона	two million	ту: мùлиън

един милиард	one milliard, billion*(am.)*	уа̀н мѝлиа:д, бѝлиън
два милиарда	two milliard	ту: мѝлиа:д
стотици хора	hundreds of people	ха̀ндридз ъв пѝ:пъл
хиляди хора	thousands of people	*т*а̀узъндз ъв пѝ:пъл
редни	***ordinal***	***о̀:диньл***
първи,-а,-о	first	фъ:ст
втори,-а,-о	second	сѐкънд
трети,-а,-о	third	*т*ъ:д
четвърти,-а,-о	fourth	фо:*т*
пети,-а,-о	fifth	фиф*т*

шести,-а,-о	sixth	сикс*т*
седми,-а,-о	seventh	сѐвън*т*
осми,-а,-о	eighth	ей*т*
девети,-а,-о	ninth	нàйн*т*
десети,-а,-о	tenth	тен*т*
единадесети,-а,-о	eleventh	илѐвън*т*
дванадесети,-а,-о	twelfth	туѐлф*т*
тринадесети,-а,-о	thirteenth	*тъ*:тѝ:н*т*
четиринадесети,-а,-о	fourteenth	фо:тѝ:н*т*
петнадесети,-а,-о	fifteenth	фифтѝ:н*т*
шестнадесети,-а,-о	sixteenth	сикстѝ:н*т*
седемнадесети,-а,-о	seventeenth	севънтѝ:н*т*
осемнадесети,-а,-о	eighteenth	ейтѝ:н*т*
деветнадесети,-а,-о	nineteenth	найнтѝ:н*т*
двадесети,-а,-о	twentieth	туѐнтий*т*
двадесет и първи,-а,-о	twenty-first	туѐнти фъ:ст
тридесети,-а,-о	thirtieth	*тъ*:тий*т*
тридесет и първи,-а,-о	thirty-first	*тъ*:ти фъ:ст
четиридесети,-а,-о	fortieth	фо:тий*т*
деветдесет и девети,-а	ninety-ninth	нàйнти найн*т*
предпоследен,-а,-о	last but one	ла:ст бат уàн
последен,-а,-о	last	ла:ст

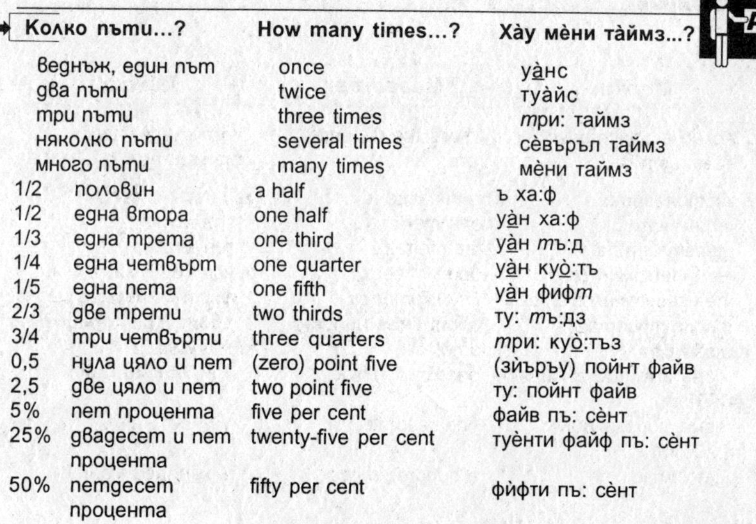

Колко пъти...? | How many times...? | Хàу мèни тàймз...?

	веднъж, един път	once	уа̀нс
	два пъти	twice	туàйс
	три пъти	three times	*три:* таймз
	няколко пъти	several times	сèвърът таймз
	много пъти	many times	мèни таймз
1/2	половин	a half	ъ ха:ф
1/2	една втора	one half	уа̀н ха:ф
1/3	една трета	one third	уа̀н *тъ:*д
1/4	една четвърт	one quarter	уа̀н куо̀:тъ
1/5	една пета	one fifth	уа̀н фиф*т*
2/3	две трети	two thirds	ту: *тъ:*дз
3/4	три четвърти	three quarters	*три:* куо̀:тъз
0,5	нула цяло и пет	(zero) point five	(зѝъръу) пойнт файв
2,5	две цяло и пет	two point five	ту: пойнт файв
5%	пет процента	five per cent	файв пъ: сèнт
25%	двадесет и пет процента	twenty-five per cent	туèнти файф пъ: сèнт
50%	петдесет процента	fifty per cent	фѝфти пъ: сèнт
	един чифт ...	a pair of ...	ъ пèъ ъв ...

Мерки	Measures	Мѐжъз
Колко е разстоянието от ... до ...?	What's the distance from... to...?	Уо̀тс дъ дѝстънс фром... ту:...?
Разстоянието е ...	The distance is ...	дъ дѝстънс из ...
един метър	one metre	уа̀н мѝ:тъ
десет метра	ten metres	тен мѝ:тъз
един километър	one kilometre	уа̀н кѝлоумѝ:тъ
петдесет километра	fifty kilometres	фѝфти кѝлоумѝ:тъз
около триста километра	about three hundred kilometres	ъба̀ут *три:* ха̀ндрид кѝлоумѝ:тъз
една английска миля (=1609 m)	one English mile	уа̀н йнглиш майл
една морска миля (=2206 m)	one sea mile	уа̀н си: майл
сто мили	a hundred miles	ъ ха̀ндред майлз

Каква е ...?	What's the ...?	Уòтс дъ ...?
дължината	length	ленгт
широчината	width	уйдт
височината	height	хайт
дебелината	thickness	тѝкнес
дълбочината	depth	дептт

Дължината е...	The length is ...	дъ ленгт из ...
един милиметър	one millimetre	уа̀н мѝлимѝ:тъ
петнадесет милиметра	fifteen millimetres	фифтѝ:н мѝлимѝ:тъз
един сантиметър	one centimetre	уа̀н сѐнтимѝ:тъ
петдесет сантиметра	fifty centimetres	фѝфти сѐнтимѝ:тъз
един инч (=2,5 cm)	one inch	уа̀н ѝнч
два инча	two inches	ту: ѝнчиз
един фут(=30,48 cm)	one foot	уа̀н фут
два фута	two feet	ту: фи:т
един ярд (=91,44 cm)	one yard	уа̀н йа̀:д
сто и двадесет ярда	a hundred and twenty yards	ъ ха̀ндрид ӕнд туѐнти йа̀:дз

един метър	one metre	уа̀н мѝ:тъ
десет метра	ten metres	тен мѝ:тъз
триста метра	three hundred metres	*три:* ха̀ндрид мѝ:тъз
➡ Каква е площта на...?	What's the area of…?	Уо̀тс *ди* ѐриъ ъв…?
парцела	the plot	*дъ* плот
имота	the property	*дъ* про̀пъти
терена	the ground	*дъ* гра̀унд
Площта на ... е ...	The area of … is …	*ди* ѐриъ ъв … из …
един квадратен метър	one square metre	уа̀н скуѐъ мѝ:тъ
сто квадратни метра	one hundred square metres	уа̀н ха̀ндрид скуѐъ мѝ:тъз
един хектар	one hectare	уа̀н хѐкта:
двадесет хектара	twenty hectares	туѐнти хѐкта:з
един кв. километър	one square killometre	уа̀н скуѐъ кѝломѝ:тъ
десет кв. километра	ten square killometres	тен скуѐъ кѝломѝ:тъз
хиляда квадратни километра	one thousand square killometres	уа̀н *т*а̀узънд скуѐъ кѝломѝ:тъз
един кв.инч(=6,45cm²)	one square inch	уа̀н скуѐъ инч

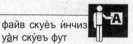

пет квадратни инча	five square inches	файв скуѐъ ѝнчиз
един кв.фут (=929cm²)	one square foot	уа̀н ску̀еъ фут
осем кв.фута	eight square feet	ейт скуѐъ фи:т
един кв.ярд(=0,836 m²)	one square yard	уа̀н ску̀еъ йа:д
петдесет кв. ярда	fifty square yards	фѝфти скуѐъ йа:дз
един акр (=0,405 хектара	one acre	уа̀н ѐйкъ
тридесет акра	thirty acres	тъ:ти ѐйкъз
една кв.миля (=259 хектара)	one square mile	уа̀н скуѐъ майл

Каква е вместимостта на...?	What's the capacity of...?	Уѐтс дъ къпǽсъти ъв...?
Вместимостта е...	The capacity is...	дъ къпǽсъти из ...
един литър	one litre	уа̀н лѝ:тъ
три литра	three litres	три: лѝ:тъз
петдесет литра	fifty litres	фѝфти лѝ:тъз
един пинт (= 0,568 l)	one pint	уа̀н пайнт
един куарт (=1,136 l)	one quart	уа̀н куѐ:т

три куарта	three quarts	*три*: куò:тс
един галон (=4,544 l)	one gallon	уàн гæ̀лън
седем галона	seven gallons	севн гæ̀лънз
един куб. метър	one cubic metre	уàн кю:бик мѝ:тъ
десет куб. метра	ten cubic metres	тен кю:бик мѝ:тъз
един куб. инч (=16,387 cm³)	one cubic inch	уàн кю:бик инч
един куб.фут (=0,028 m³)	one cubic foot	уàн кю:бик фут
един куб.ярд (= 0,765 m³)	one cubic yard	уàн кю:бик йа:д

Колко тежи това?	How much does it weigh?	Хàу мач даз ит уèй?
Какво е теглото на...?	What is the weight of ...?	Уòт из ðъ уèйт ъв ...?

Теглото е ...	The weight is...	ðъ уèйт из ...:
един грам	one gram	уàн грæм
шест грама	six grams	сикс грæмз
един килограм	one kilogram	уàн кѝлоугрæм
десет килограма	ten kilograms	тен кѝлоугрæмз
един тон	one ton	уàн тан

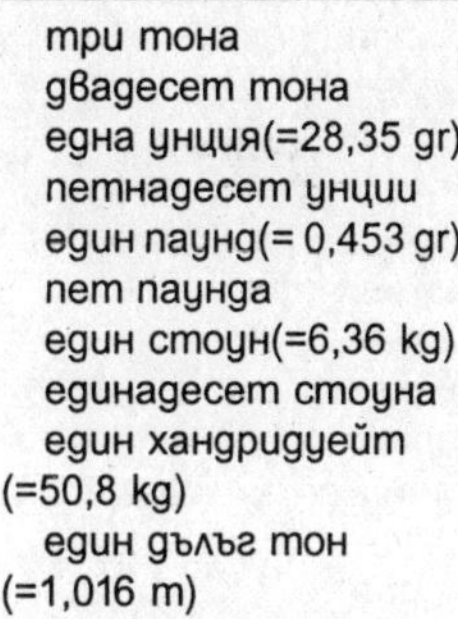

три тона	three tons	*три*: танз
двадесет тона	twenty tons	туѐнти танз
една унция(=28,35 gr)	one ounce	уа̀н а̀унс
петнадесет унции	fifteen ounces	фифтѝ:н а̀унсиз
един паунд(= 0,453 gr)	one pound	уа̀н па̀унд
пет паунда	five pounds	файв па̀ундз
един стоун(=6,36 kg)	one stone	уа̀н сто̀ун
единадесет стоуна	eleven stones	илѐвън сто̀унз
един хандридуейт (=50,8 kg)	one hundredweight	уа̀н ха̀ндридуейт
един дълъг тон (=1,016 m)	one long ton	уа̀н лонг тан
един къс тон (=907,18 kg)	one short ton	уа̀н шо:т тан

Цветове	*Colours*	*Ка̀лъз*
цвят	**colour**	**ка̀лъ**
бежов	beige	бейж
бял	white	уа̀йт
виолетов	violet	ва̀йълът
жълт	yellow	йѐлоу
зелен	green	гри:н
кафяв	brown	бра̀ун
лилав	purple	пъ:пъл
небесносин	sky-blue	скай блу:
оранжев	orange	о̀ринджж
розов	pink	пинк
сив	grey	грей
син	blue	блу:
светлосин	light blue	ла̀йт блу:
червен	red	ред
черен	black	блæк

светъл, ярък	bright	брайт
тъмен	dark	да:к
златист	gold	гòулд
сребрист	silver	сѝлвъ
цветен	coloured	кàлъ:д
безцветен	colourless	кàлълис
едноцветен	one-colour, plain	уàн кàлъ, плейн
многоцветен	many-coloured	мèни кàлъд
мургав	dark	да:к
рус	fair	фèъ
кестеняв	brown	брàун
... цвят,-ове	... colour,-s	... кàлъ,-з
крещящ,-и	flashy	флæ̀ши
съчетан,-и	matched	мæчт
контрастен,-и	contrasting	кънтрà:стинг
смесен,-и	mixed	микст
пастелен,-и	pastel	пæ̀стъл
ярък,-ки	bright	брайт

Време: часове, дни, месеци, години	**Time: hours, days, months, years**	**Тайм: а̀уъз, дейз, мантс, йиъз**
Колко е часът, моля?	What's the time, please?	Уо̀тс дъ тайм, пли:з?
Часът е ...	It's ...	Итс ...
един	one o'clock	уан ъ кло̀к
два и половина	half past two	ха:ф па:ст ту:
два и тридесет	two thirty	ту *тъ*:ти
три и четвърт	quarter past three	куо̀:тъ па:ст *три*:
осем без двадесет	twenty to eight	туѐнти ту: ейт
В колко часа ...?	(At) what time ...?	(æт) уо̀т тайм...?
Имам среща ...	I have an appointment ...	Ай хæв ън ъпо̀интмънт...
в един часа	at one o'clock	æт уан ъ кло̀к
в три и половина	at half past three	æт ха:ф па:ст *три*:
точно в пет	at five o'clock sharp	æт файв ъ кло̀к ша:п
към осем часа вечерта	about eight p.m.	ъба̀ут ейт пи: ем

Зает,-а съм ...	I'm busy...	Айм бѝзи ...
от десет до дванадесет часа сутринта	from ten to twelve a.m. (in the morning)	фром тен ту туѐлв ей ем (ин дъ мо̀:нинг)
между три и четири часа следобед	between three and four p.m. (in the afternoon)	битуй:н *три*: æнд фо: пи: ем(ин *ди* а̀фтъ:ну:н)
от шест до девет вечерта	from six to nine p.m. (in the evening)	фром сикс ту найн пи: ем (ин *ди* ѝ:внинг)
В колко часа отваря (затваря)...?	(At) what time does the ...open (close)?	(æт) уо̀т тайм да̀з дъ... о̀упън (кло̀уз)?
магазинът	the shop	дъ шоп
банката	the bank	дъ бæнк
В колко часа започва (свършва)...?	(At) what time does the ... start (finish)?	(æт) уо̀т тайм да̀з дъ ... ста:т (фѝниш)?
предаването	the programme	дъ про̀уграм
телевизионното шоу	the TV show	дъ ти:ви: шо̀у
представлението	the performance	дъ пъфо̀:мънс
В колко часа пристига (заминава)...?	(At) what time does the...arrive (depart)?	(æт) уо̀т тайм да̀з дъ... ъра̀йв (дипа̀:т)?
автобусът	the bus	дъ бас
самолетът	the plane	дъ плейн

влакът	the train	*д*ъ трейн
фериботът	the boat	*д*ъ бо̀ут
Можеш ли да дойдеш...?	Can you come ...?	Кæн ю: кам ...?
след двадесет минути	in twenty minutes	ин туѐнти мѝнитс
след половин час	in half an hour	ин ха:ф ън а̀уъ
след два часа	in two hours	ин ту: а̀уъз
утре сутринта	tomorrow morning	тъмо̀роу мо̀:нинг
по обед	at noon	æт ну:н
към обед	about lunch time	ъба̀ут ланч тайм
вечерта	in the evening	ин *д*и ѝ:внинг

Ще дойда ...	I'll come ...	Айл ка̀м ...
следобед	this afternoon	*д*ис а̀:фтъну:н
вдругиден	the day after tomorrow	*д*ъ дей а̀:фтъ тъмо̀роу
(!) след два дни	in two days	ин ту: дейз
след една седмица	in a week	ин ъ уѝ:к
след десет дни	in ten days	ин тен дейз
след един месец	in a month	ин ъ ман*т*

Пристигнах,-ме току-що.	I(We)'ve just arrived.	Ай(уѝ:)'в джаст ъра̀йвд.

Пристигнах,-ме ...	I(We) arrived ...	Ай(уй:) ъраивд ...
преди час	an hour ago	ън àуъ ъгòу
снощи	last night	ла:ст найт
вчера	yesterday	йèстъдей
завчера	the day before yesterday	дъ дей бифò: йèстъдей
преди три дни	three days ago	*три*: дейз ъгòу
преди две седмици	two weeks ago	ту: уй:кс ъгòу
Още е рано.	It's still early.	Итс стил ъ:ли.
Вече е късно.	It's already late.	Итс ò:преди лейт.

Кой ден е днес?	What day is it today?	Уòт дей из ит тъдèй?
Днес е ...	Today is ...	Тъдèй из ...
понеделник	**Monday**	мàндей
вторник	**Tuesday**	тю:здей
сряда	**Wednesday**	уèнздей
Ще се видим...	I'll see you ...	Айл си: ю: ...
в **четвъртък**	on **Thursday**	он *тъ*:здей
в **петък**	on **Friday**	он фрàйдей
в **събота**	on **Saturday**	он сæтъдей

Ще се срещнем ...	I'll meet you ...	Айл ми:т ю: ...
довечера	tonight	тънàйт
по-късно	later	лèйтъ
скоро	soon	су:н
утре	tomorrow	тъмòроу
Очаквах те ...	I expected you ...	Ай икспèктид ю:...
по-рано	earlier	ъ̀:лиъ
преди два дни	two days ago	ту: дейз ъгòу
онзи ден	the day before yesterday	дъ дей бифò: йèстъдей
от понеделник до сряда	from Monday to Wednesday	фром мàндей ту уèнздей
миналата седмица	last week	ла:ст уй:к
Можете ли да дойдете ...?	Can you come ...?	Кæн ю кам... ?
в десет часа сутринта	at ten o'clock in the morning	æт тен ъ клок ин дъ мò:нинг
през следващата седмица	next week	некст уй:к
в **неделя**	on **Sunday**	он сàндей

Можете да дойдете ...	You can come...	Ю: кæн кам...
след три дни	in three days	ин *три*: дейз
утре вечерта	tomorrow evening	тъмòроу ѝ:вининг
след обяд	this afternoon	*д*ис à:фтъну:н
На ваше разположение съм ...	I'm at your service ...	Айм æт йо: съ:вис...
утре през целия ден	tomorrow all day long	тъмòроу о:л дей лонг
всеки ден	every day	èври дей
през уикенда	at the weekend	æт *д*ъ уй:кенд
Коя дата сме днес...?	What's the date today?	Уòтс *д*ъ дейт тъдèй?
Днес е...	Today is...	Тъдèй из...
първи март	the first of March / March the first	*д*ъ фъ:ст ъв ма:ч / ма:ч *д*ъ фъ:ст
десети март	the tenth of March / March the tenth	*д*ъ тен*т* ъв ма:ч / ма:ч *д*ъ тен*т*
двадесет и трети юли	the twenty-third of July / July the twenty-third	*д*ъ туèнти-*тъ*:д ъв джулàй / джулàй *д*ъ туèнти-*тъ*:д

В Англия ли сте...?	Are you in England…?	А: ю: ин ѝнглънд…?
през **януари**	in **January**	ин джæ̀нюъри
през **февруари**	in **February**	ин фѐбруъри
през **март**	in **March**	ин ма:ч
през **април**	in **April**	ин ѐйприл
Ще се върнем тук ...	We'll come back …	Уй:л кам бæк …
през **май**	in **May**	ин мей
през **юни**	in **June**	ин джу:н
през **юли**	in **July**	ин джулàй
през **август**	in **August**	ин ò:гъст
Бях много зает,-а ...	I was very busy …	Ай уъз вѐри бѝзи…
през **септември**	in **September**	ин сиптѐмбъ
през **октомври**	in **October**	ин октòубъ
през **ноември**	in **November**	ин ноувѐмбъ
Коледа е през **декември**.	Christmas is in **December**.	Крѝсмъс из ин дисѐмбъ.
Пристигам,-е ... на първи май	I(we) arrive … on the first of May / May the first	Ай(уѝ:) ърàйв ... он дъ фъ:ст ъв мей / мей дъ фъ:ст

на трети септември	on the third of September / September the third	он *д*ъ *т*ъ:д ъв сиптѐмбъ / сиптѐмбъ *д*ъ *т*ъ:д
на двадесет и втори този месец	on the twenty-second of this month	он *д*ъ туѐнти-сѐкънд ъв *д*ис ман*т*
Кога ...? През коя година ...?	When ...? What year ...?	Уѐн ... ? Уòт йиъ ...?
През 1812 година	In 1812 (eighteen twelve)	Ин ейтѝ:н туѐлв
През 1900 година	In nineteen hundred	Ин нàйнти:н хàндрид
През 1999 година	In 1999 (nineteen ninety-nine)	Ин нàйнти:н нàйнти найн
През 2002 година	In 2002 (two thousand and two)	Ин ту: *т*àузънд æнд ту:
През 2006 година	In 2006 (two thousand and six)	Ин ту: *т*àузънд æнд сикс
През седемдесетте години на XX век	In 1970s (nineteen seventies)	Ин нàйнти:н сѐвънтис
През миналия век	In the last century	Ин *д*ъ ла:ст сѐнчъри
През този век	In this century	Ин *д*ис сѐнчъри
През следващия век	In the next century	Ин *д*ъ некст сѐнчъри

➡ Кога си роден,-а?	When were you born?	Уѐн уъ: ю: бо:н?
Роден,-а съм ...	I was born...	Ай уъз бо:н...
на седемнадесети юни 1961 година	on the seventeenth of June nineteen sixty-one	он дъ сѐвънти:нт ъв джу:н нàйнти:н сѝксти уàн
на първи април 1977 година	on the first of April nineteen seventy-seven	он дъ фъ:ст ъв ѐйприл нàйнти:н сѐвънти сѐвън
➡ На колко си (сте) години?	How old are you?	Хàу òулд а: ю:?
Аз съм ...	I'm ...	Айм ...
на тридесет и пет години	thirty-five (years old)	тъ:ти файв (ѝ:ъз оулд)
на четиридесет и осем години	forty-eight (years old)	фò:ти ейт(ѝ:ъз òулд)
На колко години е ...?	How old is ...?	Хàу òулд из...?
Той (тя) е на...	He(she) is ...	Хи:(ши:) из ...
на петнадесет години	fifteen (years old)	фифтѝ:н (ѝ:ъз òулд)
на петдесет години	fifty (years old)	фѝфти (ѝ:ъз òулд)
➡ Колко време беше (бяхте) ...?	How long were you...?	Хàу лонг уъ: ю: ...?
в чужбина	abroad	ъбрò:д

във Великобритания	in (Great) Britain	ин (грейт) брѝтън
в България	in Bulgaria	ин балгѐъриъ
Бях,-ме там ...	I was / We were there ...	Ай уъз / Уи: уъ: дѐъ...
шест месеца	for six months	фо: сикс мантс
една година	for one year	фо: уа̀н йиъ
около две години	for some two years	фо: сам ту: йиъз
три години и половина	for three and a half years	фо: три: ænд ъ ха:ф йиъз
Срещнахме се в Оксфорд ...	We met in Oxford ...	Уи: мет ин о̀ксфъд ...
миналата година	last year	ла:ст йиъ
тази година	this year	дис йиъ
през **лятото**	in **summer**	ин са̀мъ
през **есента**	in **autumn, fall** *(ам.)*	ин о̀:тъм, фо:л
случайно	by chance	бай чæнс
Смятам да поработя в Англия ...	I'm going to work in England ...	Айм гоуинг ту уъ:к ин ѝнглънд ...
догодина	next year	некст йи:ъ
през **зимата**	in **winter**	ин уѝнтъ
през **пролетта**	in **spring**	ин спринг

Метеорологично време	*The weather*	*дъ уèдъ*
Какво е времето днес?	What's the weather today?	Уòтс дъ уèдъ тъдèй?
Днес е ...	The weather is ...	дъ уèдъ из ...
топло	hot	хот
студено	cold	кòулд
задушно	close	клоуз
Днес ...	It's ... today.	Итс...тъдèй.
вали дъжд	raining	рèйнинг
ръми	drizzy	дрùззи
има лек вятър	brizzy	брùззи
вали сняг	snowing	снòуинг
вали град	hailing	хèйлинг
е облачно	cloudy	клàуди

е слънчево	sunny	са̲ни
е влажно	wet	уѐт
е ветровито	windy	уѝнди
е мъгливо	foggy	фо̀ги

Каква е температурата днес?	What's the temperature today?	Уòтс дъ тèмпръчъ тъдèй?
Температурата е ...	The temperature is ...	дъ тèмпръчъ из ...
Термометърът показва...	The thermometer shows ...	дъ тъмòмитъ шòуз ...
тридесет градуса над нулата	thirty degrees above zero	тъ:ти дигрѝ:з ъбàв зѝъроу
два градуса под нулата	two degrees below zero	ту: дигрѝ:з билòу зѝъроу
по Целзий	Centigrade(C)	Сентигрèйт
по Фаренхайт	Fahrenheit(F)	Фǽрънхайт
Каква е прогнозата за времето?	What's the weather forecast?	Уòтс дъ уèдъ фò:ка:ст?
Утре времето ще бъде ...	Tomorrow the weather will be ...	Тъмòроу дъ уèдъ уйл би: ...
хубаво	fine	файн
лошо	bad	бæд
хладно	cool	ку:л
горещо	hot	хот

топло	warm	уò:м
облачно	cloudy	клàуди
Ще има ...	It's going to be ...	Итс гòуинг ту би: ...
големи горещини	extremely hot	икстрѝ:мли хот
страшни студове	terribly cold	тèрибли кòулд
буря	stormy	стò:ми
гръмотевици	thundery	*т*а̀ндъри
Вчера времето беше...	The weather was ... yesterday.	*д*ъ уè*д*ъ уъз ... йèстъдей.
Времето ще се задържи ...	The weather is going to stay ...	*д*ъ уе*д*ъ из гòинг ту стей ...
Ще се задържи ...	It's going to stay ...	Итс гòинг ту стей ...
дъждовно	rainy	рèйни
мъгливо	foggy	фòги
ясно	clear	клѝъ
променливо	changeable	чèйнджъбъл

Тук климатът е ...	The climate is ... here.	дъ кла̀ймит из ... хѝъ.
континентален	continental	ко̀нтинѐнтъл
умерен	temperate	тѐмпърит
средиземноморски	Mediterranean	медитърѐйниън
суров	severe	сивѝъ
сух	dry	драй
влажен	humid	хю̀мид
горещ	hot	хот

Във Великобритания и повечето англоговорящи страни измерването на ***температурата*** *става по скалата на* ***Фаренхайт****(F). Ако по скалата на* ***Целзий****(C) водата замръзва при 0°, а кипи при 100°, то по скалата на Фаренхайт(F) тя замръзва съответно при 32°, а кипи при 212°. За да разберем каква е температурата по Целзий, ако ни е известна по Фаренхайт, използваме следната формула: C=5(F-32):9.*

За превръщането на температурата по Фаренхайт формулата е F=9C:5+32.

Обръщения	Forms of Address	Фо:мз ъв ъдрѐс
Господине!	Sir!	Съ:!
Уважаеми господине!	Dear Sir!	Дѝъ съ:!
Господин ...!	Mr. ...!	Мѝстъ!
Господа!	Gentlemen!	Джѐнтлмен!
Госпожо!	Madam!	Мæ̀дъм!
Уважаема госпожо!	Dear Madam!	Дѝъ мæ̀дъм!
Госпожи!	Ladies!	Лѐйдиз!
Дами и господа!	Ladies and Gentlemen!	Лѐйдиз æнд джѐнтлмен!
Госпожице!	Miss! / Young Lady!	Мис! / Йанг лѐйди!
Госпожице ... !	Miss ...!	Мис ...!
Госпожо ...!	Mrs. ...!	Мѝсиз ...!
Скъпи приятелю!	Dear friend!	Дѝъ френд!
Скъпи приятели!	Dear friends!	Дѝъ френдз!
Уважаеми колеги!	Dear colleagues!	Дѝъ кòли:гз!
Господин президент!	Mr. President!	Мѝстъ прѐзидънт!

Поздрави и пожелания	Greetings	Грѝ:тингз
Здравей,-те!	Hello!	Хѐлъу!
Здрасти!	Hi!	Хай!
Добро утро!	Good morning!	Гуд мо̀:нинг!
Добър ден!	Good afternoon!	Гуд а̀:фтъну:н!
Добър вечер!	Good evening!	Гуд ѝ:внинг!
Довиждане!	Good bye!	Гуд ба̀й!
Чао!	Bye-bye! / Bye! / See you!	Бай ба̀й! / Бай! / Си: ю:!
Лека нощ!	Good night!	Гуд на̀йт!
Добре дошъл,-ли!	Welcome!	Уѐлкъм!
За много години!	Many happy returns (of the day)!	мӕ̀ни хӕ̀пи ритъ̀:нз (ъв дъ дей)!
Как си(сте)?	How are you?	Ха̀у а: ю:?
Как си(сте)?	How is it going?	Ха̀у из ит го̀уинг?
Какво правиш,-те?		

Благодаря, ...	... , thank you.	..., *тæнк* ю:.
добре	Fine	Файн
зле	Not very well	Нот вѐри уѐл
горе-долу	So-so	Сѝу-сѝу

До скоро виждане!	See you (soon)!	Си: ю: (су:н)!
Наздраве!	Cheers!	Чѝъ:з!
Бог да ви благослови!	(God) bless you!	(Год) блес ю:!

Всичко хубаво!	All the best!	О:л дъ бест!
Честит рожден ден!	Happy birthday!	Хæ̀пи бъ:дей!
Приятно пътуване!	Have a nice trip /journey!	Хæв ъ найс трип /джъ:ни!
Приятно прекарване!	Have a nice time!	Хæв ъ найс тайм!
Приятна почивка!	Have a nice rest!	Хæв ъ найс рест!
Приятен ден	Have a nice day!	хæв ъ найс дей!
Приятна вечер	Have a nice evening!	хæв ъ найс и:внинг!
Приятни сънища!	Sleep well!	Сли:п уѐл!
	Sweet dreams!	Суит дри:мз!
На добър час! / Късмет!	Good luck!	Гуд лак!
Скорошно оздравяване!	Recover soon!	Рика̀въ су:н!
	Get well soon!	Гет уѐл су:н!
Весели празници!	Happy holidays!	Хæ̀пи хо̀лидейз!
Моите поздравления!	Congratulations!	Кънгрæ̀тюлѐйшънз!
Поздравявам ви за ...	Congratulations on ...	Кънгрæ̀тюлѐйшънз он...
успеха ви	your success	йо: съксѐс
празника	the holiday	дъ хо̀лидей
годишнината	the anniversary	ди æнивъ:съри
Поздравете го (я, ги) от мен.	Give my regards to him (her, them).	Гив май рига̀:дз ту хим (хъ:, дъм).

Много поздрави ... от мен (нас).	Say "Hi" from me. *(разг.)*	Сей хай фром ми.
	Remember me (us) to ...	Римѐмбъ ми(ас) ту...
на семейството ти (ви)	your family	йо: фǽмили
на приятелите	our friends	ѝуъ френдз
Пожелавам ви(ти) ...	I wish you ...	Ай уйш ю: ...
щастие	happiness	хǽпинис
много успехи	much success	мач съксѐс
много здраве	much health	мач хел*т*

Съгласие. Отказ	**Agreement. Refusal**	**Ъгрѝ:мънт. Рифю̀:зъл**
Да	Yes	Йѐс
Да, точно така.	That's right.	ƍæтс райт.
Разбира се.	Of course./ Sure.	Ъв ко:с./ Шу̀ъ.
Правилно!	Right!	Райт!
Отлично!	Excellent!	ѐксълънт!
С удоволствие!	With pleasure!	Уѝƍ плѐжъ!
(Много) добре.	Very well. / Very good.	Вѐри уѐл. / Вѐри гуд.
Всичко е наред.	Everything is all right.	ѐвриmинг из о:л райт.
Точно / Именно.	Exactly.	Игзæ̀ктли.
Разбира се./ Несъмнено.	Certainly!	Съ:тънли!
Съгласен,-а съм ...	I agree ...	Ай ъгрѝ: ...
с теб, с вас	with you	уѝƍ ю:
с него, с нея	with him, with her	уѝƍ хим, уѝƍ хъ:
Нямам нищо против.	I don't mind.	Ай до̀унт майнд.

Мисля, че това е (много) добра идея.	I think that's a (very) good idea.	Ай *т*инк *д*æтс ъ (вѐри) гуд айдѝъ.
(Приемам) С удоволствие.	I would love to. (*при отговор*)	Ай у:д лав ту.
Според мен ...	In my opinion ...	Ин май ъпѝниън ...
Естествено.	Naturally	Нæ̀чърърли
Няма значение.	It doesn't matter.	Ит дà̲знт мæ̀тъ.
Имаш (имате) право.	You're right.	Йуъ рàйт.
Несъмнено.	No doubt	Нòу дàут
Може би.	Maybe. / Perhaps.	Мèйби:. / Пъхæ̀пс.
Не, благодаря.	No, thank you.	Нòу, *т*æнк ю:.
Изключено е.	By no means.	Бай нòу мѝ:нз.
Няма начин.	No way.	Нòу уèй.
Не съм съгласен,-а.	I don't agree.	Ай дòунт ъгрѝ:.
Не мога.	I can't.	Ай кà:нт.
Не можем.	We can't.	Уѝ: кà:нт.
Невъзможно е.	It's impossible.	Итс импòсибъл.
Не искам.	I don't want.	Ай дòунт уòнт.
Не е правилно.	It's not right. (It isn't right.)	Итс нòт рàйт. (Ит ѝзънт райт.)

Не е необходимо.	It's not necessary (It isn't necessary).	Итс нот нѐсъсъри. (Ит ѝзънт нѐсъсъри).
Не си (сте) прав.	I don't think so.	Ай до̀унт *т*инк со̀у.
И дума не може да става.	It's out of the question.	Итс а̀ут ъв *д*ъ куѐсчън.
За нищо на света!	No way!	Но̀у уей!
Мисля, че не е точно така.	I think it's not quite right.	Ай *т*инк итс нот куа̀йт райт.
Съмнявам се.	I doubt it.	Ай да̀ут ит.
Жалко!	It's a pity!	Итс ъ пѝти!
Колко жалко!	What a pity!	Уо̀т ъ пѝти!
Не пуша.	I don't smoke.	Ай до̀унт смо̀ук.
Грешиш,-те.	You're wrong.	Йуъ ро:нг.
Не е истина.	It isn't true.	Ит ѝзънт тру:.
Съжалявам, но не мога да приема.	I'm sorry, but I can't accept it.	Айм со̀ри, бат ай ка:нт ъксѐпт ит.

Запознанство	Meeting People	Mѝ:тинг пѝ:пъл
➡ Как се казвате?	What's your name?	Уѐтс йо: нейм?
Позволете ми да ви се представя.	May I introduce myself?	Мей ай интръдю̀:с майсѐлф?
➡ Казвам се ...	My name's …	Май неймз …
Как е ... ви?	What's your ...?	Уѐтс йо: ... ?
името	name	нейм
презимето	middle name	мѝдъл нейм
фамилията	surname	съ:нейм
➡ Името (презимето, фамилията) ми е...	My name (middle name, surname) is …	Май нейм (мѝдъл нейм, сънейм) из ...
Позволете ми да ви представя на ...?	May I introduce you to…?	Мей ай интръдю̀:с ю: ту ...?
господин …	Mr.…	мѝстъ…
госпожа ...	Mrs.…	мѝсиз…

Бих искал,-а да ви представя …	I would like you to meet…	Ай у:д лàйк ю: ту мѝ:т…
моя съпруг	my husband	май хàзбънд
моята съпруга	my wife	май уàйф
моя приятел	my friend	май френд
моята приятелка	my girlfriend	май гъ:лфренд
моя съдружник	my partner	май пà:тнъ

Приятно ми е! *(при запознаване)*	How do you do?	Хàу ду: ю: ду:?
Приятно ми е да се запознаем.	Nice to meet you.	Найс ту ми:т ю:.
Удоволствието е изцяло мое.	The pleasure is all mine.	дъ плѐжъ из о:л мàйн.

Познаваме ли се?	Have we met before?	Хæв уѝ: мет бифò:?
Познавате ли господин (госпожа) ...?	Do you know Mr.(Mrs.)...	Ду: ю: нòу мѝстъ (мѝсиз)...?
	Have you met Mr. (Mrs.)...	Хæв ю: мет мѝстъ (мѝсиз)...?

От къде сте?	Where do you come from?	Уѐъ ду: ю: кам фром...?
	Where are you from?	Уѐъ а: ю: фром...?
От България съм (сме).	I(we) come from Bulgaria.	Ай(уѝ:) кам фром балгѐриъ.
	I'm (we are) from Bulgaria.	Айм (уѝ: а:) фром балгѐриъ.
Говорите ли английски?	Do you speak English?	Ду: ю спи:к ѝнглиш?

Някой говори ли български?	Does anyone here speak Bulgarian?	Даз æниуан хѝъ спи:к бългѐъриън?
Извинете лошия ми английски.	Excuse my poor English.	Икскю̀:з май пу̀ъ ѝнглиш.
Разбирам ви напълно (идеално).	I understand you (perfectly).	ай андъстæ̀нд ю: (пъ:фектли).
Говоря малко английски.	I only speak a little English.	Ай о̀унли спи:к ъ лѝтъл ѝнглиш.
Не говоря.	I don't speak.	Ай до̀унт спи:к.
Сега уча английски.	I'm learning English now.	Айм лъ:нинг ѝнглиш на̀у.
Не ви разбирам.	I don't understand you.	Ай до̀унт андъстæ̀нд ю:.
Говорете по-бавно, моля!	Would you speak more slowly, please?	Уу̀д ю: спи:к мо: сло̀ули, пли:з?
На почивка ли сте в Англия?	Are you on holiday in England?	А: ю: он хо̀лидей ин ѝнглънд?
На почивка съм.	I'm on holiday.	Айм он хо̀лидей.
Турист съм.	I'm a tourist.	Айм ъ ту̀ърист.
Тук съм по работа.	I'm here on business.	Айм хѝъ он бѝзнис.
Работя тук.	I work here.	Ай уъ:к хѝъ.
На гости съм при приятели.	I'm staying with friends.	Айм стѐинг уѝд френдз.

(За) колко време сте тук ?	How long are you here for?	Хàу лонг а: ю: хѝъ фо:?
Тук съм (за) ...	I'm staying / I'm here ...	Айм стèинг / Айм хѝъ...
няколко дни	for a couple of days	фо: ъ кàпъл ъв дейз
няколко седмици	for a few weeks	фо: ъ фю: уѝ:кс
два месеца	for two months	фо: ту: мантс
Харесва ли ви Великобритания?	How do you like Great Britain?	Хàу ду: ю: лайк грейт брѝтън?
Да, много ми харесва.	I like it very much.	Ай лàйк ит вèри мач.
Бих искал,-а да ви поканя ...	I'd like to invite you ...	Айд лàйк ту инвàйт ю:...
вкъщи	to my place	ту май плейс
на вечеря	to dinner	ту дѝнъ
в хотела (в който съм отседнал,-а)	to the hotel (I'm staying)	ту дъ хоутèл (айм стèинг)
утре вечер	tomorrow evening	тъмòроу ѝ:внинг
тази вечер	tonight	тънàйт
➡ Беше ми приятно!	It's been a pleasure!	Итс би:н ъ плèжъ!

Бихте ли ми дали адреса си, моля?	Would you give me your address, please?	Уу̀д ю: гив ми: йо: ъдрѐс, пли:з?
Бихте ли ми написали адреса си, моля?	Would you write (down) your address, please?	Уу̀д ю: райт (да̀ун) йо: ъдрѐс, пли:з?
Адресът ми е ...	My address is ...	Май ъдрѐс из ...
Телефонът ми е ...	My (tele)phone number is ...	Май (тѐли)фо̀ун на̀мбъ из ...
Заповядайте визитката ми.	Here's my business card.	Хѝъз май бѝзнис ка:д.
Беше ми приятно да се запознаем.	It was nice meeting you.	Ит уас на̀йс ту ми:т ю:.
Кога ще се видим отново?	When will I see you again?	Уѐн уйл ай си: ю: ъгѐйн?
Ще се радвам да се видим пак.	I'd be happy(glad) to see you again.	Айд би хѐпи(глæд) ту си: ю: ъгѐйн.
Надявам се да се видим скоро.	Hope to see you soon.	Хо̀уп ту си: ю: су:н.

Благодарност	*Gratitude*	*Грæтитю:g*
Благодаря Ви (ти)...	Thank you...	*т*æнк ю: ...
много	very much	вѐри мач
горещо	with all my heart	уи*т* ол май ха:*т*
за топлия прием	for your cordial welcome	фо: йо: кò:диъл уѐлкъм
за гостоприемството	for your hospitality	фо: йо: хоспит*æ*лити
за вниманието	for your attention	фо: йо: ътѐншън
за всичко	for everything	фо: ѐври*т*инг
за пожеланията Ви	for your wishes	фо: йо: уйшиз
за помощта Ви	for your help	фо: йо: хелп
Благодаря, подобно.	Thank you, same to you.	*т*æнк ю:, сейм ту ю:.
Няма защо.	Not at all.	Нот æт о:л.
	That's all right.	*g*æтс о:л райт.
Много мило от ваша страна.	It's very kind of you.	Итс вѐри кайнд ъв ю:.
Задължен съм Ви.	I owe you.	Ай оу ю:.

Безкрайно съм ти (ви) задължен,-а.	I'm most obliged to you.	Айм мо̀уст ъбла̀йджд ту ю:.
Не знам как да ви благодаря.	I don't really know how to thank you.	Ай до̀унт рѝъли но̀у ха̀у ту *т*æнк ю:.
Никога няма да забравя това.	I'll never forget that.	Айл нѐвъ фъгѐт *д*æт.

Молба. Разрешение	***Request. Permission***	***Рикуѐст. Пъмѝшън***
Моля, ...!	(Would you) please...?	(Уу̀д ю:) пли:з ...
дайте (ми) ...	give (me) ...	гив ми:...
почакайте ...	wait for a while	уѐйт фо: ъ уа̀йл
изпратете (ми) ...	send (me)...	сенд (ми:) ...
покажете (ми)...	show (me)...	шо̀у (ми:)
отворете ...	open...	о̀упън ...
затворете ...	close...	кло̀уз ...
повикайте ...	call...	ко:л ...
повторете ...	say that again ...	сей *д*æт ъгѐйн ...
помогнете (ми)	help (me) ...	хелп (ми:) ...
телефонирайте(ми)	call (me)	ко:л (ми:)

Разрешете ми ...!	Would you allow me ...?	Уу̀д ю: ълàу ми:...?
Имате ли нещо против...?	Would you mind if I...	Уу̀д ю: майнд иф ай ...
да вляза	come in	кам ин
да изляза за малко	go out for a while	гòу àут фо: ъ уàйл
да мина	pass	па:с
да кажа	tell	тел
да попитам	ask	а:ск
да пуша	smoke	смòук
Придружете ме, моля до ... !	Would you accompany me to ...?	Уу̀д ю: ъкàмпъни ми: ту...?
хотела	the hotel	дъ хоутѐл
полицията	the police	дъ пълѝ:с
Българското посолство	the Bulgarian Embassy	дъ балгѐриън ѐмбъси
Имиграционните служби	the Immigration Office	ди имигрѐйшън òфис
Мога ли да ви помоля?	Can I ask you? May I ask you?	Кæн ай а:ск ю:? Мей ай а:ск ю:?
Бихте ли ми казали ...?	Would you tell me, please ...?	Уу̀д ю: тел ми:, пли:з...?

Разрешено ли е да ...?	Is it allowed to ...?	Из ит ълàуд ту: ...?
	Is it permitted to ...?	Из ит пъмѝтид ту:?
Да, разбира се.	Yes, of course.	Йес, ъв кò:с.
Не е разрешено.	It's not allowed(permitted).	Итс нот ълàуд (пъмѝтид).
Не пушете, моля!	Don't smoke, please!	Дòунт смòук, пли:з!
Забранено е!	It's prohibited!	Итс пръхѝбитид!
Бих искал,-а ...	I'd like ...	Айд лайк ...
Искам ...	I want ...	Ай уòнт ...
Желая ...	I wish ...	Ай уйш ...
да ти(ви) благодаря	to thank you	ту *т*æнк ю:
да си отпочина	to have a rest	ту хæв ъ рèст
да поспя малко	to have some sleep	ту хæв сам слѝ:п
да ме събудите	you to wake me up	ю: ту уейк ми: ап
в ... часа	at ... o'clock	æт ... ъклòк
да се измия	to have a wash	ту хæв ъ уòш
да отида до тоалетната	to go to the toilet,	ту гòу ту *д*ъ тòйлит,
	to go to the bathroom	ту гòу ту *д*ъ бà:*т*рум
да се изкъпя	to have a bath	ту хæв ъ ба:*т*
да взема душ	to have a shower	ту хæв ъ шàуъ

да те (ви) поканя ...	to invite you...	ту инвàйт ю:...
да се видим ...	to meet you ...	ту ми:т ю: ...
да ми се обадиш,-ите	you to ring me up	ю: ту рингг ми: ап
да ме почакаш,-ате	you to wait for me	ю: ту уèйт фо: ми:
да те (ви) почерпя	to treat you	ту три:т ю:
да ти (ви) направя подарък за ...	to make you a present for...	ту мейк ю: ъ прèзънт фо: ...
да ми направите една услуга	you to do me a favour	ю: ту ду: ми: ъ фèйвъ
да ме изпратите до вкъщи	to take me home / to walk me home	ту тейк ми: хòум / ту уò:к ми: хòум

Извинения. Съжаление	**Apologies. Regrets**	**Апòлъджиз. Ригрèтс**
Извинете!	Sorry!	Сòри!
Извинете ме.	Excuse me.	Икскю̀:з ми:.
Извинете ...	Sorry ...	Сòри ...
не ви чух	I didn't hear you	ай дѝдънт хѝъ ю:
не ви разбрах	I didn't understand you	ай дѝдънт андъстæ̀нд ю:
за закъснението	for being late	фо: би:нг лейт
Извинете ме за безпокойството.	Excuse me for disturbing you.	Икскю̀:з ми: фо: дистъ̀:бинг ю:.
Сбърках.	I made a mistake.	Ай мѐйд ъ мистѐйк.
Без да искам.	I didn't mean it.	Ай дѝдънт ми:н ит.
Моля да ми простите.	Please, forgive me.	Пли:з, фъгѝв ми:.
Не беше по моя вина.	It wasn't my fault.	Ит уòзънт май фò:лт.
Няма значение.	It doesn't matter.	Ит дàзънт мæ̀тъ.
Жалко!	It's a pity!	Итс ъ пѝти!
Колко жалко!	What a pity!	Уòт ъ пѝти!

Съжалявам (много)!	I'm very sorry!	Айм вѐри сòри!
Разбирам ви.	I understand you.	Ай андъстǽнд ю:.
Съчувствам ти (ви).	I sympathize with you.	Ай сѝмпътàйз уѝд ю:.
Колко неприятно.	What a nuisance!	Уòт ъ нѝо:сънс!
Какво нещастие!	What a bad luck!	Уòт ъ бæд лàк!
За съжаление ...	Unfortunately ...	Ънфò:чънътли ...
не ми достигат пари	I'm short of money	Айм шо:т ъв мàни
нямам време	I'm short of time	Айм шо:т ъв тайм
нямам възможност да	I'm not able to...	Айм нот ейбл ту...

Покани, срещи, посещения	Invitations, meetings, visits	Инвитѐйшънз, мѝ:тингз, вѝзитс
Приятно ми е да те (ви) видя!	It's nice to see you!	Итс нàйс ту си: ю!
Свободен,-а ли сте ...? в петък на трети този месец	Are you free ...? on Friday on the third of this month	А: ю: фрѝ: он ...? он фрàйдей он дъ тъ:д ъв дис мàнт
Какво ще правите ...? довечера утре	What will you do ...? tonight tomorrow	Уòт уйл ю: ду: ...? тънàйт тъмòроу
Свободен,-на съм. Не съм зает, -а. Съжалявам, но съм зает,-а.	I'm free. I'm not busy. I'm sorry I'm busy.	Айм фрѝ:. Айм нòт бѝзи. Айм сòри айм бѝзи.

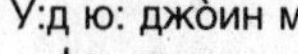

Ще ... ли с мен?	Would you join me ... ?	У:д ю: джо̀ин ми:...?
обядвате	for lunch	фо: ланч
вечеряте	for dinner	фо: дѝнъ
Искам да ви поканя...	I'd like to invite you...	Айд лайк ту инва̀йт ю: ...
вкъщи	to my place	ту май плейс
на кино	to the cinema	ту *д*ъ сѝнимъ
на театър	to the theatre	ту *д*ъ *т*ѝътъ
да отидем на ресторант	to go to a restaurant	ту го̀у ту ъ рѐстърънт
на венчавката ми	to my wedding	ту май уѐдинг
на сватбата ми	to my wedding party	ту май уѐдинг па̀:ти
на рождения ми ден	to my birthday party	ту май бъ:*т*дей па̀:ти
на парти	to a party	ту ъ па̀:ти

Ако имате възможност	If it's possible for you ...	Иф итс пòсибъл фо: ю: ...
заповядайте вкъщи	why don't you come to my place	уай донт ю кам ту май плейс
заповядайте на чай следобед	come to tea this afternoon	кам ту ти: *д*ис а:фтънỳ:н
заповядайте да изпием по едно кафе	why don't you come and have a cup of coffee	уай донт ю кам æнд хæв ъ кап ъв кòфи
Благодаря ти (ви) за поканата.	Thank you for the invitation.	*т*æнк ю: фо: *д*и инвитèйшън.
Бихте ли ми показали къде е тоалетната?	Could you show me the toilet, please?	Кỳд ю: шòу ми: *д*ъ тòилит, пли:з?
Мога ли да те (ви) почерпя ...	May I treat you ...? May I buy you ...	Мей àй три:т ю: ...? Мей àй бай ю: ...?
нещо	something	сàм*т*инг
едно кафе	a cup of coffee	ъ кап ъв кòфи
един сладолед	an ice cream	ън айс кри:м
един сок	some juice	сам джу:с
С удоволствие.	I'd love to.	Айд лав ту.
Благодаря, нищо друго.	Thank you, nothing more.	*т*æнк ю:, нà*т*инг мò:.

Кога ...	When ...	Уѐн ...
В колко часа ...	What time ...	Уо̀т тайм ...
Къде ...	Where...	Уѐъ ...
предпочитате да се срещнем?	would you prefer to meet me?	уу̀д ю: прифъ: ту ми:т ми?
Бих предпочел,-а ...	I'd prefer ...	Айд прифъ: ...
в хотела	at the hotel	æт *дъ* хоутѐл
в кафето на улица ...	at the cafè on... street	æт *дъ* кæ̀фей он ... стри:т
на ъгъла на улица ... и улица ...	at the corner of ... street and ... street	æт *дъ* ко̀:нъ ъв ... стри:т æнд ... стри:т
на площад	in ... square	ин ... скуѐъ
в 10 часа сутринта	at ten o'clock a.m.	æт тен ъкло̀к ей ем
точно в 7 часа вечерта	at seven o'clock p.m. sharp	æт сѐвън ъ кло̀к пи ем ша:п
Бих искал,-а ...	I would like ...	Ай уу̀д лайк ...
да се срещнем	to meet you	ту ми:т ю:
да се поразходим	to have a walk with you	ту хæв ъ уо̀:к уѝ*д* ю:
да ми се обадите по телефона	you to phone me	ю: ту фо̀ун ми:

да ме почакате малко	you to wait for me a little bit	ю: ту уѐйт фо: ми: ъ лѝтъл бит
да излезем навън	to go out with you	ту гòу àут уѝд ю:
да отидем някъде довечера	to go to some place with you tonight	ту гòу ту сам плейс уѝд ю: тънàйт
Имате ли нещо против, да изпием по чаша чай/ кафе?	Do you mind if we have a cup of tea / coffee?	Ду ю мàйнд иф уѝ: хæв ъ кап ъф ти: / кòфи?
Имам среща с господин (госпожа) ...	I've got an appointment with Mr. (Mrs.)...	Айв гот ън ъпòинтмънт уѝд мѝстъ (мѝсиз) ...
Той (тя) кога ще се върне?	When will he (she) be back?	Уѐн уйл хи:(ши:) би: бæк?
Мога ли да го (я) почакам?	May I wait for him(her)?	Мей ай уѐйт фо: хим (хъ:)?
Мога ли да оставя бележка?	Can I leave a message?	Кæн ай ли:в ъ мѐсидж?
Бихте ли му (ѝ) дали, моля, ...?	Would you give him(her), ...please?	Уỳ:д ю: гив хим(хъ:) ... пли:з?
това писмо	this letter	дис лѐтъ
тази бележка	this message	дис мѐсидж
този пакет	this package	дис пǽкидж
телефонния ми номер	my (tele)phone number	май (тѐли)фòун нàмбъ

Кажете му (ѝ), че ... господин (госпожа)...	Would you tell him (her), that Mr.(Mrs.) ..., please?	Уўд ю: тел хим (хъ:), gæт мѝстъ (мѝсиз) ..., пли:з?
се е обаждал,-а	(has) called	(хæз) ко:лд
е идвал,-а	came	кейм
Търся го (я) от името на господин(госпожа)..	Mr. (Mrs.) ... is sending me.	Мѝстъ(мѝсиз) ... из сѐндинг ми:.
Кога ще дойдете отново?	When will you come again?	Уѐн уйл ю: кам ъгѐйн?
Кога ще ви видя пак?	When will I see you again?	Уѐн уйл ай си: ю: агѐйн?
Мога ли да ви видя пак?	May I see you again?	Мей ай си: ю: ъгѐйн?
Доволен,-на ли сте от..?	Are you pleased with...?	А: ю: пли:зд уѝg...?
Много съм доволен,-на от...	I'm very pleased with...	Айм вѐри пли:зд уѝg...
моя престой тук	my stay here	май стѐй хѝъ
срещата	the appointment	gи ъпѝнтмънт
посещението	the visit	gъ вѝзит
Ще ви телефонирам.	I'll phone you.	Айл фѝун ю:.
Ще ви се обадя.	I'll call you.	Айл ко:л ю:.
Скоро пак ще се чуем.	We'll hear from each other soon.	Уи:л хѝъ фром и:ч àgъ су:н.

Ще ви изпратя факс.	I'll send you a fax.	Айл сѐнд ю: ъ фӕкс.
Ще ви пиша.	I'll write to you.	Айл рàйт ту ю:.

Семейство. Роднини / Family. Relatives / Фӕмили. Рѐлътивз

Аз съм ...	I'm ...	Айм ...
женен, омъжена	married	мӕрид
разведен,-а	divorced	дивò:ст
ерген	single	сйнгъл
неженен, неомъжена	not married	нот мӕрид
сгоден,-а	engaged	ингѐйджд
вдовец	a widower	ъ уйдоуъ
вдовица	a widow	ъ уйдоу

Колко деца имате?	How many children have you got?	Хàу мѐни чѝлдрън хæв ю: гот?
Имате ли братя и сестри?	Do you have brothers or sisters?	Ду ю: хæв брàдъз о: сѝстъз?
Имам,-е ...	I(we) have got ...	Ай(уй:) хæв гот ...
едно дете	one child	уàн чайлд
... деца	... children	... чѝлдрън

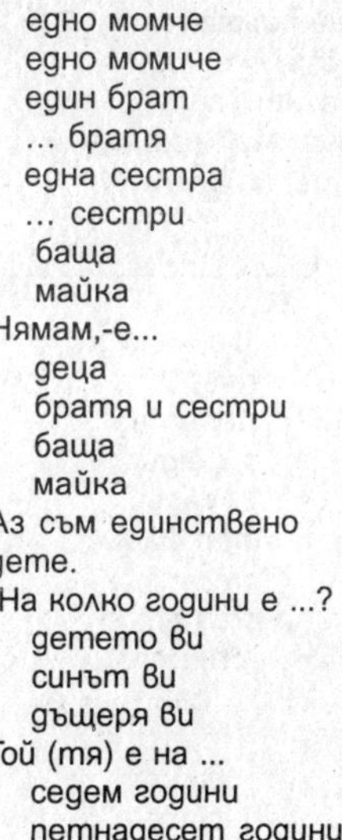

едно момче	one boy	уа̀н бой
едно момиче	one girl	уа̀н гъ:л
един брат	one brother	уа̀н бра̀дъ
... братя	... brothers	...бра̀дъз
една сестра	one sister	уа̀н сѝстъ
... сестри	... sisters	...сѝстъз
баща	father	фа̀:дъ
майка	mother	ма̀дъ
Нямам,-е...	I(we) haven't got ...	Ай(уѝ:) хæ̀вънт гот ...
деца	any children	ѐни чѝлдрън
братя и сестри	any brothers or sisters	ѐни бра̀дъз о: сѝстъз
баща	father	фа̀:дъ
майка	mother	ма̀дъ
Аз съм единствено дете.	I'm an only child.	Айм ън о̀унли чайлд.
На колко години е ...?	How old is ...?	Ха̀у о̀улд из ...?
детето ви	your child	йо: чайлд
синът ви	your son	йо: сан
дъщеря ви	your daughter	йо: до̀:тъ
Той (тя) е на ...	He(she) is ...	Хи:(ши:) из...
седем години	seven (years old)	сѐвън (йъ̀:з о̀улд)
петнадесет години	fifteen (years old)	фифтѝ:н (йъ̀:з о̀улд)

Родителите ми ...	My parents ...	Май пѐърънтс ...
са живи	are alive	а: ъла̀йв
починаха	are not alive	а: нот ъла̀йв
Жив,-а е само баща ми (майка ми).	Only my father(my mother) is alive.	о̀унли май фа̀:дъ (май ма̀дъ) из ъла̀йв.

семейство	family	фа̀емили
родители	parents	пѐърънтс
роднини	relatives	рѐлътивз
баща, татко	father	фа̀:дъ
майка	mother	ма̀дъ
пастрок	step-father	степ фа̀дъ
мащеха	step-mother	степ ма̀дъ
доведена дъщеря	step-daughter	степ до̀:тъ
доведен син	step-sun	степ са̀н
син	son	сан
дъщеря	daughter	до̀:тъ
брат	brother	бра̀дъ
сестра	sister	сѝстъ

съпруг	husband	ха̀збънд
съпруга	wife	уа̀йф
съпружеска двойка	couple	ка̀пъл
дядо и баба	grandparents	грæ̀нпеърънтс
дядо	grandfather, grandpa, granddad	грæ̀нфа:дъ, грæ̀нпа:, грæ̀ндæд
баба	grandmother,grandma, granny	грæ̀нмадъ, грæ̀нма:, грæ̀ни
внуче	grandchild	грæ̀нчайлд
внук	grandson	грæ̀нсан
внучка	granddaughter	грæ̀ндо:тъ
внуци	grandchildren	грæ̀нчилдрън
дете	child, kid	чайлд, кид
деца	children, kids	чѝлдрън, кидз
зет	son-in-law	са̀нинло:
булка	bride	брайд
снаха	daugther-in-law	до̀:тъинло:
девер, шурей	brother-in-law	бра̀:дъинло:
зълва, балдъза, етърва	sister-in-law	сѝстъинло:
свекър, тъст	father-in-law	фа̀:дъинло:

свекърва, тъща	mother-in-law	мàдъинло:
чичо, вуйчо	uncle	àнкъл
леля, вуйна	aunt	а:нт
племенник	nephew	нèфю:
племенница	niece	ни:с
братовчед,-ка	cousin	кàзън
кум, кръстник	godfather	гòдфа:дъ
кумица, кръстница	godmother	гòдмадъ
годеник	fiancè	фиа:нсèй
годеница	fiancèe	фиа:нсèй
църковен брак	church marriage	чъ:ч мæ̀ридж
граждански брак	civil marriage	сѝвил мæ̀ридж
венчавка	wedding	уèдинг
сватба	wedding party	уèдинг пà:ти
раждане	birth	бъ:*т*
кръщение	christening	крѝсънинг
развод	divorce	дивò:с
погребение	funeral	фю:нърък

Страни, народи, езици	*Countries, Nationalities, Languages*	*Кàнтриз, нæшънæ̀лътиз, лæ̀нгуиджиз*
➡ От къде сте?	Where are you from?	Уèъ а: ю: фром?
	Where do you come from?	Уèъ ду: ю: кам фром?
От коя страна сте?	What country are you from?	Уòт кàнтри а: ю: фром?
➡ Аз съм (ние сме) от ...	I'm (we're) from…	Айм (уѝъ) фром ...
	I (we) come from…	Ай (уѝ:) кам фром …
България	Bulgaria	балгèъриъ
Обединено Кралство	the United Kingdom	дъ юнàйтид кѝнгдъм
Великобритания	(Great Britain)	(грейт брѝтън)
Англия	England	ѝнглънд
Уелс	Wales	уèйлз
Шотландия	Scotland	скòтлънд
Северна Ирландия	Northern Ireland	нò:дън àйълънд

Той (тя) е от ...	He (she) is from...	Хи: (ши:) из фром ...
	He (she) comes from...	Хи: (ши:) камз фром...
Австрия	Austria	ò:стриъ
Албания	Albania	æлбèйниъ
Белгия	Belgium	бèлджъм
Германия	Germany	джъ̀:мъни
Гърция	Greece	гри:с
Дания	Denmark	дèнма:к
Испания	Spain	спейн
Италия	Italy	ѝтъли
Канада	Canada	кæ̀нъдъ
Кипър	Cyprus	сàйпрьс
Куба	Cuba	кю̀:бъ
Полша	Poland	пòлæнд
Португалия	Portugal	пò:тюгъл
Румъния	Romania	ру:мèйниъ
Русия	Russia	рàшъ
Словакия	Slovakia	слоув æ̀киъ
Словения	Slovenia	слоувѝ:ниъ
САЩ (Съединени американски щати)	the U.S.A.(the United States of America)	дъ ю: ес ей(дъ юнàйтид стейтс ъв ъмèрикъ)

Сърбия	Serbia	съ:биъ
Турция	Turkey	тъ:ки
Украйна	Ukraine	ю:крѐйн
Франция	France	фра:нс
Холандия	Holland	хо̀лънд
Хърватска	Croatia	кроуѐйшъ
Чехия	Czech Republic	чек рипа̀блик
Швейцария	Switzerland	суйтсълънд
Швеция	Sweden	суй:дън
Югославия	Yugoslavia	ю:гоусла̀:виъ
Япония	Japan	джъпа̀ен

Били ли сте някога в ...?	Have you ever been to...?	Хæв ю: ѐвъ би:н ту ...?
Никога не съм бил,-а в...	I have never been to ...	Ай хæв нѐвъ би:н·ту...?
Вие англичанин,-ка ли сте?	Are you English?	А: ю: ѝнглиш?
Да.	Yes, I am.	Йес, ай æм.
Не, не съм.	No, I'm not.	Но̀у, айм нот.

7.

Какъв си(сте) по народност?	What nationality are you?	Уòт нǽшънǽлъти а: ю:?
Аз съм ...	I'm ...	Айм ...
българин,-ка	Bulgarian	ба̲лгѐъриън
англичанин,-ка	English	ѝнглиш
Той (тя) е ...	He(she) is ...	Хи:(ши:) из ...
австриец,-ка	Austrian	ò:стриън
американец,-ка	American	ъмѐрикън
арабин,-ка	Arabian	ърѐйбиън
белгиец,-ка	Belgian	бѐлджън
германец,-ка	German	джъ̀:мън
датчанин,-ка	Danish	дǽниш
италианец,-ка	Italian	итǽлиън
испанец,-ка	Spanish	спǽниш
кипърец,-ка	Cyprian	сѝприън
китаец,-йка	Chinese	чайнѝ:з
кубинец,-ка	Cuban	кю̀:бън
поляк,-иня	Polish	пòлиш
румънец,-ка	Romanian	ру:мѐйниън
руснак, рускиня	Russian	ра̲̀шън

словак,-чка	Slovakian	слоув ǽкиън
сърбин, сръбкиня	Serbian	съ:биън
турчин, туркиня	Turkish	тъ:киш
унгарец,-ка	Hungarian	ханѓѐъриън
французин,-ойка	French	френч
финландец,-ка	Finnish	фѝниш
циганин,-ка	Gypsy	джѝпси
швейцарец,-ка	Swiss	суѝс
швед,-ка	Swedish	суѝ:диш
японец,-ка	Japanese	джæпънѝ:з

континент	**continent**	**кòнтинънт**
Европа	Europe	ю̀ъръп
европеец,-йка	European	юъръпѝ:ън
Азия	Asia	ѐйшъ
азиатец, -тка	Asian	ѐйшън
Америка	America	ъмѐрикъ
американец,-нка	American	ъмѐрикън
Африка	Africa	ǽфрикъ
африканец,-ка	African	ǽфрикън
Австралия	Australia	острѐйлиъ
австралиец,-йка	Australian	острѐйлиън

Какви езици говориш, -ите?	What languages do you speak?	Уòт лæнгуиджиз ду: ю: спи:к?
Говориш,-ите ли...?	Do you speak ...?	Ду: ю: спи:к ...?
български	Bulgarian	балгѐриън
английски	English	ѝнглиш
Говоря...	I speak...	Ай спи:к ...
английски	English	ѝнглиш
руски	Russian	рàшън
френски	French	френч
немски	German	джъ:мън
италиански	Italian	итæлиън
испански	Spanish	спæниш
гръцки	Greek	гри:к
Съжалявам.	I'm sorry.	Айм сòри.
Не говоря ...	I don't speak ...	Ай дòунт спи:к ...
английски	English	ѝнглиш
Говоря езика трудно.	I speak the language with difficulty.	Ай спи:к дъ лæнгуидж уѝд дѝфикалти.
Едва разбирам.	I can hardly understand.	Ай кæн хà:дли андъстæ̀нд.

Разбирам,	I understand	Ай андъстæ̀нд,
но не мога да говоря.	but I can't speak.	бат ай ка:нт спи:к.
Не разбирам	I don't understand	Ай дòунт андъстæ̀нд
въобще.	at all.	æт о:л.
Разбирам малко.	I understand a little.	Ай андъстæ̀нд ъ лѝтъл.
Обяснете ми, моля!	Would you explain to me,	Уѝд ю: иксплѐйн ту ми:,
	please?	пли:з?
Покажете ми	Would you show it to me	Уѝд ю: шòу ит ту ми: ин
в речника, моля!	in the dictionary, please?	дъ дѝкшънри, пли:з?
Говорете по-бавно,	Please speak more	Пли:з спи:к мо:
моля!	slowly.	слòули.
Как е на английски ...,	What's the English for...,	Уòтс ди ѝнглиш фо: ... ,
моля?	please?	пли:з?
Как казвате ...	How do you say ...	Хàу ду: ю: сей ...
на английски, моля?	in English?	ин ѝнглиш?
Как се произнася	How do you pronounce	Хàу ду: ю: пръна̀унс ...
на английски ...?	... in English?	ин ѝнглиш?
тази дума	this word	дис уъ:д
Какво означава	What does this	Уòт дàз дис
думата?	word mean?	уъ:д ми:н?

Бихте ли я написали, моля?	Would you write it down, please?	Уу̀д ю: райт ит да̀ун, пли:з?
Какво каза той (тя)?	What did he(she) say?	Уо̀т дид хи:(ши:) сей?
Какво казва той (тя)?	What is he(she) saying?	Уо̀т из хи:(ши:) сѐи:нг?
Преведете ми..., моля!	Translate ..., please!	Тра:нслѐйт..., пли:з!
Повторете, моля!	Please repeat.	Пли:з рипѝ:т.
Повторете ..., ако обичате!	Would you repeat ..., please! / Say it again please!	Уу̀д ю: рипѝ:т ..., пли:з!/ Сей ит ъгѐйн пли:з!
думата	the word	гъ уъ:рд
фразата	the phrase	гъ фрейз
Сега разбирате ли ме?	Do you understand me now?	Ду: ю: андъстѐнд ми: на̀у?
Да, разбирам ви.	Yes, I understand you.	Йес, ай андъстѐнд ю:.
Правилно ли го казах?	Did I say it right?	Дид ай сей ит райт?
Харесва ли ви произношението ми?	How do you like my pronunciation ?	Ха̀у ду: ю: лайк май прънѐнсиѐйшън?
Имате ли нужда от преводач?	Do you need an interpreter?	Ду: ю: ни:д ън интъ:притъ?
Имам нужда от преводач.	I need an interpreter.	Ай ни:д ън интъ:притъ.

Празници и церемонии | Holidays and Ceremonies | Хòлидейз æнг сèримониз

празник	holiday	хòлидей
годишнина, юбилей	anniversary	æнивъ:сри
рожден ден	birthday	бъ:*т*дей

Приятно прекарване на празника!	Have a nice holiday!	Хæв ъ найс хòлидей!
Коледа	Christmas	Крѝсмъс
Честита Коледа!	Merry Christmas!	Мèри крѝсмъс!
Нова година	New Year	Ню: ѝъ
Честита Нова година!	Happy New Year!	Хæ̀пи ню: ѝъ:!
Да си жив и здрав!	God bless you!	Год блес ю:!
Поздравления!	Congratulations!	Кънгр æ̀тюлèйшънз!

кръщение	christening	крѝсънинг
погребение	funeral	фю:нрърл
Моите (нашите) съболезнования!	My (our) condolences!	Май (àуъ) кънд̀оулънсиз!
Бог да го (я) прости!	Let him (her) rest in peace!	Лет хим(хъ:) рест ин пи:с!
Великден	Easter day	й:стъ дей
Страстна седмица	Holy Week	Х̀оули уѝ:к
Разпети петък	God Friday	Год фрàйдей
Възкресение Христово	Easter	й:стъ
Възнесение	Ascension (Day)	Ъсѐншън (дей)
Заговезни	Shrovetide	Шр̀оувтàйд
Успение Богородично	The Assumption	ди ъсàмпшън
Богоявление	Epiphany	Ипѝфъни
Бъдни вечер	Christmas Eve	Крѝсмъс и:в

ОФИЦИАЛНИ ПРАЗНИЦИ:

Нова Година
(New Year's Day) *- 1 януари*
Великден
(Easter Monday)
Първият понеделник от май
(Bank Holiday)
Последният понеделник от май
(Whit Monday)
Последният понеделник от август
(August Bank Holiday)
Коледа
(Christmas) *- 25-26 декември*

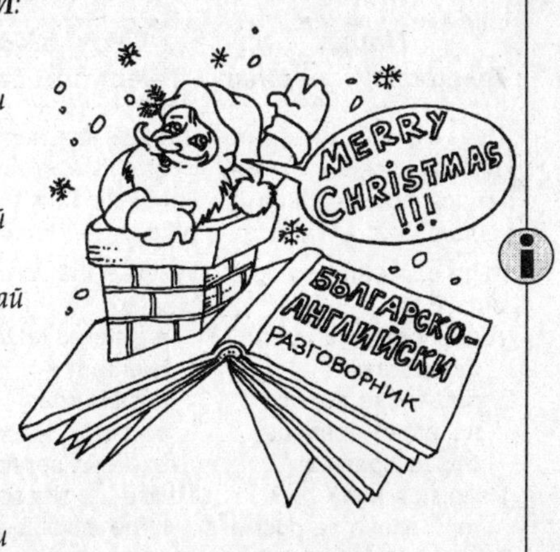

УСЛУГИ И РАЗВЛЕЧЕНИЯ

Поща. Телефон. Интернет	Post office. Telephone. Internet	Пòуст òфис. Тèлифòун.Интънет
Къде е най-близката пощенска станция, моля?	Where's the nearest Post Office, please?	Уèъз ɡъ нѝърист пòуст òфис, пли:з?
Търся пощенската станция.	I'm looking for the post office.	Айм лỳ:кинг фо: ɡъ пòуст òфис.
Къде е гишето за..., моля?	Where's the … counter, please?	Уèъз ɡъ … кàунтъ, пли:з?
препоръчани писма	registered letter	рèджистъд лèтъ
телеграми	telegram	тèлиграæм
пощенски записи	postal order	пòустъл ò:дъ
колетни пратки	parcel	пà:съл
бързи пратки	express service	икспрèс съ:вис
Искам да купя ...	I'd like …, please.	Айд лайк, ...пли:з?
три плика за писма	three envelopes	*три*: ѐнвълоупс
хартия за писма	some sheets of paper	сам ши:тс ъв пèйпъ

няколко марки	some stamps	сам стæмпс
четири картички	four postcards	фо: пòусткa:дз
Искам да изпратя ...	I'd like to send ...	Айд лайк ту сенд...
едно писмо	a letter	ъ лèтъ
един колет	a parcel	ъ пà:съл
един факс	a fax	ъ фæкс
един пощенски запис	a postal order	ъ пòустъл ò:дъ
до България	to Bulgaria	ту балгѐъриъ
до град ...	to the town of ...	ту gъ тàун ъв ...
Трябват ми марки за въздушна поща за две писма.	I need stamps for two air-letters.	Ай ни:д стæмпс фо: ту: ѐъ лèтъ:з.

ЛОНДОН

Централна поща:	***Пощенски клон:***
King Edward Building,	*24-28 William IV St.,*
King Edward St.,	*London WC2N*
(метро St.Paul's)	*(метро Charing Cross)*

Колко струва ... до България?	How much is it for ... to Bulgaria?	Хау мач из ит фо: ... ту Българиъ?
писмо	a letter	ъ лѐтъ
картичка	a postcard	ъ пѝуст ка:д

Колко трябва да платя за ... писмо?	How much is the postage for a ... letter?	Хàу мàч из дъ пòустидж фо: ъ ... лѐтъ?
обикновено	regular	рѐгюлъ
препоръчано	registered	рѐджистъд
с обратна разписка	recorded delivery	рикò:дид дилѝвъри
въздушна поща	(an) air mail	(ън) ѐъ мейл
писмо до поискване	poste restante	пòуст рѐста:нт
с наложен платеж	cash on delivery	кæш он дилѝвъри

Моля, попълнете тук!	Please, fill in here!	Пли:з, фил ин хѝъ!
Подпишете се ..., моля!	Sign ..., please!	Сайн ..., пли:з!
тук	here	хѝъ
на лицевата страна	on the front side	он дъ франт сайд
на обратната страна	on the back side	он дъ бæк сайд
Напишете ...!	Write down...!	Рàйт дàун...!
адреса на получателя	the recipient's address	дъ рисѝпиънтс ъдрѐс
адреса на подателя	the sender's address	дъ сѐндъз ъдрѐс

името	the first name	дъ фъ:ст нейм
фамилията	the surname	дъ съ:нейм
улицата	the street	дъ стри:т
номера на улицата	the street number	дъ стри:т нàмбъ
града	the name of the town	дъ нейм ъв дъ тàун
селото	the name of the village	дъ нейм ъв дъ вѝлидж
страната	the country	дъ кàнтри
пощенския код	the postal code	дъ пòустъл кòуд
с печатни букви	in block letters	ин блок лèтъз
Колко ви дължа?	How much is it?	Хàу мач из ит?
Има ли колет на мое име от България?	Is there a parcel for me from Bulgaria, please?	Из дѐъ ъ пà:съл фо: ми: фром балгѐриъ, пли:з?

адрес	address	ъдрѐс
подател	sender	сѐндъ
получател	recipient	рисѝпиънт
бланка	form	фо:м
квитанция	receipt	рисѝ:т
подпис	signature	сѝгнъчъ
печат	seal	си:л

попълвам	fill in	фил ин
подписвам	sign	сайн
подпечатвам	seal	си:л
запечатвам	seal	си:л
пощальон	postman	пòустмън
пощенска кутия	mailbox	мèилбокс
абонаментна пощ. кутия	P.O. Box	пи: òу бокс
пощенски такси	postage	пòустидж

Откъде мога да се обадя по телефона?	Where can I make a phone call?	Уеъ кæ̀н ай мейк ъ фòун ко:л?
Има ли наблизо телефон?	Is there a public (tele)phone nearby?	Из ∂èъ ъ пàблик (тèли)фòун нѝъбай?

Мога ли да се обадя...?	May I (tele)phone ...?/ May I call ...?	Мей àй (тèли)фòун...?/ Мей ай ко:л ...?
Трябва да позвъня ...	I have to call ...	Ай хæв ту ко:л ...
в Лондон	London	лàндън
в София	Sofia	сòуфиъ
на децата си	my children	май чѝлдрън
на съпругата си	my wife	май уàйф

на съпруга си	my husband	май хàзбънд
на този номер	this number	дис нàмбъ
веднага	right now	рàйт нàу
непременно	at any cost	æт æни кост
спешно	urgently	ъ:джънтли
Имате ли телефонен указател?	Have you got a phone book(directory)?	Хæв ю: гот ъ фòун бук (дирèктъри)?
Какъв е кодът за ...?	What is the area code for ... ?	Уот из ди èъриъ кòуд фо: ...?

Колко е една минута … телефонен разговор?	What's the … call charge per minute ?	Уо̀тс дъ … ко̀:л ча:дж пъ мѝнит?
➡ градски	local	ло̀укъл
междуградски	long-distance	лонг дѝстънс
международен	international	ѝнтънæ̀шънъл
Бих искал,-а да поръчам разговор за чужда сметка.	I would like to make a reverse-charge call (*brit.*)/ a collect call (*am.*)	Ай уу̀д лайк ту мейк ъ ривъ̀:с ча:дж ко:л. (*бр.*)/ ъ кълект ко:л (*ам.*)
Кой е номерът на телефона ви?	What's your phone number?	Уо̀тс йо̀: фо̀ун на̀мбъ?
Номерът е …	The number is …	дъ на̀мбъ из …
23 05 76	23 05 76	ту: *три:* о̀у файв сѐвън сикс
Имате ли …?	I'd like …	Айд лайк …
дребни за телефон	some change for the phone	сам чейндж фо: дъ фо̀ун
фонокарта	a pre-paid phone card	ъ прѝ:пейд фо̀ун ка:д

Ало!	Hello!	Хѐлоу!
Ало, телефонни услуги ли сте?	Hallo, is that directory enquiries?	Хѐлоу, из ðæт дирѐктъри инкуа̀йъриз?
Бихте ли ми дали номера на ..., моля?	Would you give me the number of ..., please?	У:д ю: гив ми: ðъ н<u>а</u>мбъ ъв ..., пли:з?

*Всички **телефони** са снабдени с достатъчно ясни инструкции. Ако се обаждате някъде и не желаете разговорът да прекъсне, купете си фонокарта. Те се продават на най-различни места, включително в пощите и от вестникарските будки, откъдето може да закупите и фонокарти за компании от типа на Swiftlink, които предлагат по-ниски тарифи за международните позвънявания от British Telecom (BT).*

*Всички мобилни оператори предлагат изгодни международни разговори през централа а за вътрешни **разговори с мобилен телефон** най-евтино е да се снабдите със SIM карта от 5 или 10 лири(напр. на Oringe или Vodafone).*

*Местните телефонни указатели се наричат **Yellow Pages**.*

Бихте ли ми казали как да се свържа с ..., моля?	Would you tell me how I can reach ..., please?	Уѝд ю: тел ми хàу ай кæн ри:ч ..., пли:з?
Свържете ме с ..., моля!	Put me through to..., please!	Пут ми: *тру:* ту ..., пли:з!
вътрешен номер 273	Extension 273	икстѐншън ту: сѐвън *три:*
Кой е на телефона?	Who's speaking?	Ху:з спѝ:кинг?
➡ С кого разговарям?	To whom am I speaking?	Ту хум æм ай спѝ:кинг?
Кой го (я) търси?	Who's calling?	Ху:з кò:линг?
Търся господин (госпожа) ...	I'm looking for Mr. (Mrs.)...	Айм лỳкинг фо: мѝсть (мѝсиз)...
Бих искал,-а да разговарям с	I'd like to speak to	Айд лайк ту спи:к ту ...
Бихте ли ме свързали ➡ с някой, който говори български (руски, ...)?	Could you put me through to someone who speaks Bulgarian (Russian ...), please?	Куд ю: пут ми тру: ту сàмуан ху спи:кс бългѐриън (рàшън, ...), пли:з?
Един момент!	Hold on, please!	Хòулд он, пли:з!
Изчакайте, моля.	Hold on the line, please.	Хòулд он *дъ* лайн, пли:з.
Не е вкъщи.	He(she)'s out.	Хи:(ши:)з àут.

Той (тя) не е тук.	He(she)'s not in.	Хи:(ши:)з нот ин.
Кога ще се върне?	When will he (she) be back?	Уѐн уѝл хи:(ши:) би: бæк?
➡ Кога да се обадя пак?	When can I call back?	Уѐн кæн ай ко:л бæк?
Обадете се …	Call back ..., please.	Ко:л бæк…,пли:з.
след един час	in an hour	ин ън ѝуъ
утре	tomorrow	тъмòроу
след осем часа довечера	tonight after 8 p.m.	тънàйт à:фтъ ейт пи: ем
Бихте ли му (ѝ) казали да се обади на …, моля?	Would you tell him (her) to call …, please?	Уýд ю: тел хим (хъ:) ту ко:л…, пли:з?
на господин (госпожа) …	Mr. (Mrs.)...	мѝстъ (мѝсиз) …
в хотел …	at the … Hotel	æт ɡъ ... хоутѐл
Номерът не отговаря.	Sorry, no reply.	Сòри, нòу риплàй.
Линията е заета.	The line is engaged.	ɡъ лайн из ингѐйджт.
Съжалявам, набрали сте грешен номер.	Sorry, you've dialed the wrong number.	Сòри, ю:в дàйълд ɡъ ронг нaмбъ.

Чува ли се?	Are you through?	А: ю: *тру*:?
Чувам ви добре.	I can hear you well.	Ай кæн хѝъ ю: уèл.
Чувам ви съвсем слабо.	I can hardly hear you.	Ай кæн хà:рдли хѝъ ю:.
Не ви чувам.	I can't hear you.	Ай кà:нт хѝъ ю:.
Затворете, моля!	Hang up, please!	Хæнг àп, пли:з.
Ще ви избера отново.	I'll call you again.	Айл ко:л ю: ъгèйн.
Връзката се разпадна.	We've been cut off.	Уѝв би:н кат оф.
Не мога да се свържа.	I can't get through.	Ай кà:нт гет *тру*:.
Ще ви се обадя по-късно.	I'll call back later.	Айл ко:л бæк лèйтъ.
Имате ли факс?	Have you got a fax?	Хæв ю: гот ъ фæкс?
Включете на факс, моля!	Swich on fax, please!	Суич он фæкс, пли:з!
Кой е ... моля?	What's ..., please?	Уòтс ..., пли:з?
кода на страната	the country code	*д*ъ кàнтри кòуд
кода на града	the area code	*д*ъ èъриъ кòуд
домашният ви телефон	your home number	йо: хòум нàмбъ
служебният ви телефон	your office number	йо: òфис нàмбъ
номера на вашия факс	your fax number	йо: фæкс нàмбъ

адреса на електронната ви поща	your E-mail address	йо: и: мейл ъдрѐс
адреса ви в Интернет	your Internet address	йо: ѝнтънет ъдрѐс
телефона на ...	the telephone of...	дъ тѐлифо̀ун ъв...
Отговаря само телефонният секретар.	There is an answering machine on.	дѐър из ън а̀:нсъринг мъшѝ:н он.
Ще ви изпратя електронна поща.	I will e-mail you.	Ай уѝл ѝ-мейл ю:?
Извинете, къде е найблизкото Интернет кафе?	Excuse me, where is the nearest Internet cafè?	Икскю̀:з ми, уѐъ из дъ нѝърест ѝнтънет кæ̀фей?
Кажете ми, моля, вашата уеб страница!	Tell me, please, your web site!	Тел ми:, пли:з, йо: уеб сайт!

Днес повечето хотели разполагат с факсове и предлагат ***Интернет*** *срещу приблизително една лира. Някои магазини също предлагат факс услуги, което става ясно от знака на витрината. За да прочетете електронната си поща, влезте в някой от многобройните Интернет клубове. Все повече кафенета предоставят Интернет през IR порт.*

Банка. Пари	Bank. Money	Бæнкс. Мàни
Извинете, къде се намира ... банка?	Excuse me, where's the ...Bank, please?	Икскю:з ми:, уèъз gъ ... бæнк, пли:з?
Какво е работното време на банката?	What are the working hours of the bank?	Уòт à: gъ уъ:кинг àуъз ъв gъ бæнк ?
Кога ... банката?	When does the bank ...?	Уèн даз gъ бæнк ...?
отваря	open	òупън
затваря	close	клòуз
Искам да обменя ...	I would like to change...	Ай уỳд лàйк ту чèйндж...
левове	some levas	сам лèваз
долари	some US dollars	сам ю: ес дòлъз
в английски лири	into British pounds	ѝнту брѝтиш пàундз
в долари	into US dollars	ѝнту ю: ес дòлъз
в евро	into euro	ѝнту ю:роу

Може ли да обменя пътнически чекове?	Can I change traveler's checks?	Кæн ай чèйндж трæвълъ:з чекс?
Има ли наблизо обменно бюро?	Is there a currency exchange office nearby?	Из деъ ъ кàрънси иксчèйндж òфис нѝъбай?
Какъв е курсът на ... днес?	What's the exchange rate for ... today?	Уòтс ди иксчèйндж рейт фо: ... тъдèй?
еврото	the euro	дъ ю:роу
американския долар	the US dollar	дъ ю: ес дòлъ
английската лира	the British pound	дъ брѝтиш пàунд
Един долар (евро, лира) прави ... лева.	A dollar (euro, pound) exchanges for ... levs.	Ъ дòлъ (ю:роу, пàунд) иксчèйнджиз фо:...лèвз.

*Банките във Великобритания са отворени от 9.30 до 16.30 от понеделник до петък. Обикновено те предлагат по-добри курсове за обмен на валута от частните бюра (**bureaux de change**), където трябва да се внимава за комисионните и курса. Бюрата на международните летища са изключение от правилото. Те вземат по-малко от повечето големи банки.*

Искам да купя (лири) ...	I'd like to buy (pounds) ...	Айд лайк ту бай (пàундз)...
Какъв е курсът (Каква е стойността) на долара?	How much is the dollar worth?	Хàу мач из дъ дòлъ уъ:т ?
Къде да се подпиша?	Where do I sign?	Уèъ ду: ай сайн?
Бихте ли ми дали по-дребни банкноти?	Can you give me small bills / change?	Кæн ю: гив ми смо:л билз / чейндж?
Комисионната е ... процента.	The commission is ... per cent.	дъ къмѝшън из ... пъ сèнт.

Валутен курс	Currency rate	Кàрънси рейт
курс купува	buy (rate)	бай (рейт)
курс продава	sell (rate)	сел (рейт)

Искате ли разписка?	Would you like a receipt?	Уùд ю: лàйк ъ рисѝ:т?
Да, дайте ми.	Yes, please.	Йес, пли:з.
Мога ли да си открия (да закрия)...?	Can I open (close)…?	Кæн ай òупън (клòуз)…?
влог	a bank deposit	ъ бæнк дипòзит
сметка	an account	ън ъкàунт
текуща сметка	a current account	ъ кàрънт ъкàунт

Колко пари са необходими?	How much do I need?	Хàу мач ду: ай ни:д?
Искам да преведете тази сума на сметката на господин (госпожа) ...	I'd like you to transfer this money on the account of Mr. (Mrs.) ...	Айд лайк ю: ту трǽнсфъ: дис мàни он ди ъкàунт ъв мѝстъ (мѝсиз) ...
в ... банка	to... Bank	ту... бǽнк
в клона на вашата банка в България	to your branch in Bulgaria	ту йо: брǽнч ин балгѐъриъ
Очаквам паричен превод на мое име от ... банка.	I am expecting a money order on my name from... Bank.	Ай ǽм икспѐктинг ъ мàни о̀:дъ он май нейм фром ... бǽнк.

__Банкова сметка__ се отваря трудно, но ако възнамерявате да работите, тя може да се окаже крайно необходима. Взаимоспомагателните каси (__building societies__) по правило са по-добронамерени и често предлагат по-изгодни лихви. Ще се нуждаете от постоянен адрес, а нещата ще вървят много по-леко, ако разполагате с референция от банката, в която държите парите си, заедно със справка за финансовото ви състояние през последната година. Във Великобритания ще ви бъдат много полезни __кредитните/дебитните карти__.

Имате ли ...?	Have you got ...?	Хæв ю: гот ...?
банкова сметка	a bank account	ъ бæнк ъка̀унт
чекова книжка	a cheque book	ъ чек бук
кредитна карта	a credit card	ъ крѐдит ка:д
Номерът на сметката ми е ...	My account number is ...	Май ъка̀унт на̀мбъ из...
Искам да ... тази сума.	I'd like to... this sum.	Айд лайк ту ... дис са̀м.
внеса	deposit	дипо̀зит
изтегля	draw	дро̀:
преведа	transfer	тр æ̀нсфъ:
Заповядайте...	Go to..., please!	Го̀у ту ..., пли:з!
на каса номер ..	cash-desk number...	кæш деск на̀мбъ ...
на гише номер ...	teller's desk number...	тѐлъз деск на̀мбъ ...
при касиера	the teller	дъ тѐлъ
Бихте ли ми дали формуляр, моля?	Could you hand me a form, please?	Куд ю: хæнд ми ъ фо:м пли:з?
Попълнете!	Fill out, please!	Фил а̀ут, пли:з!
с печатни букви	in block letters	ин блок лѐтъ:з
Подпишете тук!	Sign here, please!	Са̀йн хѝъ, пли:з!

Дайте си паспорта, моля!	Let me have your passport, please!	Лет ми: хæв йо: па̀:спо:т, пли:з!
Моля, поставете кредитната си карта и въведете вашия ПИН-код.	Please insert your credit card in and punch your PIN.	пли:з инсъ:т йо: крѐдит ка:д ин æнд панч йо: пи: ай ен.

внасям пари	deposit money	дипо̀зит ма̀ни
тегля пари	draw money	дро̀: ма̀ни
банкомат	cashpoint, ATM	кæ̀шпойнт, ей ти: ем
кредитирам	credit	крѐдит
трансферирам пари	transfer money	трæ̀нсфъ: ма̀ни
осребрявам чек	cash a cheque	кæш ъ чек
сключвам заем	contract a loan	ко̀нтрæкт ъ ло̀ун
чекова книжка	cheque book	чек бук
паричен превод	money transfer	ма̀ни трæ̀нсфъ:
акредитив	letter of credit	лѐтъ ъв крѐдит
кредит	credit	крѐдит
на кредит	on credit	он крѐдит
лихва	interest	ѝнтрист
лихвен процент	interest rate	ѝнтрист рейт
за сметка на...	on account of...	он ъка̀унт ъв ...

Пари	money	мàни
Валута	currency	кàрънси
обмен	exchange	иксчèйндж
монета	coin	кòин
банкнота	banknote	б æ̀нкноут
дребни	change	чейндж

Развалете ми, моля ...!	Can you change, please!	Кæн ю: чейндж, пли:з..!
тази банкнота	this (bank)note	дис (бæнк)нòут
десет лири	ten pounds	тен пàундз

Валутата във Великобритания е ***лирата стерлинг*** *(£). Една лира е съставена от 100 пенса (p). Монетите от* ***1p*** *и* ***2p*** *са медни; монетите от* ***5p, 10p, 20p*** *и* ***50p*** *са сребърни; голямата монета от* ***£1*** *е оцветена златисто, а новата монета от £2 в златисти и сребристи тонове. Думата* ***пенс*** *се използва рядко в разговорния език и вместо това се съкращава на "****пи****".*

Банкнотите са от ***£5, £10, £20 и £50*** *и се различават по цвят и големина.*

Възможно е да ви върнат други банкноти, които се издават от шотландски банки, в това число и банкнота от £1. Тези пари са законно платежно средство от двете страни на границата, макар че магазинерите в Англия и Уелс може да откажат да ги приемат. В такъв случай влезте в някоя банка и ги разменете.

Британска парична система	British Monetary System	Бр̀итиш мо̀нетъри сѝстем
монети	**coins**	**amount** *(стойност)*
1 пени	a penny	a penny
2 пени	a twopenny piece	two pence
5 пени	a fivepenny piece	five pence
10 пени	a tenpenny piece	ten pence
20 пени	a twentypenny piece	twenty pence
50 пени	a fiftypenny piece	fifty pence
1 лира	a pound coin	a pound
банкноти	**(bank)notes**	
5 лири	a five pound note	five pounds
10 лири	a ten pound note	ten pounds
20 лири	a twenty pound note	twenty pounds
50 лири	a fifty pound note	fifty pounds

Великобритания е скъпа страна с висок стандарт, да не говорим за Лондон. Докато сте там, разчетете разходите си на около £30 до £40 дневно за най-елементарни нужди. Разглеждането на забележителности, храненето в заведение и нощният живот ще увеличат значително размера на тази сума.

В хотела	*At the hotel*	*æт gъ хоуmèл*
Къде се намира хотел...?	Where's the ... Hotel, please?	Уèъз gъ ... хоутèл, пли:з?
Как да стигна до хотел ...?	How do I get to the ... Hotel, please?	Хàу ду: ай гет ту gъ ... хоутèл, пли:з?
В кой хотел сте отседнали?	What hotel are you staying at?	Уòт хоутèл а: ю: стейинг æт?
На рецепцията	**At the Reception Desk**	**æт gъ рисèпшън деск**
Какво ще обичате?	Can I help you?	Кæн ай хелп ю:?
Имате ли свободни стаи?	Have you got any vacancies?	Хæв ю гот æни вèкънсиз?
Имате ли свободни стаи за тази нощ?	Do you have any rooms available for tonight?	Ду: ю: хæв æни ру:мз ъвèйлъбъл фо: тунàйт?
Искам стая за тази вечер.	I'd like a room for tonight.	Айд лайк ъ ру:м фо: тунàйт.
Съжалявам, няма места.	I'm sorry, we are full.	Айм сòри, уи: а: фул.

Има ли друг хотел наблизо?	Is there another hotel near here?	Из деъ ънàдъ хоутѐл нѝъ хѝъ?
Имам резервирана ...	I've got a reservation for ...	Айв гот ъ рѐзървѐйшън фо: ...
Искам да наема ...	I'd like to rent ...	Айд лайк ту рент ...
Искам да запазя...	I'd like to book ...	Айд лайк ту бук ...
единична стая	a single room	ъ сѝнгъл ру:м
двойна стая	a double room	ъ дàбъл ру:м
две единични стаи	two singles	ту: сѝнгълз
стая с двойно легло	a twin bed room	ъ туѝн бед ру:м
апартамент	a suite	ъ суѝ:т
Казвам се ...	My name is...	Май нейм из ...
Предпочитам...стая...	I'd prefer ...room ...	Айд прифъ̀:...ру:м...
спокойна	a quiet	ъ куàйът
слънчева	a sunny	ъ сàни
светла	a bright	ъ брàйт
с телефон	with a telephone	уйд ъ тѐлифòун
с баня	with a bath	уйд ъ ба:т
с душ	with a shower	уйд ъ шàуъ
с климатик	with an air-conditioner	уйд ън ѐъ къндѝшънъ

на втория етаж	on the second floor	он gъ сѐкънд фло:
на приземния етаж	on the ground floor	он gъ гра̀унд фло:
на последния етаж	on the top floor	он gъ топ фло:
Искам нещо ...	I'd like something...	Айд лайк са̀мтинг...
по-добро	better	бѐтъ
по-евтино	cheaper	чѝ:пъ
по-скъпо	more expensive	мо: икспѐнсив
Заповядайте паспорта ми.	Here's my passport.	Хѝъз май па̀:спо:т
Попълнете адресната карта!	Fill in the registration form, please!	Фил ин gъ рѐджистрѐйшън фо:м, пли:з!
Колко време ще останете?	How long do you intend to stay?	Ха̀у лонг ду: ю: интѐнд ту стей?
Ще остана ...	I'm staying ...	Айм стѐи:нг
Ще останем ...	We are staying ...	Уѝ: а: стѐи:нг...
една нощ	for a night	фо: ъ найт
две нощи	for two nights	фо: ту: найтс
до четвъртък	until Thursday	ънтѝл тъ:здей
една седмица	for a week	фо: ъ уѝ:к

НАСТАНЯВАНЕ

За препоръчване е да си направите **резервация**, където желаете да отседнете още от България. Ако предпочитате да контактувате директно с хотела, може да направите такава с факс, по телефона или чрез имейл. Обикновено се изисква някаква гаранция като кредитна карта или депозит за няколко вечери.

Удачно е да се възползвате и от услугите на реномирана туристическа агенция в България.

Ако по една или друга причина не сте успели да резервирате още от България, може да направите това на летището или жп гарата в специализираните служби - Accommodation, Hotels, B&B и др., като уточните цената, която сте готови да плащате, колко време възнамерявате да останете и района, където желаете да отседнете.

В туристическите центрове и бюра, срещу минимална такса, можете да получите информация за настаняване в хотели, общежития, квартири, да направите резервация за нощувка, пътуване или посещение на театър, да се включите в организирана обиколка на града и др. Бихте могли да отседнете и в частни домове, предлагани от собствениците, на туристи (**www.homebase-hols.com**).

При желание, бихте могли да направите резервация за хотел самостоятелно по телефона и чрез Интернет, но в този случай могат да ви поискат номера на кредитната Ви карта или депозит.

Не забравяйте до 24 часа преди датата да потвърдите или откажете направената резервация!

Ето някои полезни уеб страници:
www.ehi.com
www.expedia.co.uk
www.visitlondon.com
www.visitbritain.com
www.holiday-inn.com
www.londontown.com
www.travelinn.co.uk
www.thegoodwebguide.co.uk

Britain & London Visitor Centre

1 Regent St, Piccadilly Circus SW1Y 4PQ. Това е голям и шумен информационен и резервационен център, на две минути път от Piccadilly Circus. Той предлага екскурзии, обменно бюро, билети за театрите, билети за влакове и самолети и оферти за коли, настаняване, магазин за карти и справочници и информация за Шотландия, Уелс и Ирландия. Винаги е пълно с хора и работи ежедневно: от понеделник до петък от 9 часа сутринта до 6.30 часа вечерта, в събота и неделя от 10 часа сутринта до 4.30 часа следобед.

Лондонски туристически информационни центрове

Такива има на четирите терминала на Heathrow, на летища Gatwick, Luton *и Stansted, в залата на пристигащите връзки на международния терминал на гара Waterloo и на метростанция Liverpool St.*

Главният център във фоайето на гара Victoria предлага резервации за места за настаняване, информация и магазин за книги и карти. Той е отворен всеки ден, като често е препълнен с хора. Запитвания по пощата може да правите на адрес 26 Grosvenor Gardens SW1W 0DU.

Хотелски резервационни центрове

Резервации за същия ден се правят в TIC(Tourist Information Centre) на гара Victoria и Heathrow, но има комисионна от £5 за резервация за хотели и B&B и £1.50 за общежития. Друга възможност е да отидете в някои от частните хотелски резервационни центрове на гара Victoria (един в главната зала и друг отвън, близо до стъпалата за подземната железница), които вземат £5 на резервация.

Каква е цената на нощувка?	How much is the rate per night?	Хàу мач из ðъ рейт пъ: найт?
полупансион	half-board	ха:в бо:д
пълен пансион	full-board	фул бо:д
Каква е цената на стаята ...?	How much is the room…?	Хàу мач из ðъ ру:м…?
за едно денонощие	for a night	фо: ъ нàйт
за три денонощия	for three nights	фо: *т*ри: найтс

В цената влиза ли...?	Does the price include...?	Даз дъ прайс инклу̀:д...?
закуската	the breakfast	дъ брѐкфъст
обслужването по стаите	the room service	дъ ру̀:м съ:вис
В колко часа е ...?	What time is ...?	Уо̀т тайм из ...?
закуската	the breakfast	дъ брѐкфъст
вечерята	the dinner	дъ дѝнъ
Мога ли да закуся в стаята си?	Can I have my breakfast in my room?	Кæн ай хæв май брѐкфъст ин май ру:м?
Имате ли сейфове?	Do you have safe boxes?	Ду ю: хæв сейф бо̀ксиз?
Бих желал,-а ...	I'd like to ...	Айд лайк ту ...
да наема сейф	rent a safe box	рент а сейф бо̀кс
да оставя това в сейфа	leave this in your safe	ли:в дис ин йо: сейф
Има ли намаление за ...?	Is there a reduction for ...?	Из деъ а рида̀кшън фо: ... ?
деца	children	чѝлдрън
съпрузи на сватбено пътешествие	couples on honeymoon	ка̀пълз он ха̀ни му:н
Има ли агенция за коли под наем в хотела?	Is there a car hire agency in the hotel?	Из деъ ъ ка: хайъ ѐйджънси ин дъ хоутѐл?

Има ли някакви съобщения за мен?	Are there any messages for me?	А: ∂еъ ѐни мѐсиджиз фо: ми:?
Кога трябва да напусна стаята?	When do I have to check out?	Уѐн ду: ай хæв ту чек а̀ут?
➡ Кога трябва да платя?	When do I have to pay?	Уѐн ду: ай хæв ту пей?
Кой номер е стаята ми?	Which my room number?	Уйч из май ру:м на̀мбъ?
На кой етаж е?	Which floor is it on?	Уйч фло: из ит он?
Имам нужда от носач.	I need a porter.	Ай нѝ:д ъ пò:тъ.
Може ли някой да занесе куфарите ми горе?	Can somebody please bring my cases up?	Кæн са̀мбоди пли:з бринг май кѐйсиз ап?
Моля изпратете куфарите ми в стаята.	Please have my bags sent up to my room.	Пли:з хæв май бæгз сент ап ту май ру:м.
Моля свалете багажа ми долу.	Please have my luggage brought downstairs.	Пли:з хæв май ла̀гидж бро:т да̀унстеъ:з
Бих желал,-а да видя стаята!	I'd like to see the room, please!	Айд лайк ту си: ∂ъ ру:м, пли:з!
Харесва ми.	I like it.	Ай лайк ит.
Не ми харесва.	I don't like it.	Ай дòунт лайк ит.
Ще я взема.	I'll take it.	Айл тейк ит.
Няма да я взема.	I'm not going to take it.	Айм нот гòинг ту тейк ит.

Дайте ми, ако обичате, ключа от стая номер 215.	Can I have the key of room 215, please?	Кæн ай хæв дъ ки: ъв ру:м ту:, уа̀н, файв, пли:з?
Аз съм в стая ...	I'm in room ...	Айм ин ру:м ...
Ключът ми, моля.	My key, please.	Май ки: пли:з.
Ако ме потърси един господин (една госпожа), извикайте ме, моля!	Would you please call me if a gentleman (a lady) asks for me!	Уу̀д ю: пли:з ко:л ми: иф ъ джѐнтълмън (ъ лѐйди) а:скс фо: ми:!
Събудете ме, ако обичате ... сутринта.	Would you wake me up ... in the morning.	Уу̀д ю: уѐйк ми: ап ... ин дъ мо̀:нинг.
в шест часа	at six (o'clock)	æт сикс (ъкло̀к)
Искам да се обадя в България.	I'd like to make a call to Bulgaria.	Айд лайк ту мейк ъ ко:л ту балгѐъриъ.
Може ли да изперете и изгладите тези дрехи?	May I have these clothes washed and pressed?	Мей а̀й хæв ди:з кло̀удз уо̀шт æнд прест?
Мога ли да изгладя ризата си сам?	May I iron my shirt myself?	Мей а̀й а̀йън май шъ:т майсѐлф?

Искам да се оплача.	I want to make a complaint.	Ай уòнт ту мейк ъ къмплèйнт.
Има проблем с ...	There's a problem with ...	*g*èъз ъ прòублъм уѝ*g* ...
Не е в ред ...	Something's wrong with..	С<u>а̀</u>м*т*инг*з* ронг уѝ*g*...
климатикът	the air-conditioner	*g*и èъ кънд*ѝ*шънъ
телевизорът	the TV	*g*ъ ти: ви:
хладилникът	the fridge	*g*ъ фридж
душът	the shower	*g*ъ шàуъ
тоалетната	the toilet	*g*ъ тòйлит
ваната	the bathtub	*g*ъ бà:*т*т<u>а</u>б
вратата	the door	*g*ъ до:
ключалката	the lock	*g*ъ лок
ключа	the key	*g*ъ ки:
отоплението	the heat	*g*ъ хи:т
телефонът	the (tele)phone	*g*ъ (тèли)фòун
асансьорът	the lift	*g*ъ лифт
Няма ...	There is no ...	*g*èъ из нòу ...
топла (студена) вода	hot(cold) water	хот (кòулд) уòтъ
осветление	lighting	лàйтинг
отопление	heating	хѝ:тинг

Имам нужда от ...	I need ...	Ай ни:д ...
одеало	a blanket	ъ блæнкит
възглавница	a pillow	ъ пѝлоу
чаршафи	sheets	ши:тс
хавлия	a towel	ъ тàуъл
сапун	soap	сòуп
тоалетна хартия	some toilet paper	сам тòйлит пèйпъ
крушка	a bulb	ъ балб

Изчезнаха мои вещи.	My things are missing.	Май *т*инг з а: мѝсинг.
Изчезнаха ми парите.	My money is gone.	Май мàни из гон.
Извикайте полицията!	Call the police!	Ко:л *д*ъ пълѝ:с!

Кога заминавате?	When are you leaving?	Уèн а: ю: лѝ:винг?
Заминавам ...	I'm leaving ...	Айм лѝ:винг ...
Заминаваме ...	We're leaving ...	Уѝъ лѝ:винг ...
следобед	this afternoon	*д*ис à:фтъну:н
утре	tomorrow	тъмòроу
Аз (ние) ще остана,-ем още една нощ.	I(we)'d like to stay one more night.	Ай(уѝ:)д лайк ту стей уàн мо: найт.
Пригответе ми сметката, моля!	Could I have the bill, please?	Куд ай хæв *д*ъ бил, пли:з?

Бихте ли ми извикали едно такси?	Would you get me a taxi, please?	Уўд ю: гет ми: ъ тæкси, пли:з?
Мога ли да платя ...?	Can I pay ...?	Кæн ай пей ...?
в брой	cash	кæш
с кредитна карта	by credit card	бай крèдит ка:д
Благодарим много.	Thank you very much.	тæнк ю: вèри мач.

Цените на **ХОТЕЛИТЕ** *на Великобритания са едни от най-високите в Европа. Взависимост от това дали сте направили ранна резервация или отивате направо в хотела, може да се случи да платите за стая два пъти повече. Практика в Лондон е да се показват цени на нощувки без ДДС (VAT 17.5 %). За да не останете изненадани, прочетете дребния шрифт или попитайте. В повечето хотели цената е за стая, а не за човек. Внимавайте за скрити надценки(напр. на телефонните разговори от стаята). Много хотели предлагат отстъпки за престой през уикенда или по времето на различни официални празници. Във всеки случай си заслужава да опитате да договорите отстъпка от цената с мотива, че хотелът не е пълен, плащате в брой или няма да закусвате. Кажете на английски:* ***Can I get any discount?***

Хотелите във Великобритания обикновено предлагат ***закуска****, която може да бъде "Английска" или "Континентална". "Английската" включва: пържени яйца с бекон или шунка, овесени ядки или "Corn Flakes" с кисело мляко, препечен хляб, сок, чай/кафе. Ако Ви предложат "Continental Breakfast", ще закусите кроасан или*

друг вид кифличка, масло, конфитюр, сок, чай или кафе. В някои по-скъпи хотели имате възможност да избирате между двата типа закуски.

Стаите се освобождават до 11 на обяд, освен ако предварително не сте договорили друго време.

Нощувка и закуска (Bed and Breakfast; B&B)

Обикновено това са семейни хотелчета поместени в къщи. Те са малко по-скъпи от общежитията, но по-тихи и с по-малко хора. В стаята обикновено има баня и тоалетна.

Цената им варира от 15 до 50 лири.

Общежитие (Hostel)

Удобни и евтини за току-що пристигналите в Лондон. Много от тях предлагат намаление за престой от седмица и повече. Някои приемат кредитни карти, а други работят само с пари в брой. Цените варират между 80 и 100 лири за човек на седмица в двойна стая с осигурена закуска.

Престой при приятели

Ако ви посрещне приятел и отседнете при него, нормално е да предложите около 5 лири на вечер. Помогнете с каквото можете в жилището и не оставайте по-дълго от предварително уговорения срок.

Търся **къмпинг**	I'm looking for	Айм лу̀:кинг фо:
с питейна вода.	**a campsite**	ъ кæ̀мпсайт
	with drinking water.	уиg дрѝнкинг уò:тъ.
Къде е рецепцията?	Where is the reception,	Уеъ из gъ рисѐпшън,
	please?	пли:з?
Има ли паркинг?	Is there a car park?	Из gèъ ъ ка: па:к?
Имате ли място за ...?	Do you have room for ...?	Ду ю: хæв ру:м фо: ...?
каравана	a caravan	ъ кæ̀ръвæн
палатка	a tent	ъ тент
Къде са ...?	Where are ...?	Уèъ а: ...?
тоалетните	the toilets	gъ тòйлетс
душ кабините	the shower blocks	gъ шàуъ блокс
контейнерите за отпадъци	the dustbins	gъ дàстбинс
Има ли магазин	Is there a shop	Из gèъ ъ шоп
в къмпинга?	on the camp site?	он gъ кæмп сайт?
Има ли електрическа	Is there an electric	Из gèъ ън илѐктрик
връзка за караваната	connection for	ка̲нѐкшън фо:
ни?	our caravan?	ауъ кæ̀ръвæн?

В ресторанта	At the Restaurant	æт gъ рѐстърънт
Бихте ли ми препоръчали ...?	Could you recommend me...?	Куд ю: рекъмѐнд ми...?
някой по-евтин ресторант	a cheaper restaurant	ъ чѝ:пъ рѐстърънт
ресторант с национална кухня	a traditional British meals restaurant	ъ трѝдишънъл брѝтиш ми:лз рѐстърънт
ресторант за бързо хранене	a fast food restaurant	ъ фа:ст фу:д рѐстърънт
Къде се намира най-близката закусвалня?	Where is the nearest fast food restaurant?	Уѐъ из gъ нѝърест фа:ст фуд рѐстора:нт?
Мога ли да ви поканя ...?	Can I invite you ...?	Кæн ай инвàйт ю: ...?
на обяд	to lunch	ту ланч
на вечеря	to dinner	ту дѝнъ
Искаме една маса за...	We need a table for...	Уѝ: ни:д ъ тѐйбъл фо:..
двама	two	ту:
трима	three	три:

Имате ли маса за шестима?	Have you got a table for six?	Хæв ю: гот ъ тѐйбъл фо: сикс?
Имам запазена маса на името на ...	I have a table reserved in the name ...	Ай хæв ъ тѐйбъл ризъ:вд ин ₫ъ нейм ...
Нека седнем на тази маса!	Let's sit at this table.	Летс сит æт ₫ис тѐйбъл.
Извинете, имаме нужда от още един стол.	We need one more chair, please.	Уй: ни:д уа̲н мо: чѐъ, пли:з.
Извинете, местата свободни ли са?	Excuse me, are these seats taken?	Икскю̀:з ми, а: ₫и:з си:тс тѐйкън?
➡ сервитьор,-ка	a waiter, a waitress	ъ уѐйтъ, ъ уѐйтрис
Може ли менюто!	Can I have the menu, please?	Кæн ай хæв ₫ъ мѐню: пли:з?
Мога ли да видя листа с вината?	May I see the wine list?	Мей ай си: ₫ъ уайн лист?
Бихме желали да поръчаме.	We'd like to order.	Уйд ла̀йк ту о̀:дъ.
(Не сме) готови сме да поръчаме.	We're (not) ready to order yet.	Уйъ (нот) рѐди ту о̀:дъ йет.

Какво ще поръчате?	Can I take your order?	Кæн ай тейк йо: о̀:дъ?
Искам да опитам нещо	I want to try something...	Ай уо̀нт ту трай са̀мтинг
ново	new	ню:
традиционно	traditional	тръди̇̀шънъл
екзотично	exotic	игзо̀тик
Какъв е специалитетът на заведението?	What is the speciality of the house?	Уот из дъ спешиæ̀лити ъв дъ хаус?
Предлагате ли вегетариански ястия?	Do you offer got any vegetarian dishes?	Ду: ю: офъ: æ̀ни веджитѐъриън ди̇̀шиз?
Необходими са още едни прибори.	We need one more setting, please.	Уй: ни:д уа̀н мо: сѐтинг, пли:з.
Не съм гладен,-на.	I'm not hungry.	Айм нот ха̀нгри.
Не ям по това време.	I don't eat at this time.	Ай до̀унт и:т æт дис тайм.
Аз съм вегетарианец,-ка.	I am a vegetarian.	Ай æм ъ вѐджитѐъриън.
За мен само зеленчуци.	Only vegetables for me, please.	о̀унли вѐджитъбълз фо: ми:, пли:з.
Не пия алкохол.	No alcohol for me.	Но̀у æ̀лкъхол фо: ми:.
За мен само плодове.	Some fruit for me only.	Сам фру:т фо: ми: о̀унли.
Аз съм на диета.	I'm on a diet.	Айм он ъ да̀йът.

Кафе, моля!	Coffee, please!	Ко̀фи, пли:з.
За мен чай, моля.	Tea for me, please.	Тѝ: фо: ми:, пли:з.
Още ...	Some more ...	Сам мо: ...
Имате ли ...?	Have you got ...?	Хæв ю: гот ...?
Бих предпочел,-а ...	I would rather have...	Ай уу̀д ра̀:дъ хæв..
Какво бихме ни препоръчали ...?	What would you recommend us ...?	Уо̀т уу̀д ю: рекъмѐнд ас...?
за начало	to start with	ту ста:т уйд
за аперитив	for appetizers	фо: æ̀питайзъз
за предястие	as a starter	ес ъ ста̀:тъ
за основно ястие	for main courses	фо: мейн ко̀:сиз
за пиене	for drinks	фо: дринкс
за десерт	for desserts	фо: дизъ̀:тс

За предястие бих искал,-а ...	To start, I would like ...	Ту ста:т ай уу̀д лайк ...
За основно ястие бих искал,-а ...	For the main course, I would like ...	Фо: дъ мейн ко:с ай уу̀д лайк ...
За десерт ще взема ...	For dessert, I'll have ...	Фо: дизъ̀:т айл хæв ...
За пиене бих искал,-а ...	To drink, I would like some ...	Ту дринк ай уу̀д лайк сам ...

Бих,-ме искал,-а, -и...	I (we)'d like ..., please?	Ай (уй:)д лайк ..., пли:з?
една салата	a salad	ъ сǽлъд
... салати	... salads	... сǽлъдз
една супа	some soup	сам су:п
... супи	... soups	... су:пс
една пържола	a steak	ъ стейк
... пържоли	... steaks	... стейкс
няколко филии хляб	some slices of bread	сам сла̀йсиз ъв бред
една бутилка	a bottle	ъ бо̀тъл
... бутилки вино	... bottles of wine	... бо̀тълз ъв уа̀йн
Това не е каквото поръчах.	That's not what I ordered.	Дæтс нот уо̀т ай о̀:дъ:д.
Желая ви ...!	Enjoy your ...!	Инджо̀й йо: ...!
добър апетит	meal	ми:л
приятна закуска	breakfast	брѐкфъст
приятна обяд	lunch	ланч
приятна вечеря	dinner	дѝнъ
Наздраве!	Cheers!	Чѝъз!

В Англия ще се убедите, че кръчмите са на всеки ъгъл. Те са една от туристическите атракции на страната. Повечето от тях затварят до 11 часа и само някои имат разрешение да работят до по-късно. Кръчми като ***The Slug and the Lettu-ce, All Bar One, Firkin, Corney and Barrow, Pitcher and Piano*** *могат да се намерят из цял Лондон и обикновено предлагат добро обслужване и разнообразие от напитки.*

В Лондон, както и в цялата страна може да посетите кафета от световноизвестната верига **SPORTS CAFÉ** ***(www.thesportscafe.com)***.

*Особено посещавани са ресторантите, които предлагат различна по националност кухня: индийски(**Khan's** на спирка Bayswater), италиански, ливански, поортугалски и др. Много предпочитана верига с английска кухня е* ***Angus Steak House***.

Английската кухня днес е малко по-различна от мазната риба и пържени картофки. Лондон се превръща в една от столиците на световната кухня. Туристическите ресторанти предлагат разнообразие както в атмосферата, така и в менюто, но и цените са по-високи.

Много интересни са ресторантите от типа **Eat as much as you can** (Изяж, колкото можеш). В тях плащаш еднократно и си вземаш от предлаганата храна колкото пъти искаш.

Сохо (Soho) и Чайна таун (China Town) (Gerrard Street) са пълни с малки ресторантчета, предлагащи храна на разумни цени. Не пренебрегвайте и традиционното меню в кръчмите. Оставянето на бакшиш е задължително. Ако сте много доволни от обслужването, може да оставите около 10 % от сметката.

Все пак погледнете в менюто, тъй като има ресторанти които включват обслужването в цената на сметката.

Странни за вкуса на българина ястия:

Spotted Dick (Шарения Дик) торта която прилича на гъба, украсена с боровинки **Yorkshire Pudding** (Йоркширски пудинг) хляб който прилича на тесто и се сервира с говеждо и сос

Black Pudding (Черен пудинг) наденица в която има сушена свинска кръв

Cock-a-Leakie (Кок а лики) супа направена от пиле и пресен лук

Wet Nelly- Ует Нели (Мократа Нели) - трохи от сладкиш натопени в сироп

Сметката, ако обичате!	The bill, please!	дъ бѝл, пли:з!
Мисля, че има грешка в сметката.	I think there is a mistake in the bill.	Ай тинк деъ из ъ мистѐйк ин дъ бил.
Искаме да платим поотделно.	We would like to pay separately.	Уи: уу̀д лайк ту пей сѐпъртли.
Задръжте рестото, моля.	Keep the change, please!	Кѝ:п дъ чѐйндж, пли:з!

Прибори	**Cutlery**	**Кàтлъри**
нож	knife	найф
лъжица	spoon	спу:н
вилица	fork	фо:к
солница	salt-cellar	сò:лт сѐлъ
чаша *(стъклена)*	glass	гла:с
чиния	plate	плейт
чаша *(за кафе и чай)*	cup	кап
бутилка	bottle	бòтъл
кана	jug	джаг
свещник	candlestick	кæ̀ндлстик
свещ	candle	кæ̀ндъл
салфетка	napkin	нæ̀пкин
пепелник	ash-tray	æш трей
клечки за зъби	tooth-picks	тỳ:*т* пикс

Закуска	Breakfast	Брèкфъст
Да отидем да закусим.	Let's go and have breakfast.	Лèтс гòу æнд хæв брèкфъст.
Къде ще закусим?	Where shall we have breakfast?	Уèъ шæл уй: хæв брèкфъст?
Какво желаете за закуска?	What would you like for breakfast?	Уòт у:д ю: лайк фо: брèкфъст?
➡ Дайте ми, моля...!	I'd like ..., please?	Айд лайк ..., пли:з?
едно ... кафе	a (cup of) ... coffee	ъ (кап ъв)...кòфи
турско	Turkish	тъ:киш
нес	instant	йнстънт
единично / двойно	single, regular / double	сингъл, рèгюлъ: / дàбъл
еспресо	espresso	испрèсоу
с (без) захар	with(without) sugar	уйд (уидàут) шỳгъ
с мляко	with milk (white)	уйд милк (уàйт)
без мляко	without milk (black)	уидàут милк (блæк)
със сметана	with cream	уйд кри:м
(чаша) чай	a (cup of) tea	ъ (кап ъв) ти:

(чаша) какао	a (cup of) cocoa	ъ (кап ъв) кòукоу
малко мляко	some milk	сам милк
кисело мляко	yoghurt	йòгът
препечена филия	toast	тòуст
шунка	ham	хæм
сирене	cheese	чи:з
мед	honey	хàни
масло	butter	бàтъ
маргарин	margarine	ма:джърѝ:н
сметана	cream	кри:м
сладко	jam	джæм
варено яйце	boiled egg	бòйлд ег
кашкавал	yellow cheese	йѐлоу чи:з
сандвич	sandwich	сæ̀ндуич
бекон с яйце	bacon and egg	бѐйкън æнд ег
овесени ядки	pouridge	пòридж
кренвирши	sausages	сòсиджис
риба тон	tuna fish	тю̀на фиш

Обяд	**Lunch**	***Ланч***
Кога / Къде ... ще обядваме?	What time / Where ... shall we have lunch?	Уо̀т тайм / Уѐъ ... шæл уй: хæв ланч?
Мога ли да би поканя на обяд?	Do you mind if I invite you to lunch?	Ду: ю: майнд иф ай инва̀йт ю: ту ланч?
Благодарим ви за чудесното ядене.	Thank you for the wonderful meal.	*т*æнк ю: фо: *д*ъ уа̀ндъфул ми:л.
... супа	... soup	... су:п
пилешка	chicken	чѝкън
рибена	fish	фиш
бульон	bouillon	бу̀:йон
крем	cream	кри:м
шкембе	tripe	трайп
зеленчукова	vegetable	вѐджитъбъл
телешка	veal	ви:л

риба	**fish**	**фиш**
пушена	smoked, kippers	смòукт, кѝпъз
варена	boiled	бòйлд
печена	roasted / baked	рòустид / бейкт
пържена	fried	фрайд
маринована	pickled	пѝкълд
скумрия	mackerel	мæ̀кръл
шаран	carp	ка:п
треска	cod	код
пъстърва	trout	тра̀ут
октопод	octopus	òктъпъс
омари	lobsters	лòбстъз
калкан	turbot	тъ:бът
риба тон	tuna fish	тю̀:нъ
сьомга	salmon	сæ̀лмън
сепия	cuttle fish	кæ̀тъл
херинга	whitebait	уа̀йтбейт
хек	hake	хейк
змиорка	eel	и:л
щука	pike	пайк
костур	perch	пъ:ч

раци	crabs	крæбз
миди	clams, mussles	клæмз, ма̀сълс
скариди	shrimps	шримпс
стриди	oysters	о̀истъз

▶ Ястия с месо — Meat Dishes — Ми:т дѝшиз ◀

месо	**meat**	**ми:т**
пържено	fried	фрайд
печено	roasted	ро̀устид
на скара	grilled	грилд
задушено	stewed	стю:д
телешко	veal	ви:л
свинско	pork	по:к
агнешко	lamb	лæм
овнешко	mutton	ма̀тън
говеждо	beef	би:ф
питомен заек	rabbit	рæ̀бит
с ориз	with rice	уѝд ра̀йс
с картофи	with potatoes	уѝд пътѐйтоуз

с грах	with peas	уѝд пи:з
със зеле	with cabbage	уѝд кæ̀бидж
със зеленчуци	with vegetables	уѝд вѐджитъбълз
с гъби	with mushrooms	уѝд ма̀шру:мз
ребра	ribs	рибз
бъбреци	kidneys	кѝдниз
черен дроб	liver	лѝвъ
шницел	cutlet	ка̀тлит
пържола *(с кокъл)*	chop	чоп
тел. пържола	steak	стейк
по-крехка	rare	рѐъ
по-препечена	well done	уѐл дан
бифтек	beefsteak	бѝ:фстейк
сарми със зелев лист	stuffed cabbage	стафт кæ̀бидж
пълнени чушки	stuffed peppers	стафт пѐпъз
кюфтета	meat balls	ми:т бо:лз
пиле	**chicken**	**чѝкън**
печено пиле	roasted / grilled chicken	ро̀устид / грилд чѝкън
пилешки гърди	chicken breast	чѝкън брест

пилешко бутче	chicken drumstick	чѝкън дра̀мстик
пилешка пържола	chicken fillet	чѝкън фѝлит
дивеч	**game**	**гейм**
яребица	grouse	гра̀ус
фазан	pheasant	фѐзънт
дива патица	wild duck	уа̀йлд дак
заек	hare	хѐъ
сърна	deer, venison	дѝъ, вѐнзън
глиган	boar	бо:

▶ Постни ястия — Vegetable Dishes — Вѐджтъбъл дѝшиз ◀

фасул яхния	dried beans	дра̀йд би:нз
зелен фасул яхния	string beans	стринг би:нз
леща	lentils	лѐнтилз
гъби	mushrooms	ма̀шру:мз
грах	peas	пи:з
зеле	cabbage	кæ̀бидж
броколи	broccoli	брòкъли
гювеч	hotch-potch	хоч поч

► **Предястия**	**Starters**	**Стà:тъз** ◄
омлет ...	... omelette	... òмлит
със сирене	cheese	чи:з
яйца на очи	fried eggs	фрàйд егз
бъркани яйца	scrambled eggs	скрæ̀мбълд егз
пържени картофи	French fries, chips	фрèнч фрайз, чипс
наденица	sausage	сò:сидж
луканка, суджук	flat sausage	флæт сò:сидж
филе	fillet	фѝлит
хайвер	caviar	кæ̀виа:
език	tongue	танг
... мозък	... brain	... брейн
телешки	calf's	ка:фс
овчи	sheep's	ши:пс
зеленчуци	**vegetables**	**вèджитъбълз**
домати	tomatoes	тъмà:тоуз
краставици	cucumbers	кю̀:камбъз
маруля	lettuce	лèтис
репички	radishes	рæ̀дишиз

моркови	carrots	кæрътс
маслини	olives	òливз
целина	celery	сèлъри
магданоз	parsley	пà:сли
кромид	onions	àниънз
чесън	garlic	гà:лик
спанак	spinach	спѝнич
тиквички	marrows	мæроуз
карфиол	cauliflower	кòлифлауъ
броколи	broccoli	брòкъли
царевица	sweet corn	суѝ:т ко:н
брюкселско зеле	Brussels sprouts	бр<u>à</u>сълз спрàутс
аспержи	asparagus	ъспæрългъс
цвекло	beetroot	бѝ:тру:т
пащърнак	parsnip	пà:снип

► Салати — Salads — Сæлъдз ◄

мешана	mixed	микст
зеленчукова	vegetable	вèджтъбъл
плодова	fruit	фру:т

▶ Подправки	Spices	Спàйсиз ◀
сол	salt	со:лт
оцет	vinegar	вùнигъ
олио	vegetable oil	вèджитъбъл ойл
зехтин	olive oil	òлив ойл
червен пипер	paprika	пàприка
черен пипер	pepper	пèпъ
кетчуп	ketchup	кèчап
захар	sugar	шỳгъ
горчица	mustard	мàстъд
майонеза	mayonnaise	мейънèйз
целина	celery	сèлъри
мащерка	(wild) thyme	(уàйлд) тайм
алкохолни напитки	**strong drinks**	**стронг дринкс**
уиски ...	whisky...	уùски...
с лед	on the rocks	он дъ рокс
със сода	and soda	æнд сòудъ
водка	vodka	вòдка
коняк	cognac	кòняк
бренди	brandy	брæнди

гроздова ракия	grape brandy	грейп брæнди
джин	gin	джин
с тоник	and tonic	æнд тòник
вермут	vermouth	вѐ:мът
коктейл	cocktail	кòктейл
бира	beer	бѝъ
малка халба бира	half a pint of beer	ха:ф ъ пайнт ъв бѝъ
голяма халба бира	a pint of beer	ъ пайнт ъв бѝъ
наливна бира	beer on draught	бѝъ он дра:фт
бутилка бира	a bottle of beer	ъ бòтъл ъв бѝъ
... питие	... drink	... дринк
малко	a small	ъ смо:л
голямо	a double	ъ дàбъл
безалкохолни	**soft drinks**	**софт дринкс**
сода	soda - water	сòудъ уòтъ
обикновена минерална вода	still mineral water	стил мѝнърл уò:тъ
газирана	sparkling	спà:клинг
тоник	tonic	тòник
сок	fruit juice	фру:т джу:с
прясно изстискан сок	fresh squeezed juice	фреш скуѝ:зд джу:с
доматен сок	tomato juice	томàтоу джу:с

Вина	Wines	Уàйнз
Какво вино предпочитате?	What wine do you prefer?	Уòт уàйн ду: ю: прифъ?
Какви вина имате?	What sorts of wine have you got?	Уòт со:тс ъв уàйн хæв ю: гот?
Харесва ми ... вино.	I like… wine.	Ай лайк … уàйн.
Нека поръчаме бутилка ... вино.	Let's have a bottle of ... wine.	Летс хæв ъ бòтъл ъв ... уàйн.
бяло	white	уàйт
червено	red	ред
сухо	dry	драй
полусухо	medium dry	мѝ:диъм драй
десертно	sweet	суѝ:т
розе	rosè, pink	рòузей, пинк
шампанско	champagne	шæмпèйн
Благодаря, ...	…, thank you.	… , *т*æнк ю:
не пия вино	I don't drink wine	Ай дòунт дринк уàйн
ще пийна само малко	I'll have just a little	Айл хæв джаст ъ лѝтъл
Искате ли още малко?	Would you have some more…?	У:д ю: хæв сам мо:?

Десерти	Desserts	Дизъ̀:тс
Какви десерти имате?	What have you got for dessert?	Уòт хæв ю гот фо: дизъ̀:тс?
..., моля!	..., please!	..., пли:з!
Сладолед	Ice cream	Айс кри:м
Плодова салата	Fruit salad	Фру:т сæ̀лъд
Сладкиш - пудинг	Pudding	Пу̀дин[г]
Сладкиш - пай	Pie	Пай

Вечеря	*Dinner*	*Дѝнъ*
лека вечеря	supper	са̀пъ
Къде ще вечеряме?	Where shall we go for dinner?	Уèъ шæл уй: гòу фо: дѝнъ?
Какво ще поръчаме за вечеря?	What shall we order for dinner?	Уòт шæл уй: ò:дъ фо: дѝнъ?
Благодаря ти (ви) за чудесната вечер!	Thank you for the wonderful evening!	*т*æнк ю: фо: *д*ъ уа̀ндъфул ѝ:внин[г]!

➡ Искате ли да отидем...?	Would you like to come ... with me?	Уу̀д ю лайк то кам... уйт ми?
в някой бар	to a pub	ту ъ паб
в някой нощен клуб	to a night club	ту ъ на̀йт клаб
да пием кафе	to have some coffee	ту хæв сам ко̀фи
да пием бира	to have some beer	ту хæв сам бйъ
да хапнем по една пица	to have a pizza	ту хæв ъ пѝ:цъ
да потанцуваме	to a disco	ту ъ дѝскоу
да се забавляваме	somewhere and have fun	са̀муеъ æнд хæв фан
Искам да отида на нощен клуб.	I'd like to go to a nightclub.	Айд лайк ту гоу ту ъ найтклаб.
Искам да отида на танци.	I'd like to go dancing.	Айд лайк ту гоу да̀:нсинг.
Обичате ли да танцувате?	Do you like dancing?	Ду: ю: лайк да̀:нсинг?
Да, обичам да танцувам.	Yes, I do.	Йес, ай ду:.
Искате ли да потанцуваме?	May I have the dance?	Мей ай хæв ђъ да:нс?

Този ... е много добър,-а.	This … is very good.	*д*ис… из вѐри гуд.
певец,-ица	singer	сѝнгъ
танцьор,-ка	dancer	дà:нсъ
Оркестърът е изключителен!	The band is superb!	*д*ъ бæнд из сю:пъб!
Как сте?	How are you feeling?	Хау а: ю фѝ:лингъ?
Благодаря, добре.	I am fine, thank you.	Ай ем файн, *т*енк ю
Прекарахме една незабравима вечер (нощ).	We've had an unforgettable evening(night).	Уй:в хæд ън àнфъгѐтъбъл ѝ:внинг(найт).
Забавлявахме се много.	We had a lot of fun.	Уй: хæд ъ лот ъв фан.

Театър, музика, кино	Theatre, music, cinema	тѝътъ, мю:зик, сѝнъмъ
Как прекарвате вечерите тук?	What do you usually do in the evenings here?	Уо̀т ду ю: ю̀:жуъли ду ин ди ѝ:внинг з хѝъ?
Има ли наблизо ...?	Is there ... nearby?	Из дѐъ ... нѝъбай?
кино	a cinema	ъ сѝнъмъ
театър	a theatre	ъ тѝътъ
Може ли да ми препоръчате нещо за деца?	Can you recommend me something for children?	Кæн ю: рекъмѐнд ми: са̀мтинг фо: чѝлдрън?
Искаме да видим ...	I would like to see ...	Ай у:д лайк ту си: ...
пиеса от Шекспир	a Shakespeare play	ъ шѐйкспиъ плей
постановка на	a performance	ъ пъфо̀:мънс
Кралския театър	at the Royal Theatre	æт дъ ро̀йъл тѝътъ
мюзикъл	a musical	ъ мю̀:зикъл
Харесва ли ти (ви)...?	Do you like...?	Ду: ю: лайк ...?
пиесата	the play	дъ плей
музиката	music	мю:зик

операта	the opera	ди òпъръ
оперетата	the musical comedy	дъ мю̀:зикъл кòмиди
балетът	the ballet	дъ бǽлей
концертът	the concert	дъ кòнсът
... ми харесва много.	I like ... very much.	Ай лайк ... вѐри мач.
Коя музика предпочитате?	What sort of music do you like?	Уòт со:т ъв мю̀:зик ду: ю: лайк?
Предпочитам ...	I like…	Ай лайк…
класическа музика	classical music	клǽсикъл мю̀:зик
симфонична музика	symphonic music	симфòник мю̀:зик
народна музика	country(folk) music	кàнтри(фòук) мю̀:зик
камерна музика	chamber music	чѐймбъ мю̀:зик
Харесва ми също ...	I (we) also like ... I am fond of..., as well.	Ай (уй) òлсоу лайк... Ай ем фонд ъф..., ес уел.
джаза	jazz	джæз
рока	rock	рок
рок балади	rock ballads	рок бǽлъдз
Какво играят в театъра?	What's on at the theatre?	Уòтс он æт дъ тѝътъ?
Играе се ...	It's ...	Итс ...
една комедия	a comedy	ъ кòмиди
една трагедия	a tragedy	ъ трǽджиди

една драма	a drama	ъ дра̀:мъ
една историческа пиеса	a historical play	ъ хисто̀рикъл плей
Кой играе в главната роля?	Who plays the leading part?	Ху: плейз gъ лѝ:динг па̀:т?
Ще играе ли ...?	Will ... be playing?	Уѝл...би плѐйинг?
Ще пее ли ...?	Will ... be singing?	Уѝл...би сѝнгинг?
... изпълнява главната роля.	... plays the leading part.	... плейз gъ лѝ:динг па:т.
Кой играе ролята на ...?	Who plays the part of...?	Ху: плейз gъ па:т ъв...?
В кои други спектакли играе този актьор (тази актриса)?	What other performances does this actor(actress) take part in?	Уо̀т а̀gъ пъфо̀:мънсиз даз gис ǽктъ(ǽктрис) тѐйк па:т ин?
Кой е ...?	Who's ...?	Ху:з ...?
авторът на пиесата	the playwright	gъ плѐйрайт
режисьорът на спектакъла	the director	gъ дирѐктъ
диригентът	the conductor	gъ кънда̀ктъ

Имате ли билети за ...?	Have you got any tickets for...?	Хѐв ю гот ѐни тѝкитс фо:?
Дайте ми, моля, два билета и една програма.	I'd like two tickets and a programme, please.	Айд лàйк ту: тѝкитс æнд ъ прòуграм, пли:з.
Колко струва билетът?	How much is one ticket?	Хàу м<u>а</u>ч из у<u>à</u>н тѝкит?
Искам четири места едно до друго.	I'd like four seats together, please.	Айд лàйк фо: си:тс тъгѐ*д*ъ:, пли:з.
Имаме само единични места.	There are only single seats.	*д*еъ а: òунли сѝнгъл си:тс.
Всички билети са продадени.	All the tickets are sold out.	Ол *д*ъ тѝкитс а: солд àут.
Мога ли да видя билетите ви, моля?	May I see your tickets, please?	Мей ай си: йò: тѝкитс, пли:з?
Гардеробът е насам.	The cloakroom is this way.	*д*ъ клòукру:м из *д*ис уѐй.
Къде е ..., моля?	Where's ..., please?	Уѐъз ... , пли:з?
дамската тоалетна	the ladies room	*д*ъ лѐйдиз ру:м
мъжката тоалетна	the men's room	*д*ъ менз ру:м
пушалнята	the smoking room	*д*ъ смòукинг ру:м
бюфетът	the buffet	*д*ъ бỳфей
гримьорната	the dressing room	*д*ъ дрѐсинг ру:м

Местата ни са...	Our seats are...	àуъ си:тс а:...
на трети ред	in the third row	ин дъ тъ:д ρòу
на предните редове	in the stalls	ин дъ сто:лз
на крайните редове	in the pit	ин дъ пит
на балкона	on the balcony	он дъ бæ̀лкъни
на първия балкон	in the dress circle	ин дъ дрес съ:кьл
на втория балкон	in the upper circle	ин дъ àпъ съ:кьл
на третия балкон	in the gallery	ин дъ гæ̀лъри
в ложата	in the box	ин дъ бокс
В колко часа започва (свършва) ...?	What time does this ... start (finish)?	Уòт тайм даз дис ... ста:т (фѝниш)?
спектакълът	performance	пъфò:мънс
пиесата	play	плей
концертът	concert	кòнсъ:т
филмът	film	филм
Не виждам оттук добре	I can't see ... well from here.	Ай кà:нт си: ... уèл фром хйъ.
сцената	the stage	дъ стейдж
екрана	the screen	дъ скри:н
Колко ще продължи антракта?	How long is the interval?	Хàу лонг из ди интъ̀:вьл?

Какво мислиш,-ите за спектакъла?	What do you think of the performance?	Уòт ду ю *т*инк ъв дъ пъ:фò:мънс?
Кога започва второто действие?	When does the second act start?	Уèн даз *д*ъ сèкънд æкт стà:т?
Хареса ли ти (ви) ...?	Did you enjoy ...?	Дид ю: инджòи … ?
шоуто	the show	*д*ъ шòу
концертът	the concert	*д*ъ кòнсът
Да, беше ...	Yes, it was ...	Йес, ит уъз …
отлично	excellent	èксълънт
страхотно	terrific	търѝфик
изключително	perfect	пъ:фект
Не, беше ...	No, it was ...	Нòу, ит уъз …
скучно	boring	бò:рингг
ужасно	terrible	тèрибъл
Хайде да отидем на кино!	Let's go to the cinema!	Летс гоу ту *д*ъ сѝнемъ!
Какъв е филмът?	What kind of film is it?	Уот кайнд ъв филм из ит?
комедия	a comedy	ъ кòмеди
романтичен	a romance	ъ роумæ̀нс
научно-фантастичен	a science-fiction	ъ сàйънс фѝкшън
криминален	a crime	ъ крайм

Искам да гледам	I'd like to see	Айд лайк ту си: ... .
трилър	a thriller	ъ *трѝлъ:*
психотрилър	a suspense	ъ сàспенс
драма	a drama	ъ дрǽмъ
уестърн	a western	уèстъ:н
Филмът на английски ли е?	Is the film in English?	Из *дъ* филм ин ѝнглиш?
Дублиран ли е?	Is it dubbed?	Из ит дàбд?
Със субтитри на английски ли е?	Is it subtitled in English?	Из ит сàбтайтълд ин ѝнглиш?
Какво дават в киното?	What's on at the cinema?	Уòтс он æт *дъ* сѝнемъ?
Кога започва последната прожекция?	When does the last performance begin?	Уен даз *дъ* ла:ст пъфò:мæнс бигѝн?
Колко е дълга?	How long does it last?	Хау лонг даз ит ла:ст?
Кога свършва филма?	When does the film end?	Уен даз *дъ* филм енд?
Колко струва място на балкона?	How much is it on the balcony?	Хау мач из ит он *дъ* бà/елкони?
Искам места ...	I want seats ...	Ай уòнт си:тс ...
отпред	in the front	ин *дъ* фронт
някъде в средата	somewhere in the middle	самуеъ ин *дъ* мѝдъл
не съвсем отзад	not too far back	нот ту: фа: бæк
Филмът бе чудесен.	It was a wonderful film.	Ит уаз ъ уàндъ:фул филм.

режисьор	director	дирèктъ
драматург	playwright	плèйрайт
писател, автор	writer, author	рàйтъ, ò:тъ
композитор	composer	къмпòузъ
сюжет	plot	плот
роля	part, role	па:т, рòул
ария	aria	à:риъ
певец,-ица	singer	сѝнгъ
глас	voice	войс
сцена	stage	стейдж
сцена *(при игра)*	scene	си:н
танц	dance	да:нс
турне	tour	тỳ:ъ
ансамбъл, трупа	company	кàмпъни
афиш	poster	пòустъ
аплодирам	applaud	ъплò:д
аплодисменти	applause	аплò:з
зрител	spectator	спектèйтъ

комик	comedian	къмѝ:диън
балерина	ballerina	бæлърѝ:нъ
бис	curtain call	къ:тън ко:л
дует	duet	дюѐт
музикант	musician, player	мю:зѝшън (плѐйъ)
игрален филм	feature film	фѝ:тчъ филм
анимационен филм	cartoon	ка:тỳ:н
поп група	pop group	поп гру:п
премиера	first night performance	фъ:ст найт пъфò:мънс
продуцент	producer	пръдю̀:съ
репертоар	repertoire	рѐпътуа:
сценарий	script	скрипт

Музеи. Забележителности	*Museums. Sightseeing*	*Мю:зѝъмз. Са̀итси:нг*
Къде се намира...?	Where is ..., please?	Уѐъ из ..., пли:з?
катедралата "Свети Павел"	St. Paul's Cathedral	Сент По:лз Къ*т*ѝдрълл
Уестминстърското абатство	Westminster Abbey	Уестмѝнстъ ǽби
площад Трафалгар с колоната на адмирал Нелсън	Trafalgar Square with Admiral Nelson's Column	Тръфǽлгъ Скуѐъ уѝ*д* ǽдмиръл Нѐлсънз Кòлъм
Бъкингамският дворец	Buckingham Palace	Бъкингъм Пǽлис
Лондонската кула	the Tower of London	*д*ъ Тàуъ ъв Ла̀ндън
Националната галерия	the National Gallery	*д*ъ Нǽшънъл Гǽлъри
Британският музей	the British Museum	*д*ъ Брѝтиш Мю:зѝъм

МУЗЕИ

Несъмнено най-голям от всички е **Британският музей (The British Museum)** с несравнимите си египетска, месопотамска, гръцка и римска колекции. Главният лондонски музеен район обаче е **Kensington**, непосредствено на север от метростанция South Kensington; особено ви препоръчваме брилянтния **Victoria & Albert Museum** (декоративно изкуство) и обновените **Музей на науката** и **Природонаучния музей** (рисунки на динозаври и интерактивни експозиции).

Британският музей
(www.thebritishmuseum.ac.uk), Great Russell St WC1 (метро: Russell Sq), разполага с най-богатата в света колекция от антични артефакти. Той е отворен от 10 часа сутринта до 5 часа следобед от понеделник до събота. В неделя входът е свободен.

Victoria & Albert Museum
(www.vam.ac.uk), Cromwell Rd SW7 (метро: South Kensington), притежава най-богатата в света колекция декоративно изкуство, в това число дрехи от различни епохи. Той е отворен от 10 часа сутринта до 5.45 часа следобед от вторник до неделя и от обяд до 5.45 часа следобед в понеделник, а входът е £5. Във V&A се намира най-доброто музейно кафене в Kensington.

Природонаучният музей (www.nhm.ac.uk), Cromwell Rd SW7 (метро: South Kensington), обхваща чудесните Галерии на живота и земята, които са посветени съответно на естествената история и геологията. Тук всеки септември се провежда и London Fashion Week. Отворен е от понеделник до събота от 10 часа сутринта до 5.50 часа следобед, а входната такса е £6/3.

Музеят на науката (www.sciencemuseum.org.uk) Exhibition Rd SW7 (метро: South Kensington) е напълно преобразен и разполага с достатъчно стари влакове (сред тях "Puffing Billy" – "пухтящият Били") и коли, за да развлича истински децата. Отворен е ежедневно от 10 часа сутринта до 6 часа вечерта. Входът е £5.95/3.20.

Музеят на Лондон, 150 London Wall EC2 (метро: St Paul's), представя историята на Лондон от римско време до бунтовете срещу данъка на глава от населението през 90-те години на настоящия век. Той е отворен от 10 часа сутринта до 6 часа вечерта от вторник до събота и от обяд до 6 часа вечерта в неделя, а входът е £4.

Имперският военен музей, Lambeth Rd SE1 (метро: Lambeth North), предлага удивителни възстановки (най-интересна е "Blitz Experience"). Работното му време е от 10 часа сутринта до 6 часа вечерта всеки ден, а входната такса £4.70.

Занимателният **Музей на подвижния образ** (Museum of the Moving Image;

MOMI), South Bank Centre SE1 (метро: Embankment, а после пресечете пешеходния и железопътен мост над Темза), проследява историята на киното и телевизията с интерактивни експонати. Може да го посетите ежедневно от 10 часа сутринта до 6 часа вечерта срещу £6.25.

ГАЛЕРИИ

В **Националната галерия** (www.nationalgallery.org.uk), Trafalgar Square (метро: Charing Cross), са събрани шедьоври от всички водещи европейски школи от XIII до XX век. Работното ѝ време е от 10 часа сутринта до 6 часа вечерта от понеделник до събота и от 2 часа следобед до 6 часа вечерта в неделя, а входът все още е свободен. Следете също и за безплатни обиколки с екскурзовод.

Галерията на Института Курто (Courtauld Institute Gallery), Somerset House, Strand (метро: Temple), представя възхитителна колекция постимпресионисти (Сезан, Гоген, Ван Гог). Тя е отворена от 10 часа сутринта до 6 часа вечерта от понеделник до събота и от 2 часа следобед до 6 часа вечерта в неделя, а входът е £3.

Галерията Тейт, Millbank SW1 (метро: Pimlico), се съсредоточава върху историята на британската живопис и преди всичко Търнър, както и върху световната модерна живопис. Може да я посетите безплатно от 10 часа сутринта до 5.50 часа следобед от понеделник до събота и от 2 до 5.50 часа следобед в неделя.

Кои ... могат да се видят днес в Лондон?	What ... can we see today in London?	Уòт … кæн уѝ си: тъдèй ин Лàндън?
изложби	exhibitions	екзибѝшънз
панаири	fairs	фèъз
Има ли тук някакви местни ...?	Are there any local ...?	А: *д*èъ èни лòукъл …?
фестивали	festivals	фèстъвълз
изложения	shows	шòуз
Искам да разгледам ...	I'd like to see ...	Айд лайк ту си: … .
художествените галерии	the art galleries	*д*и а:т гæлърис
замъка	the castle	*д*ъ кà:съл
битпазара	the flea market	*д*ъ фли: мà:кит
историческите забележителности	the historic sights	*д*ъ хистòрик сайтс
кралския дворец	the royal palace.	*д*ъ рòйъл пæлис

Колко струва входният билет?	How much is the admission?	Хàу мач из *д*и ъдмѝшън?
вход свободен	free admission	фри: ъдмѝшън

Мога ли да фотографирам?	Is taking photographs allowed?	Из тèйкинг фòутъ-гра:фс ълàуд?
Бихте ли ни снимали?	Would you take our picture?	Уỳд ю: тейк àуъ пѝкчъ:?
Интересува ме...	I'm interested in...	Айм ѝнтристид ин ...
живописта	painting	пèйнтинг
скулптурата	sculpture	скàлпчъ
архитектурата	architecture	à:китекчъ
съвременното изкуство	modern art	мòдън а:т

Харесват ми ...	I like ...	Ай лайк ...
античните майстори	the ancient masters	ди èйншънт мà:стъз
художниците от Ренесанса	the Renaissance painters	дъ рънèйсънс пèйнтъз
импресионистите	the impressionists	ди импрèшънистс
модернистите	the modernists	дъ мòдънистс
абстракционистите	the abstractionists	ди ъбстр æкшънистс
Кои художници	Which painters	Уйч пèйнтъз
Кои живописни школи	Which Schools of Art	Уйч ску:лз ъв а:т
Кои шедьоври	Which masterpieces	Уйч мà:стъпи:сиз
... са представени в	...are represented in	... а: рèпризèнтид ин
тази галерия (музей)?	this gallery (museum)?	дис г æлъри(мю:зйъм)?
Кой е рисувал ...?	Who painted ...?	Ху: пèйнтид ... ?
тази картина	this painting	дис пèйнтинг
този портрет	this portrait	дис пò:трит
този пейзаж	this landscape	дис л æндскейп
Кой е направил ...	Who made ...?	Ху: мейд ...?
тази скулптура	this sculpture	дис скàлпчъ
тази статуя	this statue	дис ст æтю:

*Посещението на музеите и забележителностите във Великобритания обикновено става срещу входен билет около 10 лири, но много от тях предлагат и свободен вход (**free admission**) през определени дни на седмицата или в определено време на деня.*

Ето някои от тях:

*- **The British Museum** - неделя следобед, до 18 часа*

*- **Victoria & Albert Museum** - ежедневно след 16,30 часа*

*- **Imperial War Museum** - ежедневно от 16,30 до 18 часа*

*- **Science Museum** - ежедневно след 16,30*

*Ако възнамерявате да разглеждате много забележителности, туристическите бюра продават картата **London White Card**, с която може да посетите безплатно 15 музея и галерии. Цената ѝ е £15 за три дни или £25 за седем дни. Семейните карти, предлагащи безплатен вход за двама възрастни и четири деца, струват £30 и £50.*

*Включени са музеите: **Apsley House (Wellington Museum), Barbican Art Gallery, Courtauld, Музеят на дизайна, Hayward Gallery, Имперският военен музей, Лондонският транспортен музей, Музеят на Лондон, Музеят на подвижния образ, Националният морски музей (със Старата кралска обсерватория и Queen's House), Природонаучният музей, Кралската академия, Музеят на науката, Театралният музей и Victoria & Albert Museum.***

Тази творба ... ли е?	Is this work...?	Из дис уъ:к ...?
оригинал	original	ърѝджънъл
копие	a copy	ъ кòпи

музей	museum	мю:зѝъм
екскурзовод,-ка	guide	гайд
храм	temple	тèмпъл
манастир	monastery	мòнъстъри
кула	tower	тàуъ
замък	castle	кà:съл
дворец	palace	пǽлис
паметник	monument	мòнюмънт
статуя	statue	стǽтю:
галерия	gallery	гǽлъри
изложба	exhibition	ексибѝшън
художник	painter	пèйнтъ
картина	painting, picture	пèйнтинг, пѝкчъ
скулптура	sculpture	скàлпчъ
скулптор	sculptor	скàлптъ

ЦЕНТЪРЪТ НА ЛОНДОН *лесно ще изследвате пеша. Обиколката, която ще ви предложим, може да осъществите в рамките на ден, но няма да имате време да разгледате подробно отделните забележителности.*

Започнете с **катедралата Св. Павел (St Paul),** *завършения през 1710 година шедьовър на Кристофър Рен. Входът е £7.50, ако искате да видите галериите (и да се насладите на прекрасна панорама от Лондон), и £4, ако ви интересуват единствено катедралата и криптата. Хванете метрото от метростанция St Paul's до* **Covent Garden** *(в западна посока по централната линия до Holborn и след това пак в западна посока по линията за* **Piccadilly***).*

Площадът пред **Covent Garden***, някогашния лондонски плодов и зеленчуков пазар, е превърнат в оживена туристическа атракция. Това е едно от малкото места в Лондон, предадено изцяло в ръцете на пешеходците, където може да слушате уличните музиканти срещу няколко монети.*

Върнете се на метростанцията и завийте вляво по **Long Acre.** *Продължете през* **Charing Cross Rd** *до* **Leicester Square** *с кината и скъпите хранителни магазини.*

Продължете по **Coventry St** *покрай* **Trocadero** *и* **Rock Circus***, докато стиг-*

нете до **Piccadilly Circus**, където се намира **Tower Records**, по всеобщо признание най-добрият лондонски музикален магазин. Оттам тръгнете по **Shaftesbury Ave**. Тази осеяна с театри артерия върви до **Soho**, където работят безброй ресторанти. **Regent St** се отбива от северозападния край.

Продължете на запад по **Piccadilly** до Кралската академия на изкуствата и **St James's Church**. Отскочете до вечната **Burlington Arcade** непосредствено след академията и вижте как пазаруват богатите хора.

Върнете се на **Piccadilly** и продължете, докато вляво видите **St James's St**. Тя отвежда до **St James's Palace**, кралския дворец от 1660 до 1837 година, когато той е счетен за недостатъчно внушителен.

Завийте зад източната му страна и ще стигнете до **Pall Mall**.

Trafalgar Square е на изток, а **Бъкингамският дворец** - на запад. Дворецът е отворен за посещения ежедневно от 9.30 часа сутринта до 4.30 часа следобед от началото на август до началото на октомври. Входът е £9.50. Билети се продават от каса на спирката на метрото в Green Park, но може да резервирате и с кредитна карта ✆ 0171-321 2233. От 3 април до 3 август смяната на караула пред Бъкингамския дворец става ежедневно в 11.30 часа сутринта, а от август до април в 11.30 часа сутринта през ден. Най-доброто място за наблюдение е край портите на Бъкингамския дворец, но тълпите са невероятни.

Поемете обратно към **St James's Park**, най-красивия парк в Лондон, и следвайте езерото до източния му край. Завийте вдясно по **Horse Guards Rd**. Той минава покрай Военните зали (Cabinet War Rooms; £4.40), където ще видите изключително изложение на тема тъмната епоха на Втората световна война.

Продължете по **Horse Guards Rd** и завийте вляво по **Great George St**, която ще ви изведе до красивото **Уестминстърско абатство**, сградата на парламента и **Westminster Bridge**.

Сградата на парламента (The House of Parlament) и часовниковата кула (всъщност камбаната ѝ), **Big Ben**, са строени през XIX век в псевдо-средновековен стил.

Отдалечавайки се от **Westminster Bridge**, завийте вдясно по **Parliament St**, която преминава в **Whitehall**. В обикновената наглед сграда на **№ 10 Downing St** вляво живее министър-председателят със семейството си. По-нататък вдясно се намира проектираната от Иниго Джоунс **Banqueting House**, пред която е обезглавен Чарлз I. Продължете покрай конния караул **(Horse Guards)**, където по-спокойно може да наблюдавате смяната на караула в 11 часа сутринта от понеделник до събота и в 10 часа сутринта в неделя.

Накрая ще стигнете до **Trafalgar Square** с **Нелсъновата колона** и до безплатните **Национална галерия** и **Национална портретна галерия**, които са от северната страна.

Спорт	Sports	Спо:тс
Къде се намира..., моля?	Where's ..., please?	Уѐъз ..., пли:з?
стадионът	the stadium	гъ стѐйдиъм
спортната зала	the gym hall	гъ джѝм хо:л
гимнастическият салон	the gym	гъ джим
пистата	track, the speedway	тræк, гъ спѝ:дуей
басейнът	the swimming pool	гъ суйминг пу:л
спортният клуб	the sports club	гъ спо̀:тс клаб
тенискортът	the tennis court	гъ тѐнис ко:т
пресцентърът	the press center	гъ прѐс сѐнтъ
Хайде да отидем до стадиона!	Let's go to the sports stadium!	Летс гоу ту дъ спо:тс стѐйдиъм!
На мен ми харесва ...	I like ...	Ай лайк ...
футболът	football	фу̀тбо:л
гимнастиката	gymnastics	джимна̀стикс
баскетболът	basketball	ба̀:скитбо:л
автомобилизмът	motoring	мо̀утъринг

Бихме искали да отидем на футболен мач.	We would like to go to a football match.	Уи: уу̀д лайк ту гоу ту ъ фу̀тбо:л мæч.
Кой играе?	Who's playing?	Хуз плейинг?
Кои са отборите?	What are the teams?	Уот а: дъ ти:мз?
Спортувате ли нещо?	Do you train/practice any sports?	Ду ю трѐйн/прæ̀ктиз ѐни спо:тс?
Да, ...	Yes, I ...	Йес, ай ...
играя тенис	play tennis	плей тѐнис
играя баскетбол	play basketball	плей бà:скитбо:л
плувам	go swimming	гòу суйминг
тренирам карате	practise karate	прæ̀ктиз кърà:ти
карам ски	ski	ски:
ходя на уроци по езда	take riding lessons	тѐйк рàйдинг лѐсънз
посещавам фитнес-център	go to the fitness center	гòу ту: дъ фѝтнис сѐнтъ
Занимавам се с ...	I train/practice ...	Ай трѐйн/прæ̀ктис ...
лека атлетика	field-and-track events	филд енд трæк ивѐнтс
бокс	boxing	бòксинг
борба	wrestling	рѐслинг
джудо	judo	джу̀:доу
шах	chess	чес

Желаете ли да ... ?	Would you like to ...?	Уўд ю: лайк ту...?
играем тенис	play tennis	плей тенис
караме ски	go skiing	гоу ски:инг
Искам да наема ...	I'd like to rent ...	Айд лайк ту рент ...
ски оборудване	ski equipment.	ски: икуйпмънт
Има ли писти за ...?	Are there slopes for ...?	А: дѐъ слòупс фо: ...?
начинаещи	beginners	бигѝнъ:з
средно-напреднали	intermediates	ѝнтъ:мѝдиътс
експерти	experts	èкспъ:тс
Кога ще започне (ще завърши)...	When does ... begin (finish)?	Уѐн даз ... бигѝн (фѝниш)?
играта	the game	дъ гѐйм
състезанието	the race	дъ рѐйс
мачът	the match	дъ мæч
Кога (къде) е ...?	When (where) is...?	Уѐн (уѐъ) из...?
стартът / финалът	the start / the finish	дъ стà:т / дъ фѝниш
Привърженик съм на отбора на ...	I am a fan of ...	Айм ъ фæн ъв ...
домакините	the hosts	дъ хòустс
гостите	the guests	дъ гестс

Той (тя) е … шампион.	He(she) is a… champion.	Хи:(ши:) из ъ…чæ̀мпиън.
национален	national	нæ̀шънъл
европейски	European	юъръпѝън
световен	World	уъ:лд
олимпийски	an Olympic	ън ълѝмпик
Това е нов … рекорд.	This is a new … record.	*д*ис из ъ ню: … рѐко:д.
световен	World	уъ:лд
олимпийски	Olympic	ълѝмпик

Отборът ...	The team ...	*д*ъ ти:м ...
спечели / загуби	won / lost	уàн / лост
Какъв е резултатът?	What's the score?	Уòтс *д*ъ скò:?
Резултатът е ...	The score is...	*д*ъ скò: из ...
равен	a draw	ъ дрò:
2 на 0	two - nil	ту: нил
1 на 3	one - tree	уàн *т*ри:
в полза на гостите	for the guests	фо: *д*ъ гестс
в полза на домакините	for the hosts	фо: *д*ъ хòустс
в полза на противника	for the opponent	фо: *д*и ъпòунънт
за отбора на ...	for the team of ...	фо: *д*ъ тѝ:м ъв ...
Кой победи?	Who won?	Ху: уàн?
Кой загуби?	Who lost?	Ху: лост?
Кой взе ...?	Who won ...?	Ху: уàн ...?
първо място	the first place	*д*ъ фъ:ст плейс
второ място	the second place	*д*ъ сèкънд плейс
трето място	the third place	*д*ъ *т*ъ:д плейс
златен медал	a gold medal	ъ гòулд мèдъл
сребърен медал	a silver medal	ъ сѝлвъ мèдъл
бронзов медал	a bronze medal	ъ брòнз мèдъл
купата	the cup	*д*ъ кàп

футбол	**football** *(brit.)*, **socker** *(am.)*	**фу̀тбо:л** **со̀:къ**
футболист	football-player	фу̀тбо:лъ
капитан	captain	кǽптън
треньор	coach	ко̀уч
съдия	referee	рефърѝ:
защитник	defender	дифѐндъ
полузащитник	midfilder	мѝдфѝ:лдъ
нападател	forward, striker	фо̀:уъд, стра̀йкъ
вратар	goal-keeper	го̀ул кѝ:пъ
гол	goal	го̀ул
топка	ball	бо:л
удар	shot, kick	шот, кик
пас	pass	па:с
фал	free-kick	фрѝ:кик
засада	off-side	о̀ф сайд
ъглов удар	corner kick	ко̀:нъ кик
дузпа	penalty kick	пѐнълти кик

резултат	score	скò:
полувреме	half time	ха:ф тайм
тренировка	training, practice	трèйнинг, прæктис
тренирам	train	трèйн
треньор	trainer, coach	трèйнъ, кòуч
турнир	tournament	тỳ:намънт
състезател	competitor	кълпèтитъ
противник	opponent	опòунънт
отбор	team	ти:м
старт	start	ста:т
финал	final	фàйнъл
финал на първенство	play off	плей оф
стадион	stadium	стèйдиъм
игрище	field	фи:лд
шампионат	championship	чæмпиъншип
шампион	champion	чæмпиън
равенство	draw	дро:
жълт картон	yellow card	йèлоу ка:д
червен картон	red card	ред ка:д

... гимнастика	**gymnastics, gym**	**джимнæстикс, джим**
спортна	athletic gym	æтлѐтик джим
художествена	eurythmics	ю:рѝтмикс
висилка	horizontal bar	хоризòнтъл ба:
успоредка	parallel bars	пæ̀рълел ба:з
халки	rings	рингз

вдигане на тежести	**weight-lifting**	**уѐйт лѝфтинг**
тежкоатлет	weight-lifter	уѐйт лѝфтъ
щанга	barbell	бà:бел
изхвърляне	two hand clean and jerk	тỳ: хæнд клѝ:н æнд джъ:к
изтласкване	two hand snatch	тỳ: хæнд снæч

борба	**wrestling**	**рѐслинг**
свободна борба	free-style-wrestling	фри: стайл рѐслинг
класическа борба	Graeco-Roman style	грѐкоу рòумън стайл
борец	wrestler	рѐслъ
тепих	carpet	кà:пит

бокс	**boxing**	**бòксинг**
боксьор	boxer	бòксъ
боксови ръкавици	boxing gloves	бòксинг главз
ринг	ring	ринг
рунд	round	рàунд
точка	point	пòинт
нокдаун	knock down	нòк даун
нокаут	knock out	нòк аут
волейбол	**volley-ball**	**вòлибо:л**
волейболист	volley-baller	вòлибо:лъ
мрежа	volleyball net	вòлибо:л нет
игрище	volley-ball court	вòлибо:л ко:т
сервис	service	съ:вис
смяна на сервиса	change of the service	чèйндж ъв *д*ъ съ:вис
блок	block	блок
удар	shot	шот
баскетбол	**basketball**	**бà:скитбо:л**
баскетболист	basketball player	бà:скитбо:л плèйъ
кош	basket	бà:скит
пас	pass	па:с
точка	point	пòинт

тенис на корт	**tennis**	**тèнис**
играч	tennis player	тèнис плèйъ
ракета	(tennis)-racket	(тèнис) рæкит
мрежа	net	нет
сет	set	сет
гейм	game	гейм

алпинизъм	**alpinism, rock-climbing**	**æлпинизм, рок клàйминг**
планинарство	mountaineering	маунтинѝъринг

Лека атлетика	**Track and Field Events**	**Трæк æнд фи:лд ивèнтс**
бягане ...	running...	рàнинг...
на къси разстояния	sprint	спринт
на средни разстояния	a middle distance running	ъ мѝдъл дѝстънс рàнинг
на дълги разстояния	a long distance running	ъ лонг дѝстънс рàнинг
с препятствия	hurdles	хъ:дълз
маратон	a Marathon race	ъ мæрътън рейс

скок	... jump	... джамп
на дължина	a long jump	ъ лònг джамп
на височина	a high jump	ъ хàй джамп
троен	a hop-step-and-jump	ъ хоп степ æнд джамп
овчарски	pole-vault	пòул волт
тласкане на гюле	shot put	шот пут
хвърляне на диск	discus-throwing	дѝскъс трòуинг
хвърляне на копие	javelin-throwing	джæ̀влин трòуинг
хвърляне на чук	hammer-throwing	хæ̀мъ трòуинг
зимни спортове	winter sports	уйнтъ спо:тс
ски	skiing	ски:нг
слалом	slalom race	слà:лъм рейс
ски скок	ski jump	ски джамп
спускане	down sloping	дàун слòупинг
фигурно пързаляне	figure skating	фѝгъ скèйтинг
пързаляне с кънки	ice-skating	àйс-скèйтинг
пързаляне с шейни	sledging	слèджинг
плуване	swimming	суѝминг
кроул	crawl (-stroke)	крò:л (-стрòук)
бруст	breast-stroke	брèст стрòук
бътерфлай	butterfly	бàтъфлай

скокове във вода	diving	дàйвинг
гребане	rowing	рòуинг
водни ски	water-skiing	уò:тъ ски:нг
ветроходство	yachting	йò:тинг
яхта	yacht	йо:т
лодка	boat	бòут
сърфинг	surf-riding	съ:ф рàйдинг
сърф	surf-board	съ:ф бо:д
стрелба	shooting	шỳ:тинг
стрелба с пушка	rifle practice	рàйфъл прǽктис
стрелба с пистолет	pistol shooting	пѝстъл шỳ:тинг
стрелба с лък	archery	à:чъри
фехтовка	fencing	фѐнсинг
конен спорт	horse riding	хò:с рàйдинг
лов	hunting	хàнтинг
риболов	fishing	фѝшинг
петобой	pentathlon	пент ǽтлън
голф	golf	гòлф
хокей на лед	ice hockey	àйс хòки

Козметичен салон.	***Beauty Parlour.***	***Бю:ти пà:лъ.***
Фризьорски салон.	***Hairdresser's.***	***Хѐъдресъз.***
Бръснарница	***Barber's***	***Бà:бъз***
Бих искал,-а ...	I'd like ...	Айд лайк ...
прическа	a hair-style	ъ хѐъ стайл
фризура	a hair-do	ъ хѐъ ду:
къдрене	a perm	ъ пъ:м
изсушаване	a blow dry	ъ блòу драй
подстригване	a haircut	ъ хѐъкат
Сложете ми ...!	Fix it with ..., please!	Фикс ит уѝд ..., пли:з!
гел	some gell	сам гел
лак за коса	some hair-spray	сам хѐъ спрей
Едно подстригване, моля!	A hair-cut, please!	Ъ хѐъ кат, пли:з!
Как да ви подстрижа?	What haircut would you like?	Уòт хѐъкат уỳд ю: лайк?
Подстрижете ме ...!	Cut ... !	Кат ...!
късо	it short	ит шо:т
не много късо	it not too much (off)	ит нот ту: мач (оф)

Само я оформете.	I want just a trim.	Ай уòнт джаст ъ трим.
Вземете я още малко …	Take a little more off …	Тейк ъ лѝтъл мò: оф…
отстрани	the sides	gъ сайдз
отпред	the front	gъ фрàнт
отзад	the back	gъ бæк
отгоре	on top	он топ
➡ Обръснете ме, моля!	I'd like a shave, please.	Айд лайк ъ шейв, пли:з!

Искам ...	I'd like a …	Айд лайк ъ …
боядисване	colour	кàлъ
миене	shampoo	шæ̀мпу:
масаж на лице	facial	фѐйшъл
масаж на тяло	massage	мæсà:ж
маникюр	a manicure	мæ̀никюъ
педикюр	a pedicure	пѐдикюъ

Желаете ли …?	Would you like (some)…?	Уỳд ю: лайк (сам) …?
крем	face-cream	фѐйс кри:м
лак за коса	hair-spray	хѐъ спрей
Така е добре.	That's good.	gæтс гуд.
Достатъчно.	That will do.	gæт уѝл ду:.

... коса	...hair	...хèъ
черна	black	блæк
руса	fair	фèъ
къдрава	curly	къ:ли
кестенява	brown	бра̀ун
гъста	thick	*т*ик
рядка	thin	*т*ин
суха	dry	драй
мазна	greasy	грѝ:зи
нормална	normal	нò:мъл

бръснене	**shaving**	**шèйвинг**
бръсна се	shave	шейв
мустаци	moustache	мъстà:ш
брада	beard	бѝъд
бакембарди	whiskers	уѝскъз
самобръсначка	safety razor	сèйфти рèйзъ

електро самобръсначка	an electric shaver	ън илѐктрик шѐйвъ
ножче за бръснене	a razor blade	ъ рѐйзъ блейд
огледало	mirror	мѝръ
гребен	comb	кѐум
ножица	scissors	сѝзъз
четка	brush	браш
крем	cream	кри:м
боя за коса	hair dye	хѐъ дай
къна	henna	хѐнъ
лак за коса	hair spray	хѐъ спрей

Химическо чистене	*Dry Cleaner's*	*Драй клѝ:нъз*
Къде се намира ...?	Where's the ..., please?	Уѐъз ḍъ ..., пли:з?
пералнята	launderette	ло:ндрѐт
ателието за химическо чистене	dry cleaner's	дрàй клѝ:нъз
Искам да дам ...	I want to have ...	Ай уòнт ту хæв ...
тези дрехи	these clothes	ḍи:з клòуḍз
това бельо	this underwear	ḍис а̀ндъуеъ
тези панталони	these trousers	ḍи:з трàузъз
тези ризи	these shirts	ḍи:з шъ:тс
това сако	this jacket	ḍис джæ̀кит
този костюм	this suit	ḍис сю:т
тази рокля	this dress	ḍис дрес
за пране	washed	уòшт
за гладене	pressed (ironed)	прест (àйънд)
за химическо чистене	dry-cleaned	дрàй кли:нд

Дали може да се изчисти това петно?	Could this stain be removed?	Куд дис стѐйн би: риму̀:вд?
Желая да дам ... поръчка.	I want to make...order.	Ай уо̀нт ту мейк...ò:дъ.
обикновена	a regular	ъ рѐгюлъ
бърза	an express	ън икспрѐс
Колко струва...?	How much does the ... cost?	Хàу мач даз дъ ... кост?
прането	washing	уо̀шинг
гладенето	ironing	àйънинг
химическото чистене	dry cleaning	дрàй клѝ:нинг
Кога ще бъде готово?	When will my things be ready?	Уѐн уйл май тѝнгз би: рѐди?
Трябва ли да платя сега?	Do I have to pay now?	Ду: ай хæв ту пей нàу?

*Автоматична пералня в **ЛОНДОН** има на всяка главна улица. Средната цена за един барабан дрехи е £1.50 за изпиране и около £1 за изсушаване.*

пера	wash	уо̀ш
гладя	iron	àйън
чистя	clean	кли:н
петно	stain	стейн
изцапан	dirty	дъ:ти

На море	***At the seaside***	***æт gъ сѝ:сайд***
Колко дни е отпускът ви тази година?	How long is your leave this year?	Хàу лонг из йо: ли:в *g*ис йиъ?
Кога е отпускът ви тази година?	When are you taking your leave this year?	Уèн а: ю: тèйкинг йо: ли:в *g*ис йиъ?
Къде ще прекарате ваканцията си?	Where are you going on holiday?	Уèъ а: ю: гòуинг он хòлидей?
Тази година ще отида (ще отидем) ...	I'm (we're) going ...	Айм (уйъ) гòуинг ...
на море	to the seaside	ту *g*ъ сѝ:сайд
на планина	to the mountains	ту *g*ъ мàунтинз
на екскурзия в чужбина	on an excursion abroad	он ън икскъ:шън ъбрò:д
на минерални бани	to a spa	ту ъ спà:
със семейството ми	with my family	уѝ*g* май фæ̀мили
с приятеля,-ката ми	with my boy(girl) friend	уѝ*g* май бòй(гъ:л) френд
със приятели	with friends	уѝ*g* фрèндз

Имате ли свободни места?	Have you got any vacancies?	Хæв ю: гот èни вèйкънсиз?
Ще останем ...	We are staying ...	Уй а: стèинг...
само тази нощ	just overnight	джаст òувънайт
една седмица	for a week	фо: ъ уй:к
десет дни	for ten days	фо: тен дейз
Колко се плаща за една палатка за един ден?	How much do you charge a camping-site a day?	Хàу мач ду ю: ча:дж ъ кæмпинг сайт ъ дей?
Какво е разстоянието от хотела до плажа?	How far is it from the hotel to the beach?	Хау фа: из ит фром дъ хоутèл ту ðъ би:ч?
Къде в района е най-хубавият плаж?	Where's the best beach near here, please?	Уèъз ðъ бест би:ч нѝъ хѝъ, пли:з?
Как се стига дотам?	How can I get there?	Хàу кæн ай гет ðèъ?
Какъв е пясъкът на плажа?	What's the sand like on the beach?	Уòтс ðъ сæнд лайк он ðъ бѝ:ч?
Разрешено ли е къпането?	Is swimming allowed?	Из суйминг ълàуд?
Къпането е забранено.	No swimming!	Нòу суйминг!
Заплаща ли се ...?	Do I pay ...?	Ду: ай пей...?
престоят на плажа	a beach fee	ъ бѝ:ч фи:
ползването на душа	for the showers	фо: ðъ шàуъз

Разрешен ли е риболовът?	Is fishing allowed?	Из фѝшинг ъла̀уд?
Скалисто ли е дъното?	Is the bottom rocky?	Из дъ бо̀тъм ро̀ки?
Има ли ...?	Are there ...?	А: дѐъ ...?
подводни течения	any undercurrents	ѐни а̀ндъкарънтс
опасни скали	dangerous reefs	дѐйнджъръс ри:фс
медузи	jelly-fish	джѐли фиш
акули	sharks	ша:кс
много водорасли	a lot of sea-weeds	ъ лот ъв сѝ: уй:дз

Искам да наема ...	I'd like to rent ...	Айд лайк ту рѐнт...
лодка	a boat	ъ бѐут
водно колело	a pedal boat	ъ пѐдъл бѐут
водни ски	water skis	уѐтъ ски:з
шезлонг	a chaise-longue	ъ шѐйзлѐнг
чадър/слънчев чадър	an umbrella/a parasol	ън амбрѐлъ / ъ пæ̀ръсол

Не забравяй да си донесеш ...	Don't forget to bring ...	Донт фо:гѐт ту бринг ...
слънчеви очила	sunglasses	сѐнгла:сиз
слънцезащитен лосион	suntan lotion	сѐнтæн лѐушън
Трябва да купим няколко топки.	We need to buy some balls.	Уи ни:д ту бай сам бо:лз.
Къде е спасителят?	Where is the lifeguard?	Уѐъ из дъ лайфга:д?
Къде е басейнът?	Where is the pool?	Уѐъ из дъ пу:л?
Басейна на открито ли е?	Is the pool outdoors?	Из дъ пу:л ѐутдо:з?
Аз почернявам ...	I tan ...	Ай тæн ...
много бързо	very easily	вѐри ѝ:зили
не много бързо	not easily	нот ѝ:зили

Плувам много добре.	I swim very well.	Ай суйм вèри уèл.
Не умея да плувам.	I can't swim.	Ай ка:нт суйм.
Не искам да влизам много навътре.	I wouldn't go too far in.	Ай ỳдънт гòу ту: фа: ин.
Не влизай навътре!	Don't go too far in!	Дòунт гòу ту: фа: ин!
Какво ще кажеш,-ете...?	How about ...?	Хàу ъбàут...?
Хайде ... !	Let's go for ...!	Летс гоу фо: ... !
да поплуваме	a swim	ъ суйм
да се гмуркаме	a dive	ъ дайв
да се разходим с лодка	going boating	гòуинг бòутинг
да вземем душ	a shower	ъ шàуъ
Извикайте спасителя!	Get the lifeguard!	Гèт ðъ лàйфга:д!
Един човек се дави.	A man is drowning.	Ъ мæн из дрàунинг.
Внимание!	Caution!	Кò:шън!
Мъртво вълнение.	Ground swell.	Грàунд суèл.

море	sea	си:
остров	island	àйлънд
крайбрежие	shore	шòъ
морски бряг	coast	кòуст
плаж	beach	би:ч
пясък	sand	сæнд
пояс	life-belt	лàйф белт
спасителна жилетка	life-jacket	лàйф джæ̀кит
слънцезащитен лосион	sun tan lotion	сан тæн лòушън
слънчеви очила	sun glasses	сан глà:сиз
бански костюм	swimming costume	суйминг кòстю:м
шнорхел	snorkel	снòркъл
маска	diving mask	дàйвинг ма:ск
плавници	fins, flippers	финс, флѝпъ:з
неопренов костюм	neoprene, wetsuit	нѝ:ъпрѝ:н, уèтсю:т

СТОКИ И ПОКУПКИ

Магазини	*Shops*	*Шопс*
Супермаркет	Supermarket	Сю:пъма:кит
Хранителен магазин	Grocer's	Грòусъз
Кулинарен магазин	Culinary Produce	Калинъри пръ̀дю:с
	Takeaway Shop	Тѐйкъуей шоп
Консервирани храни	Tinned Goods	Тинд гудз
Дамски дрехи	Ladies' Clothes	Лѐйдиз клòуgз
Мъжки дрехи	Men's Clothes	Менз клòуgз
Детски дрехи	Children's Clothes	Чѝлдрънз клòуgз
Обувки	Shoes, Footwear	Шу:з, Фу̀туеъ
Платове	Fabrics (Textiles)	Фæ̀брикс (Тѐкстайлз)
Домашни потреби	Household Goods	Ха̀усхоулд гудз
Уреди за дома	Electrical Appliances	Илѐктрикъл ъпла̀йънсиз
Кожени изделия	Leather Goods	Лѐgъ: гудз
Пътни стоки	Travelling Accessories	Трæ̀влинг ъксѐсъриз
Електроника	Electronics	Илектрòникс
Електроматериали	Electrical Appliances	Илѐктрикъл ъпла̀йънсиз

Цветарски магазин	Florist's	Флòристс
Книжарница *(за книги)*	Bookshop	Бỳкшоп
Книжарница *(за канцеларски стоки)*	Stationery	Стѐйшънъри
Спортни стоки	Sports Goods (Ware)	Спо:тс гудз (Уѐъ)
Оптика	Optician	Оптѝшън
Стъкларски изделия	Cut Crystal and Glass Ware	Кат крѝстъл æнд гла:с уѐъ
Бижутерия	Jewellery	Джỳ:ълри
Часовници	Watches, Clocks	Уòчиз, Клокс
Парфюмерия	Perfumery	Пъ:фю̀:мъри
Козметика	Cosmetics	Козмѐтикс
Сватбен магазин	Wedding Boutique	Уѐдинг бу:тѝ:к
Антикварни стоки	Antiques	æ̀нти:кс
Галантерия.Кинкалерия	Haberdashery	Хæ̀бъдæшъри
Мебели	Furniture	Фъ:ничъ
Месарница	Butcher's	Бỳчъз
Хлебарница	Baker's	Бѐйкъз
Фурна	Bakery	Бѐйкъри
Плодове и зеленчуци	Greengrocer's	Грѝ:нгроусъз
Риба и рибни продукти	Fishmonger	Фѝшмангъ
Сладкарница	Confectionery	Кънфѐкшънъри

Пазар	Market	Mа̀:кит
Книги на втора ръка	Second-hand Books	Сѐкънд хæнд букс
Изложба-базар	Show-sale	Шо̀у сейл
Магазин за шапки	Hats, Millinery	Хæтс, Мѝлинъри
Конфекция	Ready-made Clothes	Рѐди мейд кло̀уgз
Дом на модата	House of Fashion	Ха̀ус ъв фæ̀шън
Нагледни пособия	Visual Aids	Вѝжуъл ейдз
Цигари	Tobacconist's	Тъб æ̀кънистс
Безистен	Arcade	а̀:кейд
Рибарски принадлежности	Fishing Tackle	Фѝшинг тæ̀къл
Плетиво и трикотаж	Knitted Goods	Нѝтид гудз
Продажба на кредит	Sale on credit	Сѐйл он крѐдит
Обща разпродажба	Clearance sale	Клѝърънс сейл
Поръчки и доставки вкъщи	Order-and-Delivery Service	О́:дъ æнд дилѝвъри съ:вис
Благотворителна съботна разпродажба	Jumble Sale	Джа̀мбъл сейл
Магазин с намаление	Discount shop	Дѝскаунт шоп
Магазин със стоки втора употреба	Second hand shop	Сѐкънд хæнд шоп

Ателиета	Ateliers	æтèлиейз
Бързи поправки	Everyday Repairs	èвридей рипèъз
Направи си сам	Do-it-yourself Atelier	Ду: ит йò:селф æтèлией
Бързо почистване	Fast Cleaning	Фà:ст клѝ:нинг
Часовникар	Watchmaker's	Уòчмейкъз
Обущар	Shoe Maker's	Шỳ:мейкъз
Експресно фото	Snapshots	Сн æ̀пшотс
Фото ателие	Photographer's	Фътòгръфъз
Ремонт телевизори	TV Repairs	Тѝ: ви: рипèъз
Заложна къща	Pawn shop	Пò:н шоп

Къде се намира магазинът за ...?	Where's the … shop?	Уèъз ðъ … шоп?
Има ли наблизо магазин за …?	Is there a … shop nearby?	Из ðèъ а … шоп нѝъбай?
алкохолни напитки	spirits	спѝритс
фотоматериали	photography	фътòгръфи
спортни стоки	sports goods	спò:тс гудз

кожени изделия	leather goods	лѐ:дъ гудз
музикални инструменти	musical instruments	мю:зикъл ѝнструмънтс
платове	fabrics	фǽбрикс
играчки	toys	тойз
диетични храни	diet foods	дàйът фу:дз
подаръци	souvenirs	су:вънѝъз

Наблизо ли е?	Is it near here?	Из ит нѝъ хѝъ?
Съвсем наблизо е.	It's very near.	Итс вѐри нѝъ.
На около 5 минути пеша.	It's about five minutes on foot.	Итс ъба̀ут файв мѝнитс он фут.
Какво е работното време?	What are the opening hours?	Уо̀т а: дъ о̀упънинг а̀уъз?
Искам да купя ...	I'd like to buy ...	Айд ла̀йк ту бай ...
Искам да продам ...	I'd like to sell ...	Айд ла̀йк ту сел ...
Търся ...	I am looking for ...	Ай æм лу̀кинг фо: ...
Къде мога да намеря...?	Where can I find ...?	Уѐъ кæн ай фа̀йнд ...?
Можете ли да ми кажете къде мога да купя ..., моля?	Can you tell me where I can buy ..., please.	Кæн ю: тел ми: уеъ ай кæн бай ..., пли:з?
Ще го купя.	I'll take it.	Айл тѐйк ит.
Покажете ми, моля ...	Would you, please, show me ...?	Уу̀д ю:, пли:з, шо̀у ми:...?
Имате ли...?	Have you got...?	Хæв ю: гот ...?

Мога ли да го(я) видя?	Can I have a look at it?	Кæн ай хæв ъ лук æт ит?
Мога ли да видя нещо друго?	Can I have a look at something else?	Кæн ай хæв ъ лук æт сàмтинг елс?
Правите ли отстъпка?	Do you give any discounts?	Ду: ю: гив èни дѝскаунтс?
➡ Колко струва това?	How much is it?	Хàу мач из ит?
Заповядайте.	Here you are.	Хѝъ ю: а:.
Мога ли да подменя това с друго?	Can I exchange this with another one, please?	Кæн ай иксчèйндж *д*ис уй*д* ънà*д*ъ уàн, пли:з?
Мога ли да го премеря?	May I try it on?	Мей àй трàй ит он?
Къде мога да премеря това?	Where can I try this on?	Уèъ кæн ай трàй *д*ис он?
Не, това не е онова, което търся.	No, it's not quite what I'm looking for.	Нòу, итс нот куàйт уòт айм лỳкинг фо:.
Този материал ... ли е?	Is this material ...?	Из *д*ис мътѝъриъл ...?
естествен	natural	нæ̀чърън
синтетичен	synthetic	син*т*èтик

Бих искал,-а нещо ...	I want something ...	Ай уòнт сàмтинг ...
в различен цвят	in a different colour	ин ъ дѝфрънт кàлъ
в по-тъмен тон	in a darker shade	ин ъ дà:къ шейд
в по-светъл тон	in a lighter shade.	ин ъ лàйтъ шейд
Може ли да разгледаме?	Can we have a look around?	Кæн уи: хæв ъ лу:к ърàунд?
Само разглеждам, -е.	I'm (we're) just looking.	Айм (уиъ:) джаст лỳ:кинг.
Тук ли се плаща или на касата?	Do I pay here or at the cash desk?	Ду: ай пей хѝъ о: æт дъ кæш деск?
Къде е касата, моля?	Where's the cash desk, please?	Уèъз дъ кæш деск, пли:з?
Бихте ли го (я) опаковали, моля?	Would you wrap it up for me, please?	У:д ю: рæп ит ап фо: ми:, пли:з?
Бихте ли ги опаковали заедно?	Would you wrap everything together, please?	У:д ю: рæп èвритинг тъгèдъ, пли:з?
Може ли да го изпробвате?	Can I see how it works?	Кæн ай си: хàу ит уъ:кс?
Какъв подарък може да ми препоръчате ...?	What can you suggest for a present ...?	Уòт кæн ю: съджèст фо: ъ прèзънт ...?
за жена / за мъж	for a lady / for a man	фо: ъ лèйди / фо: ъ мæн

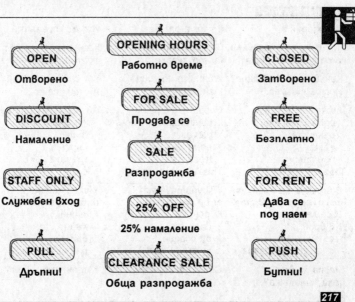

OPEN
Отворено
OPENING HOURS
Работно време
CLOSED
Затворено
FOR SALE
Продава се
DISCOUNT
Намаление
FREE
Безплатно
SALE
Разпродажба
STAFF ONLY
Служебен вход
FOR RENT
Дава се
под наем
25% OFF
25% намаление
PULL
Дръпни!
CLEARANCE SALE
Обща разпродажба
PUSH
Бутни!

За подарък е.	It's for a present.	Итс фо: прѐзънт.
Бихте ли го опаковали като подарък, моля?	Can you gift-wrap it for me, please.	Кæн ю: гѝфт-рап ит фо: ми:, пли:з?
Какъв размер носите?	What size do you take?	Уо̀т сайз ду: ю: тейк?
Нося ... размер.	I take size ...	Ай тѐйк са̀йз ...
Бих искал,-а чифт ...	I would like a pair of ...	Ай у:д ла̀йк ъ пѐъ ъв ...
удобни обувки	comfortable shoes	ка̀мфътъбъл шу:з
ръкавици	gloves	главз
обеци	earrings	ѝърингз
панталони	trousers	тра̀узъз
Това ми става.	This fits me perfectly.	дис фѝтс ми пъ:фиктли.
В брой ли ще платите или с кредитна карта?	Will you pay cash or by credit card?	Уѝл ю: пѐй кæш о: бай крѐдит ка:д?
Ще платя ...	I'll pay ...	Айл пей ...
в брой	cash	кæш
с чек	by cheque	бай чѐк
с кредитна карта	by credit card	бай крѐдит ка:д
Бихте ли ми дали чантичка?	Could I have a bag?	Куд ай хæв ъ бæг?

купувам	buy	бай
продавам	sell	сел
плащам	pay	пей
поръчвам	order	ò:дъ
избирам	choose	чу:з
разглеждам	have a look at	хæв ъ лỳк æт
отварям	open	òупън
затварям	close	клòуз
търся	look for	лỳк фо:
отивам на покупки	go shopping	гòу шòпинг
пазарувам	shop	шоп
пазар	market	мà:кит
пазаруване	shopping	шòпинг
артикул	article	à:тикъл
стоки	goods	гудз
поръчка	order	ò:дъ
магазин	shop	шоп
отдел *(в магазин)*	department	дипà:тмънт

склад	store	стò:
търговия	trade	трейд
търговец	trader	трèйдъ
търговец на едро	merchant, wholesale dealer	мъ̀:чънт, хòулсèйл дѝ:лъ
търговец на дребно	retailer	ритèйлъ
собственик	owner	òунъ
продавач,-ка	shop assistant	шоп ъсѝстънт
клиент	customer, client	кàстъмъ, клàйънт
касиер	cashier	кæшѝъ
каса	cash desk	кæш деск
касова бележка	receipt	рисѝ:т

цена	**price**	**прайс**
цена на дребно	market price	мà:кит прайс
цена на едро	trade price	трèйд прайс
продажна цена	offer price	òфъ прайс
висока цена	high price	хàй прайс
ниска цена	low price	лòу прайс
продажба	sale	сейл
покупко-продажба	sale-trade	сèйл трейд
сделка	business, deal	бѝзнис, дѝ:л

Храни и напитки	*Food and drinks*	*Фу:g æнg gринкс*
Дайте ми ...!	I'd like ...!	Айд лàйк ...!
това парче	this piece	gис пи:с
... грама	... grams of ...	... грæмз ъв ...
половин килограм ...	half a kilo of ...	ха:ф ъ кѝ:лоу ъв ...
един килограм ...	a kilo of ...	ъ кѝ:лоу ъв ...
... килограма ...	...kilos of ...	... кѝлоуз ъв ...
една опаковка ...	a package of ...	ъ пæ̀кидж ъв ...
... опаковки ...	...packages of ...	... пæ̀киджиз ъв ...
една кутия ...	a box of ...	ъ бòкс ъв ...
... кутии ...	...boxes of ...	... бòксиз ъв ...
Прясно ли е ...?	Is the ...fresh?	Из gъ ... фрѐш?
Произведено в ...	Made in ...	Мѐйд ин ...
Да се консумира преди ...	Best before ...	Бѐст бифò: ...

... хляб	**...bread**	**...бред**
бял	white	уа̀йт
черен	wholemeal	хо̀улми:л
пшеничен	wheaten	уй:тън
ръжен	rye	рай
мек	soft	софт
изпечен	well baked	уѐл бейкт
един хляб	a loaf of bread	ъ ло̀уф ъв бред
франзела	French roll	Фрѐнч ро̀ул

... месо	**...meat**	**...ми:т**
прясно	fresh	фреш
замразено	chilled	чилд
пушено	smoked	смо̀укт
свинско	pork	по:к
телешко	veal	ви:л
агнешко	lamb	лæм
овнешко	mutton	ма̀тън
говеждо	beef	би:ф
дивеч	game	гейм
кайма	mince	минс

свински бут	a leg of pork	ъ лѐг ъв пѐ:к
филе	fillet	фѝлит
ребра	ribs	рибз
език	tongue	танг
мозък	brain	брейн
телешка пържола	beef steak	бѝ:ф стейк
пържола	chop	чоп
домашни птици	**poultry**	**пѐултри**
пиле	chicken	чѝкън
кокошка	hen	хен
гъска	goose	гу:с
пуйка	turkey	тъ:ки
патица	duck	дак
колбаси	**sausages**	**сѐсиджиз**
салам	salami	сълà:ми
кренвирш	sausage	сѐсидж
шунка	ham	хæм
пастет	paste	пѐйст

... риба	...fish	...фиш
морска	sea	си:
сладководна	freshwater	фрѐшуò:тъ
прясна	fresh	фреш
замразена	chilled	чилд
пушена	smoked, kippered	смòукт, кѝпъд
солена	salt	со:лт
скумрия	mackerel	мæ̀кърал
херинга	herring	хѐринг
сардела	sardine	са:дѝ:н
сьомга	salmon	сæ̀мън
пъстърва	trout	тра̀ут
омар	lobsters	лòбстъз
октопод	octopus	òктъпъс
калкан	turbot	тъ:бът
миди	mussles	ма̲̀сълс
раци	crabs	крæбз
скариди	shrimps	шримпс
стриди	oysters	òйстъз
черен хайвер	caviar	к æ̀виа:

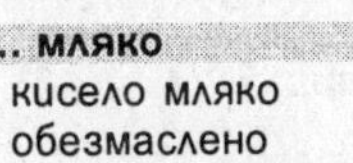

... мляко	... milk	... милк
кисело мляко	yoghurt	йо̀гът
обезмаслено	skimmed	скимд
пастьоризирано	pasteurized	пæстърайзд
мляко на прах	milk powder	мѝлк пàудъ
сирене	cheese	чи:з
кашкавал	yellow cheese	йѐлоу чи:з
масло	butter	бàтъ
маргарин	margarine	ма:джърѝ:н
сметана	cream	кри:м
майонеза	mayonnaise	мейънѐйз
извара	pot cheese	по̀т чи:з

Продукти и подправки	*Foodstuffs and Spices*	*Фу̀:дстафс æнд спàйсиз*
олио	vegetable oil	вѐджитъбъл ойл
зехтин	olive oil	о̀лив ойл
оцет	vinegar	вѝнигъ
сол	salt	со:лт
захар	sugar	шу̀гъ
червен пипер	paprika	пæприкъ

черен пипер	pepper	пѐпъ
горчица	mustard	мạстъд
яйца	eggs	егз
фиде	vermicelli	въ:мисѐли
нишесте	farina	фърѝ:нъ
макарони, спагети	pasta	пàста
свинска мас	lard	ла:д
ориз	rice	райс
брашно	flour	флàуъ
тесто	dough	доу
пастет	paste	пейст
грис	semolina	семълѝ:нъ
мая	yeast	йи:ст
консерва	canned food	кǽнт фу:д
плодове	**fruit(s)**	**фру:т(с)**
лимони	lemons	лѐмънз
портокали	oranges	ỏринджиз
мандарини	tangerine	тǽнджърѝ:н
смокини	figs	фигз
ябълки	apples	ǽпълз

ягоди	strawberries	стрò:бъриз
маслини	olives	òливз
круши	pears	пèъз
грозде	grapes	грейпс
къпини	blackberries	блæ̀кбъриз
малини	raspberries	рà:збъриз
череши	cherries	чèриз
вишни	morello cherries	мърèлоу чèриз
праскови	peaches	пѝ:чиз
кайсии	apricots	èйприкотс
диня	watermelon	уò:тъмелън
пъпеш	melon	мèлън
сливи	plums	пламз
дюли	quinces	куѝнсиз
банани	bananas	бънà:нъз
ананас	pine-apple	пàйн æ̀пъл
фурми	dates	дейтс
тиква	pumpkin	пàмпкин
черница	mulberries	мàлбъриз
боровинки	blueberries	блỳ:бъриз
червени боровинки	cranberries	крæ̀нбъриз

френско грозде	red currants	рèд кàрънтс
касис	black currants	блæк кàрънтс
грейпфрут	grapefruit	грèйпфру:т
нар	pomegranate	помгрæ̀нит
ядки	**nuts**	**натс**
орехи	walnuts	уò:лнатс
бадеми	almonds	à:мъндз
кестени	chestnuts	чèснатс
лешници	hazelnuts	хèйзълнатс
фъстъци	ground-nuts	грàунд-натс
зеленчуци	**vegetables**	**вèджитъбълз**
зеле	cabbage	кæ̀бидж
домати	tomatoes	тъмà:тоуз
краставици	cucumbers	кю̀:камбъз
маруля	lettuce	лèтис
репи	radishes	рæ̀дишиз
кромид лук	onion	àниън
праз	leeks	ли:кс
чесън	garlic	гà:лик
чушки	peppers	пèпъз

целина	celery	сѐлъри
цветно зеле	broccoli	брòкъли
моркови	carrots	кæрътс
копър	dill, fennel	дил, фѐнъл
магданоз	parsley	пà:сли
бакла	broad beans	брò:д би:нз
боб, зрял фасул	beans	би:нз
зелен фасул	string beans	стрѝнг би:нз
леща	lentils	лѐнтилз
грах	peas	пи:з
картофи	potatoes	пътѐйтоуз
тиквички	marrows	мæроуз
червено цвекло	beetroot	бѝ:тру:т
спанак	spinach	спѝнич
хрян	horse radish	хò:с рæдиш
карфиол	cauliflower	кòлифлауъ
гъби	mushrooms	мàшру:мз
бамя	okra	òукръ
джоджен	mint	минт
туршия	pickles	пѝкълз
син домат	aubergine	òубъджи:н

захар	**sugar**	**шу̀гъ**
мед	honey	ха̀ни
шоколад	chocolate	чо̀кълът
млечен шоколад	milk chocolate	милк чо̀кълът
горещ шоколад	hot chocolate	хот чо̀кълът
бонбони	sweets	суѝ:тс
бисквити	biscuits	бѝскитс
локум	Turkish Delight	тъ:киш дила̀йт
сладки	sweeties	суѝ:тиз
мармелад	marmalade	ма:мълѐйд
сладко	jam	джæм
торта	cake	кейк
пасти	pastry	пѐйстри
кекс	cake, pie	кейк, пай
пудинг	pudding	пу̀динг
желе	jelly	джѐли
сироп	syrup	сѝръп
сладолед	ice cream	а̀йс кри:м

Напитки	*Drinks*	*Дринкс*
алкохолни напитки	**strong drinks**	**стронг дринкс**
уиски	whisky	уѝски
водка	vodka	вòдка
коняк	cognac	кòнйæк
гроздова ракия	grape brandy	грейп брæнди
джин	gin	джин
бира	beer	бѝъ
вино	**wine**	**уàйн**
червено	red	ред
бяло	white	уайт
шампанско	champagne	шæмпèйн
безалкохолни напитки	**soft drinks**	**софт дринкс**
... кафе	**...coffee**	**...кòфи**
печено	baked/roasted	бейкт, рòустид
мляно	ground	грàунд
нес	instant	инст<u>а</u>нт

единично / двойно еспресо	single(*brit.*), regular (*am.*)/ double espresso	сѝнгъл, рѐгюлъ:/ дàбъл испрѐсоу
какао	cocoa	кòукоу
чай	tea	ти:
сода	soda water	сòудъ уò:тъ
тоник	tonic	тòник
минерална вода	mineral water	мѝнърлл уò:тъ
доматен сок	tomato juice	томàтоу джу:с
прясно изстискан сок	fresh squeezed juice	фреш скуѝ:зд джу:с
натурален плодов	fruit juice	фру:т джу:с
цигари	**cigarettes**	**сигърѐтс**
Дайте ми един пакет цигари.	I'd like a packet of cigarettes, please.	Айд лàйк ъ пæ̀кит ъв сигърѐтс, пли:з.
Имате ли ...?	Have you got ...?	Хæв ю: гот ...?
огънче	a light	ъ лайт
запалка	a lighter	ъ лàйтъ
кибрит	any matches	ѐни мæ̀чис
Пушите ли?	Do you smoke?	Ду: ю: смòук?
Пуша.	I smoke.	Ай смòук.
Не пуша.	I don't smoke.	Ай дòунт смòук.
Отказах ги.	I gave up smoking	Ай гѐйв ап смоу̀кинг.

пушене	smoking	смòукинг
цигара	cigarette	сигърèт
пура	cigar	сигà:
кутия	box	бокс
пакет	packet	пǽкит
стек	carton	кà:тън
лула, цигаре	pipe	пайп
запалка	a lighter	ъ лàйтъ
камъчета за запалка	flintstones	флѝнтстòунз
тютюн	tobacco	тъбǽкоу
пепелник	ash tray	æш трей

Дрехи, обувки, аксесоари	***Clothes, Shoes, Accessories***	***Клòудз, шу:з, ъксѐсъриз***
Търся магазин за ...	I'm looking for a…shop.	Айм лỳкинг фо: ъ ...шоп.
дамски дрехи	women's clothes	уйминз клòудз
мъжки дрехи	men's clothes	менз клòудз
детски дрехи	children's clothes	чѝлдрънз клòудз
Нося ... номер ...	I take … size …	Ай тейк … сайз …
костюм	suit	сю:т
рокля	dress	дрес
дамски костюм	tailored suit	тѐйлъд сю:т
панталон	trousers	тра̀узъз
блуза	blouse	бла̀уз
риза	shirt	шъ:т
слип	briefs	бри:фс
сутиен	bra	бра:

Бих искал,-а	I'd like	Айд лàйк
да пробвам...	to try ... on.	ту трай ... он.
джинсите	the jeans	дъ джѝ:нз
костюма	the suit	дъ сю:т
роклята	the dress	дъ дрèс
Харесва,-т ми.	I like it(them).	Ай лайк ит(дъм).
Ръкавите са къси.	The sleeves are short.	дъ сли:вз а: шò:т.
Панталонът е	The trousers are	дъ трàузъз а:
малко (доста) ...	a little bit (too)...	ъ лѝтъл бит (ту:) ...
тесен	tight.	тайт
широк	loose	лу:с
Роклята е	The dress is	дъ дрèс из
малко (доста) ...	a little bit (too)...	ъ лѝтъл бит (ту:)...
дълга	long	лонг
къса	short	шо:т
Ризата ... ли е?	Is it a ... shirt?	Из ит ъ ... шъ:т?
памучна	cotton	кòтън
копринена	silk	силк
Пуловерът ... ли е?	Is it a ... sweater?	Из ит ъ ... суèтъ?
вълнен	woolen	уỳлън
синтетичен	synthetic	синтèтик

Съответствие на номерата по британския и европейския стандарт

Дамски дрехи

британски	6	7/8	9/10	11/12	13/14	15/16	17/18
европейски	34	36	38	40	42	44	46

Мъжки ризи

британски	14	14.5	15	15.5	16	16.5	17	17.5
европейски	36	37	38	39/40	41	42	43	44

Детски дрехи

британски	2	4	6	8	10	12
европейски	40-45	50-55	60-65	70-75	80-85	90-95

Дамски обувки

британски	3	4	5	6	7	8	9	10	11
европейски	36	37	38	39	40	41	42	43	44

Мъжки обувки

британски	5.5	6.5	7.5	8.5	9.5	10.5
европейски	39	41	42	43	45	46

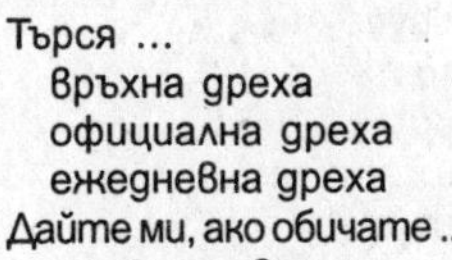

Търся ...	I'm looking for ...	Айм лу̀кинг фо: ...
връхна дреха	an overcoat	ън о̀увъкоут
официална дреха	formal wear	фо̀:мъл уѐъ
ежедневна дреха	daily wear	дѐйли уѐъ
Дайте ми, ако обичате ...	I'd like ..., please.	Айд лайк ..., пли:з.
нещо по-евтино	something cheaper, less expensive	са̀минг чѝ:пъ, лес икспѐнсив
един чифт ...	a pair of ...	ъ пѐъ ъв ...
два чифта ...	two pairs of ...	ту: пѐъз ъв ...
... размер	size ...	сайз ...
по-малък номер	a smaller size	ъ смо̀:лъ сайз
по-голям номер	a larger size	ъ ла̀:джъ сайз

Дамски дрехи и аксесоари	***Women's Clothes and Accessories***	***Уѝминз клоудз æнд ъксѐсъриз***
блуза	blouse	блауз
пола	skirt	скъ:т
дамски костюм	tailored suit	тѐйлъд сю:т
сако	jacket	джæ̀кит
рокля ...	dress...	дрес ...
с къс ръкав	with short sleeves	уѝд шо̀:т слѝ:вз
с дълъг ръкав	with long sleeves	уѝд ло̀нг слѝ:вз

поло	polo-neck	пòулоу нек
манто	top coat	тòп кòут
палто	coat	кòут
късо палто	short coat	шò:т кòут
нощница	night gown	нàйт гàун
бельо	underwear	à̲ндъуеъ
бикини	pants	пæнтс
сутиен	bra	бра:
чорапогащник	tights	тайтс
престилка	apron	èйпрън
кожено палто *(с косъм)*	fur coat	фъ: кòут
халат	dressing gown	дрèсинг гàун
шапка	hat	хæт
шал	scarf	ска:ф
ръкавици	gloves	гла̲вз
колан	belt	белт
дамска чанта	handbag	хæ̀ндбæг
портмоне	purse	пъ:с
очила	glasses	глà:сиз

Мъжки дрехи и аксесоари	Men's Clothes and Accessories	Менз клоудз æнд ъксèсъриз
риза	shirt	шъ:т
костюм	suit	сю:т
елек	sleeveless jacket	слѝ:влис джæ̀кит
жилетка	waistcoat	уèйсткоут
панталони	(a pair of) trousers	(ъ пèъ ъв) трàузъз
сако ...	jacket ...	джæ̀кит...
едноредно	single-breasted	сѝнгъл брèстид
двуредно	double-breasted	дàбъл брèстид
джинси, дънки	Denim jeans	дèним джи:нз
джинси *(от кадифе)*	velvet jeans	вèлвит джи:нз
пуловер	sweater	суèтъ
шлифер	raincoat	рèйнкоут
дъждобран	mackintosh	мæ̀кинтош
палто, манто	overcoat, coat	òувъкòут, кòут
шапка	hat	хæт
шал	muffler, scarf	мàфлъ, ска:ф

папийонка	bow-tie	бо̀у тай
вратовръзка	tie	тай
бомбе	bowler hat	бо̀улъ хæт
каскет	(cloth) cap	(клот) кæп
чадър	umbrella	амбрѐлъ
ръкавици	gloves	главз
чорапи	socks	сокс
пижама	a pair of pyjamas	ъ пѐъ ъв пиджæ̀мъз
бельо	underwear	а̀ндъуѐъ
потник	undershirt	а̀ндъшъ:т
слип	briefs	бри:фс
бастун	cane	кейн
часовник	watch	уо̀ч
копче	button	ба̀тън
копчета *(за ръкавели)*	cuff-links	каф линкс
портфейл	wallet	уо̀лит
папка *(за книжа)*	folder	фо̀улдъ
дипломатически куфар	briefcase	брѝ:фкейс
куфар	suitcase	сю̀:ткейс

Детски дрехи и играчки	Children's Clothes and Toys	Чѝлдрънз клòудз æнд тойз
еднократни пелени, памперси	diapers, pampers, nappies	дàйъпъз, пæ̀мпъз, нàпиз
биберон	baby's comforter, dummy	бèйбиз кàмфътъ, дàми
шише за хранене	feeding-bottle	фѝ:динг бòтъл
гащички	baby's pants	бèйбиз пæнтс
камизолка	wrapover vest	рæ̀поувъ вест
потник	singlet	сѝнглит
лигавник	bib	биб
терлички	bootees	бỳ:ти:з
ританки	tights	тàйтс
шапчица	bonnet	бòнит
грейка	snowsuit	снòусю:т
ръкавички	mittens	мѝтънз
гащиризон	playsuit	плèйсю:т
детска ваничка	baby bath	бèйби ба:*т*

люлка	cradle	крѐйдъл
детско легло	crib	криб
кошарка	playpen	плѐйпън
детска количка	buggy	ба̀ги
играчка	toy	тòи
дрънкалка	rattle	рæ̀тъл
кукла	doll	до:л
топка	ball	бо:л
барабанче	drum	драм
балон	balloon	бълу̀:н

Обувки	Shoes	Шу:з
Искам да купя един чифт ... обувки.	I'd like a pair of … shoes.	Айд ла̀йк ъ пѐъ ъв … шу:з.
дамски	women's	уѝминз
мъжки	men's	менз
детски	children's	чѝлдрънз
Бих искал...	I'd like …	Айд лайк …
по-голям номер	a larger size	ъ ла̀:джъ сайз
по-малък номер	a smaller size	ъ смо̀:лъ сайз
чифт обувки номер...	a pair of shoes size…	ъ пѐъ ъв шу̀:з са̀йз…
Ще ги купя.	I'll take them.	Айл тейк дъм.
Къде могат да поправят обувките ми?	Where can I have my shoes mended?	Уѐъ кæн ай хæв май шу̀:з мѐндид?
Можете ли да поправите обувките ми?	Coud you mend my shoes, please?	Куд ю: менд май шу̀:з, пли:з?

обувки	**shoes**	**шу:з**
летни	summer	са̀мъ
зимни	winter	уйнтъ
спортни	sports	спо:тс
официални	formal	фо̀:мъл
с нисък ток	low / flat heeled	ло̀у / флæт хи:лд
с висок ток	high heeled	ха̀й хи:лд
от кожа	leather	лѐ:gъ
от велур	Suede, buckskin	суѐйд, ба̀кскин
от плат	fabric	фæ̀брик
подметка ...	sole...	...со̀ул
гумена	rubber	ра̀бъ
гьон	leather	лѐ:gъ
ботуши	boots	бу:тс
пантофи	slippers	сли̇̀пъз
сандали	sandals	сæ̀ндълз
връзки за обувки	laces	лѐйсиз
боя за обувки	shoe dye	шу̀: дай
четка	shoe brush	шу̀: браш

... кожа	**... leather**	**... lè:gъ**
естествена	real	рѝъл
изкуствена	artificial	à:тифѝ:шъл
свинска	pigskin	пѝгскин
телешка	calfskin	кà:фскин
кожена яка	fur collar	фъ: кòлъ
кожено яке	leather jacket	лѝ:gъ джǽкит

платове	**fabrics**	**фǽбрикс**
Колко струва един метър?	How much is a metre?	Хàу мач из ъ мѝ:тъ?
Колко е широк?	How wide is it?	Хàу уàйд из ит?
Искам ... метра плат.	I'd like ... metres of cloth.	Айд лàйк ... мѝ:тъз ъв кло*т*.

... плат	**... cloth**	**... кло*т***
памучен	cotton	кòтън
вълнен	woolen	уỳлън
копринен	silk	силк
ленен	linen	лѝнън

изкуствена коприна	synthetic silk	синтѐтик силк
естествена коприна	natural silk	нǽчърл силк
кадифе	velvet	вѐлвит
подплата	lining	лѝнинг
райе	stripe	страйп
каре	check	чек
лице на плата	right side	рàйт сайд
опако на плата	wrong side	рòнг сайд
прежда	yarn, thread	я:н, тред
килим	carpet	кà:пит

Парфюмерия и бижутерия	Perfumery and Jewellery	Пъфю:мъри æнд джỳ:ълри
парфюм	perfume	пъ:фю:м
крем ...	...cream	...кри:м
за лице	facial	фѐйшъл
за ръце	hand	хæнд
дневен / нощен	day / night	дѐй / нàйт
за суха кожа	for dry skin	фо: дрàй скин
за мазна кожа	for greasy/fat skin	фо: грѝ:зи/фæт скин
за нормална кожа	for normal skin	фо: нò:мъл скин

шампоан	shampoo	шæмпу̀:
сапун	soap	со̀уп
одеколон	eau-de-Cologne	о̀удъкъло̀ун
дезодорант	deodorant	ди:о̀удърънт
лак за нокти	nail-polish	нѐйл по̀лиш
червило	lipstick	лѝпстик
грим	make-up	мѐйк ап
молив	make-up pencil	мѐйкап пѐнсъл
спирала за мигли	mascara	мæска̀:ра
пудра	powder	па̀удъ
самобръсначка	razor, shaver	рѐйзъ, шѐйвъ
ножче за бръснене	razor blade	рѐйзъ блейд
крем за бръснене	shaving cream	шѐйвинг кри:м
боя за коса	hair dye	хѐъ дай
лак за коса	hair spray	хѐъ спрей

бижу	**jewellery**	**джу̀:ълри**
скъпоценен камък	precious stone	прѐшъс сто̀ун
пръстен	ring	ринг
злато, златен	gold	го̀улд

златно украшение	gold jewel	гòулд джỳ:ъл
сребро, сребърен	silver	сѝлвъ
платина	platinum	плæ̀тинъм
обици	earrings	ѝърин́з
брошка карфица	pin	пин
гривна	bracelet	брѐйслит
верижка	chain	чѐйн
колие	necklace, pendant	нѐклис, пѐндънт
огърлица	necklace	нѐклис
часовник	clock	клок
ръчен часовник	watch	уòч

Стоки за дома. Електроуреди	*Household Goods. Electrical Appliances*	*Хàусхоулд гудз. Илѐктрикъл ъплàйънсиз*
Бих искал,-а да купя...	I'd like ..., please.	Айд лàйк ..., пли:з.
сервиз за хранене	a dinner set	ъ дѝнъ сет
телефизор	a TV set	ъ Тѝ: Вѝ: сет
хладилник	a fridge	ъ фридж
фритюрник	an electric fryer	ън илѐктрик фрàйъ
Какъв е гаранционният срок?	How long is the guarantee period?	Хàу лонг из дъ гæрънтѝ: пѝъриъд?
Бих искал,-а гаранционна карта?	I'd like a guarantee card, please?	Айд лàйк ъ гæрънтѝ: ка:д, пли:з.
Покажете ми ..., моля!	Show me ..., please.	Шòу ми: ..., пли:з.
Може ли да чуя ...?	Can I listen to ...?	Кæн ай лѝсън ту ...?
диска	the CD	дъ си: ди:
касетофона	the cassette recorder	дъ късѐт рикò:дъ

Бихте ли го изпробвали?	Would you try it out?	Уд ю: трай ит аут?
Ще взема ...	I'll take ...	Айл тѐйк ...
тази кафемелачка	this coffee-mill	дис кòфи мил
четири батерии	four batteries	фо: бæ̀търиз
тази видеокасета	this video cassette	дис вѝдиоу късѐт

кафеварка	coffeemaker	кòфимѐйкъ
хладилник с камера	fridge with a frozen food compartment	фридж уѝд ъ фрòузън фу:д къмпà:тмънт
фризер	freezer	фрѝ:зъ
пералня	washing machine	уòшинг мъшѝ:н
съдомиялна машина	dishwasher	дѝшуошъ
електрическа печка	electric cooker	илѐктрик кỳкъ
скара	grill	грил
ютия	iron	àйън
шевна машина	sewing machine	сòуинг мъшѝ:н
прахосмукачка	vacuum cleaner	вæ̀кю:м клѝ:нъ

бойлер	boiler, water heater	бо̀йлъ, уо̀:тъ хѝ:тъ
антена	aerial	ѐъриъл
телевизор	TV set, television	Тѝ: Вѝ: сет, тѐливижън
видеокамера	video camera	вѝдиоу кǽмъръ
цифрова камера	digital camera	дѝджитал кǽмъръ
видеокасетофон	videocassette recorder	вѝдиоукъсѐт рико̀:дъ
видеокасета	video cassette	вѝдиоу късѐт
радиоапарат	radio	рѐйдиоу
касетофон	cassette recorder	късѐт рико̀:дъ
касетка	audio cassette	о̀:диоу късѐт
фотоапарат	camera	кǽмъръ
батерия	battery	бǽтъри
полюлей	chandelier	шǽндълѝъ
лампа	lamp	лæмп
електрическа крушка	bulb	балб
контакт	socket	со̀кит
щепсел	plug	плаг
прекъсвач	switch	суйч
кабел	cable	кѐйбъл
жица	wire	уа̀йъ
предпазител	(safety)-fuse	(сѐйфти)-фю:з

електротабло	switchboard	суйчбо:д
електромер	electrometer	илектрòми:тъ
водомер	water-meter	уò:тъ мѝ:тъ
адаптер	adapter	ъдæ̀птъ
трансформатор	transformer	трънсфò:мъ

офис-обзавеждане	**office-equipment**	**òфис-екуйпмънт**
бюро	desk	деск
шкаф, секция	cabinet	кæбинит
стол	chair	чèъ
въртящ стол	swivel chair	суѝвъл чèъ
фотьойл	arm chair	à:м чèъ
малка масичка	coffee table	кòфи тèйбъл
библиотека	bookcase	бỳккейс
компютър	computer	камптю̀тъ
лаптоп	laptop	лæ̀птоп
електронен бележник	electronic notebook	илектрòник нòутбук
монитор	monitor	монѝтъ:
клавиатура	keybord	кѝ:бод
мишка	mouse	мàус

кутия за компютър	tower case	та̀уъ кейс
дънна платка	main board	мейн бо:д
процесор	processor	пръцѐсъ:
твърд диск	hard disk	ха:д диск
памет	memory	мѐмъри
... модем	... modem	... модѐм
вътрешен	internal	интъ̀:нъл
външен	external	икстъ̀:нъл
ди-ви-ди плеър	DVD player	ди ви ди плѐъ
... принтер	... printer	... прѝнтъ
лазерен	laser jet	лѐйзъ джет
мастилено-струен	ink jet	инк джет
матричен	matrix	мѐйтрикс
тонер касета	toner cartridge	то̀нъ ка̀ертридж
факс-апарат	fax	фæкс
копирен апарат	copier	копѝъ
скенер	scaner	ска̀енъ
калкулатор	calculator	ка̀елкюлейтъ
мобилен телефон	mobile *(brit.)*	мо̀байл
	cellular /cellphone *(am.)*	сѐлюлъ /сѐлфоун
пишеща машина	typewriter	та̀йпрайтъ

канцеларски материали	office materials	о̀фис мътѝриълз
папка	folder	фо̀лдъ
бележник	notepad	но̀утп ӕ̀д
настолен календар	desk diary	деск да̀йъри
химикалка	pen	пен
папка, класьор	file	файл
печат	seal	си:л
сейф	safe	сейф
гума за триене	rubber	ра̀бъ
телбод	stapler	стѐйплъ
телчета за телбод	staples	стѐйпълз
перфоратор	punch	панч
кламер	paper clip	пѐйпъ клип
тиксо	adhesive tape	ъдхѐсив тейп
ножици	scissors	сѝ:зъс
копирна хартия	copier paper	копѝъ пѐйпъ
лепило	glue	глу

съдове и прибори за хранене	china and cutlery	чàйна æнд кàтлъри
чиния	plate	плейт
чиния за супа	soup plate	сỳ:п плейт
чинийка	saucer	сò:съ
тенджера	pot, saucepan	пот, сò:спън
тава, тепсия	tin	тин
тиган	frying pan	фрàйинг пæн
чайник	kettle	кèтъл
каничка за кафе	coffee pot	кòфи пот
каничка за чай	tea pot	тѝ: пот
чаша *(стъклена)*	glass	гла:с
чаша *(за чай, кафе и др.)*	cup	кап
лъжица	spoon	спу:н
вилица	fork	фо:к
нож	knife	найф
сервиз ...	...set	... сет
за хранене	dinner	дѝнъ
за чай	tea	ти:
за кафе	coffee	кòфи

Книги, вестници, списания	***Books, Newspapers, Magazines***	***Букс, нѝо:зпейпъз, мӕгъзѝ:нз***
Търся...	I'm looking for…	Айм лу̀кинг фо: …
английско-български речник	an English-Bulgarian dictionary	ън ѝнглиш балгѐъриън дѝкшънри
❗ английски тълковен речник	a one-language dictionary	ъ уа̀н лӕ̀нгуидж дѝкшънри
английска граматика	an English Grammar book	ън ѝнглиш грӕ̀мъ бук
Искам да купя...	I'd like to buy …	Айд лайк ту бай …
някой роман от английски автор	a novel by an English author	ъ нѐвъл бай ън ѝнглиш о̀:тъ
календар	a calendar	ъ кӕ̀лъндъ
списание за мода	a fashion magazine	ъ фӕ̀шън мӕ̀гъзи:н
карта на града	a town map	ъ та̀ун мӕп
последния брой от ...	the latest issue of…	дъ лѐйтист ѝшу: ъв...
Как излиза ...?	How often does ... come out?	Ха̀у о̀фън даз … кам а̀ут?
това списание	this magazine	дис мӕ̀гъзи:н
този вестник	this newspaper	дис нѝо:зпейпъ

Седмичен,-но (месечен, -но) ли е?	Is it a weekly (monthly)?	Из ит ъ уй:кли (мàнтли)?
Дайте ми...	I'd like ...	Айд лàйк ...
един туристически справочник	a tourist guide-book	ъ тỳърист гайд-бук
една картичка	a post card	ъ пòуст ка:д
две тетрадки	two note books	ту: нòут букс
една писалка	one pen	уàн пен
Колко струва ...?	How much is ...?	Хàу мач из ...?

книга, учебник	book, text book	бук, тѐкст бук
речник	dictionary	дѝкшънъри
справочник	guide-book	гайд бук
пътеводител	road-book	рѐуд бук
наръчник	manual	мæ̀нюъл
брой	issue	ѝшу:
том	volume	вѐлюм
тираж	circulation	съ:кюлѐйшън
екземпляр	copy	кѐпи
издание	edition, issue	идѝшън, ѝшу:
издателство	publishers	па̀блишъз
географска карта	map	мæп
хартия	paper	пѐйпъ
печат, преса	the press	дъ прес
будка, павилион	kiosk, stall, stand, newsstand, bookstall	киѐск, сто:л, стæнд, нѝо:зстæнд, бу̀ксто:л

вестник	newspaper	нѝю:зпейпъ
... списание	... magazine	... мæгъзѝ:н
илюстровано	illustrated	ѝлъстрейтид
за мода	fashion	фæ̀шън
техническо списание	technical journal	тѐкникъл джъ:нъл
приложение	supplement	са̀плмънт
статия	article	а̀:тикъл
съобщение	announcement	ънàунсмънт
реклама	advertisement	ъдвъ̀:тизмънт
заглавие	title	та̀йтъл
корица *(на книга)*	cover	ка̀въ
ежедневник	daily	дѐйли
седмичник	weekly	уѝ:кли
месечник	monthly	ма̀н*т*ли

ПЪТУВАНЕ

Митница	The Customs	дъ кàстъмз
паспортна проверка	**Passport Control**	**пà:спо:т кънтрòул**
От коя страна идвате?	What is the country of departure?	Уòт из дъ кàнтри ъв дипà:чъ?
Идвам,-е от ...	I'm (we are) coming from..	Айм (уйъ) кàминг фром..
България	Bulgaria	Балгèъриъ
Великобритания	Great Britain	Грèйт Брѝтън
Паспортът ви, моля!	Your passport, please!	Йò: пà:спо:т, пли:з!
Заповядайте!	Here you are!	Хйъ ю: а:!
Визата ми е ...	I have got ...visa.	àй хæв гот ... вѝ:зъ.
туристическа	a tourists'	ъ тỳъристс
транзитна	a transit	ъ трæ̀нзит
работна	a business	ъ бѝзнис
многократна	a multiple entry	ъ мàлтипъл èнтри

Колко души сте?	How many are you?	Хàу мèни а: ю:?
Сам,-а съм.	Me alone.	Ми: ълòун.
Пътувам ...	I am ...	Ай æм ...
с моята съпруга	with my wife	уѝд май уàйф
с моя съпруг	with my husband	уѝд май хàзбънд

с моето семейство	with my family	уѝд май фǽмъли
с туристическа група	with a tour group	уѝд ъ тỳъ гру:п
Попълнете ..., моля!	Fill in ..., please!	Фѝл ин..., пли:з!
този бланка	this form	дис фò:м
тази декларация	this declaration	дис деклърèйшън
фамилия	surname	съ:нейм
име / презиме	name / middle name	нейм / мѝдъл нейм
година на раждане	date of birth	дèйт ъв бъ:т
гражданство	citizenship	сѝтизъншип
националност	nationality	нǽшънǽлити
цел на пътуването	purpose of the trip	пъ:пъс ъв дъ трип
Каква е целта...?	What's the purpose of…?	Уòтс дъ пъ:пъс ъв…?
на пътуването ви	your trip	йо: трѝп
на престоя ви	your visit	йо: вѝзит
туризъм	tourism	тỳъризъм
работа	business	бѝзнис
командировка	business trip	бѝзнис трип
частно посещение	private visit	пра̀йвит вѝзит
учение	study	ста̀ди

Отивам ...	I'm going ...	Айм гòуинг ...
Отиваме ...	We are going ...	Уѝ а: гòуинг ...
на екскурзия	on an excursion	он ън икскъ:шън
на почивка	on holiday	он хòлидей
по работа	on business	он бѝзнис
да работя,-им	to work	ту уъ:к
да уча,-им	to study	ту стàди
на конференция	to a conference	ту ъ кòнфърънс
на състезание	to a competition	ту ъ кòмпитѝшън
Имам,-е ...	I(we)'ve got ...	Ай(уѝ:)в гот ...
покана от приятели	an invitation from friends	ън ѝнвитèйшън фром френдз
делова среща	a business appointment	ъ бѝзнис ъпòйнтмънт
Колко време възнамерявате да останете?	How long do you intend to stay?	Хàу лонг ду: ю: интèнд ту стей?
Ще остана,-ем в страната ...	I'm (we're) going to stay in the country ...	Айм(уѝъ) гòуинг ту стей ин *д*ъ кàнтри ...
една седмица	for a week	фо: ъ уѝ:к
две седмици	for two weeks	фо: ту̀: уѝ:кс
един месец	for a month	фо: ъ мàн*т*
шест месеца	for six months	фо: сикс мàн*тс*

Всичко е наред.	Everything is alright.	ѐври*т*инг из òлрайт.
Приятно пребиваване в страната ни.	Have a nice stay in our country.	Хæв ъ нàйс стей ин àуъ кàнтри.
Минавайте, моля!	You may pass on.	Ю: мей пà:с он.

Митнически контрол	**The Customs**	**дъ кàстъмз**
Имате ли нещо за деклариране?	Have you got anything to declare?	Хæв ю: гот ѐни*т*инг ту диклѐъ?
Колко валута носите?	How much money have you got?	Хàу мач мàни хæв ю: гот?
Носите ли ценни предмети?	Have you got anything of value?	Хæв ю: гот ѐни*т*инг ъв вæ̀лю:?
Това не е разрешено...	That's forbidden to be...	*д*æтс фъбѝдън ту би...
за внос	imported	импò:тид
за износ	exported	експò:тид
Трябва да платите мито.	You must pay a duty.	Ю: маст пѐй ъ дю̀:ти.
Колко мито трябва да платя?	How much duty must I pay?	Хàу мач дю̀:ти маст ай пѐй?

Тези вещи се конфискуват.	We are confiscating these things.	Уй а: кòнфискей-тинг *д*и:з *т*ùнгз.
Колата ви застрахована ли е?	Is your car insured?	Из йо: ка: иншùъд?
Покажете застраховката на колата си!	May I have your car insurance, please?	Мей àй хæв йо: кà: иншùърънс, пли:з?
Нямам нищо за деклариране.	Nothing to declare.	Н<u>à</u>*т*инг ту диклèъ.
Нося ... долара (евро, лири).	I have got ... dollars (euro, pounds).	Ай хæв гот ... дòлъз (ю:роу, пàундз).
Не пренасям ...	I'm not carrying ...	Айм нот кæрииинг ...
наркотици	any narcotics	èни на:кòтикс
ценни предмети	anything of value	èни*т*инг ъв вæлю:
Имам разрешение за внос / износ на тези стоки.	I have got an import / export licence for these goods.	Ай хæв гòт ън ùмпо:т / èкспо:т лàйсънс фо: *д*ù:з гудз.
Това са подаръци (за мои приятели).	These are gifts (for friends of mine).	*д*ù:з а: гùфтс (фо: фрèндз ъв майн).

Колко цигари (бутилки алкохол) ...?	How many cigarettes (bottles of spirits) ...?	Хàу мèни сигърèтс (бòтълз ъв спѝритс) ...?
са разрешени за внос	are allowed for import	а: ълàуд фо: ѝмпо:т
не се обмитяват	are duty free	а: дю:ти фри:
Заплатих митото.	I've paid the duty.	Айв пейд дъ дю:ти.
Ето квитанцията.	Here's the receipt.	Хѝъз дъ рисѝ:т.
Имам застраховка за колата.	I have got a car insurance.	Ай хæв гòт ъ ка: иншỳърънс.
Това ли е багажът ви?	Is this your luggage?	Из дис йо: лàгидж?
Отворете ...!	Open…!	òупън …!
този куфар	this suitcase	дис сю:ткейс
онази чанта	that bag	дæт бæг
багажника	the boot	дъ бỳ:т
Багажът ви е обработен.	Your luggage is passed.	Йо: лàгидж из па:ст.
Това какво е?	What's this?	Уòтс дис?
Елате с мен, моля!	Come with me, please!	Кам уѝд ми:, пли:з!
Чакайте тук, моля!	Wait here, please!	Уèйт хѝъ, пли:з!

Имиграционните власти на митницата са много педантични. При влизане в страната се облечете прилично и носете нещо, с което да докажете, че имате достатъчно средства за съществуване. Някои посетители са били връщани, тъй като носят документи, по които може да се съди, че възнамеряват да работят нелегално. Когато пристигате в Обединеното Кралство, служителят по имиграционните въпроси може да ви зададе въпроси, така че носете всички важни документи в ръчния си багаж и предварително си подгответе убедителни отговори.

Ако основната цел на посещението ви е да работите, най-често ще трябва да ви спонсорира някоя британска компания. Когато пътувате с образователна цел, ще се наложи да убедите властите, че разполагате с достатъчно пари, за да си платите билета за връщане и сте в състояние да се издържате самостоятелно.

Къде мога да обменя валута?	Where can I change some foreign currency?	Уѐъ кæн ай чѐйндж сам фòрин кàрънси?
Искам да се обадя ... в Българското посолство	I'd like to call ... the Bulgarian Embassy	Айд лàйк ту ко:л ... дъ Балгѐъриън ѐмбъси
Протестирам.	I protest.	Ай пръ̀тѐст.
Извинете.	I am sorry.	Ай æм сòри.
Не знаех.	I didn't know.	Ай дѝдънт нòу.

митница	the Customs	дъ кàстъмз
граница	frontier	фрàнтиъ
КПП (контролно-пропускателен пункт)	(CCP) Control Checkpoint	(Си: Си: Пи:) Кънтрòул Чѐкпойнт
полиция	police	пълѝ:с
полицай	policeman	пълѝ:смън

митничар	customs officer	кàстъмз òфисъ
паспорт	passport	пà:спо:т
право на пребиваване	right to stay	рàйт ту стей
удължаване на престоя	visa extension	вѝ:зъ икстѐншън
престой	stay	стей
местоживеене	residence	рѐзидънс
временно пребиваване	sojourn	сòджъ:н
нелегален, незаконен	illegal	илѝ:гъл
законен	legal	лѝ:гъл
наказание	punishment	пàнишмънт
бланка	form	фо:м
декларация	declaration	деклърѐйшън
декларирам	declare	диклѐъ
мито	duty	дю̀:ти
подлежащ на обмитяване	liable to duty	лàйъбъл ту дю̀:ти
безмитен	duty free	дю̀:ти фрѝ:

разрешено е	it's allowed	итс ъла̀уд
забранено е	it's forbidden	итс фъбѝдън
внос, внасям	import	ѝмпо:т, импо̀:т *(глаг.)*
износ, изнасям	export	ѐкспо:т, експо̀:т *(глаг.)*
застраховка	insurance	иншу̀ърънс
имиграционна служба	Immigration Service	имигрѐйшън съ:вис
имиграционен служител	immigration officer	имигрѐйшън о̀фисъ
разрешение	import / export	ѝмпо:т / ѐкспо:т
за внос / износ	licence	ла̀йсънс
разписка, квитанция	receipt	рисѝ:т

Транспортни средства	**Means of Transportation**	**Ми:нз ъв трæнспо:тѐйшън**
Пътуване с автомобил	***Travelling by car***	***Трæвълинг бай ка:***
Кога	When	Уѐн
За колко време	How long	Хàу лонг
... заминаваш,-ате?	... will you be off?	... уйл ю: би: оф?
Кога се връщаш,-ате?	When will you be back?	Уѐн уйл ю: би: бæк?
Ще пристигнем ...	We're arriving…	Уйъ ърàйвинг…
в ... часа	at … o'clock	æт … ъ клок
утре вечерта	tomorrow evening	тъмòроу ѝ:вниng
вдругиден	the day after tomorrow	дъ дей à:фтъ тъмòроу
Това ли е пътят за ...?	Is this the road to …?	Из дис дъ рòуд ту …?
Извинете ме, ➡ кой е пътят за...?	Excuse me, which is the road to…?	Икскю:з ми, уйч из дъ рòуд ту…?
Кой е най-прекият път до ...?	Which is the shortest way to …?	Уйч из дъ шò:тист уѐй ту …?

Това ли е правилният път за ...?	Are we on the right road to ...?	А: уй: он ðъ райт ро̀уд ту: ...?
Бихте ли обяснили как да стигна до ..., моля?	Could you tell me the way to ... , please?	Куд ю: тел ми ðъ уѐй ту ..., пли:з?
Тръгнали сте по грешен път.	You've taken the wrong road.	Ю:в тѐйкън ðъ ронг ро̀уд.
Карайте направо до края на този път и тогава завийте ...	Go straight on to the end of this road and then turn ...	Го̀у стрейт он ту ðи енд ъв ðис ро̀уд ӕнд ðен тъ:н ...
наляво / надясно	left / right	лефт / райт
Движете се по този път и ще стигнете до..	Take this road and you'll reach ...	Тѐйк ðис ро̀уд ӕнд ю:л рѝ:ч ...
Далече ли е ...?	Is it far?	Из ит фа̀:?
Далеч е оттук.	It's a long way from here.	Итс ъ ло̀нг уѐй фром хѝъ.
Близо е.	It's near by.	Итс ниъ бай.
Кой път излиза от града?	Which road goes out of the city?	Уѝч ро̀уд го̀уз а̀ут ъв ðъ сѝти?
Колко километра са от ... до...?	How many kilometres is it from ... to ...?	Ха̀у мѐни кѝлоумѝ:тъз из ит фром... ту...?
Къде има паркинг?	Where's the car park?	Уѐъз ðъ ка: па:к?

Наем на автомобил	Rent a Car	рент ъ ка:
Бих искал,-а да наема ...	I'd like to rent ...	Айд лайк ту рент ...
автомобил	a car	ъ ка:
джип	a jeep	ъ джи:п
мотоциклет	a motorbike	ъ мòтъ:байк
скутер	a scooter	ъ скỳ:тъ
велосипед	a bike	ъ байк
Каква е цената за ...?	How much does it cost ...?	Хау мач даз ит кост ...?
ден	per day	пъ: дей
седмица	per week	пъ: уи:к
Какъв е депозитът?	What is the deposit?	Уот из дъ дипòзит?
Възможно ли е да върна автомобила в ...?	Is it possible to leave the car in ...?	Из ит пòсибъл ту ли:в дъ ка: ин ...?

автомобил	automobile	ò:тъмъби:л
кола	car	ка:
пътуване	trip, travelling	трип, трæвълинг
магистрала	motorway *(brit.)*, highway *(am.)*	мòутъуей, хàйуей
път, шосе	way, road	уèй, рòуд
паркинг	parking (lot)	пà:кинг (лот)
паркинг-часовник	parking meter	пà:кинг мѝ:тъ
задръстване	a traffic jam	ъ трæфик джæм
пътна такса	tall	тол
свидетелство за управление	driving licence	дрàйвинг лàйсънс
завой	turn	тъ:н
заледен участък	icy road	àйси рòуд
мъгла	fog	фог
пътна детелина	fly-over	флàй òувъ
правила за движение	traffic rules	трæфик ру:лз

Бензиностанция	Petrol Station	Пѐтрълстѐйшън
Къде е най-близката бензиностанция, моля?	Where's the nearest petrol station, please?	Уѐъз дъ нѝърист пѐтрлстѐйшън, пли:з?
Сипете ми ... литра...!	I need ... litres of ...	Ай нѝ:д ... лѝтъз ъв ...
бензин	petrol	пѐтрл
безоловен	unleaded	анлѐдид
супер	super	сю:пъ
дизел	diesel	дѝ:зъл
газ	petroleum	питрòулиъм
Сипете ми бензин за 20 лири, моля!	I'd like petrol for 20 pounds, please.	Айд лàйк пѐтръл фо: туѐнти пàундз, пли:з.
Напълнете ми резервоара, моля!	Can you fill it up, please?	Кæн ю: фил ит ап, пли:з?

Дайте ми ... , моля.	I'd like ..., please.	Айд лàйк ... ,пли:з.
моторно масло	some (motor) oil	сам (мòутъ) ойл
антифриз	some antifreeze	сам æнтифрѝ:з
дистилирана вода	some distilled water	сам дистѝлд уòтъ
спирачна течност	some brake fluid	сам брѐйк флу̀ид

REDUCE SPEED!
Намали скоростта!
CAUTION!
Внимание!
SLOW!
Бавно!
DANGER!
Опасно!
DANGEROUS BEND!
Опасен завой!
BRIDGE
Мост
DEAD SLOW CHILDREN!
Внимание деца!
KEEP TO THE LEFT!
Движете се вляво!
KEEP TO THE RIGHT!
Движете се вдясно!
RAILROAD CROSSING
Ж.п. прелез
SLIPPERY WHEN WET
Хлъзгаво при дъжд

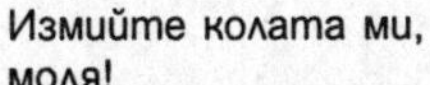

Измийте колата ми, моля!	I'd like to have my car washed.	Айд ла̀йк ту хæв май ка: уо̀шт.
Свърши ми бензинът / горивото.	I am out of petrol / fuel.	Ай ем а̀ут оф пѐтрол / фю̀ел.
Бихте ли ми проверили гумите?	Would you check my tyres up, please.	У:д ю чек май та̀йъз ап, пли:з.

произшествие	**_accident_**	**_ǽксидънт_**
Претърпях авария.	I had a breakdown.	Ай хæд ъ брѐйкдаун.
Той се блъсна в мен.	He ran into me.	Хи: рæн ѝнту ми:.
Той караше твърде бързо.	He was driving too fast.	Хи: уъз дра̀йвинг ту: фа:ст.
Той не ми даде предимство.	He didn't give way to me.	Хи: дѝдънт гив уѐй ту ми:.
Той не даде мигач.	He didn't indicate.	Хи: дѝдънт ѝндикейт.
Карах със скорост ... километра в час.	I was driving with ... -ty kilometres per hour.	Ай уъз дра̀йвинг уѝд... -ти кило̀ми:тъз пъ а̀уъ.
Пътувате с превишена скорост.	You're driving over the speed limit.	Йо: дра̀йвинг о̀увъ дъ спи:д лѝмит.

Извинете,	I am sorry.	Ай æм сòри.
вината е моя.	It's my fault.	Итс мàй фò:лт.
Не съм виновен,-на.	It's not my fault.	Итс нòт май фò:лт.
Не видях знака.	I didn't see the sign.	Ай дѝдънт си: дъ сàйн.
Колко е глобата?	How much is the fine?	Хàу мач из дъ фàйн?
Ще платя.	I'll pay.	Айл пей.
Отказвам да платя.	I refuse to pay.	Ай рифю̀:з ту пей.
Ще подпиша.	I'll sign.	Айл сàйн.
Няма да подпиша.	I won't sign.	Ай уòунт сайн.
Искам ...	I need ...	Ай нѝ:д ...
преводач	an interpreter	ън интъ̀:притъ
адвокат	a lawyer	ъ лò:йъ
представител	a representative	ъ репризѐнтътив
на посолството ни	of our embassy	ъв àуъ ѐмбъси

Извикайте ...!	Call ...!	Ко:л ...!
линейка	an ambulance	ън æ̀мбюлънс
пътната полиция	the Road Police	дъ рòуд пълѝ:с
пътна помощ	the Road Duty	дъ рòуд дю̀:ти

Има ранени.	There are injured people.	ðèъ а: ѝнджъд пѝ:пъл.
Няма ранени.	There's nobody injured.	ðеъз нòубади ѝнджъ:д.
	Nobody is hurt.	Нòубади из хъ:т.
Господинът (госпожата) е ранен,-а.	The gentleman (the lady) is injured.	ðъ джѐнтълмън (ðъ лѐйди) из ѝнджъд.
Не го(я) местете!	Don't move him (her)!	Дòунт му:в хим (хъ:)!
В коя болница го (я) карате?	Which hospital are you taking him(her) to?	Уѝч хòспитъл а: ю: тѐйкинг хим(хъ:) ту?
Намирам се на път А235.	I am on A235.	Ай æм он А235 (ей ту: *три*: файв).
Изпратете ..., моля!	Send ..., please!	Сенд ..., пли:з!
механик	a mechanic	ъ микæ̀ник
пътна помощ	Road Duty	Рòуд Дю:ти
Претърпях злополука.	I had an accident.	Ай хæд ън æ̀ксидънт.
Изтеглете ме, моля.	Give me a tow, please!	Гѝв ми: ъ тòу, пли:з!

Бихте ли ми услужили с ..., моля?	Can I borrow ..., please?	Кæн àй бòроу ..., пли:з?
лост	a jack	ъ джæк
ключ	a wrench	ъ ренч
помпа	a pump	ъ памп
аптечка	a first aid kit	ъ фъ:ст ейд кит
въже	a rope	ъ рòуп

глобявам, глоба	fine	фа̀йн
налагам глоба	impose a fine	импо̀уз ъ фа̀йн
злополука, пътно произшествие	road accident	ро̀уд ӕ̀ксидънт
катастрофа, катастрофирам	crash	крæш
пътна полиция	Road Police	ро̀уд пъли̇̀:с
пътен полицай	traffic warden	тр ӕ̀фик уо̀:дън

Сервиз. Работилница	***Car Repair Garage***	***Ка: рипѐъ г ӕ̀ридж***
Има ли сервиз наблизо?	Is there a service station nearby?	Из ðѐъ ъ съ:вис стѐйшън ни̇̀ъбай?
Колата ми се повреди.	My car broke down.	Май ка: бро̀ук да̀ун.

Не мога да запаля.	I can't start the engine.	Ай ка:нт ста:т ди енджин.
Имам проблем с ...	I think there's something wrong with ...	Ай тинк деъ сaмтинг ронг уид ...
двигателя	the engine	ди енджин
тока	the power	дъ пауъ
светлините	the lights	дъ лайтс
спирачките	the brakes	дъ брейкс
съединителя	the clutch	дъ клач
Сменете ..., моля!	Change ..., please!	Чейндж ..., пли:з!
маслото	the oil	ди ойл
свещите	the (spark) plugs	дъ (спа:к) плагз
ремъка	the (driving) belt	дъ (драйвинг) белт
бобината	the coil	дъ койл
Какви резервни части имате?	What spare parts have you got?	Уот спеъ па:тс хæв ю: гот?
Можете ли да ни помогнете?	Can you help us?	Кæн ю: хелп ас?
Бързам.	I'm in a hurry.	Айм ин ъ хари.

Проверете ..., моля!	Check..., please!	Чек..., пли:з!
акумулатора	the battery	дъ бæтъри
маслото	the oil	ди ойл
спирачната течност	the brake fluid	дъ брѐйк флѝуид
гумите	the tyres	дъ тàйъз
Имам нужда от ...	I need ...	Ай нѝ:д ...
нова гума	a new tyre	ъ ню: тàйъ
нова свещ	a new spark plug	ъ ню: спа:к плаг
Спуках гума.	I have a puncture.	Ай хæв ъ пàнкчъ.
Радиаторът тече.	The radiator is leaking.	дъ рѐйдиейтъ из лѝ:кинг.
Да, поправете го(я).	Yes, fix it, please.	Йес, фѝкс ит, пли:з.
Кога можете да поправите колата ми?	When can I have my car repaired, please?	Уѐн кæн ай хæв май ка: рипѐъд, пли:з?

сервиз	service station	съ:вис стѐйшън
работилница	car repair garage	ка̀: рипѐъ гæ̀ридж
повреда	breakdown	брѐйкдаун
ремонт, поправка	repairing, fixing	рипѐъринг, фѝксинг
ауспух	exhaust (pipe)	игзо̀:ст (пайп)
резервоар	tank	тæнк
огледало за обратно виждане	rear mirror	рѝъ мѝръ
седалка	seat	сѝ:т
предпазен колан	safety belt	сѐйфти белт
(светлинен) индикатор	indicator (light)	ѝндикейтъ(лайт)
каросерия	carriage	кæ̀ридж
шаси	chassis	шæ̀си
предно стъкло	windscreen	уѝндскри:н
чистачка	windscreen wiper	уѝндскри:н уа̀йпъ
багажник	boot	бу:т
калник	mudguard	ма̀дга:д
преден капак	bonnet	бо̀нит

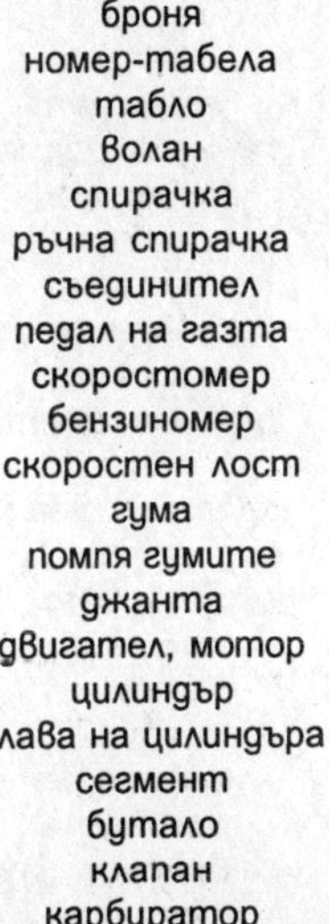

броня	bumper	ба̀мпъ
номер-табела	number-plate	на̀мбъ плейт
табло	dashboard	дæ̀шбо:д
волан	(steering) wheel	(стѝъринг) уй:л
спирачка	brake	брейк
ръчна спирачка	lever brake	лѝ:въ брейк
съединител	clutch	клач
педал на газта	accelerator pedal	ъксѐлърейтъ пѐдъл
скоростомер	speedometer	спи:дѐмитъ
бензиномер	petrol gauge	пѐтрътл гѐйдж
скоростен лост	gear lever	гѝъ лѝ:въ
гума	tyre	та̀йъ
помпя гумите	pump up the tyres	па̀мп ап дъ та̀йъз
джанта	wheel rim	уй:л рим
двигател, мотор	engine	ѐнджин
цилиндър	cylinder	сѝлиндъ
глава на цилиндъра	cylinder head	сѝлиндъ хед
сегмент	segment	сѐгмънт
бутало	piston	пѝстън
клапан	valve	вæлв
карбуратор	carburettor	ка:бюрѐтъ

скоростна кутия	gearbox	гѝъбокс
маслена помпа	oil-pump	о̀йл памп
водна помпа	water-pump	уо̀:тъ памп
бензинова помпа	gasoline-pump	гæ̀соули:н памп
радиатор	radiator	рѐйдиейтъ
перка	paddle	пæ̀дъл
акумулатор	battery	бæ̀търи
динамо	dynamo	да̀йнъмоу
свещ	spark plug	спа:к плаг
ремък	(driving) belt	(дра̀йвинг) белт
бобина	coil	койл
предни светлини	headlight / lamp	хѐдлайт / лæмп
габарити	rear lights	рѝъ лайтс
къси светлини	short lights	шо̀:т лайтс
дълги светлини	long lights	ло̀нг лайтс
мигач	blinker	блѝнкъ
задавяне	choke	чо̀ук
стартен ключ	ignition key	игнѝшън ки:
разпределител	distributor	дистрѝбютъ
ток	electricity, power	илектрѝсъти, па̀уъ
резервни части	spare parts	спѐъ па:тс

Пътуване с автобус	Travelling by Bus	Трӕвълинг бай бàс
Къде се намира автогарата, моля?	Where is the bus station, please?	Уèъ из дъ бàс стèйшън, пли:з?
В колко часа тръгва автобусът за...	What time does the bus for ... leave?	Уòт тайм даз дъ бàс фо: ... ли:в?
София	Sofia	Сòуфиъ
Лондон	London	Лàндън
Кембридж	Cambridge	Кèймбридж
Къде да си купя билет, моля?	Where can I buy a bus ticket, please?	Уèъ кæн ай бай ъ бàс тѝкит, пли:з?
Дайте ми ... за ..., моля!	I'd like ..., please!	Айд лайк ..., пли:з!
един билет	a single (ticket)	ъ сѝнгъл (тѝкит)
двупосочен билет	a return (ticket)	ъ ритъ̀:н (тѝкит)
Кога ще пристигнем?	When do we arrive?	Уèн ду: уѝ: ърàйв?
Къде ще спираме?	Where do we stop?	Уèъ ду: уѝ: стоп?

Колко трае почивката?	How long is the stopover?	Хàу лонг из ðъ стòпоувъ?
Дайте ми багажа, моля!	Can I have my luggage, please?	Кæн ай хæв май лàгидж, пли:з?

автогара	coach/bus station	кòуч/бас стèйшън
автобус (за дълги разстояния)	coach	кòуч
пътник	passenger	пæсинджъ
шофьор	driver	дрàйвъ
багажник	boot	бу:т
багаж	luggage	лàгидж

Пътуване с влак	Travelling by Train	Трæвълинг бай трèйн
Къде се намира гарата?	Where's the railway station, please?	Уèъз ðъ рèйлуèй стèйшън, пли:з?
В колко часа е влакът..?	What time is the train…?	Уòт тайм из ðъ трèйн…?
за Лондон	for London	фо: лàндън
От кой коловоз тръгва влакът ...?	Which platform does the train … leave from?	Уйч плæтфо:м даз ðъ трèйн … лѝ:в фром?
за Кеймбридж	for Cambridge	фо: кèймбридж
На кой коловоз пристига влакът от Лондон?	Which platform does the London train arrive?	Уйч плæтфо:м даз ðъ лàндън трèйн ърàйв?
В колко часа пристига влакът от ...?	What time will the train from ... arrive?	Уòт тайм уйл ðъ трèйн фром ... ърàйв?
Дайте ми ... билета за..., моля!	Can I have… to…, please!	Кæн ай хæв…ту…, пли:з!
един билет	a single (ticket)	ъ сѝнгъл (тѝкит)
два билета	two singles	ту: сѝнгълз
един билет отиване и връщане	a return (ticket)	ъ ритъ̀:н (тѝкит)

два билета отиване и връщане	two returns	ту: ритъ:нз
първа класа	first class	фъ:ст кла:с
втора класа	economy class	икòнъми кла:с
пушачи	smokers	смòукъз
непушачи	non-smokers	нòн смòукъз
Искам да резервирам едно легло.	I'd like to book a berth.	Айд лàйк ту бук ъ бъ:*т*.
Желая ...	I want ...	Ай уòнт ...
легло горе	an upper berth	ън àпъ бъ:*т*
легло долу	a lower berth	ъ лòуъ бъ*т*
Влакът ... ли е?	Is it ... train ?	Из ит ... трèйн?
➡ пътнически	a passenger	ъ пǽсинджъ
експрес	an express	ън икспрèс
Трябва ли да сменям влака?	Do I have to change trains?	Ду: ай хæв ту чèйндж трейнз?
Кога е следващият влак до ..., моля?	What time is the next train for ..., please?	Уòт тайм из *д*ъ некст трейн фо: ..., пли:з?

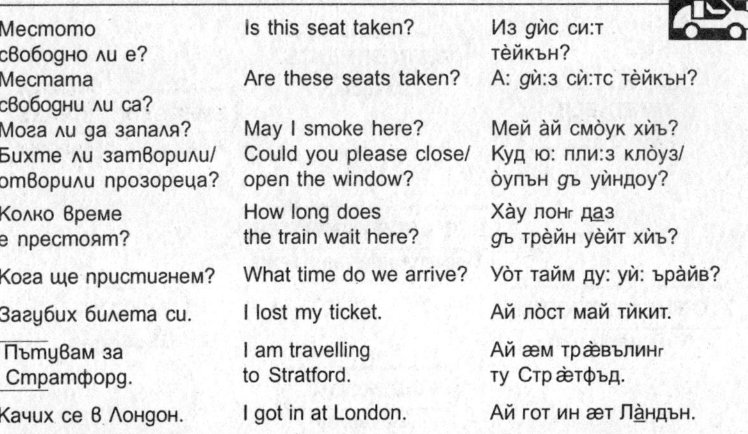

Местото свободно ли е?	Is this seat taken?	Из дѝс си:т тѐйкън?
Местата свободни ли са?	Are these seats taken?	А: дѝ:з сѝ:тс тѐйкън?
Мога ли да запаля?	May I smoke here?	Мей ѝй смо̀ук хѝъ?
Бихте ли затворили/ отворили прозореца?	Could you please close/ open the window?	Куд ю: пли:з кло̀уз/ о̀упън дъ уѝндоу?
Колко време е престоят?	How long does the train wait here?	Ха̀у лонг даз дъ трѐйн уѐйт хѝъ?
Кога ще пристигнем?	What time do we arrive?	Уо̀т тайм ду: уѝ: ъра̀йв?
Загубих билета си.	I lost my ticket.	Ай ло̀ст май тѝкит.
Пътувам за Стратфорд.	I am travelling to Stratford.	Ай æм тр æ̀вълинг ту Стр æ̀тфъд.
Качих се в Лондон.	I got in at London.	Ай гот ин æт Ла̀ндън.
Пропуснах гарата си.	I missed my station.	Ай мѝст май стѐйшън.

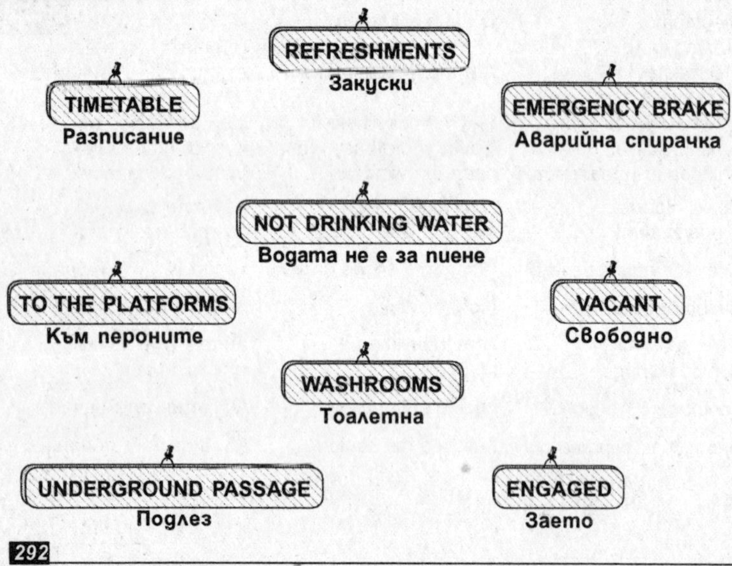
REFRESHMENTS
Закуски
TIMETABLE
Разписание
EMERGENCY BRAKE
Аварийна спирачка
NOT DRINKING WATER
Водата не е за пиене
TO THE PLATFORMS
Към пероните
VACANT
Свободно
WASHROOMS
Тоалетна
UNDERGROUND PASSAGE
Подлез
ENGAGED
Заето

влак	train	трѐйн
перон	platform	плæтфо:м
железопътна линия, коловоз	railway line	рѐйлуей лайн
заминаване	departure	дипà:чъ
пристигане	arrival	ърàйвъл
спиране, престой	stop	стоп
чакалня	waiting room	уѐйтинг ру:м
гардероб	left luggage office	лѐфт лàгидж òфис
разписание	timetable	тàймтѐйбъл
вагон	carriage	кæридж
спален вагон	sleeper	слѝ:пъ
вагон-ресторант	dining-car	дàйнинг ка:
купе	compartment	къмпà:тмънт
място ...	seat	си:т
в първа класа	first class	фъ:ст кла:с
във втора класа	economy class	икòнъми кла:с
пушачи	smokers	смòукъз
непушачи	non-smokers	нòн смòукъз
кондуктор	conductor	къндàктъ
легло, койка	berth	бъ:*т*
количка за багаж	trolley	трòли

Пътуване с кораб	Travelling by Sea	Трæвълинг бай си:
Къде е пристанището, моля?	Where's the harbour, please?	Уѐъз дъ хà:бъ:, пли:з?
Кога тръгва корабът (фериботът) за (от)...?	What time does the ship (ferryboat) leave for ...?	Уòт тайм даз дъ шип (фѐрибоут) лѝ:в фо: ...?
Един билет, (... билета) за ... моля!	One (ticket), (... tickets) to ..., please!	Уан (тѝкит), (... тѝкитс) ту ..., пли:з!
Искам каюта за ... души.	I'd like a cabin for ... people.	Айд лàйк ъ кæ̀бин фо: ... пѝ:пъл.
Бих искал,-а каюта ...	I'd like ... cabin.	Айд лàйк ... кæ̀бин.
в първа класа	a first class	ъ фъ:ст кла:с
във втора класа	a second class	ъ сѐкънд кла:с
С кола съм. Бих искал да платя и за колата.	I am with a car. I want to pay for the car, too.	Ай æм уѝд ъ кà:. Ай уòнт ту пей фо: дъ ка:, ту:.
Колко трае пътуването (рейсът)?	How long is the voyage (the crossing)?	Хàу лонг из дъ вòйидж (дъ крòсинг)?
На кои пристанища акустира корабът?	Which ports does the ship call at?	Уйч по:тс даз дъ шѝп кò:л æт?

Къде е ...?	Where's ...?	Уѐъз ...?
На коя палуба е ...?	On which deck is ...?	Он уйч дек из ...?
каютата ми	my cabin	май кǽбин
басейнът	the swimming pool	дъ суйминг пу:л
Кой е този остров (това пристанище)?	Which island(port) is this?	Уйч ȁйлънд(по:т) из дис?
Кога ще отплаваме?	When do we sail?	Уѐн ду: уй: сейл?
Колко време ще остане в пристанището корабът?	How long will the ship stay here?	Хȁу лонг уйл дъ шйп стей хйъ?
Бих искал да говоря с...	I would like to talk to ...	Ай у:д лȁйк ту тȍ:к ту...
капитана	the captain	дъ кǽптън
някого от екипажа	someone from the crew	сȁмуан фром дъ крỳ:
От къде мога да телефонирам?	Where can I make a (phone)call?	Уѐъ кæн ай мѐйк ъ (фȍун)ко:л?
Къде мога да намеря лекаря?	I'd like to see the doctor?	Айд лȁйк ту си: дъ дȍктъ?
Страдам от морска болест.	I get seasick.	Ай гет сй:сик.

кораб	ship	шип
ферибот	ferry(boat)	фѐри(бо̀ут)
котва	anchor	ǽнкъ
лоцман	pilot	па̀йлът
мачта	mast	ма̀:ст
спасителна лодка	lifeboat	ла̀йфбоут
спасителна жилетка	life-vest	ла̀йф вест
хвърлям/пускам котва	(to) cast/ drop anchor	(ту) ка:ст/ дроп ǽнкъ
пристанище	port (side)	по:т (сайд)
палуба	deck	дек
капитански мостик	captain's bridge	кǽптънз бридж
екскурзия с кораб	cruise	кру̀:з
капитан	captain	кǽптън
екипаж	crew	кру:
моряк	seaman	сѝ:мън

стюард	steward	стю̀ъд
стюардеса	stewardess	стю̀ъдис
суша	land	лæнд
... море	... sea	... сѝ:
спокойно	calm, tranquil	кà:м, трæ̀нкуил
развълнувано	rough, high	р<u>а</u>ф, хай
бурно	heavy, wild	хѐви, уàйлд
океан	ocean	ѝушън
залив	bay	бей
пристанище	port	по:т
фар	lighthouse	лàйтхаус
остров	island	àйлънд
буря	storm	сто̀:м
вълнение	a rough sea	ъ р<u>а̀</u>ф сѝ:
вълни	waves	уѐйвз
вятър	wind	уѝнд

Пътуване със самолет	Travelling by Airplane	Тр æвълинг бай ѐъплейн
Къде се намира бюрото на ...?	Where's ... office?	Уѐъз ... ѝфис?
Бритиш Еъруейз	the British Airways	ġъ Брѝтиш ѐъуейз
авиокомпания ...	the ... Airlines	ġъ ... ѐълайнз
Искам билет за ...	I'd like a ticket to ...	Айд лайк ъ тѝкит ту ...
Дайте ми място ...	I would like a seat ...	Ай уỳ:д лайк ъ си:т ...
до прозореца	by the window	бай ġъ уйндоу
по средата	in the middle	ин ġъ мѝдъл
до пътеката	by the aisle	бай ġи айл
Кога има полети за ...	When are the flights to ...?	Уѐн а: ġъ флàйтс ту ...?
Резервирах място за полет ...	I've booked a seat for the ... flight.	Айв букт ъ сѝ:т фо: ġъ ... флайт.
Има ли автобус до летището?	Is there a bus to the airport?	Из ġѐъ ъ бас ту ġи ѐъпо:т?
Можете ли да ми кажете къде е гишето за регистрация?	Can you tell me where the check-in counter is?	Кæн ю: тел ми: уѐъ ġъ чек-ин кàунтъ из?

летище	информация	разстояние до Лондон	време на пътуване с обществен транспорт	
Heathrow	0181 759 4321	23 км.	метро 40 мин.	автобус 1час
Gatwick	01293 535353	45 км.	влак 30 мин.	автобус 70 мин.

Най-лесния и бърз начин да пристигнете във Великобритания е със самолет. Директните полети София-Лондон траят около 3 часа и половина, а цената им варира между 250 и 400 щатски долари. Часовата разлика е 2 часа. Възможни са транзитни полети с престой и комбинация на няколко авиолинии. Добре е да сравните цените на билетите във вашата туристическа агенция.

1. Вземете до 20 килограма багаж, ако желаете да не доплащате и дали летищните такси са включени в цената на билета.

2. Уверете се, че багажът ви е надписан отвътре и отвън и добре заключен.

3. Не носете твърде много чанти, тъй като лесно може да забравите и загубите някоя.

4. Избягвайте дрехи, които показват, че сте чужденец и бъдете бдителен за това, което се случва около вас.

5. Не показвайте, че имате много пари или ценности. Носете паспорта и портфейла в себе си.

6. Не приемайте пакети от непознати и не пренасяйте вещи, без да сте проверили произхода и съдържанието им.

7. Не оставяйте багажа си без надзор.

Преди да се приземите ще трябва да попълните имиграционна карта, т. нар. "landing card", с името и фамилията ви, дата на раждане, националност, пол, професия и адреса, на който ще пребивавате във Великобритания.

*Ако летите транзитно през Лондон за друг град или държава, то излизайки от "ръкава" на самолета, следвайте стрелките с надписи "***FLIGHT CONNECTIONS***", след което направете справка за терминала си на големите електронни табла, които са разположени през кратки разстояния на летището.*

От летище **HEATHROW** *(LHR) до центъра на Лондон найевтино се стига с метро (London Underground) за около час.*

Ако пътувате с много багаж, а предпочитате комфорта, по-добрият избор е с Heathrow Express, специален високоскоростен влак, който свързва Heathrow и центърът на града (гара Paddington).

Airport Link *са малки автобусчета, които ви возят до посочен адрес. Транспортът е удобен поради това, че спестява време в търсенето на адреса.*

С автобус (by bus). *От централната зала за пристигащи тръгнете направо и излезте от сградата на терминала. Автобусите са редовни и ед-*

нопосочен билет до централен Лондон струва около 7 лири. Пътуването трае около час в зависимост от увижението.

С Taxi- Black Cab

С "черно" лицензирано такси пътуването в едната посока ще ви излезе около 45 лири. С "миникаб" или обикновена кола цената е около 20 до 30 лири. Таксита може да повикате от бюро информация - Information в залата на чакащите на летището.

От летище **GATWICK** (LGW), *може да се предвижите бързо с Gatwick express, който спира в центъра на гара Виктория. Пътуването трае около 30 минути. Влаковете заминават на всеки 30 минути. Таксито до центъра на града ще ви струва около £50-60.*

Често се случва **БАГАЖЪТ ви** *да не пристигне със същия полет. Не се притеснявайте, а отидете в службата* **"LOST AND FOUND LUGGAGE"**. *Там ще попълните формуляр с вида на багажа и адреса на престоя ви във Великобритания. Щом пристигне, багажът ще бъде доставен на посочения от вас адрес, за сметка на авиокомпанията, с която сте летели.*

Чекирайте ми багажа до ...	Check my luggage to ...	Чек май ла̀гидж ту ...
Кога ще излетим?	What time do we take off?	Уо̀т тайм ду: уѝ: тейк оф?
Кога трябва да кацнем?	What time do we land?	Уо̀т тайм ду: уѝ: лæнд?
Колко часа продължава полетът?	How long does the flight take?	Хàу лонг даз дъ флайт тейк?
Колко трябва да платя за свръхбагаж?	How much do I have to pay for extra luggage?	Хàу мач ду: ай хæв ту пей фо: èкстра ла̀гидж?

авиокомпания	air company	èъ ка̀мпъни
летище	airport	èъпо:т
полет	flight	флайт
отмяна на полета	cancelling of flight	кæ̀нсълинг ъв флàйт
закъснение на полета	delay of flight	дилèй ъв флàйт
изход към самолета	gate	гейт
бордна карта	boarding card	бò:динг ка:д
предпазен колан	seat belt	сѝ:т белт
наднормен багаж	extra luggage	èкстра лàгидж
екипаж	crew	крỳ:

пилот	pilot	пàйлът
стюард	flight attendant	флайт атѐндънт
стюардеса	flight attendant	флайт атѐндънт
излитане; излитам	take off	тѐйк оф
кацане	landing	лæ̀ндинг
кацам	land	лæнд
авариен изход	emergency exit	имъ̀:джънси ѐкзит
аварийна пързалка	emergency chute	имъ̀:джънси шу:т
терминал	terminal	тъ̀:минал

FASTEN SEAT BELTS!
Затегнете коланите!

CHECK-IN
Регистрация

NO SMOKING!
Пушенето забранено!

ARRIVALS
Пристигане

DEPARTURES
Заминаване

LOST AND FOUND
Загубени вещи

LUGGAGE CLAIM
Получаване на багажа

В града	In Town	Ин тàун
➡ Къде се намира ...?	Where's ..., please?	Уѐъз ..., пли:з?
центърът на града	the city centre	дъ сѝти сѐнтъ
гарата	the railway station	дъ рѐйлуей стѐйшън
кметството	the City Hall	дъ сѝти Хо:л
Полицейското управление	the police station	дъ пълѝ:с стѐйшън
пристанището	the port	дъ пò:т
Как да стигна ...?	How can I get to ...?	Хàу кæн ай гѐт ту ...?
до този адрес	this address	дис ъдрѐс
до тази улица	this street	дис стрѝ:т
до посолството на България	the Bulgarian Embassy	дъ балгѐъриън ѐмбъси
➡ Загубих се.	I am lost.	Ай æм лòст.

Покажете ми на картата ..., моля!	Could you show me ... on the map, please?	Куд ю: шòу ми: ... он ɡъ мæп, пли:з?
къде се намира това предградие	where this suburb is	уèъ ɡис сàбъ:б из
къде трябва да отида	where I should go	уèъ ай шуд гòу
къде е хотелът ми	where my hotel is	уèъ май хоутèл из
къде живеете	where you live	уèъ ю: лив
Обяснете ми, ако обичате, ...	Would you explain to me..., please?	Уỳд ю: иксплèйн ту ми: ..., пли:з?
отново	again	ъгèйн
по-подробно	more exactly	мò: игзæктли
Вървете направо, докато стигнете до ...	Go straight on until you get to ...	Гоу стрейт он антѝл ю: гет ту ...
паметника	the monument	ɡъ мòнюмънт
светофара	the traffic lights	ɡъ трæфик лайтс
Прекосете ...	Cross ...	Крос ...
моста	the bridge	ɡъ бридж
площада	the square	ɡъ скуèъ
улицата	the street	ɡъ стри:т
пазара	the market	ɡъ ма:кит

Намира се ...	It's ...	Итс ...
в началото на ...	in the beginning of ...	ин дъ бигѝнинг ъв ...
в края на ...	at the end of ...	æт ди енд ъв ...
срещу ...	opposite ...	ѝпъзит...
в близост до ...	near ...	ниъ ...
от лявата/ дясната страна на ...	on the left-hand/ right-hand side of ...	он дъ лѐфт-хæнд/ рàйт-хæнд сайд ъв ...
на ъгъла на ...	on the corner of ...	он дъ кò:нъ ъв ...
непосредствено до...	next to ...	некст ту ...

Бюра и офиси	**Bureaus and Offices**	**Бюрòуз æнд òфисиз**
Адресно бюро	Address Bureau	Ъдрѐс бюрòу
Загубени вещи	Lost Property Office	Лост прòпърти òфис
Туристическа агенция	Travel Agency	Трæвъл ѐйджънси
Информационен център	Information Center	Инфъмѐйшън Сѐнтъ

Основната географска забележителност на Лондон е **ТЕМЗА**, *смесваща водите си с приливите река, която позволява да бъде изградено добре защитено пристанище, далече от опасностите на Ла Манша. Протичайки покрай широки завои от запад на изток, тя разделя града на северна и южна половина.*

ЛОНДОН *се разпростира върху огромна територия. За щастие подземната железница (метрото) прави достъпа до повечето райони лесен. Всеки влак, движещ се отляво надясно, на картата е означен в посока изток, а всеки влак отгоре надолу е в посока юг. Всяка линия е с различен цвят.*

Повечето важни забележителности, театри, ресторанти и дори някои от евтините места за отсядане са разположени в границите на сравнително компактен правоъгълник, оформен от кръговата линия на метрото, непосредствено на север от реката. Всички международни летища са на известно разстояние от центъра на града, но транспортът до и от тях е лесен.

Лондон не се администрира като едно цяло, а се разделя на доста разнородни общини (boroughs), управлявани от местни управи, които разполагат със зна-

чителна автономия.

На свой ред общините се подразделят на райони (или предградия, ако предпочитате), които основно съответстват на първата група букви и числа на пощенския код. Буквите са съобразени с посоките на компаса от центъра на Лондон, който, според пощенските правила, се намира в близост до катедралата Св. Павел:
EC означава East Central (Източен център), WC West Central (Западен център), W West (Запад), NW North West (Северозапад) и така нататък. Числовата система след буквите не е толкова ясна: 1 е центърът на зоната, а следващите номера отговарят на азбучния ред на имената на пощенските райони, които рядко се използват във всекидневието.

Лондонското Сити и Изтокът

Със Сити се означава районът, където някога е бил разположен римският и средновековен град. Макар и да се намира в югоизточния край на кръговата линия на метрото, Сити се разглежда като центъра на Лондон. West End (Западният край; до голяма степен туристически център) се простира на запад от Сити.

***Сити** е един от най-големите финансови центрове в света. Той гъмжи от банкери и брокери през работната седмица, а след края на работното време е пусто. Същото не се отнася за разположените в района прочути забележителности: лондонския Тауър, катедралата Св. Павел и пазара Petticoat Lane.*

Отвъд кръговата линия в източна по-

сока се намира East End (Източният край), където някога са живели изключително коренящи, а сега там ще заварите смесица от различни култури. East End обхваща райони като Shoreditch и Bethnal Green, предлагащи оживени кътчета и сравнително евтини квартири.

Западът

Западно от Сити, но преди самия West End, са разположени Holborn и Bloomsbury. Holborn е юридическото сърце на Великобритания. Bloomsbury все още е синоним на литературния и издателския свят. Освен десетките специализирани магазини, тук ви очаква и несравнимият Британски музей, препълнен с плячка от всяко кътче на планетата.

Самият West End се простира западно от Tottenham Court Rd и Covent Garden, където гъмжи от туристи, но е забавно, и южно от Oxford St, безкрайна поредица от универсални магазини. Там ще откриете такива атракции като Trafalgar Square, ресторантите и клубовете на квартал Soho, прочутите кина и театри на West End около Piccadilly Circus и Leicester Square и елегантните магазини по Regent St и Bond St - без да пропускаме Mayfair, богатия аристократичен квартал.

St Jame's и Westminster са на югозапад. Тук ви очакват още Whitehall, Downing St № 10, парламентът, Big Ben, Уестминстърското абатство и Бъкингамският дворец.

Южно от гара Victoria се намира Pimlico, не особено привлекателен район, но предлагащ множество евтини, но прилични хотели, заедно със съблазнителната Галерия Тейт.

Earl's Court, South Kensington и Chelsea са в югозападния ъгъл, образуван от кръговата линия.

South Kensington е по-луксозен и модерен, с няколко световно известни музея (Victoria & Albert, Музеят на науката, Природонаучният музей). Chelsea вече е не толкова бохемски, колкото скъп и луксозен квартал. На King's Rd вече няма пънкари, но това е интересно място за младежка мода.

По на запад ще стигнете до някои много комфортни жилищни квартали от типа на Richmond и Chiswick. В западна посока си заслужава да се разходите до Hampton Court Palace, Kew Gardens и Syon House.

Северът

Notting Hill е оживен и интересен район, където живеят много преселници от Западна Индия. През деня обстановката става по-изискана, но пазарът Portobello Rd все още не е изгубил от чара си, а има и кръчми, оживени барове и интересни магазини.

Разположените на север от Kensington Gardens и Hyde Park, **Bayswater** и **Paddington** са същински туристически гета, но има изобилие от общежития, евтини и средно скъпи хотели, добри кръчми и интересни ресторанти (особено по Queensway и Westbourne Grove).

Поредицата от предградия на север от централната линия на метрото включва от запад на изток **Kilburn**, **Hampstead**, **Camden Town**, **Highgate**, **Highbury** и **Islington**.

Югът

Пресечете Темза от центъра на Лондон и ще помислите, че сте попаднали в друга страна. Това е **Лондон на работниците**, който няма нищо общо с елегантните канализирани улици на Westminster. Голяма част от Южен Лондон, особено на изток, все още тъне в страшна мизерия и разруха.

Дори и отбилите се за кратко ще предпочетат да посетят културни оазиси като **South Bank Centre** (средище на интересни изложби и концерти) и **Wimbledon** с тенис кортовете. В красивия **Greenwich** ви очакват **Cutty Sark**, превъзходна архитектура, природа, нулевият меридиан и Куполът на хилядолетието!

град	town, city	та̀ун, сѝти
център	city centre	сѝти сѐнтъ
предградие	suburb	са̲бъ:б
квартал	neighbourhood	нѐйбъхуд
покрайнини	outskirts	а̀утскъ:тс
столица	capital	кǽпитъл
район	region	рѝ:джън
улица	street	стри:т
еднопосочна улица	one-way street	уа̀н уѐй стрѝ:т
околовръстен път	ring-road	ринг ро̀уд
булевард	avenue	ǽвеню:
кръстовище	crossroads	кро̀сро̀удз
светофар	traffic lights	трǽфик лайтс
пътен знак	traffic sign, signpost	трǽфик сайн, са̀йнпоуст
пресечка	turning, crossing	тъ:нинг, кро̀синг
тротоар	pavement	пѐйвмънт

алея	lane	лейн
площад	square	скуèъ
парк	park	па:к
болница	hospital	хòспитъл
изложба	exhibition	екзибѝшън
изложение	exposition	експозѝшън
панаир	show, fair	шòу, фèъ
университет	university	ю:нивъ̀:сити
библиотека	library	лàйбрърѝ
театър	theatre	*тѝ*ътъ
Парламент	House of Parliament	Хàуз ъв Пà:лъмънт
Търговско-промишле-на палата	Chamber of Commerce	Чèймбъ ъв Камъ̀:с
музей	museum	мю:зѝъм
художествена галерия	art gallery	à:т гæлъри
пазар	market	мà:кит
телевизия	television, TV	тèливижън, Тѝ: Вѝ:
радио(станция)	radio station	рèйдиоу стèйшън
аптека	pharmacy	фà:мъси

Метро	Underground	а̀ндъгра̀унд
Къде е най-близката станция на метрото, моля?	Where's the nearest underground station, please?	Уѐъз дъ нѝърист а̀ндъгра̀унд стѐйшън, пли:з?
Трябва ми ...	I need ...	Ай ни:д ...
карта на метрото	an Underground map	ън а̀ндъгра̀унд мæп
единичен билет	a single (fare)	ъ сѝнгъл (фѐъ)
билет отиване и връщане	a return (fare)	ъ ритъ̀:н (фѐъ)
Искам да стигна до ...	I want to get to ...	Ай уо̀нт ту гѐт ту ...

__Придвижването__ в Лондон с обществения транспорт е неделима част от пребиваването в града. Транспортната система е синхронизирана мрежа от метролинии, автобуси, надземни влакове, няколко трамвайни линии, "черни" таксита и обикновени таксита -"миникаб-"ове. Ще ви трябва малко време, за да свикнете с обществения транспорт, но един път усвоите ли го, ще ви бъде лесно да достигнете до всяка една точка с минимум главоболие.

Как най-бързо да стигна до ...?	Which is the shortest way to ...?	Уйч из дъ шо̀:тист уѐй ту ...?
Вземете тази линия!	Take this line!	Тѐйк дис лайн!
Сменете тук!	Change here!	Чѐйндж хѝъ!
Това е вашата спирка.	That's your station.	дæтс йо: стѐйшън.
Колко е билетът за метрото?	What is the underground fare?	Уо̀т из ди а̀ндъгра̀унд фѐъ?

PUT YOUR TICKET IN THE SLOT
ON THE RIGHT SIDE OF THE GATE.
MAGNETIC STRIP DOWN.

Поставете билета си в отвора вдясно на вратата с магнитната лента отдолу!

STAND CLEAR OF THE GATES!

Не стойте до вратите!

MIND THE GAP!

Внимание при слизане!

Лондонското **МЕТРО (the Tube)**, *със своите 300 спирки, е едно от най-големите в света. То обслужва по-голямата част от града и го свързва с предградията 20 часа в денонощието.*

Карта на метрото **(Underground Map)**, *на която всяка линия е означена с различен цвят, можете да намерите на всяка спирка. Цените на билетите са в зависимост от зоните на пътуване. Зоните са общо шест, започвайки от централен Лондон (центърът е зони I и II) до покрайнините - VI зона . Преди да пътувате, трябва да се снабдите с редовен билет от автомат или от касата за продажба на билети* **(Booking Office)**, *в противен случай ще бъдете глобени. Почти на всяка спирка за помощ и информация можете да потърсите* **Help Points**. *За да си купите билет, отидете на гишето и кажете до къде пътувате. Служителят ще определи точната цена на билета. Ако гишето е затворено, може да закупите билет от автоматична машина, която се намира на метростанцията. Билетът ви служи за отваряне на вратичките на метростанциите. Трябва да го пъхнете в процепа на вратичката, обозначена със зелена светеща стрелка с магнитната лента надолу и да го вземете, за* *да отворите вратата. Ако пътувате без билет, глобата е 10 лири и служителите от метрото не приемат извинения. Ако билетът ви не отвори вратичката или ако имате багаж, помолете служителя, стоящ до автоматите, да ви помогне с израза:* **Can you help me, please?** *(Кæн ю: хелп ми, пли:з?) Помогнете ми, моля!*

Най-евтино ще ви излезе, ако си купите карта за пътуване в метрото - **Travel Card** *или* **Family Travel Card**, *като посочите до коя зона пътувате. Същата карта може да използвате и за автобусния транспорт в града.*

За да се ориентирате по-добре, препоръчително е да се снабдите с безплатната карта **LTM(London's Transport Map)**, *която ще намерите в туристическите информационни бюра или на гарите, а също така да си закупите и някой от следните справочници:* **London A to Z, Streetfinder, London's Street Index, Ordnance Survey ABC, London Street Atlas.**

ВИДОВЕ БИЛЕТИ И КАРТИ

Еднопосочни или двупосочни билети (One way and Return tickets)

Тези билети са валидни до посочена точка и обратно само в деня на покупката.

Еднодневни карти за пътуване (One day travel card)

Тези карти са най-евтиният и лесен начин да пътувате в централен Лондон. Билетът е валиден само от 9, 30 часа сутринта и с него може да използвате метрото, лондонските червени автобуси и надземния влак - докландс лайт рейл (DLR).

Уикенд карти (Weekend travel card)

Този билет е валиден в събота и неделя. В зависимост от зоните цената му варира.

Нощни автобуси (Night Bus)

Еднодневните и уикенд картите са валидни за нощните автобуси, които пътуват до 4 и 30 часа сутринта.

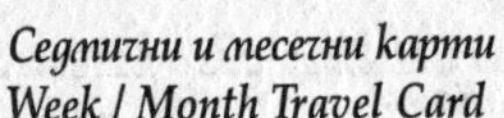

Седмични и месечни карти Week / Month Travel Card

Тези карти предлагат един удобен начин за придвижване в Лондон и ако пътувате повече дни ще спестите пари. Може да закупите и използвате седмична или месечна карта по всяко време на деня. Те са валидни за метрото, лондонските автобуси, DLR и националните железници в зависимост от зоната. За да си извадите седмична или месечна карта за пътуване ще ви трябва карта със снимка. Обяснете на служителя, че искате именно такава карта и му предоставете ваша снимка, след което той ще ви направи съответната карта. Ако си купувате месечна карта ще трябва да попълнете и бланка, в случай че я загубите и искате да ви се издаде нова.

Такси	**Taxi**	**Тӕкси**
Такси! Свободен ли сте?	Taxi! Are you free?	Тӕкси! А: ю: фрѝ:?
Може ли да ме закарате...?	Can you take me to…?	Кӕн ю: тѐйк ми: ту: …?
до хотел ...	the … Hotel	*g*ъ … хоутѐл
на този адрес	this address	*g*ис ъдрѐс
По-бързо, ако обичате! Бързам. Бихте ли шофирали по-бавно?	Faster, please. I'm in a hurry. Could you drive more slowly?	Фа̀:стъ, пли:з. Айм ин ъ ха̀ри. Куд ю: драйв мо: сло̀ули?
Моля, спрете тук!	Please, stop here!	Пли:з, стоп хѝъ!
Ще вземете ли багажа вместо мен?	Can you get my luggage for me?	Кӕн ю: тейк май ла̀гидж фо: ми:?

Черните таксита (Black Cabs), заедно с двуетажните автобуси, са се превърнали в синоним на Лондон. Те са малко по-скъпи от обществения транспорт, но превозват до 5 пътника, така че могат да се окажат доста икономични, ако пътувате в група. Таксиметърът е добре видим, така че може да следите тарифата. Бакшишът е задължителен. Закръглете сумата нагоре до най-близката лира. Незаетите таксита имат жълта светлина на покрива. За да спрете такси на улицата, просто протегнете ръка. Това не се отнася за обикновените таксита - миникабс, които обикновено работят на повикване. Максималната първоначална такса е 2 лири.

Мини таксита (Minicabs)

Това са независими фирми, които обслужват почти цял Лондон. Внимавайте при избора си на миникаб, тъй като има много фирми и водачи с лоша репутация. Ако сте само момиче, по-добре не използвайте тези таксита, а направо се насочете към **Ladycabs**.

Автобус	Bus	Бас
Къде е спирката на автобус №...?	Where's the number … bus stop please?	Уѐъз дъ на̀мбъ … бас стоп, пли:з?
Кой автобус (тролей) трябва да взема за ...	Which bus (trolley) do I take to …?	Уйч бас (тро̀ли) ду: ай тѐйк ту …?
центъра	the centre	дъ сѐнтъ
аерогарата	the airport	ди ѐъпо:т
Този автобус ходи ли до ...?	Does this bus go to …?	Даз дис ба̀с го̀у ту …?
гарата	the railway station	дъ рѐйлуей стѐйшън
площад ...	the … square	дъ … скуѐъ
Искам да стигна до ...	I want to get to …	Ай уо̀нт ту гѐт ту …
до Лондонското Сити	the City (of London)	дъ Сѝти (ъв Ла̀ндън)
до Бъкингамския дворец	Buckingham Palace	Бъкингам Пæлис
до сградата на Парламента	the Houses of Parliament	дъ Ха̀узиз ъв Па̀:лъмънт
до Хайд парк	Hyde park	Хайд па:к
Уестминстърското абатство	Westminster Abbey	Уѐстминстъ æ̀би

Вземете номер ... и слезте на ...-та спирка.	Take number ... and get off at the ... stop.	Тейк нàмбъ…æнд гет оф æт дъ … стоп.

Откъде се купуват билети?	Where can I buy a ticket?	Уèъ кæн ай бàй ъ тѝкит?
Билети се продават ...	Tickets are sold …	Тѝкитс а: сòулд…
от шофьора	by the driver	бай дъ дрàйвъ
от кондуктора	by the ticket collector	бай дъ тѝкит калèктъ

Колко е билетът?	What's the fare?	Уòтс дъ фèъ?
Колко струва ... билет?	How much is a ... ticket?	Хàу мач из ъ ... тѝкит?
еднопосочен	one way	уàн уей
двупосочен	return	ритъ:н
Кажете ми, моля, къде трябва да сляза.	Tell me where I should get off, please.	Тèл ми: уèъ ай шуд гèт оф, пли:з.
Тук ли да сляза?	Do I get off here?	Ду: ай гèт оф хѝъ?
В колко часа тръгва следващият автобус?	What time does the next bus leave?	Уот тайм даз дъ некст бас ли:в?

задръстване	traffic jam	трæфик джæм
двуетажен автобус	double-decker	дàбъл дèкъ
автобус до аерогара	airbus	èъбас

***Compulsory** (задължителна спирка) - автобусът ще спре, освен ако не е пълен*

***Request** (спирка по желание) - автобусът ще спре само, ако дадете знак с ръка на водача*

*Автобусната мрежа е много обширна и с добро покритие. Използват се старите двуетажни автобуси, както и нови едноетажни. Автобусите дори и директни могат да отнемат повече време отколкото метрото и основният проблем е да знаете къде да слезете. Кондукторите и водачите обикновено са приятелски настроени и няма да ви откажат помощ. Нощните автобуси пътуват от полунощ до 6 часа сутринта и се познават по буквата **N** преди номера на автобуса. Всички те или тръгват или минават през **Trafalgar Square**. Така че ако не знаете от къде да вземете автобус отидете там.*

Национална автобусна мрежа е много добра и повечето междуградски ав-

тобуси тръгват от автогара Виктория, която е недалече от гара Виктория.

Национални железници (BritishRail) се представляват от множество влакове, които отпътуват от ключови терминали, пръснати из цял Лондон. С тези влакове може да стигнете почти навсякъде в Англия. Може да използвате и вашата карта за пътуване от метрото, ако пътувате до някои от зоните, обозначени на нея.

Ако пътуването ви е извън зоните на картата тогава можете да си купите допълнителен билет (extension).

Основните терминали (гари) са **Waterloo, Paddington, Kings Cross, Victoria, Charing Cross, Liverpool Street**.

ENTRANCE
Вход
PRIVATE PROPERTY!
Частна собственост!
EXIT
Изход
VACANT
Свободно
NO TRESPASSING!
Не влизай без разрешение!
OCCUPIED
Заето
NO ADMITTANCE
Няма вход
WET PAINT!
Пази се от боята!
NO EXIT
Няма изход
FORBIDDEN!
Забранено!
PUBLIC CONVENIENCE
Обществена тоалетна
NO ENTRY!
Вход забранен!
LADIES
Жени
TOILET
Тоалетна
MEN
Мъже

Критични ситуации	***Crucial situations***	***Крỳ:шъл ситюѐйшънз***
Помощ!	Help!	Хелп!
Пожар!	Fire!	Фàйъ!
Извикайте полиция!	Call the police!	Ко:л ɡъ пълѝ:с!
Оставете ме на мира!	Leave me alone!	Ли:в ми: ълòун!
Ще извикам полиция!	I'll call the police!	Айл ко:л ɡъ пълѝ:с!
Опасно е!	It's dangerous!	Итс дѐйнджързс!
Внимание!	Attention!	Ътѐншън!
Спрете веднага!	Stop it now!	Стоп ит нàу!
Не пипайте!	Don't touch it!	Донт тач ит!
Бях нападнат,-а.	I was attacked.	Ай уàз ътǽкт.
Обраха ме.	I was robbed.	Ай уàз робд.
Набиха ме.	I was pummelled.	Ай уàз пàмълд.
Бях изнасилена.	I was raped.	Ай уàз рейпт.
Не видях нападателя.	I didn't see the attacker.	Ай дѝдънт си: ɡъ ътǽкъ.
Видях крадеца.	I saw the thief.	Ай со: ɡъ ти:ф.
Мога (не мога) да го позная / да го (я) опиша.	I can (can't) recognize/ describe him (her).	Ай кæн (кант) рѐкъгнайз/ дискрàйб хим (хъ:).

Разбиха колата ми.	My car was broken into.	Май ка: уа̀с бро̀укън ѝнту.
➡ Откраднаха ...	Someboby stole ...	Са̀мбъди сто̀ул ...
паспорта ми	my passport	май пæ̀спо:т
кредитната ми карта	my credit card	май крѐдит ка:д
чантата ми	my bag	май бæ̀г
портфейла ми	my wallet	май уо̀лит
➡ Загубих ...	I lost ...	Ай лост ...
документите си	my documents	май до̀кюмънтс
парите си	my money	май ма̀ни
багажа си	my luggage	май ла̀гидж
детето си	my child	май ча̀йлд
Избухна взрив.	There was explosion.	ǥеъ уа̀з ън иксплоу̀жън.
Загинаха хора.	People died.	Пѝ:пъл дайд.
Има много убити / ранени.	There are many people killed/injured.	ǥѐъ а: мæ̀ни пѝ:пъл килд / ѝнджъ:д.
Това е ...	This is ...	ǥис из ...
терористичен акт	à terrorist act (action)	ъ тѐтърист æкт (æ̀кшън)

нещастен случай инцидент катастрофа	à casualty an accident à catastrophe (a disaster)	ъ кǽжуълти ън ǽксидънт ъ кǽтǽстроф (ъ дизà:стъ)
Къде мога да намеря полицейски участък?	Where can I find a police station?	Уѐъ кæн ай файнд ъ пълѝ:с стѐйшън?
Моля, информирайте близките ми в България.	Please inform my relatives in Bulgaria.	Пли:з инфò:м май рѐлътивз ин балгѐъриъ.
Мога ли да използвам телефона ви?	May I use your telepnone?	Мей ай ю:з йо: тѐлъфоун?
Имам (нямам) здравна застраховка.	I have (don't have) health insurance.	Ай хæв (ай дòунт хæв) хел*т* иншỳърънс.
Моля, обадете се на този телефон и съобщете номера на застраховката ми.	Please call this telephone and give my insurance number.	Пли:з ко:л *д*ис тѐлифоун æнд гив май иншỳърънс нàмбъ.

ЧОВЕК И ЗДРАВЕ

Характерни черти. Състояния | *Characteristic features. Moods* | *Кæрърктърѝстик фѝ:чъз. Му:gз*

Човек	**Human being**	**Хю̀:мън бѝ:нг**
мъж	man	мæн
жена	woman	уу̀мън
gеme	child	чайлд

Аз (не) съм,	I am (not)	Ай æм (нот)
mu cu,	you are	ю: а:
moй (mя) е...	he(she) is	хи:(ши:) из
рус,-а	blond, fair	блонд, фѐъ
мургав,-а	swarthy, dark	суò:gи, да:к
кестеняв,-а	brown-haired	брàун хѐъд
къgрав,-а	curly	къ:ли
черноок,-а	black-eyed	блæк айд
синеок,-а	blue-eyed	блу̀ айд
плешив,-а	bald	бо:лд

висок,-а	tall	то:л
среден,-на на ръст	average height	æ̀въридж хайт
нисък,-ка	short	шо:т
слаб,-а	thin	*т*ин
пълен,-на	fat	фæт
тънък, елегантен,-а	slim	слим
красив,-а	beautiful	бю:тифул
красив *(за мъж)*	handsome	хæ̀нсам
грозен,-на	ugly	а̀гли
хубава	pretty, lovely	прѝти, ла̀вли
хубав *(за мъж)*	good-looking	гу̀д лу̀кинг
симпатичен,-на	nice, kind	найс, кайнд
енергичен,-на	energetic, active	ѐнъджѐтик, æ̀ктив
идеален,-на	ideal	айдѝъл
млад,-а	young	янг
стар,-а	old	о̀улд
старец	an old man	ън о̀улд мæн
старица	an old woman	ън о̀улд уу̀мън
богат,-а	rich	рич
беден,-а	poor	пу̀ъ

умен,-на	clever, cute	клèвъ, кю:т
глупав,-а	stupid	стю̀:пид
добър,-а	good	гуд
лош,-а, зъл,-а	bad	бæд
радостен,-на	glad	глæд
усмихнат,-а	all smiles	ò:л смайлз
тъжен,-на	sad	сæд
жесток,-а	cruel, brutal	крỳъл, брỳ:тъл
нежен,-на	tender, loving	тèндъ, ла̀винг
зает,-а	busy	бѝзи
свободен,-на	free	фри:
изморен,-а	tired	тàйъд
бодър,-а	fresh	фреш
отпочинал,-а	rested	рèстид
мързелив,-а	lazy	лèйзи
работлив,-а	diligent	дѝлиджънт
спокоен,-на	calm	ка:м
нервен,-на	nervous	нъ̀:във
неспокоен,-на	restless	рèстлис
търпелив,-а	patient	пèйшънт
нетърпелив,-а	impatient	импèйшънт

любезен,-на, учтив,-а	kind, polite	кàйнд, пълàйт
скромен,-на	modest	мòдист
нахален,-на	insolent, cheeky	йнсълънт, чѝ:ки
способен,-на	able, gifted	èйбъл, гѝфтид
неспособен,-на	unable	анèйбъл
страхлив,-а	coward	кàуъд
смел,-а	brave	брейв
щастлив,-а	happy	хæпи
нещастен,-на	unhappy	анхæпи
доволен,-на	pleased	плѝ:зд
недоволен,-на	displeased	дисплѝ:зд
ревнив, завистлив,-а	jealous	джèлъс
благороден,-на	noble	нòубъл
бъбрив,-а	chatty	чæти
мълчалив,-а	silent	сàйлънт
честен,-на	honest, loyal	òнист, лòйъл
безчестен,-на	dishonest	дизòнист
приятен,-на	pleasant	плèзънт
неприятен,-на	unpleasant	анплèзънт
откровен,-а	sincere	синсѝъ
лъжец, лъжкиня	liar	лàйъ

сърдит,-а	angry	æ̀нгри
удовлетворен,-а	satisfied	сæ̀тисфайд
сериозен,-на	serious	сѝъриъс
отговорен,-на	responsible	риспòнсибъл
любопитен,-на	curious	кю̀ъриъс
безразличен,-на	indifferent	индѝфрънт

➡ Гладен съм.	I'm hungry.	Айм ха̀нгри.
Не съм гладен.	I'm not hungry.	Айм нот ха̀нгри.
Нахраних се.	I've had enough.	Айв хæд инà ф.
➡ Жаден съм.	I'm thirsty.	Айм *т*ъ:сти.
Не съм жаден.	I'm not thirsty.	Айм нот *т*ъ:сти.
Страхувам се.	I'm afraid.	Айм ъфрѐйд.
Не се страхувам.	I'm not afraid.	Айм нот ъфрѐйд.

Притеснявам се.	I'm embarrassed	Айм имбæ̀ръст.
Не се притеснявай!	I feel uneasy.	Ай фѝ:л анѝ:зи.
	Take it easy!	Тейк ит ѝ:зи!
Изморих се.	I am tired.	Айм та̀йъд.
Не съм се изморил.	I'm not tired.	Айм нот та̀йъд.
Как спахте?	Did you have a good sleep?	Дид ю: хæв ъ гуд слѝ:п?
Спах добре.	I had a good sleep.	Ай хæд ъ гуд слѝ:п.
Не спах добре.	I didn't have a good sleep.	Ай дѝдънт хæв ъ гуд сли:п.
Спи ми се.	I am sleepy.	Ай æм слѝ:пи.
Пречи ли ти?	Does it bother you?	Даз ит бо̀дъ ю:?
Не ми пречи.	It doesn't bother me.	Ит да̀зънт бо̀дъ ми:.
Пречи ми.	It disturbs me.	Ит дистъ:бз ми:.
Дразни ли те (ви)?	Does it make you angry?	Даз ит мѐйк ю: æ̀нгри?
Дразни ме.	It makes me angry.	Ит мѐйкс ми: æ̀нгри.
Не ме дразни.	It doesn't make me angry.	Ит да̀зънт мейк ми: æ̀нгри.
Интересува ли те (ви)?	Are you interested?	А: ю: ѝнтристид?
Не ме (ни) интересува.	I'm(we're) not interested.	Айм(уйъ) нот ѝнтристид.
Интересува ме	I'm interested in ...	Айм ѝнтристид ин ...

Мързи ме.	I feel lazy.	Ай фѝ:л лѐйзи.
Дотяга ми.	It's boring.	Итс бо̀:рингг.
Дотегна ми.	I'm bored.	Айм бо̀:д.
Омръзна ми.	I'm fed up with It.	Айм фед ап уѝg ит.
За какво мислиш,-те?	What are you thinking about?	Уо̀т а: ю: *т*ѝнкинг ъба̀ут?
Мисля за ...	I'm thinking about...	Айм *т*ѝнкинг ъба̀ут...
Надявам се ...	I hope...	Ай хо̀уп ...
Вярвам, че ...	I believe (that)...	Ай билѝ:в (*g*æт)...
Считам / Мисля...	I consider / I think...	Ай кънсѝдъ/ Ай *т*инк...
За щастие...	Fortunately...	Фо̀:чънътли...
За съжаление...	Unfortunately...	Анфо̀:чънътли...
Какво става?	What's the matter?	Уо̀тс *g*ъ мæ̀тъ?
Какво стана?	What happened?	Уо̀т хæ̀пънд?
Съмнявам се.	I doubt it.	Ай да̀ут ит.
Не се съмнявам.	I don't doubt it.	Ай до̀унт да̀ут ит.
Не се съмнявай!	Don't doubt it!	До̀унт да̀ут ит!

Човешки отношения	Human Relations	Хю̀:мън рилѐйшънз
Имате ли нужда от ...?	Do you need ...?	Ду: ю: ни:д ...?
Имам нужда от ...	I need ...	Ай ни:д ...
помощ	help	хелп
пари	money	мàни
любов	love	лав
подкрепа	support	съпò:т
внимание	attention	ътѐншън
спокойствие	tranquillity	трæнкуйлити
разбиране	understanding	андъстæ̀ндинг
Имам (нямам) добро настроение.	I am(not) in a good mood.	Ай æм (нот) ин ъ гуд му̀:д.
Имам (нямам) ангажименти.	I have (no) engagements.	Ай хæв (нòу) ингѐйджмънтс.
Остави ме на мира! Бягай от тук!	Leave me alone! Go away! Get off!	Лѝ:в ми: ълòун! Гòу ъуѐй! Гет оф!

22.

С какво се занимавате обикновено?	What do you usually go in for?	Уòт ду: ю: ю̀:жуъли гòу ин фо:?
Когато съм свободен, -на, предпочитам ...	In my spare time I like ...	Ин май спѐъ тайм ай лàйк ...
да слушам музика	listening to music	лѝсънинг ту мю̀:зик
да гледам телевизия	watching TV	уòчинг Тѝ: Вѝ:
да пътувам (в чужбина)	travelling (abroad)	трæвълинг (ъбрò:д)
да ходя на кино (театър)	going to the cinema (theatre)	гòуинг ту *д*ъ сѝнъмъ (*т*ѝътъ)
да излизам с приятели	going out with friends	гòуинг àут уѝ*д* фрѐндз
да чета	reading	рѝ:динг
да ходя на лов	hunting	хàнтинг
да ходя за риба	fishing	фѝшинг
Умея ...	I can...	Ай кæн ...
да свиря ...	play...	плей ...
на пиано	the piano	*д*ъ пиàноу
на китара	the guitar	*д*ъ гитà:
на цигулка	the violin	*д*ъ вàйълин

да играя ...	play...	плей ...
шах	chess	чес
крикет	cricket	крѝкит
голф	golf	гòулф
боулинг	bowling	бòулинг
карти	cards	ка:дз
да пея добре	sing well	синг уèл
да работя на компютър	operate a computer	òпърейт дъ къмпю:тъ
Аз съм ...	I am ...	Ай æм ...
нумизматик	a coin collector	ъ кòин кълèктъ
филателист, колекционер на марки	philatelist, stamp collector	фил æтълист, стæмп кълèктъ
Моето любимо занимание е (са) ...	My hobby is ...	Май хòби из ...
кореспонденцията с приятели	writing letters to my friends	рàйтинг лèтъз ту май фрèндз
литературата	literature	лѝтричъ
поезията	poetry	пòуитри
музиката	music	мю̀:зик
електронните игри	computer games	къмпю:тъ геймз

Обичам ...	I like...	Ай лайк ...
да шофирам	driving	дра̀йвинг
да плувам	swimming	суѝминг
животните	animals	ӕ̀нимълз
домашните любимци	pets	пѐтс
конете	horses	хо̀:сиз
Имам,-е ...	I (we) have got ...	Ай (уѝ:) хæв гот ...
куче	a dog	ъ до̀г
котка	a cat	ъ кæт
Аз съм, ти си, той (тя) е ...	I am, you are, he (she) is ...	Ай æм, ю: а:, хи: (ши:) из ...
женен,омъжена	married	мӕ̀рид
неженен, неомъжена	single	сѝнгъл
разведен,-а	divorced	диво̀:ст
вдовец	a widower	ъ уѝдоуъ
вдовица	a widow	ъ уѝдоу
вярващ, вярваща	religious	рилѝджъс
атеист,-ка	an atheist	ън ѐй*т*иист

християнин православен	a Christian an Orthodox	ъ Крѝсчън ън ò:тъдокс
християнин	Christian	крѝсчън
католик	a Catholic	ъ кæ̀тълик
протестант	a Protestant	ъ прòтистънт
мюсюлманин	a Moslem	ъ мòзлъм
будист	a Buddhist	ъ бỳдист
Ние сме ...	We are ...	Уѝ: а: ...
колеги	colleagues	кòли:гз
добри познати	good acquaintances	гуд ъкуèйнтънсиз
приятели	friends	фрèндз
интимни приятели	intimate friends	ѝнтимит френдз
Отношенията ни са ...	Our relations are ...	àуъ рилèйшънз а: ...
служебни	official	ъфѝшъл
приятелски	friendly	фрèндли
близки	close	клòус
интимни	intimate	ѝнтимит
Живеем заедно вече ... години.	We have lived together for ... years.	Уѝ: хæв ливд тъгèдъ фо: ... йѝ:ъз.

Кога ще получа граж-данство, ако се оженя за нея (него).	When will I receive a citizenship if I marry her (him)?	Уѐн уйл ай рисѝ:в ъ сѝтизъншип иф ай мӕ̀ри хъ: (хим)?
Имам желание ...	I wish...	Ай уйш ...
Какво ще кажеш ...?	What about...?	Уо̀т ъбàут ...?
Искам ... Желая ... Бих желал,-а ...	I want ...I wish ... I'd like...	Ай уо̀нт ... Ай уйш ... Айд лàйк ...
да се разходим	to have a walk with you	ту хӕв ъ уо̀:к уйд ю:
да ви изпратя до дома ви	to take you home	ту тѐйк ю: хо̀ум
да бъдем заедно през уикенда	to spend the weekend together	ту спѐнд дъ уѝ:кенд тъгѐдъ
да се видим отново	to see you again	ту си: ю: ъгѐйн
да се оженя (омъжа) за теб	to marry you	ту мӕ̀ри ю:
да живеем заедно без брак	to live with you without getting married	ту лѝв уйд ю: уидàут гѐтинг мӕ̀рид

да те представя	to introduce	ту интрърдю:с
на родителите си	you to my parents	ю: ту май пѐърънтс
(приятелите)	(friends)	(френдз)
да правим любов	to make love with you	ту мѐйк лав уѝ*д* ю:
да имам дете от теб	to have a baby with you	ту хæв ъ бѐйби уѝ*д* ю:
Харесва ми много	I like being	Ай ла̀йк бѝ:нг
да бъдем заедно.	togeder with you.	тъгѐ*д*ъ уѝ*д* ю:.
Щастлив,-а съм с теб.	I'm happy to be with you.	Айм хæ̀пи ту би: уѝ*д* ю:.
Не мога да си предста-	I can't imagine living	Ай ка̀:нт имæ̀джин
вя живота си без теб.	without you.	лѝвинг уи*д*а̀ут ю:.
Влюбен,-а съм ...	I'm in love ...	Айм ин лав ...
в теб	with you	уѝ*д* ю
в него	with him	уѝ*д* хим
в нея	with her	уѝ*д* хъ:
Обичаш ли ме?	Do you love me?	Ду: ю: ла̀в ми:?
Обичам те.	I love you.	Ай ла̀в ю:.
Харесвам те много.	I find you very	Ай файнд ю: вѐри
	attractive.	атрæ̀ктив.

Липсвам ли ти?	Do you miss me?	Ду ю: мис ми:?
Липсваш ми много.	I miss you very much.	Ай мис ю: вѐри мач.
Ще се ожениш (омъжиш) ли за мен?	Will you marry me?	Уѝл ю: мѐри ми:?

Не те обичам вече.	I don't love you any more.	Ай дòунт лав ю: èни мо:.
Не искам да се караме.	I don't want to argue with you.	Ай дòунт уòнт ту à:гю уѝ*g* ю:.
Сърдит,-а ли си(сте)?	Are you hurt?	А: ю: хъ:т?
Обиден,-а съм.	I feel insulted.	Ай фѝ:л инсàлтид.
Искам да се разделим.	I want us to break apart.	Ай уòнт ас ту брейк ъпа:т.
Напускам те.	I'm leaving you.	Айм лѝ:винг ю:.
Искам развод.	I want a divorce.	Ай уòнт ъ дивò:с.
В живота ми има друг мъж (друга жена).	There's another man (woman) in my life.	*g*èъз ънà*g*ъ мæн (уỳмън) ин май лайф.

Части на тялото	*Parts of the Body*	*Пà:тс ъв дъ бòди*
глава	**head**	**хед**
лице	face	фейс
око, очи	eye, eyes	ай, айз
зеница	pupil	пю̀:пъл
ирис	iris	àйърис
вежди	eyebrows	àйбрауз
клепачи	eyelids	àйлидз
мигли	eyelashes	àйлæшиз
ухо, уши	ear, ears	ѝъ, ѝъз
уста	mouth	мàу*т*
устни	lips	липс
нос	nose	нòуз
бузи	cheeks	чи:кс
брадичка	chin	чин
чело	forehead	фò:хед
коса	hair	хèъ

шия	neck	нек
гърло	throat	*тро̀ут*
зъб, зъби	tooth, teeth	ту:*т*, ти:*т*
език	tongue	танг
тяло	**body**	**бо̀ди**
рамо	shoulder	шо̀улдъ
гърди, бюст	breasts	брѐстс
гърди, гръден кош	chest	чест
корем	belly	бѐли
гръб,кръст	back	бæк
таз	pelvis	пѐлвис
крайници	**limbs**	**лимз**
ръка	arm	а:м
мишница	armpit	а̀:мпит
ръка	hand	хæнд
крак	leg	лег
пръст	finger	фѝнгъ
пръст на крака	toe	то̀у
нокът	nail	нейл
лакът	elbow	ѐлбоу

длан	palm	па:м
юмрук	fist	фист
китка	wrist	рист
глезен	ankle	æ̀нкъл
задни части, таз	buttocks	ба̀тъкс
бедро	thigh	*т*ай
ханш	hip	хип
коляно	knee	ни:
прасец	calf	ка:ф
стъпало	foot	фут
пета	heel	хи:л

органи	**organs**	**ò:гънз**
мозък	brain	брейн
сърце	heart	ха:т
кръв	blood	блад
вена	vein	вейн
артерия	artery	à:търи
нерви	nerves	нъ:вз
черен дроб	liver	лѝвъ
бели дробове	lungs	лангз

черва	intestines	интѐстинз
дебело черво	large intestine	ла:дж интѐстин
бъбрек	kidney	кѝдни
стомах	stomach	ста̀мък
жлъчка	gall	го:л
далак	spleen	спли:н
кост	bone	бо̀ун
череп	scull	скал
ребро	rib	риб
скелет	skeleton	скѐлитън
мускул	muscle	ма̀съл
кожа	skin	скин

сетива	**senses**	**сѐнсиз**
слух	hearing	хѝъринг
зрение	eyesight	а̀йсайт
обоняние	(sense of) smell	(сенс ъв) смел
осезание	(sense of) touch	(сенс ъв) тач
вкус	taste	тейст

При лекаря	At the Doctor's	æт дъ дòктъз
Къде мога да намеря лекар?	Where can I find a doctor?	Уèъ кæн ай фàйнд ъ дòктъ?
Искам да отида на лекар.	I want to see a doctor.	Ай уòнт ту си: ъ дòктъ.
Трябва ми лекар, който говори ... българскu	I need a doctor who speaks ... Bulgarian	Ай ни:д ъ дòктъ ху спи:кс ... балгѐъриън
Мога ли да получа час за днес?	Can I have an appointment for today?	Кæн ай хæв ън ъпòйнтмънт фо: тъдѐй?
Аз не съм пациент тук. Чужденец,-ка съм. Нямам здравна осигуровка.	I 'm not a patient here. I am a stranger. I haven't got health insurance.	Айм нот ъ пѐйшънт хѝъ. Ай æм ъ стрѐйнджъ. Ай хæ̀въ нт гот хѐлт иншу̀ърънс.

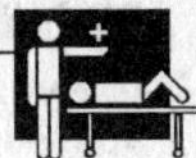

Какво ви е?	What's the trouble?	Уòтс *д*ъ тр̀абъл?
Боли,-ят ме ...	I've got ...	Айв гот ...
главата	a headache	ъ хѐдейк
гърлото	a sore throat	ъ сò: *т*рòут
стомаха	a stomachache	ъ ст̀амъкейк
бъбреците	a pain in the kidneys	ъ пѐйн ин *д*ъ кѝдниз
гърдите	a pain in the lungs	ъ пѐйн ин *д*ъ лангз
Имам ...	I have got ...	Ай хæв гот ...
хрема	a running nose	ъ р̀анинг нòуз
температура	temperature	тѐмпричъ
кръвотечение	bleeding	блѝ:динг
високо кръвно налягане	high blood pressure	хай бл̀ад прѐшъ
ниско кръвно налягане	low blood pressure	лòу блад прѐшъ
сърдечен пристъп	heart attack	ха:т ътæк
проблеми със ...	problems with ...	прòблъмз уѝ*д* ...
сърцето	my heart	май ха:т
бъбреците	my kidneys	май кѝдниз
черния дроб	my liver	май лѝвъ
жлъчката	my gall	май го:л

Имам смущения в храносмилането.	My digestion is upset.	Май дайджѐсчън из апсѐт.
Страдам от ...	I suffer from ...	Ай сафъ фром ...
Боледувал,-а съм от ...	I have suffered from ...	Ай хæв сафъд фром ...
диабет	diabetes	дайъбѝ:тис
астма	asthma	æ̀смъ
язва	ulcer	àлсъ
разстройство	diarhoea	дайърѝъ
гастрит	gastritis	гæстрàйтис
запек	constipation	констипѐйшън
Прекарал съм ...	I`ve had ...	Айв хæд ...
хепатит	hepatitis	хѐпътѐйтис
инфаркт	heart attack	ха:д ътà:к
туберкулоза	tuberculosis	тюбъ̀:кюлòусис
Кашлям непрекъснато.	I am constantly coughing.	Ай æм кòнстънтли кòфинг.
Вие ми се свят.	I feel dizzy.	Ай фѝ:л дѝзи.
Тресе ме.	I feel shivery.	Ай фѝ:л шѝвъри.
Чувствам слабост.	I feel weak.	Ай фѝ:л уѝ:к.
Нямам апетит.	I have lost my appetite.	Ай хæв лòст май æ̀питайт.

Здравната система в Англия е претоварена. Клиниките са пълни с хора и често има недостиг на персонал. Добре е да се регистрирате при GP веднага щом се настаните на постоянен адрес.

Ако не сте регистрирани, няма да може да получите лекарска помощ. В случай, че ви се наложи да потърсите спешно доктор, може да се отбиете в един от медицинските центрове на Лондон, които са за по-леки болести. Там няма да ви трябва лекарска регистрация и обслужването е безплатно. Клиниките са отворени 7 дни от сутрин до късно вечер. За да откриете къде е най-близката клиника погледнете на адрес www.doh.gov.uk

Най-близката клиника за централен Лондон е Сохо.

Soho Walk In Centre, 1 Frith Street ✆ 020 7534 6500. (метро: Covent Garden).

Аптекарите могат да ви бъдат полезни и да ви дадат съвет по много въпроси, особено при по-незначителни неразположения. Наберете ✆ 100 (безплатно) за телефонен оператор, който ще ви даде адреса на някой местен доктор или болница.

При спешни случаи за линейка позвънете на ✆ 999 (безплатно).

На тези два сайта също ще получите помощ и съвет: **www.medicdirect.co.uk; www.synergy-health.co.uk**

Изтръпва ми ...	I feel my ... stiff.	Ай фи:л май... стиф.
ръката	arm	а:м
кракът	leg	лег
Това започна ...	It started...	Ит ста̀:тид ...
преди два дни	two days ago	ту: дѐйз ъгѝу
снощи	last night	ла̀:ст найт
Счупен (изкълчен) ли е кракът (ръката) ми?	Is my arm (leg) broken (dislocated)?	Из май а̀:м (лег) брѝукън (дѝслъкѐйтид)?
Измерете ми кръвното налягане, моля!	Would you take my blood pressure, please?	У:д ю: тѐйк май блад прѐшъ, пли:з?
Мисля, че съм настинал,-а.	I think I've caught a cold.	Ай *т*инк айв ко̀:т ъ кѝулд.
Необходими ли са изследвания ...?	Do I need any ... test?	Ду: ай ни:д ѐни ...тест?
на кръвта	blood	блад
на урината	urine	ю̀рин

Необходима ли е рентгенова снимка?	Do I need an X-ray?	Ду: ай ни:д ън èкс-рей?
Не виждам добре. Не чувам добре.	I can't see well. I can't hear well.	Ай кà:нт сѝ: уèл. Ай кà:нт хѝъ уèл.
Съблечете се! Легнете тук!	Strip to the waist. Lie down here, please!	Стрѝп ту дъ уèйст. Лàй дàун хѝъ, пли:з!
Ще ви напиша рецепта.	I'll give you a prescription.	Айл гив ю: ъ прискрѝпшън.
Трябва да направите изследвания. Елате пак след ...	You have to do an analysis. You have to come in…	Ю: хæв ту ду: ън ънæ̀лисис. Ю: хæв ту кам ин …
Колко трябва да платя за прегледа?	How much do I have to pay for the examination?	Хàу мач ду: ай хæв ту пей фо: ди икзæминèйшън?
Днес се чувствам по-добре (по-лошо).	I feel better (worse) today.	Ай фѝ:л бèтъ (уъ:с) тъдèй.

лекар	**doctor**	**дòктъ**
лекуващ лекар	attending doctor	атѐндинг дòктъ
патолог	pathologist	пътòлъджист
кардиолог	cardiologist	ка:диòлъджист
гинеколог	gynaecologist	гайникòлъджист
дерматолог	dermatologist	дъ:мътòлъджист
венеролог	venereologist	виниъриòлъджист
невролог	neurologist	нюрòлъджист
гастроентеролог	gastroentereologist	гæстроуентърòлъджист
уролог	urologist	юрòлъджист
хирург	surgeon	съ:джън
ортопед	orthopaedist	ò:тоупѝ:дист
педиатър	paediatricion	пѝдиæтрѝ:шън
очен лекар	ophthalmologist	офтæлмòлъджист
лекар уши, нос, гърло	otolaryngologist	òтоулæрингòлъджист
медицинска сестра	nurse	нъ:с
санитар,-ка	hospital attendant	хòспитъл ътѐндънт

болница	hospital	хòспитъл
частна клиника	private clinic	прàйвит клѝник
поликлиника	polyclinic	поликлѝник
лекарски кабинет	surgery	съ:джъри
пациент	patient	пèйшънт
стационарно болен,-на	in-patient	ин пèйшънт
болен	ill	ил
здрав	healthy	хèлти

преглед	medical examination	мѐдикъл икзæминѐйшън
болест	disease, illness	дизѝ:з, ѝлнис
рана	wound	уу̀нд
инжекция	injection	инджѐкшън
превръзка	bandage, dressing	бæ̀ндидж, дрѐсинг
операция	operation	опърѐйшън
простуда	cold	ко̀улд
кашлица	cough	коф
грип	grippe, flu	грип, флу:
тумор ...	... tumour	... тю̀:мъ
доброкачествен	non-malignant	нон мълѝгнънт
злокачествен	malignant	мълѝгнънт
рак	cancer	кæ̀нсъ
болка	pain	пейн
алергия	allergy	æ̀лъджи
безсъние	insomnia	инсо̀мниъ

При зъболекаря	At the Dentist's	æт gъ gèнтистс
Има ли зъболекар наблизо?	Is there a dentist nearby?	Из gèъ ъ дèнтист нѝъбай?
Боли ме много един зъб.	I've got a toothache.	Айв гот ъ тỳ:тейк.
Венците ми кървят.	My gums bleed.	Май гамз блѝ:д.
Болката е тук.	I feel pain here.	Ай фѝ:л пейн хѝъ.
Този зъб ...	This tooth ...	gис ту:т ...
ме боли	hurts me.	хъ:тс ми:
не ме боли	doesn't hurt me.	дàзънт хъ:т ми:
Падна ми пломбата.	I have lost a filling.	Ай хæв лòст ъ фѝлинг.
Имате кариес.	You've got a cavity.	Ю:в гот ъ кæ̀вити.
Този зъб трябва да се извади.	This tooth must be pulled out.	gис ту:т маст би пулд àут.
Направете това, което е необходимо!	Do what is necessary, please!	Ду: уòт из нèсъсъри, пли:з!

Ще го извадите ли?	Do you have to pull it out?	Ду: ю: хæв ту пу̀л ит а̀ут?
Извадете го!	Pull it out!	Пу̀л ит а̀ут!
Ще го пломбирате ли?	Are you going to fill it?	А: ю: го̀уинг ту фил ит?
Предпочитам ...	I'd rather have ...	Айд ра̀:гъ хæв ...
с упойка	an anaesthetic	ън æнистѐтик
пломба	a filling	ъ фѝлинг
умъртвяване на нерв	the nerve removed	дъ нъ:в риму̀:вд
Отворете устата!	Open your mouth!	о̀упън йо: ма̀ут!
Не я затваряйте!	Don't close it!	До̀унт кло̀уз ит!
Затворете я!	Close it!	Кло̀уз ит!
Изплакнете устата си!	Rinse your mouth!	Ринс йо: ма̀ут!
Елате пак след два дни.	You have to come in two days.	Ю: хæв ту кам ин ту: дѐйз.

Зъболечението е безплатно, ако сте регистрирани към националната здравна служба. Спешна зъболекарска помощ може да получите безплатно от Guy Hospital Dental School от 9 до 15.30 от понеделник до петък.

При спешна нужда от зъболекар се свържете също с ***Dental Emergency Care Service*** *на ✆ 0171-955 2186 или позвънете в* ***Eastman Dental Hospital*** *(✆ 0171-837 3646), 256 Gray's Inn Rd WC1 (метро: Chancery Lane).*

При спешни случаи звънете денонощно на: ✆ 020 7867 78383, 020 7584 1008.

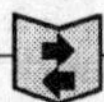

зъболекар	dentist	дѐнтист
зъболекарски кабинет	dentist's	дѐнтистс
пломбирам	fill	фил
пломба	filling	фѝлинг
абсцес	abscess	ӕ̀бсес
нерв	nerve	нъ:в
корен	root	ру:т
мост	bridge	бридж
изкуствена челюст	denture jaw	дѐнчъ джо:
челюст	jaw	джо:
горна	upper	а̀пъ
долна	lower	лѐоуъ
оток	swelling	суѐлинг
коронка	crown	кра̀ун
венец	gum	гам

В аптеката	**At the Chemist's**	**æт gъ кѐмистс**
Къgе наблизо има аптека?	Where's the nearest pharmacy, please?	Уѐъз gъ нѝърист фà:мъси, пли:з?
Дайте ми ...!	I'd like	Айд лайк ....
този антибиотик	this antibiotic	gис æ̀нтибайòтик
болкоуспокояващо	some analgesic	сам æнæлджѝ:зик
витамини	some vitamins	сам вàйтъминз
аспирин	some aspirin	сам æ̀сп(ъ)рин
разслабително	some laxative	сам л æ̀ксътив
приспивателно	a sleeping drug	ъ слѝ:пинг драг
успокоително	some sedative	сам сѐдътив
дезинфектант	some disinfectant	сам дѝсинфѐктънт
Имате ли...?	Have you got ...?	Хæв ю: гот ...?
това лекарство	this medicine	gис мѐдсин
този сироп	this syrup	gис сѝръп
спирт	spirit(s)	спѝрит(с)
бинт	bandage	б æ̀ндидж
памук	cotton-wool	кòтън уỳл
марля	gauze, lint	го:з, линт
дамски превръзки	sanitary towels	с æ̀нитъри тàуълз

Трябва ми нещо за ...	I need something for ...	Ай ни:д са̀мтинг фо: ...
настинка	a cold	ъ коулд
разстроен стомах	an upset stomach	ън апсѐт ста̀мък
главоболие	a headache	ъ хѐдейк
слънчево изгаряне	a sunburn	ъ са̀нбъ:н
ужилване	a sting	ъ стинг
Можете да вземете това лекарство само с рецепта.	You can get this medicine only with a prescription.	Ю: кæн гет дис мѐдсин о̀унли уѝд ъ прискрѝпшън.
Можете ли да изпълните тази рецепта?	Can you make up this prescription, please?	Кæн ю: мѐйк ап дис прискрѝпшън, пли:з?
Напишете ми, моля, как да ги вземам!	Would you write down how to take them, please?	У:д ю: ра̀йт да̀ун ха̀у ту тейк дъм, пли:з?
преди(след) ядене	before(after) meals	бифо̀:(а̀:фтъ) мѝ:лз
три пъти на ден	three times a day	три: та̀ймз ъ дей
по една таблетка	one tablet	уа̀н тæ̀блит
(по ... таблетки)	(... tablets)	(... тæ̀блитс)

аптека	pharmacy, Chemist's	фà:мъси, кèмистс
аптекар	pharmacist, chemist	фà:мъсист, кèмист,
лекарство	medicine	мèдсин
за външна употреба	for external use	фо: икстъ̀:нъл ю:с
за вътрешна употреба	for internal use	фо: интъ̀:нъл ю:с
рецепта	prescription	прискрѝпшън
ампула	ampule, glass tube	ǽмпю:л, глà:с тю:б
хапче, таблетка	pill, tablet	пил, тǽблит
шишенце	vial	вàйъл
прах	powder	пàудъ
крем ...	... ointment	... òйнтмънт
капки ...	... drops	... дропс
за очи	eye	ай
за нос	nose	нòус
за уши	ear	иъ:
таблетки за гърло за смучене	throat lozenges	*тр*òут лòзинджиз
лейкопласт	adhesive plaster (tape)	ъдхѝ:сив плà:стъ (тейп)
презерватив	condom	кòндъм

Образование. Професии | Education. Ocupations | Едюкѐйшън. Окюпѐйшънз

Образование. Професии	Education. Ocupations	Едюкѐйшън. Окюпѐйшънз
диплома	diploma	диплòумъ
удостоверение	certificate	съ:тѝфикит

Завършил,-а съм ...	I finished ...	Ай фѝнищт ...
начално, основно училище	a primary school	ън пра̀ймъри ску:л
средно училище	a secondary school	ъ сѐкъндъри ску:л
гимназия	high-school	хай ску:л
техникум	a technical school	ъ тѐкникъл ску:л
Завършил,-а съм ...	I graduated from ...	Ай грæ̀дюейтид фром ...
колеж	a college	ъ кòлидж
университета в	the university of ...	дъ юнивъ:сити ъф ...
консерватория	a conservatoire	ъ кънсъ:вътуа:

Имам магистърска степен по ...	I have a master's degree in ...	Ай хæв ъ мæ̀стъ:з дигрѝ: ин ...
иконоимика	economics	ѝкъ:нòмикс
медицина	medicine	мèдсин
инженерство	engineering	èнджинѝърингг
Специализирал съм...	I am specialized in ...	Ай æм спèшълайзд ин ...
ветеринарна медицина	veterinary medicine	вèтъринъри мèдисин
инженерство	engineering	èнджинѝърингг
електроника	electronics	илектрòникс
комуникации	communications	комюникèйшънс
право	law	ло:
физика	physics	фѝзикс
филология	philology	филòлъджи
теология	theology	*т*иòлъджи
химия	chemistry	кèмистри
биология	biology	байòлъджи
история	history	хѝстъри
география	geography	джиòгръфи

Сега съм ...	Now I am ...	Нàу ай æм ...
ученик,-чка	a student	ъ стю̀:дънт
студент,-ка	a student	ъ стю̀:дънт
инженер	an engineer	ън èнджиниъ
лекар,-ка	a doctor	ъ дòктъ
работник,-чка	a worker	ъ уъ̀:къ
безработен	unemployed	анимплòйд
пенсионер,-ка	retired, a pensioner	ритàйъд, ъ пèншънъ
Каква е професията ви?	What's your job?	Уòтс йо: джòб?
Какво работиш,-ите?	What do you do?	Уòт ду: ю: ду:?
Аз съм ...	I am ...	Ай æм ...
агроном	an agronomist	ън ъгрòнъмист
адвокат	a lawyer	ъ лò:йъ
актьор, актриса	an actor, an actress	ън æ̀ктъ, ън æ̀ктрис
архитект	an architect	ън à:китект
биолог	a biologist	ъ байòлъджист
бояджия	a house painter	ъ хàус пèйнтъ
бръснар	a barber	ъ бà:бъ
водопроводчик	a plumber	ъ плàмбъ

готвач,-чка	a cook	ъ кук
дърводелец	a carpenter	ъ ка̀:пънтъ
военен	a military man	ъ мѝлитъри мæн
електротехник	an electrician	ън илектрѝшън
журналист, -ка	a journalist	ъ джъ̀:нълист
земеделец, фермер	a farmer	ъ фа̀:мъ
златар	a goldsmith	ъ го̀улдсмит
издател	a publisher	ъ па̀блишъ
икономист	an economist	ън ико̀нъмист
камериер	a valet	ъ вæ̀лит
камериерка	a chambermaid	ъ чѐймбъмейд
манекен, модел	a model	ъ мо̀дъл
мебелист	a cabinet-maker	ъ кæ̀бинит мѐйкъ
месар	a butcher	ъ бу̀чъ
миньор	a miner	ъ ма̀йнъ
монтьор, механик	a fitter	ъ фѝтъ
музикант	a musician	ъ мю:зѝшън
обущар	a shoemaker	ъ шу̀:мейкъ
певец,-ица	a singer	ъ сѝнгъ
педагог	a pedagogue	ъ пѐдъгог

преводач,-ка	an interpreter	ън интъ̀:притъ
преводач,-ка*(писмен)*	a translator	ъ тра:нслѐйтъ
продавач,-чка	a shop-assistant	ъ шо̀п ъсѝстънт
проститутка	a prostitute	ъ про̀ститю:т
работник	a worker	ъ уъ̀:къ
работничка	a workwoman	ъ уъ̀:кумън
свещеник, поп	a priest	ъ при:ст
строител	a constructor	ъ кънстра̀ктъ
счетоводител,-ка	accountant	ън ъка̀унтънт
техник	a mechanic	ъ микæ̀ник
треньор	a trainer, a coach	ъ трѐйнъ, ъ ко̀уч
търговец	a trader	ъ трѐйдъ
художник	an artist	ън а̀:тист
чиновник	a clerk	ъ кла:к
чистачка	a cleaner	ъ клѝ:нъ
шофьор	a driver	ъ дра̀йвъ
шивач	a tailor	ъ тѐйлъ
шивачка	a dressmaker	ъ дрѐсмейкъ
учител,-ка	a teacher	ъ тѝ:чъ
часовникар	watchmaker	уо̀чмейкъ

Дом, адрес, наем	Home, Address, Renting	Хòум, ъдрèс, рèнтинг
Къде живееш,-ете?	Where do you live?	Уèъ ду: ю: лив?
Живея,-ем ...	I(we) live ...	Ай(уй:) лив ...
на ул. "В. Левски"	in Vassil Levski St.	ин Васѝл Лèвски стри:т
на ул. "В. Левски" 145	at 145 Vassil Levski St.	æт уа̲н фо: файв Васѝл Лèвски стри:т.
в село ...	in the village of...	ин дъ вѝлидж ъв ...
в град ...	in the town of...	ин дъ тàун ъв ...
в жилищен блок	in a block of flats / in an appartment building	ин ъ блòк ъв флæтс / ин ън ъпà:тмънт бѝлдинг
Имам,-е ...	I (we) have got ...	Ай (уй:) хæв гот ...
еднофамилна къща	a family house	ъ фæ̀мили хàус
апартамент	a flat	ъ флæт

На кой етаж?	On which floor?	Он уйч фло:?
На втория (петия) етаж.	On the second (fifth) floor.	Он *д*ъ сѐкънд (фиф*т*) фло:.
Къщата ми (ни)	My (Our) house	Май (ȁуъ) хȁус
Апартаментът ми (ни)	My (Our) flat	Май (ȁуъ) флæт
... се състои от ... ... стаи	... has got ... ... rooms	... хæз гот ... ... ру:мз
кухня	a kitchen	ъ кѝчън
трапезария	a dining room	ъ дȁйнинг ру:м
хол	a living room	ъ лѝвинг ру:м
спалня	a bedroom	ъ бѐдру:м
тераса	a balcony	ъ бæ̀лкъни
сутерен	a basement	ъ бѐйсмънт
мазе	a cellar	ъ сѐлъ
гараж	a garage	ъ гæ̀ридж
таванска стая	an attic	ън æ̀тик
баня	a bathroom	ъ бȁ:*т*рум
тоалетна	a toilet	ъ тòйлит

Имаме ...	We have got ...	Уѝ: хæв гот ...
градина	a garden	ъ га̀:дън
двор	a yard	ъ йа:д
басейн	a swimming pool	ъ суѝминг пу:л
камина	a fireplace	ъ фа̀йъплейс
➡ Имате ли свободни стаи под наем?	Have you got any rooms for rent?	Хæв ю: гот ѐни ру:мз фо: рѐнт?
Обаждам се по повод обявата за ...	I'm calling about the ... you advertised.	Айм ко̀:линг ъба̀ут ди ... ю: æдвътайзд.
стая	room	ру:м
апартамент	flat	флæт
Бих желал,-а да дойда и я (го) видя.	Is it still available? I'd like to come and see it, please.	Из ит стил ъвѐйлъбъл? Айд ла̀йк ту кам æнд си: ит, пли:з.
➡ Какъв е адресът, моля?	What's the address, please?	Уо̀тс ди ъдрѐс, пли:з?
Искам,-е да наема,-ем..	I (we) like to rent ...	Ай (уѝ:) ла̀йк ту рѐнт ...
една стая	a room	ъ ру:м
две стаи	two rooms	ту: ру:мз

малък апартамент	a small flat	ъ смò:л флæт
гарсониера	studio	стỳдио
къща	a house	ъ хàус
Влезте, моля.	Come in, please.	Кам ин, пли:з.
Ще ви покажа.	I'll show you around.	Айл шòу ю: ърàунд.
Ще го (я) наема,-ем за...	I(we)'d like to rent it for…	Ай(уй:)д лàйк ту рèнт ит фо: …
една седмица	a week	ъ уй:к
един месец	a month	ъ мант
шест месеца	six months	сйкс мантс
една година	a year	ъ йъ:

Под наем (Renting)

Отсядането под наем е за предпочитане, ако смятате да останете в Лондон или друг град за по-дълго време. Да се намери квартира не е лесна работа. Най-добре звънете сутрин рано, още щом излезе вестникът с обявите. Търпение и обикаляне са двете основни правила, ако искате да намерите това, което търсите. Вземете безплатните публикации като ***TNT*** *или* ***LAM****. Ако там не откриете нищо подходящо, купете си* ***LOOT*** *(лондонски вестник с обяви) или* ***Evening***

Standard. Вестниците имат уеб страници, където е изложена същата информация. Други сайтове предлагащи квартири са www.boulle.co.uk и www.gumtree.com.

LOOT (www.loot.com) е вестник, който излиза всеки ден. Квартирите са класифицирани според вида и цената им. Ориентирайте се по географските кодове или района, където смятате да живеете. Най-често срещаните съкращения в адресите са:

WC, EC	Централен Лондон
NW	Северозападен Лондон
SW	Югозападен Лондон
SE	Югоизточен Лондон
E	Източен Лондон
W	Западен Лондон

Квартири
Стаи (Bedsits)

Това са самостоятелни стаи с място за готвене, малък хладилник и обща баня. Обикновено в цената са включени някои разходи като газ, електричество и общинска такса (**council tax**). В зависимост от района, цените варират от 70 до 120 лири на седмица.

Студио и едностайни апартаменти (Studio and one bedroom apartments)

Те са със отделен кухненски бокс и баня. По-скъпи са от самостоятелна стая, но ако държите на спокойствието, си заслужава. Добър вариант са за двама живеещи заедно.

Колко е наемът в лири?	How much is the rent in pounds?	Хàу мач из дъ рент ин пàундз?
Наемът е ... лири ...	The rent is ... pounds ...	дъ рèнт из ... пàундз ...
на седмица	a week	ъ уй:к
на месец	a month	ъ мант
Не можем да плащаме толкова много.	We can't pay so much.	Уй: кà:нт пей сòу мач.
Ако намалите наема, съм съгласен,-на.	If you make a discount, I'll take it.	Иф ю: мейк ъ дѝскаунт, айл тейк ит.
Съгласен,-на съм.	I agree.	Ай агрѝ:.
Изгодно ми е.	It suits me.	Ит сю:тс ми:.
Не ми е изгодно.	It doesn't suit me.	Ит дàзънт сю:т ми:.
Искате ли предплата?	Would you like a deposit?	Уỳд ю: лайк ъ дипòзит?
В наема включени ли са общите разходи?	Does the rent include facilities?	Даз дъ рèнт инклỳ:д фъсѝлитиз?
ток	electricity	илектрѝсити
вода	water	уò:тъ
парно	heating	хѝ:тинг

Можете ли да го обзаведете?	Could you furnish it for me, please?	Куд ю: фъ:ниш ит фо: ми:, пли:з?
Обзаведен,-а ли е?	Is it furnished?	Из йт фъ:ништ?
Дайте ми (ни) ключа.	The key, please?	дъ кй:, пли:з?

адрес	**address**	**ъдрѐс**
номер	number	нàмбъ
улица	street	стри:т
квартал	quarter	куò:тъ
пощенски код	postal code	пòустъл кòуд
град	town	тàун
село	villige	вѝлидж
къща, дом, жилище	**house, home, lodging**	**хàус, хòум, лòджинг**
партер	ground floor	грàунд фло:
етаж	floor	фло:
сутерен	basement	бѐйсмънт
маза	cellar	сѐлъ
таван	attic	ѐтик

двор	yard	йа:д
прозорец	window	уйндоу
стълбище	staircase	стèъкейс
под	a floor	ъ фло:
коридор	corridor	кòридъ
басейн	basin	бèйсин
спалня	**bedroom**	**бèдру:м**
спалня (легло)	bed	бед
гардероб	wardrobe	уò:дроуб
одеяло	blanket	бл æ̀нкит
чаршаф	sheet	ши:т
възглавница	pillow	пѝлоу
калъф за възглавница	pillow-case	пѝлоу кейс
дюшек	mattress	м æ̀трис
хол, дневна	**sitting room**	**сѝтинг ру:м**
трапезария	**dining room**	**дàйнинг ру:м**
стол	chair	чèъ
маса	table	тèйбъл
покривка *(за маса)*	table-cloth	тèйбъл кло*т*
диван	sofa	сòуфъ

фотьойл	arm-chair	à:м чèъ
секция *(мебели)*	cabinet	кǽбинит
завеса	curtain	къ:тън
барче	liquor cabinet	лѝкъ кǽбинит
килим	carpet	кà:пит
кухня	**kitchen**	**кѝчън**
мивка	sink	синк
печка *(за отопление)*	stove	стòув
печка *(готварска)*	cooker	кỳкъ
печка *(микровълнова)*	micro-wave oven	мàйкроуèйв òувн
пералня	washing machine	уòшинг мъшѝ:н
миялна машина	dishwasher	дѝшуошъ
хладилник	fridge	фридж
фризер	freezer	фрѝ:зъ
прахосмукачка	vacuum cleaner	вǽкю:м клѝ:нъ
баня	**bathroom**	**бà:*т*ру:м**
тоалетна	toilet	тòйлът, тòйлит
вана	bathtub	бà:*т* таб
чешма, кранче	tap	тæп
мивка	wash-basin	уòш-бèйсин

разходи	**expenses**	**икспѐнсиз**
сметка ...	**... bill**	**... бил**
за водата	water	уò:тъ
за електричеството	electricity	илектрѝсити
за телефона	phone	фòун
такса	charge, fee	чà:дж, фи:
данък	tax	тæкс
водомер	water-meter	уò:тъ мѝ:тъ
електромер	electrometer	илектрòми:тъ
консумация	consumption	кънсàмпшън
депозит, предплата	deposit	дипòзит

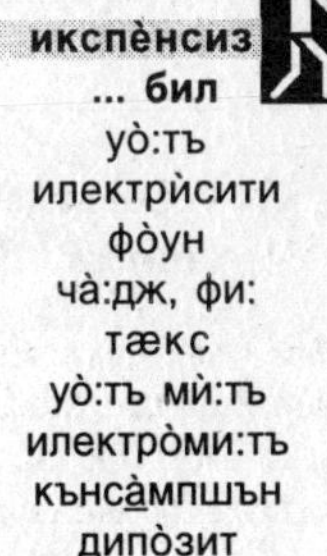

Общи квартира (House / flat share)

Това е най-популярният вариант за чужденци, пребиваващи в Лондон. Може да съберете група приятели и да наемете свободен апартамент или къща. В зависимост от района и състоянието на стаите, цените варират от 50 до 100 лири на седмица за стая. Двойка партньори трябва да очакват малко по-високи цени за стая. Практика в Лондон е да се взема четириседмичен ***депозит*** *или четири седмици* ***предплата*** *за жилището. Повечето договори за наем са за периоди от 6 до 12 месеца. В края на периода ще си получите депозита, ако жилището е предадено в същия вид, в който е получено. Преди да се нанесете в наетото жилище, се убедете, че няма неплатени сметки. Прочетете много внимателно договора за наем преди да го подпишете. Множество фирми предоставят квартири в Лондон за студенти. Обикновено това е стая или легло в стая в зависимост от бюджета ви и в цената на наема са включени общинската такса и сметките. Заслужава си да се свържете с някоя от тези фирми особено, ако бюджетът ви е малък и искате да спестите пари. Внимавайте да не ви настанят в къща с 20 или повече човека.*

Търсене на работа	***Looking for a Job***	***Лу̀кинг фо: ъ джоб***
Бюро за търсене на работа	Employment Office / Job Centre	имплòймънт òфис / джоб сѐнтъ
работя	work	уъ:к
работа	work, job, business	уъ:к, джòб, бѝзнис
Търся,-им работа.	I'm(we're) looking for a job.	Айм(уѝъ) лу̀кинг фо: ъ джоб.
Искам да постъпя на работа.	I'd like to apply for a job.	Айд лàйк ту ъплàй фо: ъ джòб.
Искам да кандидатствам за длъжността ...	I'd like to apply for a position of ...	Айд лайк ту ъплàй фо: ъ пъзѝшън ъв ...
Каква работа търсите?	What kind of job are you looking for?	Уòт кàйнд ъв джòб а: ю: лу̀кинг фо:?
Търся каквато и да е работа.	I'm looking for any kind of job.	Айм лу̀кинг фо: ѐни кàйнд ъв джòб.

Търся работа ...	I'm looking for a job…	Айм лу̀кинг фо: ъ джо̀б
в земеделието	in farming / agriculture	ин фа̀:минг / æгрика̲лчъ
в животновъдството	in stock-farming	ин сто̀к фа:минг
в туризма	in tourism	ин ту̀ъризм
Какво точно искате да работите?	What exactly do you need?	Уо̀т игзæ̀ктли ду: ю: нѝ:д?
Искам да работя като ...	I can be …	Ай кæн би: …
домашна помощница	maid	мѐйд
мияч на съдове	a dish-washer	ъ дѝш уо̀шъ
камериерка в хотел	a chambermaid	ъ чѐймбъмейд
чистачка	a cleaner	ъ клѝ:нъ
Искам да...	I want to…	Ай уо̀нт ту …
гледам някой болен човек	take care of an ill person	тѐйк кѐъ ъв ън ил пъ:сън
гледам някой възрастен	take care of an elderly person	тейк кѐъ ъв ън ѐлдъли пъ:сън
бъда детегледачка	be a baby-sitter	би: ъ бѐйби сѝтъ

работя в строителството	work on a construction	уъ:к он ъ кънстракшън
работя в някоя работилница / фабрика	work in a workshop / factory	уъ:к ин ъ уъ:кшоп: / фæктъри
Какво сте работили преди?	What's your work experience?	Уòтс йо: уъ:к икспѝъриънс?
Работил,-а съм като... *(вж. стр.367-369)*	I have worked as ...	Ай хæв уъ:кт æз ...
Мога да ...	I can...	Ай кæн ...
да карам кола	drive	дрàйв
ремонтирам коли	repair cars	рипèъ ка:з
работя на компютър	operate a computer	òпърейт ъ кълпю:тъ
да готвя	cook	кук
да шия	sew	сòу
Отдава ми се ..	I am good at...	Айм гуд æт ...
домакинството	house keeping	хàус кй:пинг
счетоводството	accounting	ъкàунтинг
секретарската работа	secretarial work	секритèъриъл уъ:к

Работя добре в колектив.	I'm a good team worker.	Айм ъ гуд ти:м уъ:къ.
Мога да работя ...	I can work ...	Ай кæн уъ:к ...
по всяко време	at any time	æт èни тайм
през работните дни	on week days	он уй:к дейз
през уикенда	at weekends	æт уй:кендз
на пълен работен ден	full time	фул тайм
на половин работен ден	part time	па:т тайм
нощна смяна	night shifts	найт шифтс
извънредно	overtime	òувътайм
с гъвкаво работно време	flexible working hours	флèксибъл уъ:кинг àуъ:з
За съжаление, в момента не можем да ви предложим нищо.	I'm sorry, we can't offer you anything at the moment.	Айм сòри, уй: ка:нт òфъ ю: èнитинг æт дъ мòумънт.
Можем да ви предложим следната работа...	We can offer you the following positions ...	Уй: кæн òфъ ю: дъ фòлоуинг пъзѝшънз ...

Ще ви наемем само временно.	We'll hire you temporarily.	Уѝ:л ха̀йъ ю: тѐмпъръри̇ли.
Съгласен,-на съм.	I agree.	Ай ъгрѝ:.
Приемам.	I accept.	Ай ъксѐпт.
Не ме устройва.	It doesn't suit me.	Ит дàзънт сю:т ми:.
Не е съвсем това, което търся.	It's not quite what I'm looking for.	Итс нот куàйт уòт айм лỳкинг фо:.
За сега ме устройва.	It suits me for the time being.	Ит сю:тс ми: фо: ðъ тайм бѝинг.
Какви документи трябва да представя?	What sort of documents should I submit?	Уòт со:т ъв дòкюмънтс шуд ай сабмѝт?
Къде ще работя?	Where shall I work?	Уѐъ шæл ай уъ:к?
Кога мога да започна работа?	When can I start working?	Уѐн кæн ай ста:т уъ̀:кинг?
Имам (нямам) ...	I have (not) got ...	Ай хæв (нот) гот ...
разрешение за работа	a work permit	ъ уъ:к пъ̀:мит
работна виза	a business visa	ъ бѝзнис вѝ:зъ
препоръки	references	рѐфърънсиз
три години стаж в ...	three years' experience in ...	три: йъ:з икспѝриънс ин ...

Визата ми изтича след...	My visa expires in ...	Май вѝ:зъ икспàйъз ин ...
три месеца	three months	*три:* м<u>а</u>н*тс*
шест месеца	six months	сикс м<u>а</u>н*тс*
Бих искал да знам...	I'd like to know...	Айд лàйк ту нòу ...
за колко време ме наемате	what the duration of my employment is	уòт *д*ъ дюърèйшън ъв май имплòймънт из
какво точно ще работя	what exactly I'm supposed to do	уòт игз ǽктли айм съпòузд ту ду:
повече подробности относно работата ми	more details regarding my job	мò: ди:тèйлз ригà:дин*г* май джòб
Ще имам ли почивен ден?	Shall I have a holiday?	Шæл ай хæв ъ хòлидей?
Мога ли да работя извънредно?	Can I work overtime?	Кæн ай уъ:к òувътàйм?
Ще имам ли трудова застраховка?	Shall I have job insurance?	Шæл ай хæв джоб иншỳрънс?
Каква ще бъде заплатата ми?	What's my salary going to be?	Уòтс май сǽлъри гòин*г* ту би:?

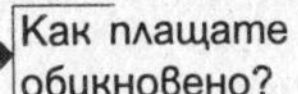

Как плащате обикновено?	How do you usually pay?	Хàу ду ю: ю:жуъли пей?
всяка седмица	every week	èври уй:к
всеки две седмици	every fortnight	èври фò:тнайт
всеки месец	every month	èври мант
Осигурявате ли ми (ни)...?	Are you going to provide ... for me (us)?	А: ю: гòуинг ту пръвàйд ... фо: ми: (ас)?
жилище (и)	lodging	лòджинг
храна	food, board	фу:д, бо:д
Осигуряваме ви...	We're going to provide ... for you	Уйъ гòуинг ту пръвàйд ... фо: ю:.
само жилище	only lodging	òунли лòджинг
само храна, ядене	only food, board	òунли фу:д, бо:д
жилище и храна	lodging and board	лòджинг æнд бо:д
Всичките разходи си поемате вие.	You undertake all the expenses.	Ю: андътèйк о:л ди икспèнсиз.

работодател	employer	имплойъ
управител	manager	мæниджъ
началник, шеф	chief, boss	чи:ф, бос
собственик	owner	оунъ
собственост	property	пропъти
работно място	working place	уъ:кинг плейс
работно време	working time	уъ:кинг тайм
извънредна работа	overtime work	оувътайм уъ:к
заплащане	payment	пеймънт
заплата	salary	сæлъри
надница	wage	уейдж
седмична заплата	week salary	уй:к сæлъри
месечна заплата	month salary	мант сæлъри
... осигуровка	insurance	... иншуърънс
трудова	job	джоб
социална	social	соушъл
здравна	health	хелт
молба, заявление	application form	æпликейшън фо:м
автобиография	CV(curriculum vitae)	Си:Ви: (кърикюлъм вайти:)
препоръки	reference	рефърънс

Делови контакти и кореспонденция	Business contasts and correspondence	Бѝзнес кòнтактс æнg кореспòнgънс
Нашата фирма е създадена през ... година.	Our firm is founded in ... year.	àуъ фъ:м из фàундид ин ... иъ:.
Главният ни офис се намира в град ...	Our headquarters is in the town of ...	àуъ хèдкуотъ:з из ин gъ тàун ъв ...
Имаме представителства в ...	We have offices in the town of ...	Уѝ: хæв òфисиз ин gъ тàун ъв ...
Основният ни предмет на дейност е (са) ...	Our main activity(-ies) is (are) ...	àуъ мейн aктѝвити(-с) из (а:) ...
търговията	trading	трèйдинг
производството	production	пръдàкшън
борсовите операции	stock exchange operations	сток иксчèйндж опърèйшънс
инвестициите	investments	инвèстмънтс

Проявяваме интерес към следните стоки ...	We are interested in the following goods ...	Уѝ: а: ѝнтрестид ин gъ фòлоуинг гудз ...
Изпращаме ви нашата оферта ...	We are sending our offer ...	Уѝ: а: сèндинг àуъ òфъ ...
по факса	by fax	бай фæкс
по електронната поща	by e-mail	бай и-мейл
Получихме вашата оферта.	We received your offer.	Уѝ: рисѝ:вт йо: òфъ:.
(Не) приемаме условията, които ни предлагате.	We (don't) accept the conditions you offer us.	Уѝ: (доунт) ъксèпт gъ кандѝшънс ю òфъ: ас.
(Не) сме съгласни с ...	We (don't) agree with ...	Уѝ: (доунт) ъгрѝй уиg ...
цената	the price	gъ прàйс
сроковете	the terms	gъ тъ:мс
Изпратете ни ...	Send us ...	Сенд ас ...
факс	fax	фæкс
официално писмо	official letter	ъфѝшъл лèтъ:

документите по регистрацията ви	the documents about your registration	дъ дòкюмънтс абàут йо: реджистрèйшън
писмо от Търговско-промишлената палата	letter from the Chamber of Commerce	лèтъ: фром дъ чæ̀мбъ: ъв комъ̀:с
Изпратете ни ...!	Send us ...!	Сенд ас ...!
незабавно мостра	a sample immidiately	ъ сæ̀мпъл имѝдиътли
електронна поща	e-mail	й-мейл
Ще се чуем по телефона.	We will hear with you by phone.	Уй: уйл хѝъ уѝд ю бай фòун
Цените ви са ...	Your prices are ...	Йо: прàйсиз а: ...
високи	high	хай
ниски	low	лоу
приемливи	acceptable	ъксèптабъл
Получихме мострата.	We received the sample.	Уй: рисѝ:вд дъ сæ̀мпъл.
Кога можем да преговаряме?	When can we negotiate?	Уен кæн уй нигòушиейт?

Бихме желали да	We would like	Уй: уѝд лайк
подпишем договор.	to sign a contract.	ту сàйн ъ кòнтрæкт.
Направихме проучване	We have examined	Уй: хæв игзæ̀минт
на пазара.	the market.	дъ мà:кит.
Условията за	The selling	дъ сèлинг
продажби са ...	conditions are ...	къндѝшънс а: ...
добри	good	гуд
незадоволителни	unsatisfying	анс æ̀тисфайнг
Искаме да станем	We would like to become	Уй: уѝд лайк ту бикàм
ваши представители...	your representatives ...	йо: репризѐнтативс ...
за България	for Bulgaria	фо: Бългæ̀риъ
за региона на ...	for the region of ...	фо: дъ рѝ:джън ъв ...
Можем ли да получим	Can we receive the	Кæн уй: рисѝ:в ди икск-
изключително право	exclusive right for the	лỳ:зив райт фо: дъ сèлинг
за продажбата	selling of ... in Bulgaria?	ъв ... ин Бългæ̀риъ?
в България на ...?		
Желаем да регистрира-	We would like to register	Уй: уѝд лайк ту рèджистъ:
ме смесено дружество.	a joint venture.	ъ джòйнт вèнчъ:.

Налага се да обсъдим всички подробности.	We have to discuss all the details.	Уй хæв ту дискàс о:л gъ дѝтейлс.
Не желаем да работим с посредници.	We don't want to work with mediators.	Уй: донт лайк ту уъ̀:к уѝg медиѐйтъ:з.
На посредника ще заплатим комисионна в размер на ... процента.	We will pay ... royalties to the mediator.	Уй: уѝл пей ... рòйалти:з gъ медиѐйтъ:
Каним ви да дойдете в България ...	We invite you to come in Bulgaria ...	Уй: инвàйт ю: ту кам ин Бългæриъ ...
в удобно за вас време	at your convenience	æт йо: кънвѝниънс
в периода от трети до осми април	in the period from April 3rd to April 8th	ин gъ пѝриъд фром тъ:д ъв ѐйприл ту ейт ъв ѐйприл
Кога ще направите доставката?	When will you make the delivery?	Уен уил ю: мейк gъ делѝвъри?
Транспортът е за ... сметка.	The tarnsport is at ... expence.	gъ трàнспорт из æт ... икспѐнс.
ваша	your	йо:
наша	our	àуъ

За митницата са необходими документите:	You will need the following documents for the customs:	Ю: уѝл ни:д gъ фо̀лоуинг до̀кюмънтс фо: gъ ка̲стъмс:
разрешително за внос	Import Licence	ѝмпорт ла̀йсънс
разрешително за износ	Export Licence	ѝкспо:т ла̀йсънс
сертификати на стоката	Commodity Certificates	късмо̀дити съ:тификитс
фактури с точно описание на стоките и количествата	Invoices with the exact description of the goods and quantities	инво̀йсиз уѝg gи игзæ̀кт дискрѝпшън ъв gъ гудс æнд куо̀нтитис
застраховка на стоките	insurance of the goods	иншу̀рънс ъв дъ гудс
Митото е в размер на ... процента.	The duty is ... %.	gъ дю̀ти из ... пърсѐнтс.
Има (Няма) акциз.	There is (not) excise duty.	gѐъ из (нот) икса̀йз дю̀ти.
Заплащат се също и допълнителни такси.	Additional charges are also paid.	Адѝшънъл ча̀:джиз а: о̀лсоу пейд.

Стоката пристигна. Освободихме я от митницата.	The goods arrived. The goods are customs cleared.	*g*ъ гудз ъра̀йвт. *g*ъ гудз а: ка̀стомс клйъ:д.
Плащането ще се извърши ...	The payment will be made ...	*g*ъ пѐймънт уйл би мейд ...
по банков път	by bank transfer	бай бæнк тра̀нсфъ:
чрез акредитив	by Letter of Credit (L/C)	бай лѐтъ: ъв крѐдит (ел си)
в брой	cash	кæш
Плащането е направено.	The payment is made.	*g*ъ пѐймънт из мейд.
Открихме сметка на Ваше име в ... банка.	We opened an account on your favour in ... bank.	Уи о̀упънт ън ъка̀унт он йо: фѐйвъ ин ... бæнк.
Номерът на банковата сметка е ...	The number of your bank account is ...	*g*ъ на̀мбъ ъв йо: бæнк ъка̀унт из ...
Можете ли да ми (ни) осигурите преводач?	Can you provide me (us) with interpreter?	Кæн ю пръва̀йд ми (ас) уѝ*g* интъ̀:притъ:?

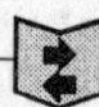

фирма	company	кòмпани
предприятие	enterprise	èнтъ:прайз
дружество	association	ъсòушиейшън
смесено дружество	joint venture	джойнт вèнчъ:
дружество с ограничена отговорност (ООД)	limited liability company (Ltd.)	лѝмитид лàйъбилити кòмпани
акционерно дружество (АД)	joint stock company	джойнт сток кòмпани
управление *(сграда)*	headquarters	хèдкуотъ:з
управител	manager	мæ̀ниджъ:
производител	producer	пръдю̀:съ
доставчик	supplier	съплàйъ
превозвач	carter	кà:тъ
клиент	client	клàйънт
търговец на едро	merchant	мъ:чънт
данък	tax	тæкс
данък добавена	value added tax (VAT)	вæ̀лю æ̀дид тæкс
стойност	value	вæ̀лю

данък общ доход	income tax	ѝнкам тæкс
данък печалба	profit tax	прòфит тæкс
приватизация	privatization	приватизèйшън
фактура	invoice	инвòйс
условия	terms	тъ:мс
за плащането	of payment	ъф пèймънт
транспорт за сметка	transport at the expence	транспорт æт ди
на купувача	of the buyer	икспèнс ъв дъ бàйъ:
(продавача)	(seller)	(сèлъ)
франко ...	free on ...	фри: он ...
описание	description	дискрѝпшън
на стоката	of the goods	ъв дъ гудз
количество	quantity	куòнтити
ценоразпис	price list	прàйс лист
цена	price	прàйс
отстъпка	discount	дѝскаунт
обща сума	total amount of ...	тòутъл ъмàунт ъф ...
местоназначение	final destination	фàйнъл дестинèйшън
стока	goods, commodity	гу:дз, комòдити
опаковам	wrap, pack	рæп, пæк
опаковка; опаковане	package; packing	пæкидж; пæкинг

пале	pallet	пàлет
кашон	carton	кà:тън
кутия	box	бокс
пакет	packet	пæ̀кит
вързоп	bundle	ба̀ндъл
количество	quantity	куо̀нтити
мостра	sample	сæ̀мпъл
изпращане на мостра	sending a sample	сѐндинг ъ сæ̀мпъл
доставка	delivery	делѝвъри
посредничество	mediator	медиѐйтъ
рекламация	claim	клѐйм
застраховка	insurance	иншу̀ъ:рънс
мито	duty	дю̀ти
такси	charges, fees	чà:джиз, фи:з
комисионна	commission, royalties	къмѝшън, ро̀йалти:з
правя поръчка	place order	плейс о̀:дъ
спешна поръчка	express order	икспрѐс о̀:дъ
изпълнявам поръчка	complete an order	къмплѝ:т ън о̀:дъ
сделка	deal, business	ди:л, бѝзнес
покупка	purchase	пъ:чейс
продажба	sale	сел

внос	import	ѝмпорт
износ	export	ѐкспорт
плащане	payment	пѐймънт
начин на плащане	way of payment	уѐй ъв пѐймънт
в брой	cash	кæш
на изплащане	instalments	инстѐлмънтс
разсрочено плащане	in instalments payment	ин инстѐлмънтс пѐймънт
акредитив	Letter of Credit (L/C)	лѐтъ: ъв крѐдит (ел/си)
банков превод	bank transfer	бæнк трæ̀нсфъ:
печалба	profit	прѐфит
акция	share, stock	шѐъ, сток
дивидент	divident	дѝвидънт
лихва	interest	ѝнтърест
лихвен процент	rate of interest	рейт ъв ѝнтърест
акционер	shareholder, stockholder	шѐъхолдъ:, стѐкхолдъ:
инвеститор	investor	инвѐстъ:

Посолство
на ОБЕДИНЕНОТО КРАЛСТВО
в България

София-1000
ул. Московска 9
✆ (359) (2) 933 9222
факс 933 9250
www.british-embassy.bg
e-mail: britembinf@mail.orbitel.bg

Посолство
на РЕПУБЛИКА БЪЛГАРИЯ
в Обединеното кралство

London SW 7 5HL
186-188 Queen's Gate
✆(0044) (0) 870 060 2350,
870 0602351
факс: (0044) -(0) 207-584-4948
www.bulgarianembassy.org.uk

РАЗСТОЯНИЯ

между някои градове във Великобритания

(в мили и километри)

ЛОНДОН										
111/179	**Бирмингам**									
150/241	102/164	**Кардиф**								
74 /119	185/298	228/367	**Доувър**							
372/599	290/466	373/600	442/711	**Единбург**						
389/626	292/470	374/602	446/750	45/ 72	**Глазгоу**					
529/851	448/721	530/853	600/966	158/254	167/269	**Инвернес**				
184/296	81/130	173/278	257/414	213/343	214/344	371/597	**Манчестър**			
274/441	204/328	301/484	343/552	107/172	145/233	265/426	131/211	**Нюкасъл**		
112/180	161/259	235/378	167/269	360/579	383/616	517/832	185/298	260/418	**Норич**	
212/341	206/332	152/261	287/462	427/784	426/785	545/1038	250/451	427/655	324/521	**Плимут**

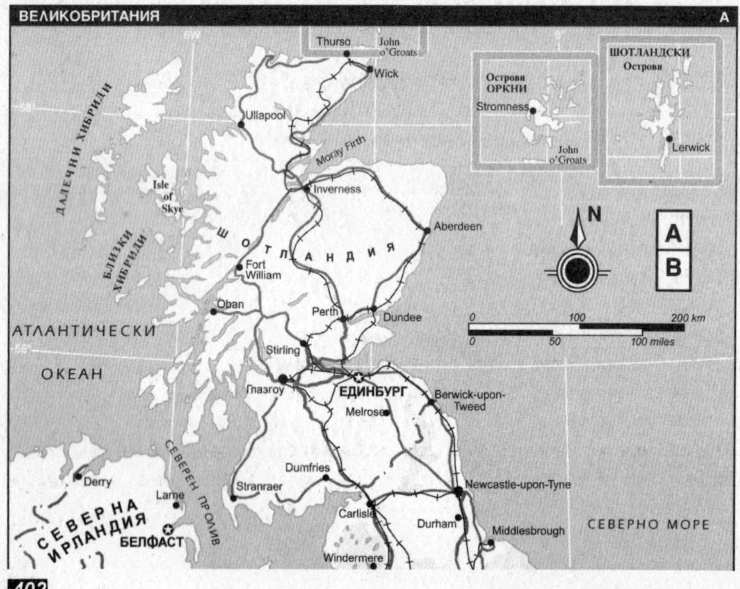
ВЕЛИКОБРИТАНИЯ
A
Thurso
John o'Groats
Wick
Ullapool
Moray Firth
Inverness
Aberdeen
Острови ОРКНИ
Stromness
John o'Groats
ШОТЛАНДСКИ Острови
Lerwick
ДАЛЕЧНИ ХИБРИДИ
Isle of Skye
БЛИЗКИ ХИБРИДИ
ШОТЛАНДИЯ
Fort William
Oban
Perth
Dundee
Stirling
АТЛАНТИЧЕСКИ ОКЕАН
Глазгоу
ЕДИНБУРГ
Berwick-upon-Tweed
Melrose
N
A
B
0
100
200 km
0
50
100 miles
Derry
Larne
СЕВЕРЕН ПРОЛИВ
СЕВЕРНА ИРЛАНДИЯ
БЕЛФАСТ
Dumfries
Stranraer
Newcastle-upon-Tyne
Carlisle
Durham
Middlesbrough
СЕВЕРНО МОРЕ
Windermere

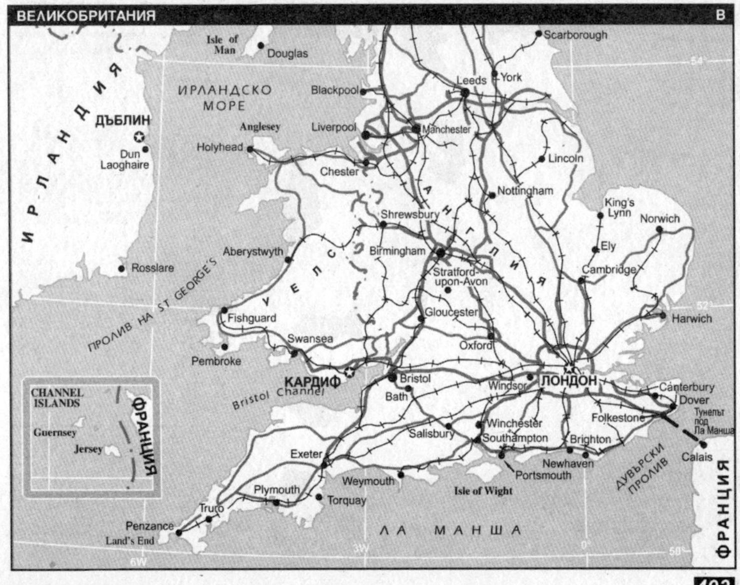
Isle of Man
Douglas
Scarborough
York
Leeds
Blackpool
ИРЛАНДСКО МОРЕ
ИРЛАНДИЯ
ДЪБЛИН
Dun Laoghaire
Anglesey
Liverpool
Manchester
Holyhead
Chester
Lincoln
Nottingham
АНГЛИЯ
King's Lynn
Norwich
Shrewsbury
Birmingham
Ely
Aberystwyth
Cambridge
Rosslare
ПРОЛИВ НА ST GEORGE'S
УЕЛС
Stratford-upon-Avon
Fishguard
Gloucester
Harwich
Swansea
Oxford
Pembroke
КАРДИФ
Bristol
Windsor
ЛОНДОН
Bristol Channel
Bath
Canterbury
Dover
CHANNEL ISLANDS
Guernsey
Jersey
ФРАНЦИЯ
Winchester
Folkestone
Тунелът под Ла Манша
Salisbury
Southampton
Brighton
Calais
Exeter
Newhaven
Portsmouth
ДУВЪРСКИ ПРОЛИВ
Weymouth
Isle of Wight
Plymouth
Torquay
Truro
Penzance
Land's End
ЛА МАНША
ФРАНЦИЯ

A C
B D
N
0 200 400 m
0 200 400 yards
към Islington
към the City
King's Cross
ST PANCRAS
CLERKENWELL
HOLBORN
Coram's Fields
Gray's Inn
Lincoln's Inn Fields
Covent Garden Piazza
Pancras Rd
Pentonville Road
King's Cross Road
Gray's Inn Road
Swinton St
Acton St
Cromer St
Judd Street
Place
Calthorpe St
Farringdon Road
Rosebery Avenue
Clerkenwell Road
Guilford Street
Great Ormond St
Theobald's Road
Red Lion St
Procter St
Southampton Row
Russell Square
Bloomsbury Way
Bloomsbury Street
High Holborn
Chancery Lane
Lincoln's Inn Fields
Kingsway
Drury Lane
Long Acre
Shelton St
Floral St
Bow St
Russell St
King St
КЪДЕ ДА ОТСЕДНЕМ
4 St Pancras International Hostel
5 Euston Hotel
8 International Students House
12 John Adams Hall
13 Passfield Hall
14 Jenkin's Hotel
15 Crescent Hotel
18 Carr Saunders Hall
21 Arran House Hotel
22 Hotel Cavendish
27 Repton Hotel
29 Museum Inn
6 Euston ML и метростанция
9 Метростанция Great Portland St
10 Метростанция Warren St
11 Метростанция Euston Square
17 London University
19 BT Tower
20 Dillons the Bookstore
23 Russell Square Tube Station
25 Goodge St Tube Station
26 Cyberia Café
30 British Museum
31 Метростанция Chancery Lane
35 Метростанция Oxford Circus
36 Council Travel
39 Astoria

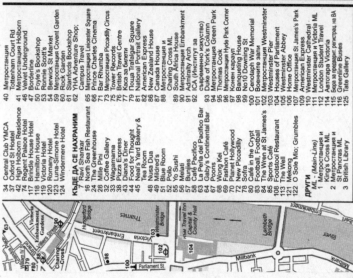

34 Central Club YMCA
37 Oxford St Hostel
42 High Holborn Residence
74 Regent Palace Hotel
117 Brindle House Hotel
118 Hamilton House
119 Victoria Hotel
120 Romany Hotel
123 Luna-Simone Hotel
124 Windermere Hotel

КЪДЕ ДА СЕ НАХРАНИМ

7 Ravi Shankar
16 North Sea Fish Restaurant
24 The Greenhouse
28 Mille Pini
32 Coffee Gallery
33 Wagamama
38 Pizza Express
43 Diana's Diner
44 Food for Thought
45 Neal's Yard Bakery & Tea Room
48 Nusa Dua
49 Mildred's
51 Blue Room
52 Pollo
55 Yo Sushi
56 Melati
57 Bunjies
58 Café Pacifico
63 La Perla del Pacifico Bar
64 Gaby's Continental Bar
67 Poons
68 Wong Kei
69 Fashion Café
70 Planet Hollywood
72 New Piccadilly
78 Sofra
80 Café in the Crypt
83 Football, Football
84 The Wren at St James's
85 Sports Café
108 Footstool Restaurant
113 The Well
121 Mekong
122 O Sole Mio; Grumbles

ДРУГИ

ML - (Main-Line)

1 Метростанция и King's Cross ML
2 Метростанция и St Pancras ML
3 British Library
40 Метростанция Tottenham Court Rd
41 Метростанция Holborn
46 Velvet Underground
47 Borderline
50 Foyle's Bookshop
53 Ronnie Scott's
54 Berwick St Market
59 Метростанция Covent Garden
60 Rock Garden
61 Stanfords Bookshop
62 YHA Adventure Shop; Campus Travel
65 Метростанция Leicester Square
66 Prince Charles Cinema
71 Bar Rhumba
73 Метростанция Piccadilly Circus
75 Tower Records
76 British Travel Centre
77 Каса за билети
79 Поща Trafalgar Square
81 National Portrait Gallery
82 American Express
86 New Zealand House
87 Canada House
88 Метростанция и Charing Cross ML
89 South Africa House
90 Метростанция Embankment
91 Admiralty Arch
92 ICA (Институт за съвременно изкуство)
93 Duke of York's Column
94 Метростанция Green Park
95 Thomas Cook
96 Метростанция Hyde Park Corner
97 Конен караул
98 Banqueting House
99 No10 Downing St
100 Cenotaph War Memorial
101 Военните зали
102 Метростанция Westminster
103 Westminster Pier
104 Houses of Parliament
105 Westminster Abbey
106 Home Office
107 Метростанция St James's Park
109 American Express
110 Westminster Cathedral
111 Метростанция и Victoria ML
112 London Student Travel
114 Автогара Victoria
115 Бюра за предварит. регистрац. на ВА
116 Greenline Buses
125 Tate Gallery

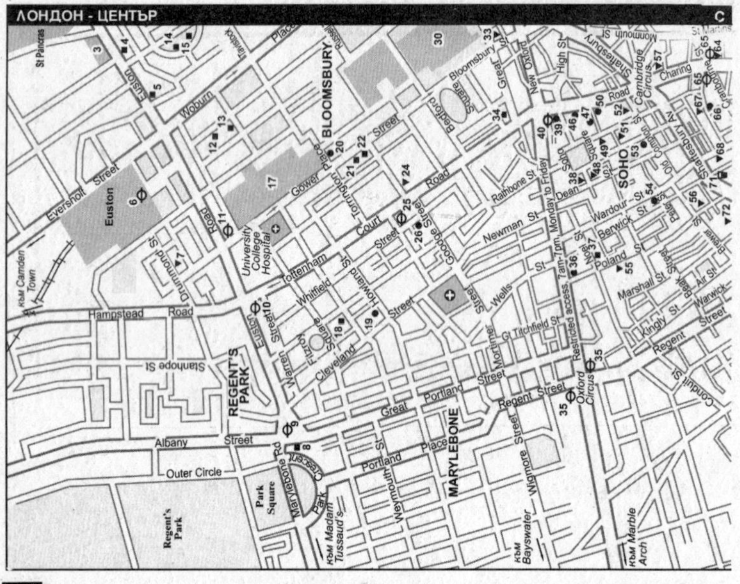
BLOOMSBURY
SOHO
MARYLEBONE
REGENT'S PARK
Regent's Park
Park Square
Euston
University College Hospital
Oxford Circus
Hampstead Road
Euston Road
Eversholt Street
Albany Street
Outer Circle
Great Portland Street
Tottenham Court Road
Gower Place
Goodge Street
Newman St
Rathbone St
Wardour St
Berwick St
Poland St
Marshall St
Regent Street
Wigmore Street
Weymouth St
Cleveland St
Fitzroy Square
Whitfield St
Howland St
Warren St
Stanhope St
Drummond St
Woburn
Bedford Square
Bloomsbury
New Oxford St
Great Russell St
High St
Shaftesbury
Charing Cross
Cambridge Circus
Monmouth St
Dean St
Soho Square
Old Compton St
Wells St
Gt Titchfield St
Mortimer Street
Conduit St
Kingly St
Warwick Street
Beak St
Air St
Brewer St
Marylebone Rd
Park Crescent
Restricted access 7am-7pm, Monday to Friday
към Camden Town
към Madam Tussaud's
към Bayswater
към Marble Arch
St Pancras
St Martins
Cranbourne

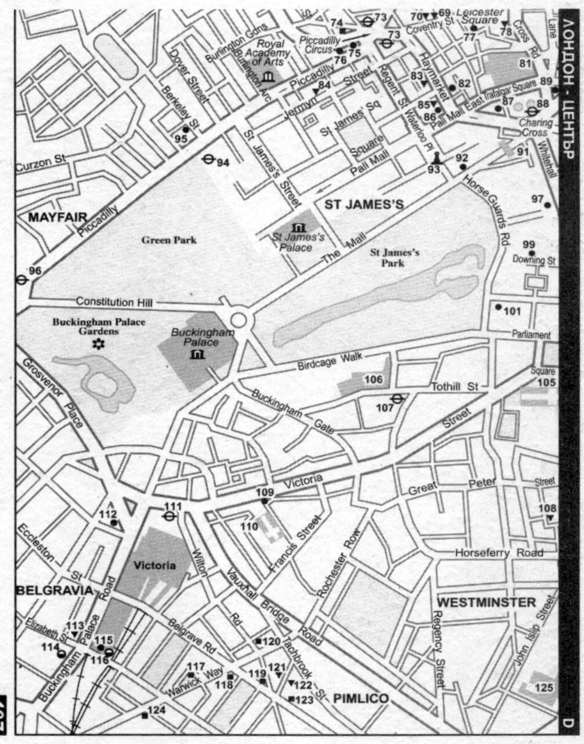
MAYFAIR
ST JAMES'S
Green Park
St James's Park
St James's Palace
Buckingham Palace Gardens
Buckingham Palace
Victoria
BELGRAVIA
WESTMINSTER
PIMLICO
Piccadilly
Constitution Hill
The Mall
Horse Guards Rd
Birdcage Walk
Buckingham Gate
Tothill St
Victoria Street
Great Peter Street
Horseferry Road
Regency Street
John Islip Street
Rochester Row
Francis Street
Vauxhall Bridge Road
Wilton Rd
Belgrave Rd
Tachbrook St
Warwick Way
Buckingham Palace Road
Elizabeth St
Eccleston St
Grosvenor Place
Curzon St
Berkeley St
Dover Street
Burlington Gdns
Burlington Arc
Royal Academy of Arts
Piccadilly Circus
Jermyn Street
St James's Street
St James's Sq
Pall Mall
Regent St
Waterloo Pl
Haymarket
Pall Mall East
Trafalgar Square
Charing Cross
Whitehall
Leicester Square
Coventry St
Cross Rd
Lane
Downing St
Parliament Square

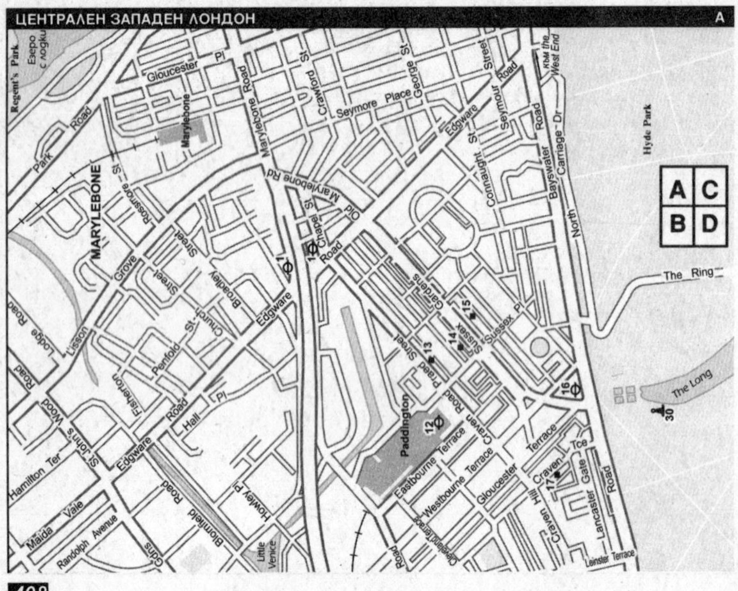
Regent's Park
Езеро с лодки
Gloucester Pl
Marylebone Road
Crawford St
Seymore Place
George St
Edgware
Seymour Road
Street
към the West End
Park Road
Marylebone
MARYLEBONE
Rossmore St
Marylebone Rd
Old Marylebone Rd
Chapel St
Road
Connaught St
Bayswater Road
Carriage Dr
North
Hyde Park
A C
B D
Street
Street
Grove
Broadley
Church St
Edgware
Gardens
Sussex
Sussex Pl
The Ring
Lodge Road
Lisson
Penfold
Praed Street
Road
Fisherton
Wood
Road
Hall Pl
Road
Paddington
Craven Road
The Long
St John's
Hamilton Ter
Edgware
Eastbourne Terrace
Westbourne Terrace
Gloucester
Terrace
Craven Tce
Maida Vale
Randolph Avenue
Gdns
Blomfield Road
Howley Pl
Little Venice
Cleveland Terrace
Road
Craven Hill
Lancaster Gate
Road
Leinster Terrace
1
12
13
14
15
16
17
30

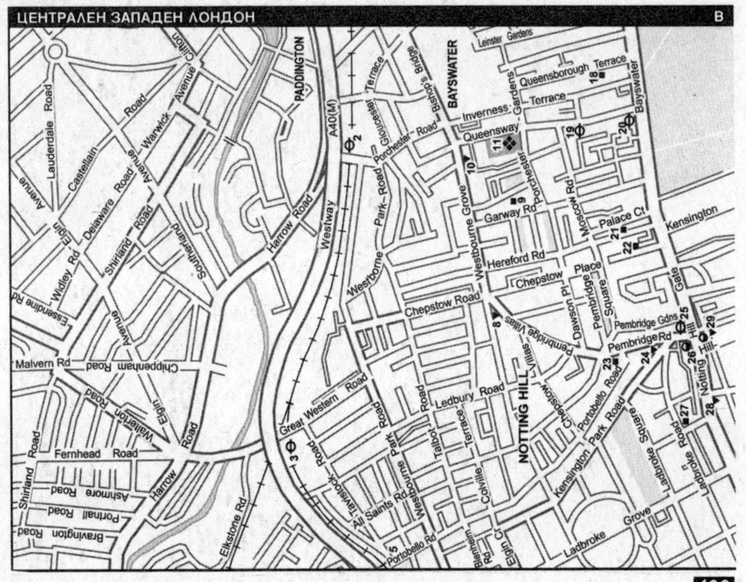
PADDINGTON
BAYSWATER
NOTTING HILL
Leinster Gardens
Queensborough Terrace
Inverness Terrace
Queensway
Bayswater
Gloucester Terrace
Bishop's Bridge
Porchester Road
A40(M)
Westway
Harrow Road
Westbourne Park Road
Westbourne Grove
Garway Rd
Porchester
Moscow Rd
Palace Ct
Kensington
Hereford Rd
Chepstow Place
Chepstow Road
Dawson Pl
Pembridge Square
Pembridge Gdns
Pembridge Villas
Pembridge Rd
Gate
Notting Hill
Villas
Ledbury Road
Great Western Road
Talbot
Terrace
Colville
Portobello Road
Kensington Park Road
Ladbroke Square
Ladbroke Road
Ladbroke Grove
Tavistock Road
All Saints Rd
Westbourne Park
Portobello Rd
Blenheim Rd
Elgin Cr
Elkstone Rd
Lauderdale Road
Castellain
Warwick Avenue
Clifton
Delaware Road
Elgin Avenue
Shirland Road
Southerland
Widley Rd
Essendine Rd
Malvern Rd
Chippenham Road
Walterton Road
Fernhead Road
Ashmore Road
Portnall Road
Bravington Road
Shirland
Harrow Road
2
3
5
8
9
10
11
18
19
20
21
22
23
24
25
26
27
28
29

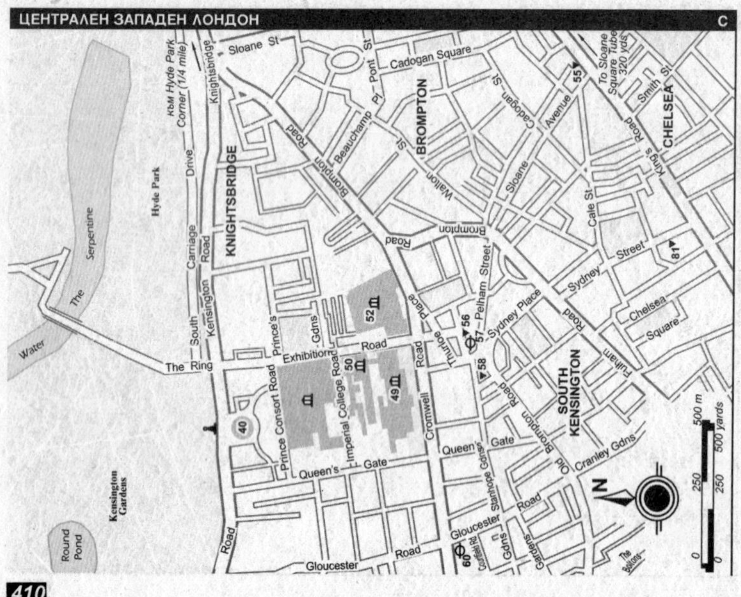

към Hyde Park Corner (1/4 mile)
Knightsbridge
Sloane St
Cadogan Square
Pont St
Beauchamp Pl
BROMPTON
Cadogan St
Avenue
55
To Sloane Square Tube 320 yds
Smith St
CHELSEA
King's Road
Brompton Road
Walton St
Sloane
Cale St
Brompton Road
Hyde Park
Carriage Drive
South Kensington Road
KNIGHTSBRIDGE
The Serpentine
Water
The Ring
Prince's Gdns
Exhibition Road
52
50
49
Prince Consort Road
Imperial College Road
Cromwell Road
Thurloe Place
56
57
58
Pelham Street
Sydney Place
Sydney Street
81
Chelsea Square
Fulham Road
SOUTH KENSINGTON
Brompton Road
Old Brompton Road
Cranley Gdns
Queen's Gate
40
Stanhope Gdns
Gloucester Road
Gloucester Road
60
Courtfield Rd
Gdns
Gardens
The Boltons
Kensington Gardens
Round Pond
Road
N
0
250
500 m
0
250
500 yards

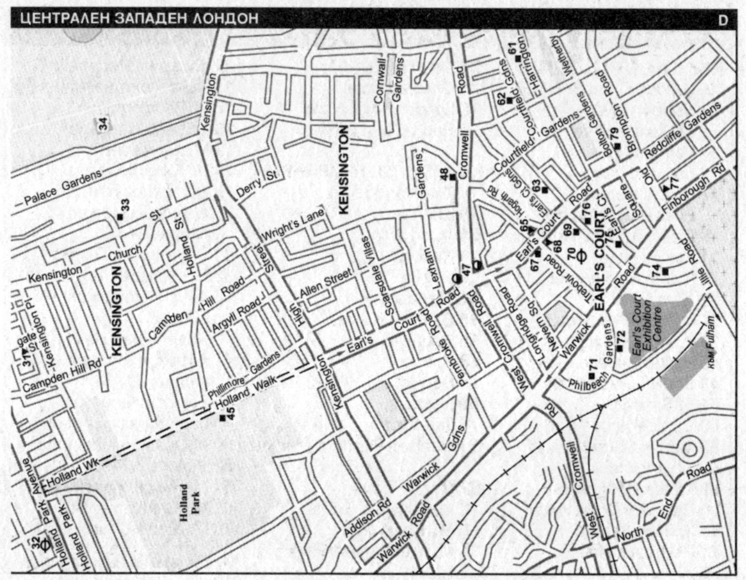
KENSINGTON
KENSINGTON
EARL'S COURT
Palace Gardens
Kensington Church St
Holland St
Derry St
Wright's Lane
Kensington High Street
Allen Street
Scarsdale Villas
Campden Hill Road
Argyll Road
Campden Hill Rd
Kensington Pl
Phillimore Gardens
Holland Walk
Holland Wk
Holland Park
Holland Park Avenue
Earl's Court Road
Pembroke Road
Warwick Gdns
Warwick Road
Addison Rd
Lexham Gardens
Cromwell Road
Cornwall Gardens
Courtfield Gardens
Harrington Gdns
Bolton Gardens
Brompton Road
Redcliffe Gardens
Finborough Rd
Old Brompton Road
Earl's Court Square
Earl's Ct Gdns
Hogarth Rd
Trebovir Road
Nevern Sq
Longridge Road
West Cromwell Road
Warwick Road
Philbeach Gardens
Lillie Road
Earl's Court Exhibition Centre
към Fulham
North End Road
West Cromwell Rd

ЦЕНТРАЛЕН ЗАПАДЕН ЛОНДОН

КЪДЕ ДА ОТСЕДНЕМ

9 Garden Court Hotel
13 Norfolk Court; St David's Hotel
14 Balmoral House
15 Europa House
17 Oxford Hotel; Sass House Hotel
18 Quest & Royal Hotels
21 Palace Hotel
22 Manor Court Hotel
23 Gate Hotel
27 Holland Park Hotel
33 Vicarage Private Hotel
45 Holland House Hostel
48 Shellbourne Hotel
61 St Simeon
62 Curzon House Hotel
63 Merlyn Court Hotel
67 Court Hotel
69 Windsor House & Regency Court Hotel
71 York House Hotel
72 Philbeach Hotel
74 Court Hotel
75 Chelsea Hotel
76 London Town Hotel
79 Earl's Court Hostel

КЪДЕ ДА СЕ НАХРАНИМ

8 The Mandola
10 Khan's
24 Modhubon
28 Nachos
29 Geales
31 Costa's Grill
55 Chelsea Kitchen
56 Daquise
58 Spago
65 Benjys
68 Nando's
77 Troubadour
81 Chelsea Farmers' Market

ДРУГИ

1 M. Edgware Rd
2 M. Royal Oak
3 M. Westbourne Park
5 пазарът Portobello Rd
11 Търг. център Whiteley's
12 M. Paddington
16 M. Lancaster Gate
19 M. Bayswater
20 M. Queensway
25 M. Notting Hill
26 Airbus, маршрут A2, спирка 14
30 Статуя на Питър Пан
32 M. Holland Park
34 Кенсингтънският дворец
40 Royal Albert Hall
47 Airbus, маршрут A1, спирка 6
49 Естествено-исторически музей
50 Музеят на науката
52 Victoria & Albert Museum
57 M. South Kensington
60 M. Gloucester Rd
70 M. Earl's Court

M. - *станция на метрото*

31 Aldgate
3 Angel
7 Baker St
30 Bank
18 Barbican
21 Bayswater
39 Blackfriars
25 Bond St
50 Borough
41 Cannon St (ML)
16 Chancery Lane
35 Charing Cross (ML)
37 Covent Garden
53 Earl's Court
14 Edgware Rd
61 Elephant & Castle (ML)
36 Embankment
4 Euston (ML)
9 Euston Square
17 Farringdon
54 Gloucester Rd
15 Goodge St
32 Green Park
44 High St Kensington
28 Holborn
46 Hyde Park Corner
60 Kennington
2 King's Cross (ML)
45 Knightsbridge
23 Lancaster Gate
34 Leicester Square
18 Liverpool St (ML)
51 London Bridge (ML)
40 Mansion House
24 Marble Arch
6 Marylebone (ML)
42 Monument
1 Mornington Crescent
20 Notting Hill Gate
5 Old St
52 Olympia (ML)
26 Oxford Circus
13 Paddington (ML)
33 Piccadilly Circus
58 Pimlico
22 Queensway
12 Royal Oak
10 Russell Square
56 Sloane Square
55 South Kensington
47 St Jame's Park
29 St Paul's
38 Temple
27 Tottenham Court Rd
43 Tower Hill (ML)
59 Vauxhall (ML)
57 Victoria (ML)
8 Warren St
49 Waterloo (ML)
11 Westbourne Park
48 Westminster

ML - *означение за станции по главната линия*

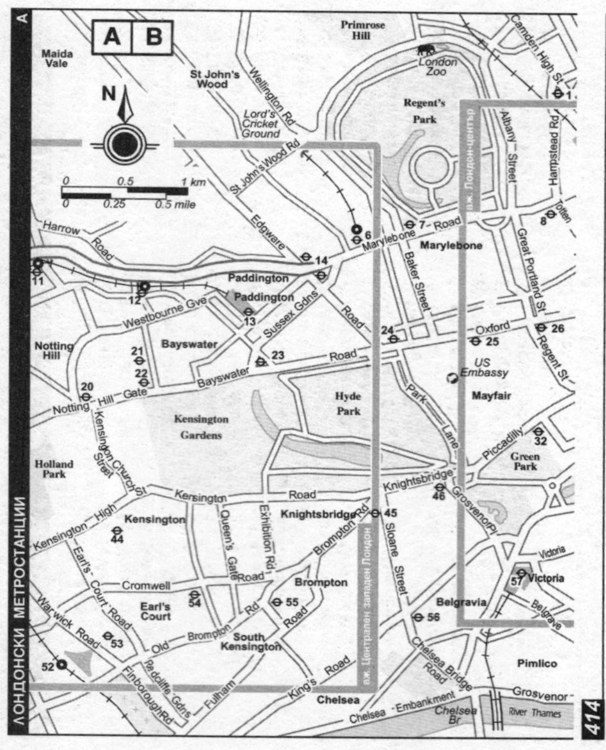
A
B
N
0 0.5 1 km
0 0.25 0.5 mile
Maida Vale
St John's Wood
Wellington Rd
Lord's Cricket Ground
St John's Wood Rd
Primrose Hill
London Zoo
Regent's Park
Camden High St
Albany Street
Hampstead Rd
Totten
вж. Лондон-център
Harrow Road
Edgware
Marylebone Road
Marylebone
Great Portland St
Baker Street
Paddington
Sussex Gdns
Westbourne Gve
Bayswater
Bayswater Road
Oxford
Regent St
US Embassy
Mayfair
Notting Hill
Notting Hill Gate
Hyde Park
Park Lane
Kensington Gardens
Piccadilly
Green Park
Holland Park
Kensington Church Street
Kensington Road
Knightsbridge
Grosvenor Pl
Kensington High
Kensington
Queen's Gate
Exhibition Rd
Brompton Rd
Sloane Street
Victoria
Cromwell Road
Brompton
Earl's Court
Earl's Court Road
Warwick Road
Old Brompton Rd
South Kensington
Belgravia
Belgrave
вж. Централен западен Лондон
Redcliffe Gdns
Finborough Rd
Fulham
King's Road
Chelsea
Chelsea Bridge Road
Pimlico
Grosvenor
Chelsea Embankment
Chelsea Br
River Thames
1
6
7
8
11
12
13
14
20
21
22
23
24
25
26
32
44
45
46
52
53
54
55
56
57

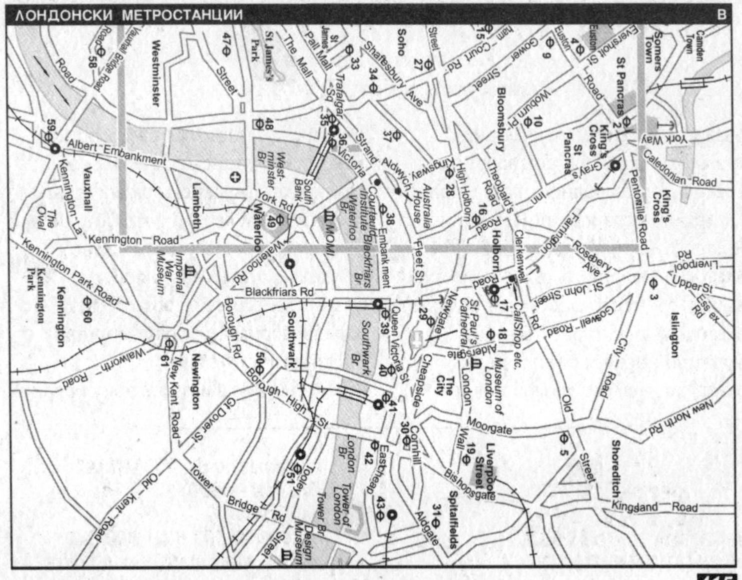
Camden Town
Somers Town
Eversholt St
Euston
Euston Rd
Gower Street
Court Rd
Soho
Shaftesbury Ave
Pall Mall
The Mall
St James's Park
Westminster
Vauxhall Bridge Road
Road
St Pancras
King's Cross
York Way
Caledonian Road
Pentonville Road
Woburn Pl
Bloomsbury
Theobald's Road
Gray's Inn
Trafalgar Sq
Strand
Aldwych
Kingsway
High Holborn
Australia House
Victoria
Albert Embankment
Westminster Br
South Bank
York Rd
Waterloo
Waterloo Br
Courtauld Institute
Blackfriars Br
Embankment
Fleet St
Holborn
Farringdon Road
Rosebery Ave
Clerkenwell
Liverpool Rd
Upper St
Essex Rd
St John Street
Goswell Road
Islington
Vauxhall
Kennington La
The Oval
Lambeth
Kennington Road
Imperial War Museum
Waterloo Rd
MOMI
Blackfriars Rd
Kennington Park Road
Kennington Park
Kennington
Borough Rd
Southwark
Southwark Br
Queen Victoria St
Newgate
St Paul's Cathedral
Aldersgate
Museum of London
City Road
Walworth Road
New Kent Road
Newington
Borough High St
Cheapside
The City
London Wall
Old Street
New North Rd
Gt Dover St
Moorgate
Cornhill
Liverpool Street
Shoreditch
Old Kent Road
Tower Bridge Rd
Tooley St
London Br
Eastcheap
Bishopsgate
Kingsland Road
Tower Br
Tower of London
Design Museum
Spitalfields
Aldgate

Други разговорници
от издателство „ГРАММА“:

"Българско - немски разговорник"
"Българско - френски разговорник"
"Българско - италиански разговорник"
"Българско - испански разговорник"
"Българско - гръцки разговорник"
"Българско - португалски разговорник"
"Българско - нидерландски разговорник"
"Българско - руски разговорник"
"Българско - чешки разговорник"
"Българско - полски разговорник"
"Българско - унгарски разговорник"
"Българско - турски разговорник"
"Българско - румънски разговорник"
"Българско - шведски разговорник"
"Българско - датски разговорник"
"Българско - арабски разговорник"
"Българско - сръбски разговорник"
"Западноевропейски разговорник"
"Bulgarian Phrasebook"
"Българско-немски бизнес разговорник"

Издателство "ГРАММА"
Плевен - 5800
ул. Сопот 9
тел. 064/ 805 682, 802 642
e-mail: gramma@el-soft.com